W9-CRW-750

Real Estate Finance

Real Estate Finance

Second Edition

John P. Wiedemer
University of Houston

Reston Publishing Company, Inc.
A Prentice-Hall Company
Reston, Virginia

Library of Congress Cataloging in Publication Data

Wiedemer, John P.
　　Real estate finance.

　　1. Real estate business—United States—Finance.
2. Mortgages—United States.　I.　Title.
HD1375.W53 1977　　　332.7'2　　　77–456
ISBN 0–87909–721–3

© 1977 by
Reston Publishing Company, Inc.
A Prentice-Hall Company
Reston, Virginia 22090

10　9　8　7　6　5　4　3　2　1

Printed in the United States of America

Contents

Introduction

The financing of real estate, which includes our homes, shopping centers, office buildings, farms, and factories, is one of the largest responsibilities of our financial system. The multifaceted operation of this system today has resulted from long experience with a great variety of requirements, from the harsh realities of the depression years of the 1930s, and from the efforts of many men and women working through private industry and governmental agencies to achieve more and better housing along with better living conditions for all of us. One might say that it is this system that attempts to match dreams with reality and make them come true.

The goal of this book is to acquaint us with the most commonly used methods of financing real property and to acquire some familiarity with the terminology used in our financial community. We recognize that differences in methods, in institutions, and even in terminology, do exist across the country, but for our purposes, and within our time limitations, this material will be focused on common practices with minimal reference to local geographic areas.

This text does not cover the "how to make a fortune in real estate your first year in business" that is popularized in some current books. It is the author's belief that well-selected land and buildings represent one of the soundest investments available, and that their value increases by two basic factors: (1) by the influx of people into any specific area, and (2) by the normal inflationary cycle we now live with. There are other influences, of course, such as the discovery of minerals, massive irrigation work, and the site selection for a major construction project; but we will concern ourselves primarily with the fundamentals and the normal pressures rather than the speculative ones.

Since World War II, the influence and power of the federal government have been an ever-increasing force in the real estate business, with many bureaus, agencies, and departments exercising authority. In this book, however, we will attempt to cover only the major procedures and programs now in use, and how they relate to the conventional capital market.

John P. Wiedemer

Foreword

Land is a scarce and limited resource. Its availability and use are so basic to human life that they form the foundation upon which societies are organized and function. Inherent in the structure of every society is a system designed to deal with the multitude of relationships concerning land.

In this society, private ownership of real property is an established and guarded right. Here too, systems have been developed that recognize this right and facilitate the individual's exercise of this right.

The economic importance of real estate transactions is obvious. So obvious, in fact, that most people are only vaguely aware of the tremendous impact of real estate transactions on the financial market. The potential size and number of these transactions give the appearance of something too complicated to understand. This appearance is both deceiving and dangerous.

An individual purchasing a home is obligating a large portion of his personal income. The real estate salesperson is concerned with the economic well-being of his or her client. Complications notwithstanding, buyers, sellers, brokers, and others are faced with an urgent need to know.

Admittedly, the field of real estate finance is in a state of continuous change; change in practices, methods, clientele, and sources. This circumstance should not be viewed with alarm, for change is inherent in progress. Professionals in real estate, like professionals in every field, must stay abreast of these changes if they are to remain professionals.

Newcomers to the field must gain a solid foundation in the basic principles and terminology of real estate finance. The real estate profession's clientele need at least a working knowledge of these same principles and terms.

In order to fulfill these needs, access to accurate, current information is necessary. The information required is available from many sources. Unfortunately, information of this type is normally presented in an obscure and unimaginative form that makes learning a labor and is of limited educational value to all but the specialist.

In this sense, Wiedemer's book is unique. Not only is the information current and technically accurate, it is presented as an informal discussion. His discussion of methods and elements of real estate finance are objective and complete.

His book contains the information necessary to fulfill the needs of the beginner and is thorough enough to be a valuable resource for the established professional. The book has been written in such a way that the novice can understand the language of the professional.

Mr. Wiedemer has been a lecturer in real estate at the University of Houston since 1970. He has brought to his classroom the knowledge and enthusiasm of a leader in his field. He approaches his teaching duties with a sincere desire for his students to learn. This approach is immediately evident in his book.

A true professional, Wiedemer wants to give back something to the profession that has been good to him. This book and his continuing work in education are overt expressions of this willingness and desire.

James C. Taylor, J.D.
Dean, Continuing Education
University of Houston

Acknowledgments

The author gratefully acknowledges the expert advice, assistance, and encouragement of the following persons who made possible the preparation and writing of this book.

Reginald C. Capshaw *Houston Sales Manager, Monarch Homes, Inc.*

Breaux B. Castleman *Vice President, Booz: Allen and Hamilton, Dallas, Texas*

Richard L. Chumbley, *Richland College, Dallas, Texas*

R. L. Cobb *Loan Guaranty Officer, Veterans Administration, Houston*

Joseph P. Conte *President, Conte Investments, Inc., Houston*

Jack W. Craddock *CLU, Great Southern Life Insurance Co.*

Jack Daniels *Chairman, Executive Committee, Fidelity National Bank, Albuquerque, New Mexico*

Bert Kadell *Executive Vice President, US Life Title Company of Houston*

Floyd Kowalski *Chief Mortgage Credit Examiner, Federal Housing Administration, Houston*

Patricia McAuliffe *Real Estate Sales, Houston*

Robert M. Megginson *Executive Vice President, Milton and Megginson Mortgage Company, Jackson, Mississippi*

Arthur Morales *Executive Vice President, San Jacinto Savings Association, Houston*

William A. Painter *Director, Houston Office, HUD, Federal Housing Administration*

James E. Murray, *General Counsel, Federal National Mortgage Association, Washington, D.C.*

Manuel A. Sanchez *President, Gulf-Tex Brokerage, Inc., Brownsville, Texas*

Rudy C. Schubert *Real Estate and Investments, Houston*

James C. Taylor, J.D. *Dean, Continuing Education, University of Houston*

Joe P. Wallace *Wallace and Associates, Realtors, Houston*

Verlyne Wallace *Wallace and Associates, Realtors, Houston*

Ben H. Ward *Real Estate Investments, Houston*

George Young *Assistant Dean, Continuing Education, University of Houston*

And a Special Acknowledgement to my wife, Margaret I. Wiedemer, for organization and editing assistance plus her kind patience.

Real Estate Finance

Chapter 1

History and Background

The history of real estate financing presents a fascinating record of man's learning to live with, and enjoy the benefits of, the land he lives on. While private ownership of land can be traced back to civilizations existing over 2500 years ago, only in the last several hundred years has it become possible for the average person to own property.

EARLY FINANCING METHODS

In ancient Rome, men of means were most often the hereditary large landlords whose land in the provinces had gained them admission to the Curia. This membership required their residence in the city, allowing them to extend their political, religious, and economic influence throughout Rome. Other members included administrators and shareholders of the tax-gathering societies whose treasuries were assured of capital funds. Of course, these societies were open only to the privileged few, unlike our modern investment institutions.

In medieval times, under the feudal system, land was owned primarily by the king, the nobility, or the church. Thus land ownership was restricted to the very few, and those who did possess rights to land could pledge their property rights as security for a loan. In these earlier times there were no savings banks or other institutions capable of accumulating investment capital, and only a few individuals of great wealth were capable of making loans. Besides the severe limitations on investment activity imposed by there being very few property owners, an equally severe limitation was caused by the lack of money —a problem that still exists with many of us today! Historically the growth of widespread land ownership parallels the increase in pools of money available for long-term loans.

With the advent of the Industrial Revolution in the eighteenth century, more individuals became capable of producing wealth with their ideas and their machinery. People began to find that they had another option opened to them; the life of a serf grubbing an existence from land owned by the nobility was no longer the only way to make a living. With the more widespread wealth came the demand for ways to make better use of accumulated money, and the seeds of our publicly owned savings institutions started to grow.

COLONIAL AMERICA

Prior to the Industrial Revolution, colonial America felt the need for capital to build its new homes and businesses. Many groups began to join together for mutual protection and mutual help. Savings were pooled in informal clubs or fraternal groups in order to provide lendable funds for members wishing to build a house, make an addition to their building, or to construct a barn. Organizations were created to provide fire protection for their members. And some groups arranged for periodic payments into the club treasury, which provided for a lump sum payment to the member's family at his death. The only problem here was that without regulation and accurate reserves based on mortality rates, the groups grew older, failed to attract younger members, and often went broke.

In spite of these setbacks, the desire for economic security and the need for the protection of capital helped spawn the banks, savings associations, and life insurance companies of the nineteenth century which have become great assets to our nation today. These older institutions, along with many younger ones, plus some exciting new pools of money such as pension funds and trust funds, are now providing us with the funds needed to own and develop our land. Table 1-1 gives a chronological outline of when the major institutions were formed in this country.

TABLE 1-1

Chronology of Key Agencies and Institutions Associated with Real Estate Finance in the United States

1759	Charter date of the oldest life insurance company in the United States. The Presbyterian Ministers Fund issued its first policy in 1761. The name was changed to Presbyterian Annuity and Life Insurance Company in 1889, thereafter insuring Protestant ministers, their wives, and theological students.
1781	Bank of North America, the oldest commercial bank in this country, opened in Philadelphia. It was chartered by the Pennsylvania legislature and incorporated by the Continental Congress for the purpose of providing money to wage the Revolutionary War against England through pooling of private and public resources.
1791	First Bank of the United States was the original effort to establish a national bank. This institution was promoted by Alexander Hamilton and chartered by the Congressional Federalists. The initial capitalization was $10 million, of which 20% was owned by the national government. The bank terminated in 1811 due to considerable opposition in Congress.
1812	The first public life insurance company was formed under the name of Pennsylvania Company for Insurance on Lives and Granting Annuities.
1816	The second Bank of the United States was established to exert some controls over private banks and to regulate the U.S. monetary system. This second attempt to establish a national banking system was successfully opposed by President Andrew Jackson and closed down in 1836.
1816	The first mutual savings bank was established and still operates under its original name–Philadelphia Savings Fund Society. The bank was organized to operate for the interests of its shareholders (its depositors) and it encouraged savings by persons of modest means.
1831	The first savings association chartered for the purpose of accumulating capital for building houses was founded by Samuel Pilling and Jeremiah Horrocks under the name of Oxford Provident Building Association in Philadelphia. The first mortgage loan for the purpose of buying a home was made to Comly Rich of Philadelphia in the amount of $375.00. Monthly payments were $4.90.
1835	New England Mutual was chartered as the first of the modern forms of life insurance companies.
1863	The federal government resumed responsibility for the regulation of currency. After the closing of the second Bank of the United States in 1836, state chartered banks had issued their own bank notes which circulated as currency.
1913	The Federal Reserve Bank was established by the federal government as a national bank to administer currency and to regulate federal chartered

(*continued*)

TABLE 1-1 (continued)

	commercial banks and any state chartered banks that met membership requirements.
1916	The government created the Federal Land Bank as a system to raise money through the sale of bonds for the purpose of making loans to farmers.
1932	Under the administration of Herbert Hoover, the Reconstruction Finance Corporation was established to provide direct government loans to private business.
1932	The Federal Home Loan Bank was created as a regulatory agency to charter national savings and loan associations and to supervise their operations.
1933	On March 6, 1933, President Franklin D. Roosevelt closed all banks in the country to halt disastrous runs. Thereafter, those deemed in satisfactory condition could reopen. Within one year, the number of operating banks in this country was reduced from 30,000 to 16,000.
1933	Securities and Exchange Commission (SEC) was established to regulate the issuance and sale of all types of securities to the general public.
1934	Federal Housing Administration (FHA) was created to utilize the credit of the federal government to insure home loans and thus encourage lending from private sources.
1934	Farmer's Home Administration (FmHA) set up a federal program to provide direct home loans to low income farmers.
1934	Federal Deposit Insurance Corporation (FDIC) provided a means to insure deposits in commercial banks against losses due to bank failure.
1934	Federal Savings and Loan Insurance Corporation (FSLIC) provided a corporate body similar to the FDIC that insures deposits in savings associations.
1937	Local Housing Authority (LHA) allowed for the creation of quasi-government agencies for the purpose of developing low-cost housing for lower income families.
1938	Federal National Mortgage Association (FNMA) was the government agency established to provide funds for the purchase of FHA insured loans.
1944	Veterans Administration (VA), created in 1930, established home loan guaranty program for veterans during World War II.
1965	Department of Housing and Urban Development (HUD) resulted from the reorganization of various government operations intended to coordinate and expand housing programs.
1968	Government National Mortgage Association (GNMA) created from the partitioning of the Federal National Mortgage Association as an agency under HUD to handle housing assistance programs and loan management functions.

TABLE 1-1 (continued)

1970	Federal Home Loan Mortgage Corporation (FHLMC) established by the Federal Home Loan Bank Board to sell bonds and use the proceeds to purchase mortgages from member savings associations.
1970	Environmental Protection Agency (EPA) created to develop rules and procedures for the improvement of our natural heritage and to enforce requirements for proper land development.
1974	Housing and Community Development Act passed by Congress consolidated a number of federal programs such as Urban Renewal, Model Cities, Neighborhood Facilities, Open Space, Water and Sewer Facilities plus some lending authority into a single program. Federal funds are made available to local communities which follow national guidelines and determine how the money is to be spent.

DEVELOPMENT OF MORTGAGE BANKING

In a growing country like the United States, the pools of lendable money were not always readily available where needed, or were not always known to a potential borrower. To help bridge the gap, a new industry gradually developed that is now known as mortgage banking. The precise date of its origin would be difficult to state because the mortgage banking business has developed from a small service or brokerage facility in the late 1800s into a major banking industry today. Initially, a lawyer, or perhaps a real estate broker with contacts in the investment world, would arrange a loan for a client and charge a service fee; and as some individuals became quite adept at this business, the placement of loans became their principal occupation. Even today, a large number of mortgage bankers come from first- or second-generation family-owned businesses.

LENDING REFORMS FROM THE GREAT DEPRESSION

In the early 1900s, potential borrowers had four main sources from which to seek a loan—a bank, a savings association, an insurance company, or a wealthy individual. Or they could minimize their search by turning their problem over to a loan broker, who usually had several potential sources of funds available for a small fee. But the rules were quite different then. A house loan might be 50% of the lender's estimate of value, to be repaid in full in five years—no amortization, no escrow account—a system that could cause an instant collapse—and did. Also, without proper regulation, an individual or company could sell mortgage bonds up to the appraised value of a projected development, say a Florida resort hotel. And the "appraisal" could be made by no less an authority than the person trying to sell the bonds! In the 1920s these were the "gold bonds," which pretty much disappeared from circulation during the Depression.

The collapse of the real estate loan market in the early 1930s brought a flood of foreclosures with farms, houses, and businesses swept away. It is the now-passing generation who determined that there must be a better way.

Many historic changes were wrought in our economy under the administration of Franklin Delano Roosevelt to prevent future economic disasters. The demand by some economists in those days to "control the economy" or to "eliminate depressions" was the source of many jokes and was not taken too seriously by most people, including much of the business community. But controls were established nonetheless.

The Securities and Exchange Commission was brought into existence to regulate the sale of all types of securities to the general public. The bankruptcy laws were revised to deter one or two creditors from destroying a cash-short business at the expense of all the other creditors.

But the area of change bearing on our special interests encompasses the sweeping reforms made in real estate finance beginning with the closing of all banks in 1933. To start patching up the economy, the Home Owners Loan Corporation was formed that same year to issue government-guaranteed bonds and to use the proceeds to refinance home owners' indebtedness. Over one million houses were refinanced through this agency, and with the new liquidity in our financial institutions, stability was gradually restored.

A year later, in 1934, the Federal Housing Administration was created to provide home loan insurance. It did not then, and does not today, make loans. It provides a loan insurance policy, insuring the lender against loss through default, if the FHA qualifications are met. However, many bankers and other lenders, inherently opposed to any government intrusion, especially in an area where character judgment was considered all important, simply refused to recognize a government-insured commitment.

Hence, a few years later, in 1938, the Federal National Mortgage Association, FNMA or "Fannie Mae," was established to buy FHA insured mortgage loans and then to resell them as markets could be found. This agency provided the real beginnings of the so-called secondary market for mortgage loans, which may be broadly defined as any purchaser of a mortgage loan who does not participate in its origination. Money to finance FNMA purchases was derived from the sale of bonds.

By 1940, the pressures of a war economy brought an expansion of FHA activities to encourage housing in defense-designated areas and to permit financing of large apartment or multifamily projects. In 1944, Congress passed legislation permitting the Veterans Administration to guarantee mortgage loans made by private lenders to veterans.

POST-WORLD WAR II EXPANSION

The post-World War II growth of government-assisted financing has paralleled and supported the growth of the mortgage banking industry. Were it not for the lubrication provided by multiservice mortgage bankers, the government would be much less efficient in spreading its insured programs to those needing loan assistance. Both the FHA and the VA lean heavily on mortgage bankers approved by these agencies as having met their standards, and who are therefore qualified (1) to disseminate correct requirements and data to the public; (2) to secure the necessary information on a loan applicant's qualifications; and (3) to arrange prompt funding for the loan upon issuance of a government commitment.

The growth of government programs has not diminished the continuing expansion of savings associations and insurance companies in providing mortgage loans, either direct to clients or through correspondents, for houses, apartments, and commercial buildings.

In addition, the recent years have seen a new pool of money entering the real estate field in pension and trust funds. Since most of these funds have little contact with the general public, such moneys move primarily through the mortgage banking industry.

FUTURE REAL ESTATE DEVELOPMENT

Looking towards the future, the demands for mortgage money should continue to grow, but at a lesser rate than in the past several decades. The largest segment of the mortgage loan market, single family housing, will decline as prices for such housing place it beyond the reach of the majority of family home purchasers. In the 1950s, approximately two-thirds of American families could afford to buy single family houses. Now, this percentage has dropped to less than one-third of the families. Government programs are recognizing this change in the housing market and are making attempts to provide lower cost loans through subsidizing a portion of the interest costs. However, money costs are only one of the factors contributing to the increased price of a house. There are also the increasing costs of land, labor, and materials that face any real estate developer plus the uncertain delays and costs brought on by the various environmental clearances presently required. A developer also may expect to face all levels of government, a variety of government agencies, plus some private local or national environmental groups which may support conflicting views. Although not yet an impossible situation, the threat of delays and legal actions discourages many developers and, in the long run, will add to the costs of future construction.

The experiment by the federal government in connection with the New Communities Development program has met with limited success. This effort, assigned to the Department of HUD, was begun in the late 1960s. Their objective was to plan and develop, in cooperation with private builders, full-scale towns on tracts of land exceeding 2,000 acres. The government subsidized certain public needs such as fire stations, and guaranteed bonds for the developer to build utilities and streets. Twenty-two major projects were undertaken on tracts of land near large urban centers. None fulfilled their growth expectations and only a few were able to meet their financial obligations after the first five years. The concept of a well-planned and attractive community that would provide a viable alternative to the over-crowded urban centers proved to be more idealistic than practical. It overlooks the basic role of a community, which is to support the work requirements of its residents. Although government assistance in the total planning of future residential developments may not be practical, some form of help may well be needed to cope with the growth in regulations designed to protect the environment.

In the private, business sector, many major companies as diverse as Westinghouse, Ford Motor Company, and Exxon Corporation have entered the real estate development field where large amounts of cash are essential. However, as some companies have learned, considerably more than money is needed to end up with successful land developments. Nonetheless, the large development companies do have an advantage in long-term resources available to handle the large investments required over a long period of time, and to attract the specialists and experts needed to carry a project through various stages to a profitable conclusion. These companies are capable of bypassing traditional financing methods and can generate their own funds through the sale of stocks and bonds, through their ability to sell commercial paper or borrow short-term funds from commercial banks without resort to mortgages.

Change in our living patterns is a continuing process brought about by economic pressures plus the human desire for betterment. The increasing costs of housing are forcing urban construction into higher density structures such as apartments, townhouses, and condominiums. However, the impetus for urban growth is not for everyone. Statistics are showing an increase in the number of families and retired people moving to the smaller communities with a more relaxed lifestyle. Development will continue to be needed in both large and small communities.

The smaller communities do not present a market of sufficient size to attract the largest builders, and, therefore, will continue to be served by the individual entrepreneur. The large development companies can flourish in the metropolitan areas with a market for housing and other construction projects suitable to their size. In an industry that has been dominated by small independent companies, there will be no substantial change. A few builders have achieved national stature, more have reached prominence in a region of the country, but because of the localized nature of the product, the need for smaller, innovative builders will continue.

QUESTIONS FOR DISCUSSION

1. From whom and under what conditions did people borrow money prior to the Industrial Revolution?

2. How did the pre-Depression methods of financing real estate contribute to the collapse of the economy in the early 1930s?

3. What do you believe is the principal contribution of the Roosevelt Administration towards stabilizing the economy in 1933?

4. Why did the Federal Housing Administration find considerable resistance from private lenders to its insured loan program?

5. How do you think real estate developments of the future will be financed?

Chapter 2

Money and Interest Rates

No commodity is more widely used and less understood than money. In a limited sense, we know very well what money can do; its value lies primarily in our confidence that other people will accept the money in exchange for their goods and services. A brief reference to history shows that money has been with us in all civilizations as a means to improve the barter system of trading goods and services among people. Commodities of high intrinsic value have always been used in trade, including precious metals, gem stones, furs, and even salt and other spices. In fact, many areas of the world still use such standards today. Our modern business, however, floats on an intangible—the trust and confidence that individuals and nations place in currency and credit lines extended for bonds or other promissory certificates issued under a recognized government's authority. Certainly, the confidence placed in a government and its international trading power is indicated by the relative values placed on a nation's money in the realm of international trade.

THE MONETARY SYSTEM

The method used to manage the nation's money is the monetary system. It is a complicated mixture of free enterprise and government controls. Every lending institution has the right to accept or reject

11

loan applications under its own requirements, which is the essence of the free enterprise system. In formulating its own requirements, each lender must conform with regulations established by both federal and state banking authorities, which often overlap. As the nation's central bank, the Federal Reserve Bank Board works to control the money supply along sound economic lines, but an effort by the board to encourage business activity through an increase in the money supply may find the bankers reluctant to make more loans for other reasons. Any plans for managing the money supply must recognize the power of Congress to alter taxing procedures and to change spending plans. The demands of the federal government for borrowed money take top priority as the Treasury can sell short-term bills and notes with no limits on the interest rate.

The monetary system was not planned—it simply grew with the country and was re-molded periodically to meet changing needs and changing political climates. Much progress has been made. Just over one hundred years ago, any state chartered bank could print its own bank notes which served as currency. In western territories, trading companies printed their own currency with which they bought furs, rugs, jewelry, and other products from people living in the area and then sold them various manufactured products and foodstuffs in return. Today there is only one legal tender which is printed and coined under the direction of the Federal Reserve Bank.

How this monetary system is managed has a direct effect on the availability of money for mortgage loans. And this in turn controls the health of the entire construction industry. So some knowledge of the mechanisms used to wield this power and the pressures that influence the direction it takes is vital to an understanding of real estate finance.

There are many problems in this system. To begin with, the operations are part free enterprise and part government owned or controlled. The large pools of money available for loans in this country are almost all owned by individual depositors, persons with insurance policies, and by private companies which in turn are owned by individuals. They cannot be forced to use their assets in a specific manner without a possible conflict with their right to due process under the law. But they can be given guidelines on how to make loans in the form of regulations directed towards the protection of the general public. Interest rates can be set by law but only one effective public rate is established. That is the interest that can be paid by a bank or a savings association to its depositors. The much publicized rate for a mortgage loan insured by the Federal Housing Administration, the insuring office of the Department of Housing and Urban Development (HUD), is not an effective rate. The actual rate is established in the marketplace.

Another problem that makes precise operation of the monetary system difficult is the lack of complete and accurate information. The Federal Reserve Bank can only demand information on cash, deposits, and loans outstanding from its member banks. The member banks number 5,775, or much less than half of the 14,632 commercial banks in the country. But they represent over 75% of the total assets as all the largest banks are members.

The increasing flow of money between major trading countries has made action by the Federal Reserve less effective. Foreign governments can buy and sell U.S. government bonds and can make deposits or withdrawals from banks in this country in large blocks that distort normal trade movements.

Probably the biggest problem in the operation of the monetary system is that so many different agencies and people can exercise an influence affecting it. The strongest power is, of course, the Congress which has taxing and spending authority, plus the power to borrow whatever is needed to cover any deficits. The Federal Reserve has to work within the laws passed by Congress and has the responsibility of managing the nation's money. The United States Treasury, operating under the direction of the politically appointed Secretary of the Treasury, is charged with the handling of the public debt. How the Treasury funds and re-funds the federal debt has a strong influence on our monetary system and the availability of money in the private sector of the economy.

In spite of the many problems with the monetary system, it should be pointed out that over the years it has proven to be an effective system. So far, this system has been able to provide the capital needed for worthy projects. There have been delays in periods of tight money and disagreement over what is considered "worthwhile." But the mixture of free enterprise, and government controls has managed to finance a nation of homeowners and an unparalleled growth in the nation's productivity.

MONEY SUPPLY

The amount of money available at any one time for use in mortgage lending is dependent on the competition for this same money, and equally important, the amount of money that is being introduced into the system by the government through its agency, the Federal

Reserve Bank. It is the increase in the money supply that is so closely watched to determine the course of Federal Reserve policies. While the activities for handling the money supply are complex and cloaked in secrecy by the Board, the basic cause and effect relationship is fairly simple.

The size of our total money supply and of the economy makes the problem appear almost beyond comprehension. For clarification, let us use a simplified example. First, remember that the value of money used today is represented by the goods and services that it can buy. If we have an economy with exactly 10,000 units of goods and services with an amount of money available to purchase these products totaling $1 million, each unit of goods and services would be worth $100. Now, by increasing productivity over several years, the economy has 20,000 units of goods and services for sale. But assume that *no increase* has been made in the available money. With twice as much to buy for the same amount of money, the price of each unit of goods and services drops to $50. If a different policy were used so that over the same period of time that our increased productivity supplied 20,000 units of goods and services, the money supply was subsequently increased to $3 million, then each unit would be worth $150. To maintain a stable pricing structure, a balance must be maintained between the money supply and the increase in productivity.

Measuring the Money Supply

In order to manage the money supply, a method of measurement is needed. Economists differ somewhat on the precise concept of money, also, the categories that are used for measurement are not too clearly defined. For example, is a NOW (Negotiable Order of Withdrawal) savings account a demand deposit? Does a large certificate of deposit (over $100,000) represent a time deposit or is it more like a security? How does a "checkless" computerized payment fit into the categories? The Federal Reserve uses several categories in their periodic reports on the money supply which are identified by the obvious letter "M." The major categories are:

1. M_1—Currency in circulation plus commercial bank demand deposits. At the end of 1975, this figure totaled $295 billion.

2. M_2—is the total of M_1 plus bank time and savings deposits other than large certificates of deposit. At the end of 1975, M_2 totaled $663 billion.

3. M_3—is the total of M_2 plus thrift institution deposits. M_3 totaled $1,092 billion at the end of 1975.

Management of the Money Supply

The actual amount of money in circulation in this country is not controlled by either the Congress or the president. It is the sole responsibility of the Federal Reserve Bank. The Federal Reserve was established by Congress on December 23, 1913 as the government's central banker and manages the nation's money through a system of 12 branches plus the commercial banks who are members of the system, a total of 5,775 banks at the end of 1975. How the Federal Reserve exercises its influence over the system is discussed later in this chapter under "Interest Rates."

The control of the money supply itself gives the Federal Reserve Board (Fed) a strong hand on the nation's economy. The crucial decisions on how much money will be added to the supply or withdrawn from circulation are made by the 12 people who comprise the Federal Open Market Committee. These are five presidents from different branch Reserve Banks and the seven governors of the Reserve Board. They meet the third Tuesday of every month in closely guarded secrecy to study indicators, receive reports, and argue among themselves as to what action should be taken. The decision is not announced to the public and is transmitted to a small staff who operate out of the New York Federal Reserve Bank and implement the Open Market Committee's decisions.

If the decision is to increase the money supply, the operation is carried out through a small number of dealers and big banks who are licensed to trade in government securities. The Federal Reserve staff handling the operation contacts one or more of these dealers and gives them a check drawn on the Federal Reserve account to buy government securities. The dealer delivers the securities and deposits the check in a bank. The check is sent back to the Fed for collection. The Fed credits the bank which now has more money on deposit and thus more money to lend. As money becomes more plentiful in the banks, it should become cheaper and encourage business activity, and this works most of the time.

But how can the Fed simply write checks like this? It is authorized by law to do so and has what amounts to an open-ended bank account. It can create money as it sees fit. Because of this power, it is easy to see why the federal government can never go bankrupt.

States and cities may become insolvent or bankrupt, but not the federal government. It is the authority to print money and create its own bank credits that gives the federal government its top of the list credit rating. Anyone buying a government bond, note, or bill knows that it will be paid off in full at due date simply by printing the money to do so, if necessary.

Effects of Money Supply Management

The ideal for the Federal Reserve to aim for with its handling of the money supply is to increase the amount of available money exactly in proportion to the growth of our economy. There is a normal need for more money as the population grows and as business activity increases along with productivity increases. In practice it doesn't work out very smoothly. Many economists believe that the key to economic stability lies in how the money supply is increased and that it has to be used as a throttle mechanism for the economy. Because of its substantial power to speed up or slow down the pace of business activity with its money supply decisions, the Federal Reserve in the past has declined to announce its money supply decisions when they are made. The results of their actions could only be determined by studying the money supply statistics released the following month—and then it was a guessing game to figure out what their moves had been. In 1975, Congress required the Fed to announce its money supply goals in advance which has reduced some of the speculation. But the announced goals have proven hard to reach. The steps taken to make adjustments in the money supply are hard to measure precisely and the results of their moves lag behind the need to know.

Further complications have arisen with the operation of the money supply in the increased velocity of money—the speed with which it can be transferred. Changes in bank clearing procedures and the use of computerized transfers have made it possible for less money to accomplish more. In addition, the substantial increase in foreign trade and the large amounts of foreign money that can move in and out of this country have sometimes worked in direct opposition to the Fed's announced policies.

At best, the management of the money supply is imprecise and depends more on expectations than on known quantities in the efforts to stabilize the economy.

ROLE OF THE FEDERAL GOVERNMENT

While the Federal Reserve Bank is considered the most influential government agency that affects the monetary system, and in turn the overall economy, there are many other governmental agencies which have a role in the movement of money to the various users. A well known government influence on real estate lending is the periodic adjustment of the FHA-VA fixed interest rates established for loans that are acceptable under their programs. However, neither the FHA or VA loan money directly to the home buyer or borrower. They try to encourage the private lending institution to make loans by issuing a default insurance policy or a guarantee of re-payment to the lender should the borrower fail to do so. So the FHA-VA established rates are more a reflection of the conventional market conditions with, perhaps, some political influence on when a change in rates is recognized. A movement of these rates either way has a psychological effect on both the lender and the borrower although the return to the lender (yield) is not affected.

Two government agencies, the Farmers Home Administration* and the Federal Land Banks, make loans with their own funds direct to farmers and for rural housing. The activities of these agencies are more fully explained under "Sources of Money" in Chapter 4.

There are several business-oriented agencies of the federal government which become involved with real estate loans and thus can have some effect on the capital and money markets. A few examples are the Small Business Administration (SBA), Rural Electrification Administration (REA), and the Government Services Agency (GSA).

Besides the government agencies that offer (1) federal insurance or guarantee programs to assist mortgage loans, (2) direct government loans for farm-related needs, and (3) business oriented loans, there is another group of agencies that exerts powerful influences in the huge secondary market for mortgage loans. One of these is the Government National Mortgage Association (GNMA) which makes purchases of certain categories of mortgage loans from loan originators to assist federal housing programs. Another is the Federal Home Loan Mortgage Corporation which is an agency established by the Federal Home Loan Bank Board for the purpose of buying loans from member savings associations. A third is the Federal National

*FmHA is designated with the "m" to reduce confusion with the abbreviation, FHA, for Federal Housing Administration which is now also designated as the Insuring Office, Department of Housing and Urban Development.

Mortgage Association (FNMA) which was established as a government agency in 1938 and was made into a private corporation in 1968. It is a large purchaser of mortgage loans in the secondary market and is still influenced in its decisions by federal government policies and programs. A separate study of these agencies is made later in this text.

The United States Treasury

In recounting the major governmental influences on the movement of money and its relation to the mortgage lending industry, a strong hand is played by the Secretary of the Treasury. The amount of money available for long-term (over 10 years) loans at any one time is limited and the next largest user of this type of money is the government. (Largest use is for mortgage loans.) So how the United States Treasury handles its requirements for money has a direct bearing on what is left for real estate loans. Increasingly, the Treasury has had to resort to short-term borrowing which is not restricted by interest rate ceilings imposed by Congress on the long-term bond issues.

Prior to 1917, every new offering of Treasury securities required specific Congressional authorization including terms and conditions of each issue. During World War I, Congress granted some leeway to the Treasury in setting terms of new issues but insisted on setting the maximum interest rate—originally at 3½ percent, reflecting the Congressional desire for low interest rates. In 1919, Congress gave the Treasury more flexibility by removing interest rate ceilings on securities that matured in five years or less but retained a 4¼ percent ceiling on new issues of longer term securities.

The restrictions provided little problem for the following half century. After all, the cost of long-term funds ranged from 2 to 6 percent through the massive economic fluctuations that occurred between 1865 and 1965. But as interest rates began to soar during the inflationary 1965–75 decade, the only way that the Treasury could sell new long-term issues was to ask Congress for higher interest rate ceilings: above 4¼ percent. Some increases were allowed for new issues during this period. Congress also changed the definition of "bond" maturity from five to seven years, and now to ten years. This effectively exempted a wider range of maturities from the ceiling and spurred the Treasury reliance on the shorter term Treasury "bills" and Treasury "notes."

The Congressional restrictions on interest rates, plus investor's unwillingness to lend long-term money during a prolonged inflationary period, has led to a continuing decline in the maturity of the Federal debt. In 1946, the average maturity of the debt was more than nine years, and longer term issues (then defined as maturities of five years or more) accounted for 54 percent of the total. In 1975, the average maturity was less than three years and long-term issues accounted for only 14 percent of the total.

Does the decline in debt maturity have any effect on the real estate mortgage market? The answer is definitely yes. The federal government is currently not soaking up funds that normally move into longer term loans as fast as the total federal borrowing would otherwise indicate. The heavy reliance that the Treasury places on short-term debt precludes them from tapping important sources of savings such as life insurance companies and pension funds which are more interested in long-term outlets. If the government demands for money continue to escalate because of deficit spending, the situation could quickly and easily change.

To give some idea of the federal needs for money and how it has escalated over the past few years, the following figures tell a threatening story. Over the entire decade of the 1960s, the Treasury raised $44 billion net in the nation's security markets. Even as late as 1974, net cash borrowing was less than $12 billion annually. By the beginning of 1976, net borrowing had soared to an annual rate of almost $85 billion. Because most of the cash came from short-term borrowings, the effect on mortgage lending was minimized. And interest rates in the short-term markets were not greatly affected because the demand for business loans remained relatively low during the period of heavy government borrowing.

To whom does the United States Treasury sell its long-term and short-term obligations when it needs money? The answer to this question has an important bearing on the nation's economy. The market has only two principal buyers—(1) the general public, and (2) the Federal Reserve Bank. The purpose of the government's borrowing is to raise money with which to buy more goods and services. It thus competes with the general public for the same goods and services. Now if the government sells its securities to the general public, it effectively takes money out of their hands and prevents competition between the general public and the government for the same goods and services. The result of government borrowing from the general public is to take purchasing power out of their hands and transfer it to the government, which is essentially non-inflationary.

But if the Treasury sells its obligations to the Federal Reserve Bank, which is the method used to increase the supply of money, there is no comparable reduction in the public's power to buy goods and services. The increase of money in government hands now competes directly with the general public for the same goods and services and presses all prices upward.

INTEREST RATES

Investment money constantly reaches for the highest yield on comparable risks. So the setting of interest rates is very important in determining the direction that money will move. Although interest is the price paid for using another's money, the price does not work quite the way it does with other commodities. An increase in the price for money does not always discourage the borrower, nor will a decrease in the interest rate by itself bring a greater demand for lendable funds. Money simply does not respond to pricing pressures in a precise and predictable manner. Where other commodities maintain something of a balance between supply and demand through price adjustments in a relatively free market, the price of money is under too much regulation to float freely and the economy operates too freely to accept regulated prices for money. The result is a blend of pressures that sets the interest rates.

The free market economy uses the basic forces of supply and demand to influence interest rates—as the demand for money increases, the cost will also increase. As the regulator of the economy with control of the monetary system, the government can establish interest rates in certain areas and pump money into programs in an effort to reduce interest costs. But neither the government nor bankers are able to set market rates of interest. The Congress could establish fixed rates of interest for various major categories of loans but this would probably require fixing prices of many other commodities at the same time. So the Congress allows the free market system to establish interest rates. Through banking regulatory agencies, only the interest rates paid by banks and savings associations to their depositors are set by law. The Federal Reserve sets the "discount rate" which is the interest rate charged by the Fed to its member banks if they borrow from the Fed.

Banks do business in a competitive market and are in the business of making a profit. They are compelled to seek the highest yields possible commensurate with the risk. But the bank's customers are free to shift their business to other banks if the bank overcharges for its loans. So in a very real sense, banks are restricted in what they can charge by the forces of competition, not by any governmental authority.

The federal government does not attempt to set a limit on maximum interest rates that may be charged, but state legislatures do exercise this authority under usury laws. States vary considerably on maximums allowed but most limit the rates in several categories. For example, short-term loans to individuals might be limited to a maximum of 10 percent interest per year, for corporations, 18 percent, for consumer-type installment loans (like car loans), 18 percent.

The federal government recognizes no limits for itself on the interest rates it will pay for money when it borrows short-term funds at the weekly Treasury bill auction. It is this power to pay any price for its short-term offerings that poses a considerable threat to other forms of private investment. When the interest rate on Treasury bills went over 9 percent in 1974, many savers withdrew their cash from savings associations and loaned their money to the federal government. The substantial outflow of cash from the savings associations dried up funds for long-term mortgage loans.

Interest Rate Indicators

There are a number of interest rates published daily in leading business magazines and newspapers and all give good clues as to the direction money costs are moving. Following are four rates that represent important indicators for the real estate mortgage business.

Federal Funds Rate. This is the most volatile of all interest rates. It is the rate charged by one bank to another for money loaned for as short a term as 24 hours. The name derives from the purpose of the loan—a bank that has funded an unusually large number of prior loan commitments on the same day, may find itself short of sufficient cash reserves to meet the federal regulations for liquidity and reserves. When this happens, a hurried call is made to another bank which has some surplus cash for that day and is willing to make the short-term loan. The rate charged has fluctuated in the past few years from a low of 4 percent to over 14 percent. It is not a nationally established rate and will vary considerably on any one day between different cities and between banks. The importance of this rate to the real estate investor is that the movement of federal funds rates in the big New York market are closely watched by the Federal Reserve Board's Open Market Committee and will give some indication of what policy the Fed is currently pursuing with its money supply targets which in turn will affect all interest rates. If the Fed permits the federal funds rate to increase over the previous weeks' before injecting new cash into the system, it is a good indication that the policy is to tighten new money supply.

Treasury Bill Rate. The cost of short-term borrowing by the federal government is clearly determined each week at the auctions of Treasury bills. The bills are sold by the Federal Reserve Bank and can be purchased from the Bank or through authorized security dealers. The return on this type of investment is expressed as a "yield" because it is determined by the difference between the purchase price and face value of the bill. For example, in a recent auction, 13-week bills were bought for 98.687 giving a yield of 5.138 percent. Expressed in dollars, a $10,000.00 face amount bill was purchased for $9,868.70. At maturity the return of $10,000.00 would give a gain of $131.30 for 13 weeks' use of the money. The percentage rates for yield on these auctions are based on the discount from par and are calculated on a 360-day year rather than the 365-day year on which the yields for bonds and other coupon securities are figured. The auctions for Treasury bills are open to anyone with investment cash (they have sold as small denominations as $1,000.00 but generally are limited to $10,000.00 denominations) and reflect the current short-term market accurately. As in all indicators, the trend, up or down, is an important guideline.

Prime Rate. This is defined as the interest rate charged by a commercial bank to its most credit-worthy customers. Each bank may set its own prime rate by any method it chooses. Some use complicated formulas and others depend on the wisdom of their Board of Directors. In practice most banks simply follow the lead of one of the major commercial banks. The prime rate is used more as a base upon which to float an interest rate for any class of loans, than as an actual lending rate. A good example is a construction loan which may be quoted at 2 points over prime—if the prime rate is 7 percent, the construction loan will be 9 percent. If the prime rate moves up to 8 percent, the construction loan automatically is increased to 10 percent and calculated from the date the prime change is announced. Another direct effect of the prime rate on the mortgage field is that warehouse lines of credit held by mortgage companies with their commercial banker are usually quoted as a point or more over prime.

FNMA Auction Yields. Every other Monday the Federal National Mortgage Association holds an auction for four-month commitments to buy home loans. The bidding is for commitments by Fannie Mae to buy mortgages during the commitment period if the originator selling the mortgages cannot get a better price elsewhere. The bid is expressed in a "yield." At a recent auction the average yield offered for FNMA cash to buy FHA–VA mortgages came to 8.967 percent. This means that the consensus of mortgage companies and other lending company participants on that particular day was that they could pay a yield of 8.967 percent for their money from the wholesale, or secondary market, and turn around to the local borrower for a little higher yield, say 9.375 percent, over the next four months. Thus yields quoted at these auctions tend to reflect lender expectations for home loan rates for the next four months. The quotations given in the results released every other Tuesday following the acceptance of bids are secondary market rates for loans purchased in larger blocks. But they accurately give an indication of future home loan rates.

Influences on Interest Rates

Since there is, as yet, no national market in mortgages with quoted rates on yields such as we find in commodity markets or the stock exchanges, the industry relies on many indicators of business activity along with the open auctions for loan commitments. To determine rates, one of the important guides is the movement of yields on other long-term investments. These include the daily published rates on government and corporate bonds. If a new government bond issue sells rapidly at its offered price, the strength is duly noted by other lenders, and there is a tendency to move interest rates upward. If an issue finds few buyers, the market tends to move downward.

The rapidly fluctuating short-term money market exerts an influence on long-term interest rates by the direction of its trend. Short-term rates tending upward eventually force long-term rates higher, or else the flow of money temporarily shifts to the short-term arena.

The interplay of influences and pressures in the economic world as they affect the rise and fall of interest rates can be outlined in the following four categories:

Supply of Money. For lending purposes, we must understand those factors that influence the flow of funds into the large sources. One of these, the inclination to save a portion of one's earnings, both by individuals and corporations, for the "rainy day," is still quite strong. As this money flows into the great pools of private funds (commercial banks, thrift institutions, and life insurance companies), their capacity for lending more money obviously increases. As our economy has grown, the increase in savings has been correspondingly steady, although more so in some years than others. Situations arise in which the movement of funds between various institutions causes periodic shortages of money in certain areas. The competitive efforts among savings associations, among banks, and between banks and savings associations to garner more deposits, mostly at each other's expense, may cause some changes in the availability of money for mortgage lending. For example, competition has surfaced in such ways as changes in interest rates offered for various types of deposits; gifts or premiums for opening new accounts or substantially enlarging old ones; and even the introduction of a checking account procedure into savings associations, currently carried on in the New England area associations by means of a Negotiable Order of Withdrawal (or NOW). Whether or not savings will be allowed to accumulate in the banks, thrift institutions, and life insurance companies' portfolios also depends on the condition of business in general. In times of increasing inflationary pressures it is often necessary to draw against savings reserves to meet rising costs. Or inflation could cause withdrawals of cash to spend on major appliances or a car before prices increase further. The element of mass psychology is inherently involved in this area and complicates the problems of analysis and prediction.

So the supply of money available in the lender's hands at any given time for a specific loan depends not only on government policies and the business climate, but also on the amount of money the lender has on hand to loan. The movement of money out of the traditional sources for mortgage money, regardless of the reason, reduces the ability of mortgage lenders to fund loans.

Demand for Money. The basic supply of money in the country does not fluctuate nearly as much as the demand. There are four major areas of demand covering both long-term and short-term needs that compete with each other for the available supply. These are:

1. *Business borrowing*—all forms of loans, inventory needs, tax requirements, long-term funds, and others.

2. *Consumer and personal loans*—installment loans, auto financing, personal requirements.

3. *Government financing*—federal, state, and municipal bond issues, short-term needs, government agency issues.

4. *Mortgage loans*—all types: construction, development, income properties, housing, and so on.

In a booming economy, all segments have needs that add to the upward pressures on interest rates in their efforts to attract the necessary financing. Regulations have been eased that previously restricted the interest rates that could be paid on bond issues by cities and states, and their issues have now become more competitive. Efforts to reduce demand by forcing acceptance of higher interest rates have not always been effective, however, because businesses can afford the higher rates if its competitors are forced to pay the same costs. The federal government is not restricted as to what interest it can pay in the bill and note markets, and Congress does not show concern for money costs when voting for a deficit spending program.

The lower end of the capability spectrum includes people on fixed incomes who are not always able to pay the extra interest costs required to purchase a car or new house. In a sagging economy, the lowering of interest rates does not in itself create much new demand for money. The inclination to borrow for an expansion of facilities or for an increase in inventory is neither strong nor urgent when business declines.

Monetary Policies of the Federal Reserve Bank. The manner in which the government handles its money supply is called monetary policies. Responsibility for these policies lies with the Federal Reserve Bank. The Board of Governors of the Federal Reserve has the power to influence and, to a substantial degree, to exercise control over interest rates. The economic tools it uses to achieve and maintain these controls are:

1. *The rate of increase in money supply.* The amount of money in circulation is a direct responsibility of the Federal Reserve. In order to maintain a stable condition, the money supply should be allowed to increase at a rate comparable to our normal economic growth. To dampen inflationary pressures, the Fed can reduce the rate of increase, which simply makes less funds available to be loaned out by our banking system. Conversely, to spur a lagging economy, the rate of increase can be accelerated to place more lendable funds in circulation.

2. *Open market operations.* By buying government bonds in the market, the Fed puts money into the accounts of sellers and thus increases bank deposits, which in turn provides more lendable funds. When the Fed sells

bonds, money is withdrawn from the bank accounts of the buyers, and this has a dampening effect on money available for loans. It is through this channel that the Fed implements its money supply targets.

3. *Changes in member bank reserve requirements.* All Federal Reserve member banks, which includes the major banks in the country, are subject to rules that specify the percentage of their assets that must be held in reserve, i.e., assets unavailable for any loans, together with the percentage of liquidity, that is, cash on hand and deposits that must be held in the Federal Reserve Bank. The reserve requirement varies at present from 7½ percent on deposits up to $10 million to 16½ percent on deposits over $400 million. By increasing the reserve requirement, the Federal Reserve is simply ordering withdrawal of a certain amount of cash from availability for loans. And by reducing this reserve requirement, more money is placed in the hands of the banking system to be loaned out.

4. *Discount rate.* The Federal Reserve member banks are permitted to borrow money from the Federal Reserve Bank system, but the loans must be fully collateralized. The use of this privilege is intended more as a standby security measure than as a normal commercial procedure. The rate that the Fed charges its member banks is called the *discount rate.* By adjusting this discount rate, the Fed tries to exercise some influence over the potential borrowings of its member banks, and the rates they charge. A change in the discount rate is an important signal to the banks, encouraging a change in their own lending rates. However, in actual practice, it has not proved to be a very effective tool. The attempt in 1973 to hold down the inflationary boom with successive increases in the discount rate proved of small value. The rate in that one year increased from 4½ percent at the beginning of the year to an all-time record of 8 percent by the following fall. The member banks managed to follow each raise with an equivalent increase in their own lending rates to all-time highs. And business demand for loans seldom wavered in the face of rising interest costs, largely because prices were increasing at a rapid enough rate to cover the costs. The effect of a lowering in the discount rate does have a positive effect, but if the business climate is not good, then businesses will not borrow money even at low rates. The need for borrowing must be present.

Fiscal Policies of the U.S. Government. The manner in which the government handles its tax and spending programs comprises the fiscal policies. The effect on interest rates is substantial. Within ill-defined bounds, an increase in taxes, primarily the income taxes on persons and corporations, will take money out of the hands of people who would otherwise spend it for more goods; whereas a decrease in taxes should serve as a spur to the economy. As for the spending side of the fiscal policy, a big deficit spending program is intended to increase a lagging economy and bring forth some inflationary pressures; whereas restricted spending programs should dampen business activity and slow down the economy. The economic inter-action isn't quite so simple as suggested, however, since deficit spend-ing creates the corresponding problem of raising the cash to finance the loss, which is done by selling more government bonds, thus soak-ing up lendable funds that might have been used for other purposes in the private sector of the economy.

INTEREST RATES ON NEW HOME MORTGAGES

Table 2-1 shows the changes that have occurred in residential mort-gage rates, maturities, and average loan amounts over the 5-year period 1971 to 1976.

MONEY MARKET—CAPITAL MARKET

Reference is made to the terms *money market* and *capital market* in this text. Investment money that moves into short-term loans is gen-erally designated for a term of less than three years. Examples of short-term loans are Treasury bills, commercial paper (corporation promissory notes), certificates of deposit, federal funds and install-ment loans. This is the *money market.*

In between the short-term money market and the long-term capital market is the *intermediate market.* The term in this market is roughly three to ten years. Examples of investment funds in this category would be Treasury notes, some debenture bonds, equip-ment notes, and the long-term certificates of deposit. The lines drawn here are generalized as definitions vary within banking institu-tions, and depend somewhat on the perspective. To a commercial banker, seven years is a long-term loan; to a savings association loan officer, seven years would be a short-term loan.

The long-term *capital market* is investment money loaned for periods of ten years or longer. This is the market that deals in mort-gage loans. Other examples of long-term loans that compete with mortgage loans for the available funds are government bonds and cor-porate bonds. For those not familiar with securities of any kind, the definition of a "bond" should be remembered as it is an acknowl-edgement of indebtedness widely used in business. A bond is an interest-bearing certificate acknowledging an indebtedness, issued by

TABLE 2-1.

Terms and Yields on New Home Mortgages

| Period | Conventional mortgages | | | | | | | | FHA-insured loans—Yield in private secondary market[5] |
| | Terms[1] | | | | | | Yields (percent) in primary market | | |
	Contract rate (percent)	Fees and charges (percent)[2]	Maturity (years)	Loan/price ratio (percent)	Purchase price (thous. of dollars)	Loan amount (thous. of dollars)	FHLBB series[3]	HUD series[4]	
1971	7.60	.87	26.2	74.3	36.3	26.5	7.74	7.75	7.70
1972	7.45	.88	27.2	76.8	37.3	28.1	7.60	7.64	7.53
1973	7.78	1.11	26.3	77.3	37.1	28.1	7.95	8.30	8.19
1974	8.71	1.30	26.3	75.8	40.1	29.8	8.92	9.22	9.55
1975	8.75	1.54	26.8	76.1	44.6	33.3	9.01	9.10	9.19
1975—May	8.63	1.63	27.0	75.5	43.5	32.2	8.90	9.05	9.16
June	8.73	1.42	26.5	76.4	43.1	32.4	8.96	9.00	9.06
July	8.66	1.40	26.0	75.9	44.1	32.9	8.89	9.00	9.13
Aug.	8.63	1.56	26.7	77.0	44.6	33.7	8.89	9.15	9.32
Sept.	8.70	1.46	26.7	75.9	45.6	34.1	8.94	9.25	9.74
Oct.	8.75	1.59	27.3	77.5	43.9	33.2	9.01	9.25	9.53
Nov.	8.74	1.65	27.6	76.5	46.4	34.8	9.01	9.20	9.41
Dec.	8.74	1.65	27.8	76.9	45.9	34.7	9.01	9.15	9.32
1976—Jan.	8.71	1.74	27.4	76.9	47.2	35.4	8.99	9.05	9.06
Feb.	8.67	1.56	26.0	75.1	45.2	33.4	8.93	9.00	9.04
Mar.	8.67	1.60	27.1	76.4	46.8	35.0	8.93	8.95	—
Apr.	8.67	1.52	27.3	75.3	48.5	35.8	8.92	8.90	8.82
May	8.76	1.32	26.5	77.3	46.5	35.2	8.98	9.00	9.03

[1] Weighted averages based on probability sample survey of characteristics of mortgages originated by major institutional lender groups (including mortgage companies) for purchase of single-family homes, as compiled by Federal Home Loan Bank Board in cooperation with Federal Deposit Insurance Corporation. Data are not strictly comparable with earlier figures beginning Jan. 1973.

[2] Fees and charges—related to principal mortgage amount—include loan commissions, fees, discounts, and other charges, but exclude closing costs related solely to transfer of property ownership.

[3] Effective rate, reflecting fees and charges as well as contract rates (as shown in first column of this table) and an assumed prepayment at end of 10 years.

[4] Rates on first mortgages, unweighted and rounded to the nearest 5 basis points.

[5] Based on opinion reports submitted by field offices of prevailing local conditions as of the first of the succeeding month. Yields are derived from weighted averages of private secondary market prices for Sec. 203, 30-year mortgages with minimum downpayment and an assumed prepayment at the end of 15 years. Any gaps in data are due to periods of adjustment to changes in maximum permissible contract interest rates.

a company authorized to do so, and secured in its repayment by (1) a mortgage on real property or equipment; (2) a designated fund; or (3) the assignment of specific income such as tax revenues.

QUESTIONS FOR DISCUSSION

1. Describe the monetary system used in this country.

2. How does the Federal Reserve increase the money supply?

3. Describe two government agencies that can influence the market for mortgage money and how they can do so.

4. How does the Treasury raise money when it has to borrow?

5. Explain the major factors that influence interest rates.

6. Explain what is meant by fiscal policies and by monetary policies.

7. Identify the four major areas of demand for money.

8. How does a change in interest rates affect business borrowing?

9. Compare the going rates of interest on mortgage loans in your community with the latest FNMA auction yields. How do the rates charged by savings associations compare with mortgage company rates?

10. Suggest ways to improve our banking system.

Chapter 3

Notes and Mortgages

Loans made with real estate as the collateral security can be traced back as far as the ancient Pharaohs of Egypt and the Romans of the pre-Christian era. Even then, some form of pledge or assignment of the property was used to ensure repayment of an obligation to the lender. The development over many centuries of this type of property assignment illustrates the interplay of individual rights, more specifically, the rights of a borrower as against the rights of a lender.

HISTORY AND DEVELOPMENT

The Mortgage as a Grant of Title to Property

In its earliest forms, a property pledge to secure a debt was an actual assignment of that property to the lender. During the term of the loan, the lender might even have the physical use of that land and was entitled to any rents or other revenues derived from the land pledged. Thus, the earliest form of land as security for a loan was the actual granting of title to the lender for the term of the loan.

Due to the primitive conditions of communication and transportation then in existence, the practice of granting title to property for a loan tended to foster a number of abuses by lenders. For example, a slight delay in payments, which might even be encouraged by the lender, easily created a default and forfeited the borrower's rights for any recovery of his land. Sometimes borrowers who felt they had been unjustly deprived of their property appealed to the king, or perhaps to an appointed minister, to seek a hearing for their grievances and to petition for just redress. And if it was subsequently determined that a wrong had been committed, the borrower might be given a chance to redeem his land with a late payment of the obligation. Thus the *right of redemption* came into being.

However, lenders were not happy with this redemption privilege and initiated a countermove by inserting a clause in future loan agreements that specifically waived the right of redemption. The borrower had to accept this clause or be denied the loan. As our civilization developed away from the unchallenged rule of an absolute monarch into written codes of law, the granting or refusal of redemption became a matter of law or of statute often referred to as *statutory redemption.* Variations in such laws among the states are substantial, going all the way from a total lack of redemption rights upon default up to two full years after default to pay off the loan and recover the property.

The Mortgage as a Lien

Another way in which land can be pledged as security for a loan is by means of granting a lien. A *lien* constitutes an encumbrance on property. It is a declaration of a claim to a parcel of land for some purpose that is recorded in the public record. In states where the lien form is prevalent, a pledge of land as security for a loan grants no title except under default of the obligation. So when a default does occur, the lender must convert his lien rights into an actual title to the property through court action, as the particular state may require.

While there is some variation in the precise usage of the lien as a form of pledge, and the limited assignment of title as another form of pledge, all property laws concerning mortgages can be classified into one form or the other. The advantages and disadvantages of each can be weighed as legal arguments, but for purposes of finance, it is important mainly to be aware of the existing differences and to know under what laws a particular property can be mortgaged.

Lenders have learned to live with various requirements, and can obtain adequate security for their loans by adapting their pledges to the many different laws. For example, they have adjusted even to the unique law spelled out in the original constitution of the State of Texas protecting a family homestead from all creditors with just three exceptions: (1) a loan for purchase of the property; (2) mechanic's and materialmen's liens and, (3) property taxes.

STATE LAWS CONTROL PROPERTY RIGHTS

Property rights in the United States are spelled out primarily under state laws, not by the federal government. Each state has written into its code of law specific rights that must be adhered to with regard to land ownership in that state. The local variations and shadings in these laws reflect the background and origins of the particular region. In the East, for example, the great body of English parliamentary law and common law guided the New England and mid-Atlantic states in setting up their constitutions and subsequent statutes. In the South, on the other hand, the French legal codes were reflected in the Louisiana Territory and were especially evident in the growing city of New Orleans. In still another section of the country, the Southwest, Spanish heritage determined the laws, and these laws recognized Catholic religious ties in marriage, as well as patriarchal protection of wife, children, and family relationships. As a result, community property statutes were enacted, and for many years special protections, as well as special limitations regarding women's property rights, were in force in this region of the country.

An attempt to cover such a broad field of law as real property rights on a national basis would be out of place in this text since it is a subject more properly handled by qualified attorneys, skilled in interpreting these rights according to the laws of each state. It can be pointed out, however, that most states have laws specifically limiting any conveyance of property rights solely to written agreements, and that all states require certain procedures to record conveyances of land in the public records. The result has been an increasingly accurate record of land titles, with a corresponding increase of protection for property owner's rights and those of any other interested parties.

THE MORTGAGE AND PROMISSORY NOTE

There are certain basic instruments used in real estate loans that have essentially the same purposes throughout the country. The most important of this group—and in fact the one that has given its name to the entire field of real estate finance—is the *mortgage.* A mortgage is simply a pledge of property to secure a loan. It is not a promise to pay anything. As a matter of fact, without a debt to secure, the mortgage itself becomes null and void by its own terms; or, as the French derivative of the word mortgage indicates, a "dead pledge." Due to the differences in state laws, the precise definition varies somewhat, but for our purposes a mortgage can best be defined as a limited conveyance of property as security for the debt recited therein, which can only be activated by failure to comply with its terms.

It is the promissory note, the actual promise to pay, which must accompany, or in some cases becomes a part of, the mortgage instrument, that is the real proof of the debt. It calls out the payment terms including the rate of interest. It is the note that defaults for nonpayment, not the mortgage instrument. The expression *mortgage default* is a technical misnomer. When the promissory note falls into default, the mortgage instrument is activated and becomes the means of protecting the lender's collateral.

In 1970, the Federal National Mortgage Association decided to expand its lending activities from exclusively FHA- and VA-underwritten loans into the larger area of conventional loans, that is to say, those loans without government underwriting. In order to provide a more uniform standard of collateral, the FNMA devised a mortgage instrument with a wider application than previously used. No one form could be used throughout the country because of variations in state laws. By way of illustration then, Figures 3-1 and 3-2 show some reproductions of forms in general usage—a note and deed of trust as used in California, and a note and mortgage as used in Michigan. The text of the mortgage instruments delineates between uniform convenants and nonuniform covenants, which simplifies a comparison.

When the Federal Home Loan Mortgage Corporation was established, it joined with FNMA in the development of standardized forms that would be acceptable to both of these organizations. This includes application forms, other forms needed to comply with new government regulations, as well as the notes and mortgage instruments reproduced on the following pages.

CLAUSES FOUND IN MORTGAGE INSTRUMENTS

Identification of *parties* in the initial clause spells out the precise names of all parties involved, the borrower or mortgagor, and the lender or mortgagee. In many states a wife must join her husband to

NOTE

US $ . . . . , California
                                                                                                    City

                                                                         . . . . , 19 . . . .

FOR VALUE RECEIVED, the undersigned ("Borrower") promise(s) to pay . . . .
. . . . , or order, the principal sum of
. . . . .Dollars, with
interest on the unpaid principal balance from the date of this Note, until paid, at the rate of . . . .
. . . . .percent per annum. Principal and interest shall be payable at . . . .
. . . . , or such other place as the Note holder may
designate, in consecutive monthly installments of . . . .
. . . . .Dollars (US $ . . . .), on the . . . .
. . . . .day of each month beginning . . . . , 19 . . . . . Such monthly installments
shall continue until the entire indebtedness evidenced by this Note is fully paid, except that any remaining indebtedness, if not sooner paid, shall be due and payable on . . . .

If any monthly installment under this Note is not paid when due and remains unpaid after a date specified by
a notice to Borrower, the entire principal amount outstanding and accrued interest thereon shall at once become
due and payable at the option of the Note holder. The date specified shall not be less than thirty days from the date
such notice is mailed. The Note holder may exercise this option to accelerate during any default by Borrower
regardless of any prior forbearance. If suit is brought to collect this Note, the Note holder shall be entitled to collect
all reasonable costs and expenses of suit, including, but not limited to, reasonable attorney's fees.

Borrower shall pay to the Note holder a late charge of . . . . .percent of any monthly
installment not received by the Note holder within . . . . .days after the installment is due.

Borrower may prepay the principal amount outstanding in whole or in part. The Note holder may require
that any partial prepayments (i) be made on the date monthly installments are due and (ii) be in the amount of that
part of one or more monthly installments which would be applicable to principal. Any partial prepayment shall be
applied against the principal amount outstanding and shall not postpone the due date of any subsequent monthly
installments or change the amount of such installments, unless the Note holder shall otherwise agree in writing. If,
within five years from the date of this Note, Borrower make(s) any prepayments in any twelve month period
beginning with the date of this Note, or anniversary dates thereof ("loan year") with money lent to Borrower by a
lender other than the Note holder, Borrower shall pay the Note holder (a) during each of the first three loan years
. . . . .percent of the amount by which the sum of prepayments made in any such loan year
exceeds twenty percent of the original principal amount of this Note and (b) during the fourth and fifth loan years
. . . . .percent of the amount by which the sum of prepayments made in any such loan
year exceeds twenty percent of the original principal amount of this Note.

Presentment, notice of dishonor, and protest are hereby waived by all makers, sureties, guarantors and endorsers
hereof. This Note shall be the joint and several obligation of all makers, sureties, guarantors and endorsers, and shall
be binding upon them and their successors and assigns.

Any notice to Borrower provided for in this Note shall be given by mailing such notice by certified mail addressed
to Borrower at the Property Address stated below, or to such other address as Borrower may designate by notice to
the Note holder. Any notice to the Note holder shall be given by mailing such notice by certified mail, return receipt
requested, to the Note holder at the address stated in the first paragraph of this Note, or at such other address as may
have been designated by notice to Borrower.

The indebtedness evidenced by this Note is secured by a Deed of Trust, dated . . . .
. . . ., and reference is made to the Deed of Trust for rights as to acceleration of the indebtedness
evidenced by the Note, including paragraph 17 which provides as follows:

"Transfer of the Property; Assumption. If all or any part of the Property or an interest therein is sold or transferred
by Borrower without Lender's prior written consent, excluding (a) the creation of a lien or encumbrance subordinate
to this Deed of Trust, (b) the creation of a purchase money security interest for household appliances, (c) a transfer
by devise, descent or by operation of law upon the death of a joint tenant or (d) the grant of any leasehold interest of
three years or less not containing an option to purchase, Lender may, at Lender's option, declare all the sums secured
by this Deed of Trust to be immediately due and payable. Lender shall have waived such option to accelerate if,
prior to the sale or transfer, Lender and the person to whom the Property is to be sold or transferred reach agreement
in writing that the credit of such person is satisfactory to Lender and that the interest payable on the sums secured
by this Deed of Trust shall be at such rate as Lender shall request. If Lender has waived the option to accelerate
provided in this paragraph 17 and if Borrower's successor in interest has executed a written assumption agreement
accepted in writing by Lender, Lender shall release Borrower from all obligations under this Deed of Trust and the
Note. If Lender exercises such option to accelerate, Lender shall mail Borrower notice of acceleration in accordance
with paragraph 14 hereof. Such notice shall provide a period of not less than 30 days from the date the notice is
mailed within which Borrower may pay the sums declared due. If Borrower fails to pay such sums prior to the
expiration of such period, Lender may, without further notice or demand on Borrower, invoke any remedies permitted
by paragraph 18 hereof."

. . . .

. . . .

. . . .
                        Property Address   *(Execute Original Only)*

CALIFORNIA—1 to 4 Family—6/75—FNMA/FHLMC UNIFORM INSTRUMENT

FIGURE 3–1a.

35

DEED OF TRUST

THIS DEED OF TRUST is made this. . . . . .day of. . . . .,
19. . . ., among the Trustor,. . . . .
. . . .(herein "Borrower"),. . . . .
. . . .(herein "Trustee"), and the Beneficiary,
. . . ., a corporation organized and
existing under the laws of. . . . ., whose address is. . . . .
. . . .(herein "Lender").

BORROWER, in consideration of the indebtedness herein recited and the trust herein created, irrevocably grants and conveys to Trustee, in trust, with power of sale, the following described property located in the County of
. . . ., State of California:

which has the address of. . . . ., ...,
                               [Street]   [City]
. . . .(herein "Property Address");
     [State and Zip Code]

TOGETHER with all the improvements now or hereafter erected on the property, and all easements, rights, appurtenances, rents (subject however to the rights and authorities given herein to Lender to collect and apply such rents), royalties, mineral, oil and gas rights and profits, water, water rights, and water stock, and all fixtures now or hereafter attached to the property, all of which, including replacements and additions thereto, shall be deemed to be and remain a part of the property covered by this Deed of Trust; and all of the foregoing, together with said property (or the leasehold estate if this Deed of Trust is on a leasehold) are herein referred to as the "Property";

To SECURE to Lender (a) the repayment of the indebtedness evidenced by Borrower's note dated. . . . .
. . . .(herein "Note"), in the principal sum of. . . . .
. . . . ,. . . . . .Dollars, with interest thereon, providing for monthly installments of principal and interest, with the balance of the indebtedness, if not sooner paid, due and payable on
. . . .; the payment of all other sums, with interest thereon, advanced in accordance herewith to protect the security of this Deed of Trust; and the performance of the covenants and agreements of Borrower herein contained; and (b) the repayment of any future advances, with interest thereon, made to Borrower by Lender pursuant to paragraph 21 hereof (herein "Future Advances").

Borrower covenants that Borrower is lawfully seised of the estate hereby conveyed and has the right to grant and convey the Property, that the Property is unencumbered, and that Borrower will warrant and defend generally the title to the Property against all claims and demands, subject to any declarations, easements or restrictions listed in a schedule of exceptions to coverage in any title insurance policy insuring Lender's interest in the Property.

CALIFORNIA—1 to 4 Family—6/75—FNMA/FHLMC UNIFORM INSTRUMENT

FIGURE 3-1b.

UNIFORM COVENANTS. Borrower and Lender covenant and agree as follows:

1. Payment of Principal and Interest. Borrower shall promptly pay when due the principal of and interest on the indebtedness evidenced by the Note, prepayment and late charges as provided in the Note, and the principal of and interest on any Future Advances secured by this Deed of Trust.

2. Funds for Taxes and Insurance. Subject to applicable law or to a written waiver by Lender, Borrower shall pay to Lender on the day monthly installments of principal and interest are payable under the Note, until the Note is paid in full, a sum (herein "Funds") equal to one-twelfth of the yearly taxes and assessments which may attain priority over this Deed of Trust, and ground rents on the Property, if any, plus one-twelfth of yearly premium installments for hazard insurance, plus one-twelfth of yearly premium installments for mortgage insurance, if any, all as reasonably estimated initially and from time to time by Lender on the basis of assessments and bills and reasonable estimates thereof.

The Funds shall be held in an institution the deposits or accounts of which are insured or guaranteed by a Federal or state agency (including Lender if Lender is such an institution). Lender shall apply the Funds to pay said taxes, assessments, insurance premiums and ground rents. Lender may not charge for so holding and applying the Funds, analyzing said account or verifying and compiling said assessments and bills, unless Lender pays Borrower interest on the Funds and applicable law permits Lender to make such a charge. Borrower and Lender may agree in writing at the time of execution of this Deed of Trust that interest on the Funds shall be paid to Borrower, and unless such agreement is made or applicable law requires such interest to be paid, Lender shall not be required to pay Borrower any interest or earnings on the Funds. Lender shall give to Borrower, without charge, an annual accounting of the Funds showing credits and debits to the Funds and the purpose for which each debit to the Funds was made. The Funds are pledged as additional security for the sums secured by this Deed of Trust.

If the amount of the Funds held by Lender, together with the future monthly installments of Funds payable prior to the due dates of taxes, assessments, insurance premiums and ground rents, shall exceed the amount required to pay said taxes, assessments, insurance premiums and ground rents as they fall due, such excess shall be, at Borrower's option, either promptly repaid to Borrower or credited to Borrower on monthly installments of Funds. If the amount of the Funds held by Lender shall not be sufficient to pay taxes, assessments, insurance premiums and ground rents as they fall due, Borrower shall pay to Lender any amount necessary to make up the deficiency within 30 days from the date notice is mailed by Lender to Borrower requesting payment thereof.

Upon payment in full of all sums secured by this Deed of Trust, Lender shall promptly refund to Borrower any Funds held by Lender. If under paragraph 18 hereof the Property is sold or the Property is otherwise acquired by Lender, Lender shall apply, no later than immediately prior to the sale of the Property or its acquisition by Lender, any Funds held by Lender at the time of application as a credit against the sums secured by this Deed of Trust.

3. Application of Payments. Unless applicable law provides otherwise, all payments received by Lender under the Note and paragraphs 1 and 2 hereof shall be applied by Lender first in payment of amounts payable to Lender by Borrower under paragraph 2 hereof, then to interest payable on the Note, then to the principal of the Note, and then to interest and principal on any Future Advances.

4. Charges; Liens. Borrower shall pay all taxes, assessments and other charges, fines and impositions attributable to the Property which may attain a priority over this Deed of Trust, and leasehold payments or ground rents, if any, in the manner provided under paragraph 2 hereof or, if not paid in such manner, by Borrower making payment, when due, directly to the payee thereof. Borrower shall promptly furnish to Lender all notices of amounts due under this paragraph, and in the event Borrower shall make payment directly, Borrower shall promptly furnish to Lender receipts evidencing such payments. Borrower shall promptly discharge any lien which has priority over this Deed of Trust; provided, that Borrower shall not be required to discharge any such lien so long as Borrower shall agree in writing to the payment of the obligation secured by such lien in a manner acceptable to Lender, or shall in good faith contest such lien by, or defend enforcement of such lien in, legal proceedings which operate to prevent the enforcement of the lien or forfeiture of the Property or any part thereof.

5. Hazard Insurance. Borrower shall keep the improvements now existing or hereafter erected on the Property insured against loss by fire, hazards included within the term "extended coverage", and such other hazards as Lender may require and in such amounts and for such periods as Lender may require; provided, that Lender shall not require that the amount of such coverage exceed that amount of coverage required to pay the sums secured by this Deed of Trust.

The insurance carrier providing the insurance shall be chosen by Borrower subject to approval by Lender; provided, that such approval shall not be unreasonably withheld. All premiums on insurance policies shall be paid in the manner provided under paragraph 2 hereof or, if not paid in such manner, by Borrower making payment, when due, directly to the insurance carrier.

All insurance policies and renewals thereof shall be in form acceptable to Lender and shall include a standard mortgage clause in favor of and in form acceptable to Lender. Lender shall have the right to hold the policies and renewals thereof, and Borrower shall promptly furnish to Lender all renewal notices and all receipts of paid premiums. In the event of loss, Borrower shall give prompt notice to the insurance carrier and Lender. Lender may make proof of loss if not made promptly by Borrower.

Unless Lender and Borrower otherwise agree in writing, insurance proceeds shall be applied to restoration or repair of the Property damaged, provided such restoration or repair is economically feasible and the security of this Deed of Trust is not thereby impaired. If such restoration or repair is not economically feasible or if the security of this Deed of Trust would be impaired, the insurance proceeds shall be applied to the sums secured by this Deed of Trust, with the excess, if any, paid to Borrower. If the Property is abandoned by Borrower, or if Borrower fails to respond to Lender within 30 days from the date notice is mailed by Lender to Borrower that the insurance carrier offers to settle a claim for insurance benefits, Lender is authorized to collect and apply the insurance proceeds at Lender's option either to restoration or repair of the Property or to the sums secured by this Deed of Trust.

Unless Lender and Borrower otherwise agree in writing, any such application of proceeds to principal shall not extend or postpone the due date of the monthly installments referred to in paragraphs 1 and 2 hereof or change the amount of such installments. If under paragraph 18 hereof the Property is acquired by Lender, all right, title and interest of Borrower in and to any insurance policies and in and to the proceeds thereof resulting from damage to the Property prior to the sale or acquisition shall pass to Lender to the extent of the sums secured by this Deed of Trust immediately prior to such sale or acquisition.

6. Preservation and Maintenance of Property; Leaseholds; Condominiums; Planned Unit Developments. Borrower shall keep the Property in good repair and shall not commit waste or permit impairment or deterioration of the Property and shall comply with the provisions of any lease if this Deed of Trust is on a leasehold. If this Deed of Trust is on a unit in a condominium or a planned unit development, Borrower shall perform all of Borrower's obligations under the declaration or covenants creating or governing the condominium or planned unit development, the by-laws and regulations of the condominium or planned unit development, and constituent documents. If a condominium or planned unit development rider is executed by Borrower and recorded together with this Deed of Trust, the covenants and agreements of such rider shall be incorporated into and shall amend and supplement the covenants and agreements of this Deed of Trust as if the rider were a part hereof.

7. Protection of Lender's Security. If Borrower fails to perform the covenants and agreements contained in this Deed of Trust, or if any action or proceeding is commenced which materially affects Lender's interest in the Property, including, but not limited to, eminent domain, insolvency, code enforcement, or arrangements or proceedings involving a bankrupt or decedent, then Lender at Lender's option, upon notice to Borrower, may make such appearances, disburse such sums and take such action as is necessary to protect Lender's interest, including, but not limited to, disbursement of reasonable attorney's fees and entry upon the Property to make repairs. If Lender required mortgage insurance as a condition of making the loan secured by this Deed of Trust, Borrower shall pay the premiums required to maintain such insurance in effect until such time as the requirement for such insurance terminates in accordance with Borrower's and Lender's written agreement or applicable law. Borrower shall pay the amount of all mortgage insurance premiums in the manner provided under paragraph 2 hereof.

Any amounts disbursed by Lender pursuant to this paragraph 7, with interest thereon, shall become additional indebtedness of Borrower secured by this Deed of Trust. Unless Borrower and Lender agree to other terms of payment, such amounts shall be payable upon notice from Lender to Borrower requesting payment thereof, and shall bear interest from the date of disbursement at the rate payable from time to time on outstanding principal under the Note unless payment of interest at such rate would be contrary to applicable law, in which event such amounts shall bear interest at the highest rate permissible under applicable law. Nothing contained in this paragraph 7 shall require Lender to incur any expense or take any action hereunder.

8. Inspection. Lender may make or cause to be made reasonable entries upon and inspections of the Property, provided that Lender shall give Borrower notice prior to any such inspection specifying reasonable cause therefor related to Lender's interest in the Property.

FIGURE 3-1c.

9. Condemnation. The proceeds of any award or claim for damages, direct or consequential, in connection with any condemnation or other taking of the Property, or part thereof, or for conveyance in lieu of condemnation, are hereby assigned and shall be paid to Lender.

In the event of a total taking of the Property, the proceeds shall be applied to the sums secured by this Deed of Trust, with the excess, if any, paid to Borrower. In the event of a partial taking of the Property, unless Borrower and Lender otherwise agree in writing, there shall be applied to the sums secured by this Deed of Trust such proportion of the proceeds as is equal to that proportion which the amount of the sums secured by this Deed of Trust immediately prior to the date of taking bears to the fair market value of the Property immediately prior to the date of taking, with the balance of the proceeds paid to Borrower.

If the Property is abandoned by Borrower, or if, after notice by Lender to Borrower that the condemnor offers to make an award or settle a claim for damages, Borrower fails to respond to Lender within 30 days after the date such notice is mailed, Lender is authorized to collect and apply the proceeds, at Lender's option, either to restoration or repair of the Property or to the sums secured by this Deed of Trust.

Unless Lender and Borrower otherwise agree in writing, any such application of proceeds to principal shall not extend or postpone the due date of the monthly installments referred to in paragraphs 1 and 2 hereof or change the amount of such installments.

10. Borrower Not Released. Extension of the time for payment or modification of amortization of the sums secured by this Deed of Trust granted by Lender to any successor in interest of Borrower shall not operate to, release, in any manner, the liability of the original Borrower and Borrower's successors in interest. Lender shall not be required to commence proceedings against such successor or refuse to extend time for payment or otherwise modify amortization of the sums secured by this Deed of Trust by reason of any demand made by the original Borrower and Borrower's successors in interest.

11. Forbearance by Lender Not a Waiver. Any forbearance by Lender in exercising any right or remedy hereunder, or otherwise afforded by applicable law, shall not be a waiver of or preclude the exercise of any such right or remedy. The procurement of insurance or the payment of taxes or other liens or charges by Lender shall not be a waiver of Lender's right to accelerate the maturity of the indebtedness secured by this Deed of Trust.

12. Remedies Cumulative. All remedies provided in this Deed of Trust are distinct and cumulative to any other right or remedy under this Deed of Trust or afforded by law or equity, and may be exercised concurrently, independently or successively.

13. Successors and Assigns Bound; Joint and Several Liability; Captions. The covenants and agreements herein contained shall bind, and the rights hereunder shall inure to, the respective successors and assigns of Lender and Borrower, subject to the provisions of paragraph 17 hereof. All covenants and agreements of Borrower shall be joint and several. The captions and headings of the paragraphs of this Deed of Trust are for convenience only and are not to be used to interpret or define the provisions hereof.

14. Notice. Except for any notice required under applicable law to be given in another manner, (a) any notice to Borrower provided for in this Deed of Trust shall be given by mailing such notice by certified mail addressed to Borrower at the Property Address or at such other address as Borrower may designate by notice to Lender as provided herein, and (b) any notice to Lender shall be given by certified mail, return receipt requested, to Lender's address stated herein or to such other address as Lender may designate by notice to Borrower as provided herein. Any notice provided for in this Deed of Trust shall be deemed to have been given to Borrower or Lender when given in the manner designated herein.

15. Uniform Deed of Trust; Governing Law; Severability. This form of deed of trust combines uniform covenants for national use and non-uniform covenants with limited variations by jurisdiction to constitute a uniform security instrument covering real property. This Deed of Trust shall be governed by the law of the jurisdiction in which the Property is located. In the event that any provision or clause of this Deed of Trust or the Note conflicts with applicable law, such conflict shall not affect other provisions of this Deed of Trust or the Note which can be given effect without the conflicting provision, and to this end the provisions of the Deed of Trust and the Note are declared to be severable.

16. Borrower's Copy. Borrower shall be furnished a conformed copy of the Note and of this Deed of Trust at the time of execution or after recordation hereof.

17. Transfer of the Property; Assumption. If all or any part of the Property or an interest therein is sold or transferred by Borrower without Lender's prior written consent, excluding (a) the creation of a lien or encumbrance subordinate to this Deed of Trust, (b) the creation of a purchase money security interest for household appliances, (c) a transfer by devise, descent or by operation of law upon the death of a joint tenant or (d) the grant of any leasehold interest of three years or less not containing an option to purchase, Lender may, at Lender's option, declare all the sums secured by this Deed of Trust to be immediately due and payable. Lender shall have waived su h option to accelerate if, prior to the sale or transfer, Lender and the person to whom the Property is to be sold or transfe·red reach agreement in writing that the credit of such person is satisfactory to Lender and that the interest payable on the sums secured by this Deed of Trust shall be at such rate as Lender shall request. If Lender has waived the option to accelerate provided in this paragraph 17, and if Borrower's successor in interest has executed a written assumption agreement accepted in writing by Lender, Lender shall release Borrower from all obligations under this Deed of Trust and the Note.

If Lender exercises such option to accelerate, Lender shall mail Borrower notice of acceleration in accordance with paragraph 14 hereof. Such notice shall provide a period of not less than 30 days from the date the notice is mailed within which Borrower may pay the sums declared due. If Borrower fails to pay such sums prior to the expiration of such period, Lender may, without further notice or demand on Borrower, invoke any remedies permitted by paragraph 18 hereof.

NON-UNIFORM COVENANTS. Borrower and Lender further covenant and agree as follows:

18. Acceleration; Remedies. Except as provided in paragraph 17 hereof, upon Borrower's breach of any covenant or agreement of Borrower in this Deed of Trust, including the covenants to pay when due any sums secured by this Deed of Trust, Lender prior to acceleration shall mail notice to Borrower as provided in paragraph 14 hereof specifying: (1) the breach; (2) the action required to cure such breach; (3) a date, not less than 30 days from the date the notice is mailed to Borrower, by which such breach must be cured; and (4) that failure to cure such breach on or before the date specified in the notice may result in acceleration of the sums secured by this Deed of Trust and sale of the Property. The notice shall further inform Borrower of the right to reinstate after acceleration and the right to bring a court action to assert the non-existence of a default or any other defense of Borrower to acceleration and sale. If the breach is not cured on or before the date specified in the notice, Lender at Lender's option may declare all of the sums secured by this Deed of Trust to be immediately due and payable without further demand and may invoke the power of sale and any other remedies permitted by applicable law. Lender shall be entitled to collect all reasonable costs and expenses incurred in pursuing the remedies provided in this paragraph 18, including, but not limited to, reasonable attorney's fees.

If Lender invokes the power of sale, Lender shall execute or cause Trustee to execute a written notice of the occurrence of an event of default and of Lender's election to cause the Property to be sold and shall cause such notice to be recorded in each county in which the Property or some part thereof is located. Lender or Trustee shall mail copies of such notice in the manner prescribed by applicable law to Borrower and to the other persons prescribed by applicable law. Trustee shall give public notice of sale to the persons and in the manner prescribed by applicable law. After the lapse of such time as may be required by applicable law, Trustee, without demand on Borrower, shall sell the Property at public auction to the highest bidder at the time and place and under the terms designated in the notice of sale in one or more parcels and in such order as Trustee may determine. Trustee may postpone sale of all or any parcel of the Property by public announcement at the time and place of any previously scheduled sale. Lender or Lender's designee may purchase the Property at any sale.

Trustee shall deliver to the purchaser Trustee's deed conveying the Property so sold without any covenant or warranty, expressed or implied. The recitals in the Trustee's deed shall be prima facie evidence of the truth of the statements made therein. Trustee shall apply the proceeds of the sale in the following order: (a) to all reasonable costs and expenses of the sale, including, but not limited to, reasonable Trustee's and attorney's fees and costs of title evidence; (b) to all sums secured by this Deed of Trust; and (c) the excess, if any, to the person or persons legally entitled thereto.

19. Borrower's Right to Reinstate. Notwithstanding Lender's acceleration of the sums secured by this Deed of Trust, Borrower shall have the right to have any proceedings begun by Lender to enforce this Deed of Trust discontinued at any time prior to five days before sale of the Property pursuant to the power of sale contained in this Deed of Trust or at any time prior to entry of a judgment enforcing this Deed of Trust if: (a) Borrower pays Lender all sums which would be then due under this Deed of Trust, the Note and notes securing Future Advances, if any, had no acceleration occurred; (b) Borrower cures all breaches of any other covenants or agreements of Borrower contained in this Deed of Trust; (c) Borrower pays all reasonable expenses incurred by Lender and Trustee in enforcing the covenants and agreements of Borrower contained in this Deed of Trust, and in enforcing Lender's and Trustee's remedies as provided in paragraph 18 hereof, including, but not limited to, reasonable attorney's fees; and (d) Borrower takes such action as Lender may reasonably require to assure that the lien of this Deed of Trust, Lender's interest in the Property and Borrower's obligation to pay the

FIGURE 3–1d.

sums secured by this Deed of Trust shall continue unimpaired. Upon such payment and cure by Borrower, this Deed of Trust and the obligations secured hereby shall remain in full force and effect as if no acceleration had occurred.

20. Assignment of Rents; Appointment of Receiver; Lender in Possession. As additional security hereunder, Borrower hereby assigns to Lender the rents of the Property, provided that Borrower shall, prior to acceleration under paragraph 18 hereof or abandonment of the Property, have the right to collect and retain such rents as they become due and payable.

Upon acceleration under paragraph 18 hereof or abandonment of the Property, Lender, in person, by agent or by judicially appointed receiver shall be entitled to enter upon, take possession of and manage the Property and to collect the rents of the Property including those past due. All rents collected by Lender or the receiver shall be applied first to payment of the costs of management of the Property and collection of rents, including, but not limited to, receiver's fees, premiums on receiver's bonds and reasonable attorney's fees, and then to the sums secured by this Deed of Trust. Lender and the receiver shall be liable to account only for those rents actually received.

21. Future Advances. Upon request of Borrower, Lender, at Lender's option prior to full reconveyance of the Property by Trustee to Borrower, may make Future Advances to Borrower. Such Future Advances, with interest thereon, shall be secured by this Deed of Trust when evidenced by promissory notes stating that said notes are secured hereby.

22. Reconveyance. Upon payment of all sums secured by this Deed of Trust, Lender shall request Trustee to reconvey the Property and shall surrender this Deed of Trust and all notes evidencing indebtedness secured by this Deed of Trust to Trustee. Trustee shall reconvey the Property without warranty and without charge to the person or persons legally entitled thereto. Such person or persons shall pay all costs of recordation, if any.

23. Substitute Trustee. Lender, at Lender's option, may from time to time remove Trustee and appoint a successor trustee to any Trustee appointed hereunder. Without conveyance of the Property, the successor trustee shall succeed to all the title, power and duties conferred upon the Trustee herein and by applicable law.

24. Request for Notices. Borrower requests that copies of the notice of default and notice of sale be sent to Borrower's address which is the Property Address.

25. Statement of Obligation. Lender may collect a fee not to exceed $15 for furnishing the statement of obligation as provided by Section 2943 of the Civil Code of California.

IN WITNESS WHEREOF, Borrower has executed this Deed of Trust.

....
—Borrower

....
—Borrower

STATE OF CALIFORNIA,.......................................County ss:

On this..............day of................, 19...., before me, the undersigned, a Notary Public in and for said State, personally appeared...

...................................., known to me to be the person(s) whose name(s)............. subscribed to the foregoing instrument and acknowledged that.................executed the same.

WITNESS my hand and official seal.   Signature:..

(Reserved for official seal)   ....
                                      Name (typed or printed)

                                      My Commission expires:

REQUEST FOR RECONVEYANCE

TO TRUSTEE:

The undersigned is the holder of the note or notes secured by this Deed of Trust. Said note or notes, together with all other indebtedness secured by this Deed of Trust, have been paid in full. You are hereby directed to cancel said note or notes and this Deed of Trust, which are delivered hereby, and to reconvey, without warranty, all the estate now held by you under this Deed of Trust to the person or persons legally entitled thereto.

Dated:........................   ....

————————————— (Space Below This Line Reserved For Lender and Recorder) —————————————

FIGURE 3–1e.

NOTE

US $ . . . . , Michigan

City

. . . . , 19 . . . .

FOR VALUE RECEIVED, the undersigned ("Borrower") promise(s) to pay . . . .
. . . . , or order, the principal sum of
. . . . .Dollars, with
interest on the unpaid principal balance from the date of this Note, until paid, at the rate of . . . .
. . . . .percent per annum. Principal and interest shall be payable at . . . .
. . . . , or such other place as the Note holder may
designate, in consecutive monthly installments of . . . .
. . . . .Dollars (US $ . . . .), on the . . . .
. . . . .day of each month beginning . . . . , 19 . . . . . Such monthly installments
shall continue until the entire indebtedness evidenced by this Note is fully paid, except that any remaining indebtedness, if not sooner paid, shall be due and payable on . . . .

If any monthly installment under this Note is not paid when due and remains unpaid after a date specified by a
notice to Borrower, the entire principal amount outstanding and accrued interest thereon shall at once become due
and payable at the option of the Note holder. The date specified shall not be less than thirty days from the date
such notice is mailed. The Note holder may exercise this option to accelerate during any default by Borrower
regardless of any prior forbearance. If suit is brought to collect this Note, the Note holder shall be entitled to collect
all reasonable costs and expenses of suit, including, but not limited to, reasonable attorney's fees.

Borrower shall pay to the Note holder a late charge of . . . . .percent of any monthly
installment not received by the Note holder within . . . . .days after the installment is due.

Borrower may prepay the principal amount outstanding in whole or in part. Any partial prepayment shall be
applied against the principal amount outstanding and shall not postpone the due date of any subsequent monthly
installments or change the amount of such installments, unless the Note holder shall otherwise agree in writing. If,
within three years from the date of this Note, Borrower make(s) any prepayments in any twelve month period
beginning with the date of this Note or anniversary dates thereof ("loan year") with money lent to Borrower by a
lender other than the Note holder, Borrower shall pay the Note holder . . . . .percent of
the amount by which the sum of prepayments made in any loan year exceeds twenty percent of the original principal
amount of this Note

Presentment, notice of dishonor, and protest are hereby waived by all makers, sureties, guarantors and endorsers
hereof. This Note shall be the joint and several obligation of all makers, sureties, guarantors and endorsers, and shall
be binding upon them and their successors and assigns.

Any notice to Borrower provided for in this Note shall be given by mailing such notice by certified mail addressed
to Borrower at the Property Address stated below, or to such other address as Borrower may designate by notice to
the Note holder. Any notice to the Note holder shall be given by mailing such notice by certified mail, return receipt
requested, to the Note holder at the address stated in the first paragraph of this Note, or at such other address as may
have been designated by notice to Borrower.

The indebtedness evidenced by this Note is secured by a Mortgage, dated . . . .
. . . ., and reference is made to the Mortgage for rights as to acceleration of the indebtedness
evidenced by this Note.

. . . .

. . . .

. . . .
Property Address   *(Execute Original Only)*

MICHIGAN—1 to 4 Family—6/75—FNMA/FHLMC UNIFORM INSTRUMENT

FIGURE 3–2a.

MORTGAGE

THIS MORTGAGE is made this.........................day of.........................,
19...., between the Mortgagor,...
...., whose address is...
...., (herein "Borrower"), and the Mortgagee,....................
...., a corporation organized and existing
under the laws of......................................, whose address is........................
....(herein "Lender").

WHEREAS, Borrower is indebted to Lender in the principal sum of.................................
....Dollars, which indebtedness is evidenced by Borrower's note
dated.........................(herein "Note"), providing for monthly installments of principal and interest,
with the balance of the indebtedness, if not sooner paid, due and payable on.............................
....................;

To SECURE to Lender (a) the repayment of the indebtedness evidenced by the Note, with interest thereon, the payment of all other sums, with interest thereon, advanced in accordance herewith to protect the security of this Mortgage, and the performance of the covenants and agreements of Borrower herein contained, and (b) the repayment of any future advances, with interest thereon, made to Borrower by Lender pursuant to paragraph 21 hereof (herein "Future Advances"), Borrower does hereby mortgage, grant and convey to Lender, with power of sale, the following described property located in the County of......................................., State of Michigan:

which has the address of.., ...,
　　　　　　　　　　　　　　　　　　[Street]　　　　　　　　　　　　　　　　　　　　　　　[City]
.........................(herein "Property Address");
　　[State and Zip Code]

TOGETHER with all the improvements now or hereafter erected on the property, and all easements, rights, appurtenances, rents, royalties, mineral, oil and gas rights and profits, water, water rights, and water stock, and all fixtures now or hereafter attached to the property, all of which, including replacements and additions thereto, shall be deemed to be and remain a part of the property covered by this Mortgage; and all of the foregoing, together with said property (or the leasehold estate if this Mortgage is on a leasehold) are herein referred to as the "Property".

Borrower covenants that Borrower is lawfully seised of the estate hereby conveyed and has the right to mortgage, grant and convey the Property, that the Property is unencumbered, and that Borrower will warrant and defend generally the title to the Property against all claims and demands, subject to any declarations, easements or restrictions listed in a schedule of exceptions to coverage in any title insurance policy insuring Lender's interest in the Property.

MICHIGAN—1 to 4 Family—6/75*—FNMA/FHLMC UNIFORM INSTRUMENT

FIGURE 3-2b.

UNIFORM COVENANTS. Borrower and Lender covenant and agree as follows:

1. Payment of Principal and Interest. Borrower shall promptly pay when due the principal of and interest on the indebtedness evidenced by the Note, prepayment and late charges as provided in the Note, and the principal of and interest on any Future Advances secured by this Mortgage.

2. Funds for Taxes and Insurance. Subject to applicable law or to a written waiver by Lender, Borrower shall pay to Lender on the day monthly installments of principal and interest are payable under the Note, until the Note is paid in full, a sum (herein "Funds") equal to one-twelfth of the yearly taxes and assessments which may attain priority over this Mortgage, and ground rents on the Property, if any, plus one-twelfth of yearly premium installments for hazard insurance, plus one-twelfth of yearly premium installments for mortgage insurance, if any, all as reasonably estimated initially and from time to time by Lender on the basis of assessments and bills and reasonable estimates thereof.

The Funds shall be held in an institution the deposits or accounts of which are insured or guaranteed by a Federal or state agency (including Lender if Lender is such an institution). Lender shall apply the Funds to pay said taxes, assessments, insurance premiums and ground rents. Lender may not charge for so holding and applying the Funds, analyzing said account, or verifying and compiling said assessments and bills, unless Lender pays Borrower interest on the Funds and applicable law permits Lender to make such a charge. Borrower and Lender may agree in writing at the time of execution of this Mortgage that interest on the Funds shall be paid to Borrower, and unless such agreement is made or applicable law requires such interest to be paid, Lender shall not be required to pay Borrower any interest or earnings on the Funds. Lender shall give to Borrower, without charge, an annual accounting of the Funds showing credits and debits to the Funds and the purpose for which each debit to the Funds was made. The Funds are pledged as additional security for the sums secured by this Mortgage.

If the amount of the Funds held by Lender, together with the future monthly installments of Funds payable prior to the due dates of taxes, assessments, insurance premiums and ground rents, shall exceed the amount required to pay said taxes, assessments, insurance premiums and ground rents as they fall due, such excess shall be, at Borrower's option, either promptly repaid to Borrower or credited to Borrower on monthly installments of Funds. If the amount of the Funds held by Lender shall not be sufficient to pay taxes, assessments, insurance premiums and ground rents as they fall due, Borrower shall pay to Lender any amount necessary to make up the deficiency within 30 days from the date notice is mailed by Lender to Borrower requesting payment thereof.

Upon payment in full of all sums secured by this Mortgage, Lender shall promptly refund to Borrower any Funds held by Lender. If under paragraph 18 hereof the Property is sold or the Property is otherwise acquired by Lender, Lender shall apply, no later than immediately prior to the sale of the Property or its acquisition by Lender, any Funds held by Lender at the time of application as a credit against the sums secured by this Mortgage.

3. Application of Payments. Unless applicable law provides otherwise, all payments received by Lender under the Note and paragraphs 1 and 2 hereof shall be applied by Lender first in payment of amounts payable to Lender by Borrower under paragraph 2 hereof, then to interest payable on the Note, then to the principal of the Note, and then to interest and principal on any Future Advances.

4. Charges; Liens. Borrower shall pay all taxes, assessments and other charges, fines and impositions attributable to the Property which may attain a priority over this Mortgage, and leasehold payments or ground rents, if any, in the manner provided under paragraph 2 hereof or, if not paid in such manner, by Borrower making payment, when due, directly to the payee thereof. Borrower shall promptly furnish to Lender all notices of amounts due under this paragraph, and in the event Borrower shall make payment directly, Borrower shall promptly furnish to Lender receipts evidencing such payments. Borrower shall promptly discharge any lien which has priority over this Mortgage; provided, that Borrower shall not be required to discharge any such lien so long as Borrower shall agree in writing to the payment of the obligation secured by such lien in a manner acceptable to Lender, or shall in good faith contest such lien by, or defend enforcement of such lien in, legal proceedings which operate to prevent the enforcement of the lien or forfeiture of the Property or any part thereof.

5. Hazard Insurance. Borrower shall keep the improvements now existing or hereafter erected on the Property insured against loss by fire, hazards included within the term "extended coverage", and such other hazards as Lender may require and in such amounts and for such periods as Lender may require; provided, that Lender shall not require that the amount of such coverage exceed that amount of coverage required to pay the sums secured by this Mortgage.

The insurance carrier providing the insurance shall be chosen by Borrower subject to approval by Lender; provided, that such approval shall not be unreasonably withheld. All premiums on insurance policies shall be paid in the manner provided under paragraph 2 hereof or, if not paid in such manner, by Borrower making payment, when due, directly to the insurance carrier.

All insurance policies and renewals thereof shall be in form acceptable to Lender and shall include a standard mortgage clause in favor of and in form acceptable to Lender. Lender shall have the right to hold the policies and renewals thereof, and Borrower shall promptly furnish to Lender all renewal notices and all receipts of paid premiums. In the event of loss, Borrower shall give prompt notice to the insurance carrier and Lender. Lender may make proof of loss if not made promptly by Borrower.

Unless Lender and Borrower otherwise agree in writing, insurance proceeds shall be applied to restoration or repair of the Property damaged, provided such restoration or repair is economically feasible and the security of this Mortgage is not thereby impaired. If such restoration or repair is not economically feasible or if the security of this Mortgage would be impaired, the insurance proceeds shall be applied to the sums secured by this Mortgage, with the excess, if any, paid to Borrower. If the Property is abandoned by Borrower, or if Borrower fails to respond to Lender within 30 days from the date notice is mailed by Lender to Borrower that the insurance carrier offers to settle a claim for insurance benefits, Lender is authorized to collect and apply the insurance proceeds at Lender's option either to restoration or repair of the Property or to the sums secured by this Mortgage.

Unless Lender and Borrower otherwise agree in writing, any such application of proceeds to principal shall not extend or postpone the due date of the monthly installments referred to in paragraphs 1 and 2 hereof or change the amount of such installments. If under paragraph 18 hereof the Property is acquired by Lender, all right, title and interest of Borrower in and to any insurance policies and in and to the proceeds thereof resulting from damage to the Property prior to the sale or acquisition shall pass to Lender to the extent of the sums secured by this Mortgage immediately prior to such sale or acquisition.

6. Preservation and Maintenance of Property; Leaseholds; Condominiums; Planned Unit Developments. Borrower shall keep the Property in good repair and shall not commit waste or permit impairment or deterioration of the Property and shall comply with the provisions of any lease if this Mortgage is on a leasehold. If this Mortgage is on a unit in a condominium or a planned unit development, Borrower shall perform all of Borrower's obligations under the declaration or covenants creating or governing the condominium or planned unit development, the by-laws and regulations of the condominium or planned unit development, and constituent documents. If a condominium or planned unit development rider is executed by Borrower and recorded together with this Mortgage, the covenants and agreements of such rider shall be incorporated into and shall amend and supplement the covenants and agreements of this Mortgage as if the rider were a part hereof.

7. Protection of Lender's Security. If Borrower fails to perform the covenants and agreements contained in this Mortgage, or if any action or proceeding is commenced which materially affects Lender's interest in the Property, including, but not limited to, eminent domain, insolvency, code enforcement, or arrangements or proceedings involving a bankrupt or decedent, then Lender at Lender's option, upon notice to Borrower, may make such appearances, disburse such sums and take such action as is necessary to protect Lender's interest, including, but not limited to, disbursement of reasonable attorney's fees and entry upon the Property to make repairs. If Lender required mortgage insurance as a condition of making the loan secured by this Mortgage, Borrower shall pay the premiums required to maintain such insurance in effect until such time as the requirement for such insurance terminates in accordance with Borrower's and

FIGURE 3-2c.

Lender's written agreement or applicable law. Borrower shall pay the amount of all mortgage insurance premiums in the manner provided under paragraph 2 hereof.

Any amounts disbursed by Lender pursuant to this paragraph 7, with interest thereon, shall become additional indebtedness of Borrower secured by this Mortgage. Unless Borrower and Lender agree to other terms of payment, such amounts shall be payable upon notice from Lender to Borrower requesting payment thereof, and shall bear interest from the date of disbursement at the rate payable from time to time on outstanding principal under the Note unless payment of interest at such rate would be contrary to applicable law, in which event such amounts shall bear interest at the highest rate permissible under applicable law. Nothing contained in this paragraph 7 shall require Lender to incur any expense or take any action hereunder.

8. Inspection. Lender may make or cause to be made reasonable entries upon and inspections of the Property, provided that Lender shall give Borrower notice prior to any such inspection specifying reasonable cause therefor related to Lender's interest in the Property.

9. Condemnation. The proceeds of any award or claim for damages, direct or consequential, in connection with any condemnation or other taking of the Property, or part thereof, or for conveyance in lieu of condemnation, are hereby assigned and shall be paid to Lender.

In the event of a total taking of the Property, the proceeds shall be applied to the sums secured by this Mortgage, with the excess, if any, paid to Borrower. In the event of a partial taking of the Property, unless Borrower and Lender otherwise agree in writing, there shall be applied to the sums secured by this Mortgage such proportion of the proceeds as is equal to that proportion which the amount of the sums secured by this Mortgage immediately prior to the date of taking bears to the fair market value of the Property immediately prior to the date of taking, with the balance of the proceeds paid to Borrower.

If the Property is abandoned by Borrower, or if, after notice by Lender to Borrower that the condemnor offers to make an award or settle a claim for damages, Borrower fails to respond to Lender within 30 days after the date such notice is mailed, Lender is authorized to collect and apply the proceeds, at Lender's option, either to restoration or repair of the Property or to the sums secured by this Mortgage.

Unless Lender and Borrower otherwise agree in writing, any such application of proceeds to principal shall not extend or postpone the due date of the monthly installments referred to in paragraphs 1 and 2 hereof or change the amount of such installments.

10. Borrower Not Released. Extension of the time for payment or modification of amortization of the sums secured by this Mortgage granted by Lender to any successor in interest of Borrower shall not operate to release, in any manner, the liability of the original Borrower and Borrower's successors in interest. Lender shall not be required to commence proceedings against such successor or refuse to extend time for payment or otherwise modify amortization of the sums secured by this Mortgage by reason of any demand made by the original Borrower and Borrower's successors in interest.

11. Forbearance by Lender Not a Waiver. Any forbearance by Lender in exercising any right or remedy hereunder, or otherwise afforded by applicable law, shall not be a waiver of or preclude the exercise of any such right or remedy. The procurement of insurance or the payment of taxes or other liens or charges by Lender shall not be a waiver of Lender's right to accelerate the maturity of the indebtedness secured by this Mortgage.

12. Remedies Cumulative. All remedies provided in this Mortgage are distinct and cumulative to any other right or remedy under this Mortgage or afforded by law or equity, and may be exercised concurrently, independently or successively.

13. Successors and Assigns Bound; Joint and Several Liability; Captions. The covenants and agreements herein contained shall bind, and the rights hereunder shall inure to, the respective successors and assigns of Lender and Borrower, subject to the provisions of paragraph 17 hereof. All covenants and agreements of Borrower shall be joint and several. The captions and headings of the paragraphs of this Mortgage are for convenience only and are not to be used to interpret or define the provisions hereof.

14. Notice. Except for any notice required under applicable law to be given in another manner, (a) any notice to Borrower provided for in this Mortgage shall be given by mailing such notice by certified mail addressed to Borrower at the Property Address or at such other address as Borrower may designate by notice to Lender as provided herein, and (b) any notice to Lender shall be given by certified mail, return receipt requested, to Lender's address stated herein or to such other address as Lender may designate by notice to Borrower as provided herein. Any notice provided for in this Mortgage shall be deemed to have been given to Borrower or Lender when given in the manner designated herein.

15. Uniform Mortgage; Governing Law; Severability. This form of mortgage combines uniform covenants for national use and non-uniform covenants with limited variations by jurisdiction to constitute a uniform security instrument covering real property. This Mortgage shall be governed by the law of the jurisdiction in which the Property is located. In the event that any provision or clause of this Mortgage or the Note conflicts with applicable law, such conflict shall not affect other provisions of this Mortgage or the Note which can be given effect without the conflicting provision, and to this end the provisions of the Mortgage and the Note are declared to be severable.

16. Borrower's Copy. Borrower shall be furnished a conformed copy of the Note and of this Mortgage at the time of execution or after recordation hereof.

17. Transfer of the Property; Assumption. If all or any part of the Property or an interest therein is sold or transferred by Borrower without Lender's prior written consent, excluding (a) the creation of a lien or encumbrance subordinate to this Mortgage, (b) the creation of a purchase money security interest for household appliances, (c) a transfer by devise, descent or by operation of law upon the death of a joint tenant or (d) the grant of any leasehold interest of three years or less not containing an option to purchase, Lender may, at Lender's option, declare all the sums secured by this Mortgage to be immediately due and payable. Lender shall have waived such option to accelerate if, prior to the sale or transfer, Lender and the person to whom the Property is to be sold or transferred reach agreement in writing that the credit of such person is satisfactory to Lender and that the interest payable on the sums secured by this Mortgage shall be at such rate as Lender shall request. If Lender has waived the option to accelerate provided in this paragraph 17, and if Borrower's successor in interest has executed a written assumption agreement accepted in writing by Lender, Lender shall release Borrower from all obligations under this Mortgage and the Note.

If Lender exercises such option to accelerate, Lender shall mail Borrower notice of acceleration in accordance with paragraph 14 hereof. Such notice shall provide a period of not less than 30 days from the date the notice is mailed within which Borrower may pay the sums declared due. If Borrower fails to pay such sums prior to the expiration of such period, Lender may, without further notice or demand on Borrower, invoke any remedies permitted by paragraph 18 hereof.

NON-UNIFORM COVENANTS. Borrower and Lender further covenant and agree as follows:

18. Acceleration; Remedies. Except as provided in paragraph 17 hereof, upon Borrower's breach of any covenant or agreement of Borrower in this Mortgage, including the covenants to pay when due any sums secured by this Mortgage, Lender prior to acceleration shall mail notice to Borrower as provided in paragraph 14 hereof specifying: (1) the breach; (2) the action required to cure such breach; (3) a date, not less than 30 days from the date the notice is mailed to Borrower, by which such breach must be cured; and (4) that failure to cure such breach on or before the date specified in the notice may result in acceleration of the sums secured by this Mortgage and sale of the Property. The notice shall further inform Borrower of the right to reinstate after acceleration and the right to bring a court action to assert the non-existence of a default or any other defense of Borrower to acceleration and sale. If the breach is not cured on or before the date specified in the notice, Lender at Lender's option may declare all of the sums secured by this Mortgage to be immediately due and payable without further demand and may invoke the power of sale hereby granted and any other remedies permitted by applicable law. Lender shall be entitled to collect all reasonable costs and expenses incurred in pursuing the remedies provided in this paragraph 18, including, but not limited to, reasonable attorney's fees.

If Lender invokes the power of sale, Lender shall mail a copy of a notice of sale to Borrower in the manner provided in paragraph 14 hereof. Lender shall publish and post the notice of sale and the Property shall be sold in the manner prescribed

FIGURE 3-2d.

by applicable law. **Lender or Lender's designee may purchase the Property at any sale. The proceeds of the sale shall be applied in the following order: (a) to all reasonable costs and expenses of the sale, including, but not limited to, reasonable attorney's fees; (b) to all sums secured by this Mortgage; and (c) the excess, if any, to the person or persons legally entitled thereto.**

19. Borrower's Right to Reinstate. Notwithstanding Lender's acceleration of the sums secured by this Mortgage, Borrower shall have the right to have any proceedings begun by Lender to enforce this Mortgage discontinued at any time prior to the earlier to occur of (i) the fifth day before sale of the Property pursuant to the power of sale contained in this Mortgage or (ii) entry of a judgment enforcing this Mortgage if: (a) Borrower pays Lender all sums which would be then due under this Mortgage, the Note and notes securing Future Advances, if any, had no acceleration occurred; (b) Borrower cures all breaches of any other covenants or agreements of Borrower contained in this Mortgage; (c) Borrower pays all reasonable expenses incurred by Lender in enforcing the covenants and agreements of Borrower contained in this Mortgage and in enforcing Lender's remedies as provided in paragraph 18 hereof, including, but not limited to, reasonable attorney's fees; and (d) Borrower takes such action as Lender may reasonably require to assure that the lien of this Mortgage, Lender's interest in the Property and Borrower's obligation to pay the sums secured by this Mortgage shall continue unimpaired. Upon such payment and cure by Borrower, this Mortgage and the obligations secured hereby shall remain in full force and effect as if no acceleration had occurred.

20. Assignment of Rents; Appointment of Receiver; Lender in Possession. Omitted.

21. Future Advances. Upon request of Borrower, Lender at Lender's option prior to release of this Mortgage, may make Future Advances to Borrower. Such Future Advances, with interest thereon, shall be secured by this Mortgage when evidenced by promissory notes stating that said notes are secured hereby.

22. Release. Upon payment of all sums secured by this Mortgage, Lender shall prepare and file a discharge of this Mortgage without charge to Borrower, and shall pay the fee for recording the discharge.

IN WITNESS WHEREOF, Borrower has executed this Mortgage.

Witnesses:

....
                                                                                                    —Borrower

....
                                                                                                    —Borrower

STATE OF MICHIGAN,..County ss:

  The foregoing instrument was acknowledged before me this...
                                                                              (date)

by ....
                              (person acknowledging)

My Commission expires: ....

                    Notary Public,..County, Michigan

This instrument was prepared by..

———————————————— (Space Below This Line Reserved For Lender and Recorder) ————————————————

FIGURE 3–2e.

44

create a binding pledge on real property. As in all such legal instruments, the parties must be legally qualified (of legal age, of sound
mind, and so on) to undertake the contract. It is important for the
lender to make sure that *all* parties holding an interest in the title to
any pledged property are a party to the mortgage pledge.

Identification of the *property* used as security must be accurately
described so as to distinguish it from any other property in the world
(see Chapter 8). A street address is never acceptable, nor are boundary lines based on physical features, such as the "big live oak by the
river bend." Accurate legal descriptions are normally used either by
"metes and bounds" (a surveyor's description of boundary lines from
a fixed starting point, thence proceeding in specific compass directions and distances around the property back to the starting point);
or more commonly in urban areas, by lot and block taken from a
subdivision plat registered and approved by a local governmental
authority. An erroneous description of the property, even a typographical error, can render the mortgage instrument void but does
not necessarily invalidate the promissory note.

Principal Amount Due

The mortgage instrument must define the property pledged as security
for the initial amount of indebtedness. But the mortgage claim cannot exceed the value of the unpaid balance of the debt. As payments
are made on the principal amount of the debt, the value of the mortgage pledge is correspondingly reduced. In this context, the word
estoppel is sometimes used. Since the mortgage instrument may have
a term of 20 or 30 years, and is recorded in the public records only
in its original form, we may ask, "How, then, does one determine the
exact balance still due on the promissory note at any point in the life
of the loan?" The balance due becomes important when a mortgage
is sold between lenders, and the estoppel form can be used. This is a
statement of the balance due as of a specific date, acknowledged by
the lender, and the borrower, and in effect, "stops" the subsequent
purchaser of the loan from claiming any greater amount due from
the borrower. While most mortgage loans are repaid on a monthly installment basis and the reduction of principal due after each payment
is accurately projected by an amortization table, there can always be
breaks in the payment pattern. A greater reduction of principal may
be made in any one year, or payments could be delinquent. So the
estoppel form is used to determine an exact balance due.

Prepayment

One of the clauses contained in most mortgages prior to 1972 provides the manner in which the loan may be paid off ahead of the full term. This particular privilege has caused many arguments and misunderstandings. From the lender's viewpoint, he is making a loan of, say $35,000 for a period of 30 years. Under the terms of the promissory note, the borrower agrees to make certain monthly payments, which include both principal and interest. The 360 payments agreed to can amount to as much as $66,000 in interest for the lender over the 30-year period.* The lender can claim a contractual right to this interest, which has obvious value. Why should the lender then be required to forfeit this right to the interest? Earlier mortgages usually provided a compromise to this position by calling for a specific payment against the unearned portion of the interest at the time of early principal payment in order to obtain a release of the mortgage claim. This *prepayment premium,* or conversely, prepayment penalty from the homeowner's viewpoint, varies widely within the industry and may run from 1 to 3 percent of the balance due at the time of prepayment up to all interest due for the first ten years of the loan. A more common provision allows up to 20 percent of the original loan to be paid off in any one year without any premium for the unearned interest, plus 1 percent of any balance in excess of the 20 percent paid in the same year.

With the rise in popularity of "consumerism," many attacks have been made on the prepayment provision insofar as residential loans are concerned. A number of lenders, following the leadership of FNMA, and supported by subsequent FHA rules eliminating prepayment premiums, have dropped all such requirements for residential loans. The reasoning behind this action is that when the principal sum has been returned to the lender, he is free to put this money back to work in a new loan and thus suffers no compensable loss.

Acceleration

One of the essential clauses in a mortgage instrument provides for the payment in full of the balance due, that is, the "acceleration" of each monthly payment to the present date in case of a default in the

---

*Monthly payment on a $35,000 loan for 30 years at 9% interest is $281.62. 281.62 × 360 = 101,383.20. To repay a $35,000 loan, the interest cost is $66,383.20 over a 30-year term.

mortgage terms. While there can be other possible reasons for a default in the mortgage terms, such as improper usage of the property, or selling of the premises without specific permission of the mortgagee, the most probable cause of default is nonpayment of the debt secured. Without an acceleration clause, it is conceivable that a lender would be forced to foreclose his claim each and every month as the installment payments came due.

The acceleration clause is sometimes referred to as the "call clause." This is not an accurate description. There are several clauses in a mortgage instrument that recite conditions which, if violated, can cause a default on the agreement and result in the calling of the loan. The acceleration clause simply makes it possible to call for the entire balance due at one time, but is not in itself a condition that can cause default.

Right to Sell

As a general rule, mortgaged property can be freely sold by the owner or mortgagor, either with an assumption of the existing debt by the new buyer, or by paying off the balance due on the existing mortgage. In a sale the common assumption is that the original borrower remains liable on the obligation along with the new buyer. Some lenders may grant a release of liability to the original borrower, but they are under no obligation to do so.

When interest remained at lower and more stable rates, lenders were more cooperative in allowing sales and assumptions of their loans. But as interest rates moved upward in the late sixties, more lenders eyed the loss of value in their older loans, which had been made at much lower rates. And many began to insert clauses in their mortgage instruments that required specific approval by the lender before the borrower could make any sale of the property. The price of that approval often proved to be an adjustment of the interest rate upward on the balance of the loan to a percentage rate closer to the then existing market rate. This interest adjustment is sometimes demanded without releasing the original borrower from the obligation.

The reservation of the right to approve a sale by the lender should not be confused with the term *interest escalation,* although this can be the result. More specifically, the escalation of interest is called for in a promissory note when payments become delinquent or when default occurs. The purpose of increasing the interest in such cases is to help offset the increased costs to the lender in collecting a delinquent account or in undertaking foreclosure proceedings.

Insurance

Mortgages require property insurance coverage for the lender's protection. This is also termed *hazard insurance.* Principally, it includes fire and extended coverage and is required by the lender where any buildings are involved in an amount at least equal to that of the loan. To make certain that insurance payments are made, the lender generally requires a full year's paid-up insurance policy before releasing the loan proceeds, plus two months of the annual premium paid into an escrow account. Then with each monthly payment, one-twelfth of the annual premium must be paid. The original policy is held by the lender, and it is part of the lender's responsibility to maintain the coverage with timely payments made from the borrower's escrow account.

Insurance companies in most states have another requirement controlling the minimum amount of coverage that can be carried to establish full coverage in case of a loss. Since most fire losses are partial in extent, it is not unusual for a property owner to carry only partial insurance hoping that any fire would be brought under control before the damage exceeds the amount of insurance coverage. To distribute the cost of insurance more equitably over all policyholders, many insurance companies require that the insured maintain insurance of not less than a given percentage of the actual cash value of the building at the time of the loss. These clauses are known variously as coinsurance clauses, average clauses, or reduced rate contribution clauses. A common minimum amount of insurance to provide full coverage is 80 percent of the actual cash value of the building at the time of the loss. By carrying less than the agreed percentage of insurance, the property owner cannot collect in full for a loss, but will have to bear a part of the loss personally. The insurance company will be liable only for such percentage of the loss as the amount of insurance carried bears to 80 percent of the actual cash value of the property at the time of the loss. The insurance company's liability may be expressed by the formula:

$$\frac{C}{R} \times L = A$$

Where   C = the amount of insurance carried
           R = the amount of insurance required
           L = the amount of the loss
           A = the amount for which the insurance
                 company is liable.

In periods of rapidly rising property values, any failure to maintain proper insurance coverage can expose the lender, as well as the property owner, to uninsured losses.

Another insurance problem to be considered in a mortgage involves determining just how the proceeds should be paid in case of an actual loss. Earlier mortgages required payment of the insurance money to the lender, who in turn then decided how to apply the funds, i.e., whether to permit the funds to be used for restoration of the property, which is the usual procedure on smaller losses, or to apply the insurance proceeds to the payoff of the loan. As time has passed, recent mortgages have given the borrower a stronger position in the distribution of insurance proceeds, as is apparent in the FNMA/FHLMC standard conventional mortgage terms.

Taxes

Lenders long ago learned that the real first lien on any property is in the hands of the property taxing authority, that is, the agency that levies the *ad valorem* property taxes. It can be categorically stated that the full documented and properly recorded "first" mortgage instrument securing the lender's position takes only a poor second place to a tax levy. And in some states, this tax levy includes an assessment by a properly authorized neighborhood maintenance association!

It is evident then, that the timely payment of property taxes becomes another essential requirement in mortgage loans. Lenders usually require that an amount equal to two months of the annual taxes be paid into an escrow account by the borrower before the loan is funded. One-twelfth of the annual taxes is also added to each monthly payment of principal and interest. In this manner, the lender accumulates sufficient cash each year to pay the borrower's property taxes directly to the tax authorities and thus is protected against any tax priority lien on the pledged property.

In regard to federal taxes, these take priority over state laws regarding property and do carry lien rights and highest priority. However, federal taxes, including federal income taxes, become property liens only when they are filed as a delinquent assessment against an individual or corporation, not when the tax liability is incurred. A federal tax lien is a general lien and may apply to any and all property owned by the taxpayer. The *ad valorem,* or property tax, is a specific lien (applying only to the designated property liable for the tax), and becomes a lien against the property from the minute the taxing authorities levy the assessment.

Foreclosure

The right of the lender to foreclose on a property is limited by the terms of the mortgage instrument and by the applicable state laws. In general, foreclosure is the last recourse of the lender, often a costly procedure and usually an open admission that an error in judgment was made in making the loan. Lenders will normally put forth considerable effort to cooperate with a borrower who has unforeseen financial problems and needs some relief. But the lender must depend on the borrower to seek the relief, and this is more easily arranged before a serious delinquency occurs. Lenders have an obligation to their own investors, depositors, insurance policy holders, trust funds, and so on, to exercise control over their borrower's accounts and not allow a property mortgage note to slide into default so that such laxity would compromise the lender's security. When failure to comply with the terms of the note and mortgage occurs on the part of the borrower, generally due to nonpayment of the obligation, then the lender must seek foreclosure of the property.

The real purpose of a foreclosure is to sell the property under the authority of a court order, usually referred to as a *sheriff's sale,* and to distribute the proceeds to the various creditors holding claims on the property. Contrary to popular belief, the lender has no more right to take title to the property than anyone else who has a claim on it, in a foreclosure proceeding.

Accordingly, the court orders a property to be sold in a foreclosure proceeding, and whoever offers the highest cash price at the subsequent public sale acquires a deed to the property by court order, in some places referred to as a *sheriff's deed.* In practice, the lender is allowed to submit a claim, that is, the balance due on the promissory note, as part or all of the cash offer for the property. In many states, the lender need not even offer the full amount of the claim if it is deemed too high.

Because the lender has a claim against the property and can use that as payment in a foreclosure sale, the lender or an agent for the lender usually ends up taking title to the foreclosed property. If the claim against the borrower is not fully satisfied from the proceeds of the sale, then the lender can seek a deficiency judgment for the balance due.

The above considerations strongly suggest that the foreclosure is apt to be a difficult, distasteful, and discouraging procedure. The lender is faced with the costs of litigation, with the possibility of an unpleasant eviction, plus the risk of property damage through owner abuse, or vandalism. In addition, the lender may have to pay the costs of renovating and maintaining the property, plus payment of delinquent taxes and insurance. Foreclosure is seldom a satisfactory solution.

TYPES OF MORTGAGES

The most common forms of mortgage instruments have some important variations, namely, in how and when they are used. The underlying purpose of providing a pledge of property as security for a loan remains the same, however. Some of the principal variations are discussed below.

Deed of Trust

The *deed of trust* introduces a third party, a trustee, into the pledging instrument. Under these terms, the borrower actually makes an assignment (the wording is very similar to a warranty deed) of the property to the trustee, but restricts the effectiveness of the assignment to when a default occurs under the mortgage terms. The trustee is normally selected by the lender with the right of substitution in case of death or dismissal.

The deed of trust form is used in many areas and is almost universally used in Texas as a means of simplifying "homestead" law procedures. It substantially reduces the problems of foreclosure, limiting the process to an action by the trustee, with proper notice and in accordance with prevailing laws, rather than by litigation conducted in a court hearing.

Open-end Mortgages

The open-end mortgage permits a lender to advance additional money under the same security and priority as the original mortgage. This type of mortgage is often employed in farm loans where the lender maintains continuing relations with his customer-borrower. As the borrower pays the mortgage principal down, he or she may wish to add a new barn, or perhaps a new loading corral to the property. The additional loan can easily be accommodated under the terms of an open-end mortgage.

In some areas a borrower may elect to leave a minimal mortgage balance of, say, one dollar outstanding on the mortgage loan. This record of balance due, no matter how small, sustains the life of the mortgage instrument and, most significantly, its priority over any other subsequent lien except, of course, property taxes. This provision gives rural banks a means of making loans to their farm- or ranch-owning customers without the expense and delay of researching a title and recording a new mortgage instrument with each loan.

Construction Mortgages

A loan to build a house or other building is a construction loan, sometimes called *interim* financing. The security requirement is the same—a first lien on real property—but in this type of loan, proceeds are disbursed as the building is constructed. Under the construction mortgage, the borrower or builder draws a portion of the total loan at various stages, or at set time intervals, such as monthly, for work completed. It takes a construction-wise lender to make sure his disbursement of funds does not exceed the value of a building at each stage of construction.

A construction loan is considered a high-risk loan. It carries high-interest rates and is never intended to extend beyond three years. Commercial projects, such as a warehouse or apartment, usually require assurance of permanent financing or a "take-out commitment," i.e., an agreement by a reputable lender that the lending organization will make a permanent loan upon completion of the project.

Homebuilders frequently build for speculative sales, in which case the construction lender must look to the actual sale of the house to pay off the construction loan. This increases the risk for the lender who may require the builder to obtain a stand-by commitment for a permanent loan before commencing construction. For additional information, see "Construction Loans," Chapter 12.

Mortgages with Release Clauses

When money is borrowed for the purpose of land development, it is necessary to have specific release procedures to enable the developer to sell lots, or a portion of the land, and deliver good title to that portion. This is the purpose of a release clause. The conditions are stated so that the developer can repay a portion of the loan and obtain a release of a portion of the land from the original mortgage. In a subdivision of building lots, the developer would be required to pay a percentage of the sales price of the lot, or a minimum dollar amount against the loan, for each lot released. The lender would calculate the pay-off so that the loan would be fully repaid when somewhere around 60 to 80 percent of the lots are sold.

Under regular mortgages, there is no provision to allow a partial sale of the property. So a development loan requires considerable negotiation to work out all the details necessary for success. The lender will want some control over the direction of the development; i.e., lots must be developed and sold in an orderly manner that will not undermine the value of any remaining land. A time pattern must be negotiated to allow realistic limits on how fast the lots must be sold. The clause that permits the release of a portion of the mortgaged land is also called a *partial release* since the remainder of the land continues to be held as security for the loan.

Junior Mortgages

The term *junior mortgages* applies to those mortgages that carry a lower priority than the prime or first mortgage. These are *second* and even *third* mortgages.

The mortgage instrument carries no designation in its text describing its lien position. The order of priority, which determines the exact order of claims against a piece of property, is established by the time of the recording of that instrument. This becomes of extreme importance in a foreclosure proceeding. For example, if a property considered to be worth $50,000 carries a first mortgage for $30,000, and a second mortgage for $8000, and that property is forced into a foreclosure sale that results in a recovery of $35,000 in cash after payment of legal fees—how, then, should the money be distributed? The priority of the liens exercises control, and assuming that no other liens, taxes, or otherwise, have shown priority, then the first mortgage holder is in a position to recover his full $30,000 from the $35,000 proceeds, and the remaining $5000 is awarded to the second mortgage holder, leaving him $3000 short of recovering his $8000 loan. Due to the promissory note, the second mortgage holder has a right to seek a deficiency judgment against the borrower to recover that $3000. However, it becomes evident that the security of the land has been wiped out in the foreclosure sale and resulting settlement.

Later in this text, the subjects of recording and of title protection, as related to the question of establishing the priority of mortgage liens, will be discussed in more detail.

Purchase Money Mortgages

Primarily, a purchase money mortgage is a mortgage taken by the seller of a property as a part of the consideration. The designation is also used in some states with homestead laws to distinguish it from any other form of mortgage that would not carry the same lien rights.

Chattel Mortgages

Although we have been discussing mortgages primarily in terms of real property as security, the term *mortgage* can also be used to describe a pledge of personal property such as furniture or a car. This personal property can be referred to as *chattel*. Chattel, then, may be defined as a movable object—any property, exclusive of land or objects permanently attached to the land. With a chattel mortgage, the pledge of personal property as security for a loan can be similar to that for real property. It is the movable quality of the collateral and the difficulty of properly identifying an object such as a table or a washing machine that make the pledge a less secure procedure than it is in regard to real property.

Nevertheless, the form is widely used in small loan companies and for installment financing. Some states, it should be noted in this connection, use a conditional sales contract procedure for installment purchases that does not legally pass title to the chattel until it is fully paid for, thus eliminating the need for a mortgage pledge.

Package Mortgages

The *package mortgage* occurs in a hybrid form and attempts to include in the mortgage indenture both real property and personal property. It is used in residential loans when considerable built-in equipment is included with the house. Such a mortgage would list various household appliances, such as an oven, a range, a dishwasher, or disposal equipment, that might be considered attached to and a part of the real property, but that can be removed rather easily. By adding these various items to the mortgage as security, the lender may better protect his complete property loan. Although the procedure is often ignored or not enforced, it is definitely a violation of the mortgage terms to sell or dispose of a mortgaged range or dishwasher without the express consent of the mortgagee.

Varying Amortization Mortgages

Two types of mortgages have been introduced in recent years that provide for variations from the constant amortization payments more commonly used. Both have been developed in an effort to cope with continuing inflation and the problems it presents to both the lender and the borrower. These are the variable rate mortgage and the graduated payment mortgage, which are described below.

Variable Rate Mortage. Under this form of mortgage agreement, the interest rate applicable to the loan is allowed to fluctuate with the rates in the capital market. The base rate used as a guide can vary with the different lending institutions but it is usually a rate indicator published by a government agency. As the indicator moves upward or downward, the interest rate for the loan follows. There is usually a restriction on changing the interest rate for the loan, such as not more often than six-month intervals, plus a restriction that may limit any increase to ½ percent each six months, but no restriction on reductions. Another feature of the variable rate mortgage is that the monthly payment itself may remain constant. The fluctuation of the interest rate is reflected in how the installment is allocated to the payment of principal and the payment of the interest due each month. This form of mortgage has found its strongest acceptance in the California markets.

Graduated Payment Mortgage. The graduated payment plan for a mortgage provides for a monthly payment at the beginning of somewhat less than would be needed to fully amortize the loan and then increasing until, in later years, a higher payment than a constant level rate would be required. The practice is not uncommon in commercial-type loans when a smaller payment is permitted in the early years for, say, the first five years based on a 30-year amortization, then a 20-year amortization, and finally a 10-year amortization rate. The intent is to permit a company or a home-buyer to make smaller payments in the beginning when their income is lower and to increase these payments as their income increases.

Most private lenders have not utilized this form of mortgage for home loans, but in November 1976, HUD announced that the FHA would insure mortgages under this graduated payment plan. Several alternative plans are being offered but essentially they provide for an initial monthly payment approximately 15 percent lower than would be required for a 30-year amortization. The payments increase about 3 percent for each succeeding year until, in the tenth year, the payments would be about 12 percent higher than normal, constant rate amortization.

One of the very real problems involved with utilizing graduated payments for a long-term loan is the high percentage of the early payment that pays for the interest only. For example, the remaining balance due on a 30-year loan at 8½ percent interest after one full year of normal, constant payments is 99.2 percent. On a $35,000 loan, after making 12 monthly payments of $269, the principal balance would be reduced by just $280. About 9 percent of the first year's payments goes to principal and the rest goes for interest costs. If the first year's payments are reduced by 15 percent as proposed by HUD, the home-buyer will end the first year owing more for his home than when he bought it.

To offset the possibility that the balance due on the insured loan will climb beyond the value of the house in the first few years, HUD requires larger down payments for loan approval. But the same home-buyer that needs smaller monthly payments to acquire the house he or she wants is probably not the one with sufficient cash on hand to make a larger down payment.

What may make graduated payment plans more acceptable to the mortgage lenders is the continuing inflation. For the past few years, home values have increased at an annual rate of approximately 10 percent. But few lenders are yet willing to concede that we will suffer this high inflation rate from now on.

Contract for Deed

In listing types of mortgages, a *contract for deed* would be considered out of place, except for the fact that many people believe this instrument to be similar to a mortgage procedure. It is not.

In essence a contract for deed is another method of selling real estate. It is exactly what its name implies, a contract for a deed, and no more. It is used to sell real property on an installment payment basis without delivering title to the property until payment has been made in full. Properly drawn, a contract for deed is enforceable against either signatory party, as is any contract under the state's codes providing for contracts. However, it is not a deed to real property and grants to the buyer only the rights of possession and enjoyment; and these rights exist only as long as the grantor holds control of the land.

If fully understood by both parties, the contract for deed can be helpful in transferring property usage when a buyer has temporary credit problems or the seller does not yet hold a fully marketable title. However, this form of contract has gained a poor reputation through abuses, failure to fully disclose the facts, and outright frauds. The real pitfall lies in the possible inability of the seller to deliver a valid title after full payment has been made. During the installment paying period, anything that might happen to the seller, such as a damage claim resulting in a heavy adverse judgment, a divorce causing property settlements, dissolution of a corporate seller through bankruptcy, or any lien filed against the property under contract, can defeat the intent of the contract and can cause the seller to be unable to deliver a good title. If the seller cannot produce a good title to the property at completion of payment, the buyer may have a claim for damages against the seller, but has no direct claim to the property involved.

Contract for deed sales are most commonly used in the sale of resort-type lots and also in smaller rent houses where a tenant becomes a buyer if he completes the payments. In the latter case, the property owner may wish to give a tenant the right to buy the house, but because of some prior credit problems or some temporary family troubles of the tenant, the owner does not want his land encumbered by the tenant buyer if a default occurs.

In regard to the resort-type lot sales, there have been flagrant abuses in the past. In 1969, the Department of Housing and Urban Development established the Office of Interstate Land Sales Registration as a policing agency for developers of property containing more than 50 lots in any one development and less than five acres per lot. The thrust of the legislation is not to establish sales patterns or minimum lot requirements, but to make sure the developer fully discloses the development plans and the legal status of the land title itself. And the buyer must acknowledge the receipt of all the information required, which also has the effect of protecting the developer against unwarranted claims from the buyer.

MORTGAGE PROCEDURES

Again, the practices and procedures by which mortgage rights are established and protected vary among the states, but certain elements are common to all. In the following discussion, the common procedures and reasons for them will be considered.

Recording

Of all the statutes written regarding ownership of land, the incentives to record a transaction have had the greatest long-range effect on improving records of land ownership. In fairly recent times and due to the lack of controlling legislation, courts have held that a valid title to land was actually passed by such procedures as a handwritten entry in the family Bible. How can a mortgage lender determine who really owns a piece of land? The answer lies in the recorded instruments of land transactions filed in the county records wherein the land is located. As the laws have made the recording of land transactions a necessary procedure and as our methods of handling this documentation have improved, the actual determination of proper title is becoming more and more accurate.

What is *recording?* In legal terms it is a form of notice—notice to the world—that a transaction of some kind has affected the title to a specific piece of land. Another form of legal notice is actual possession of the land, and historically, possession is the highest form of notice. The procedure for recording a transaction is to take the document to the record office of the county where the land is located and pay the fee for filing. The county officer responsible for the recording, copies the instrument in its entirety for the record book and certifies on the original as to the time, date, volume, and page or pages that contain the record.

Most state laws that relate to instruments affecting land titles and the recording of them do not challenge the contractual rights of any parties to buy, sell, or encumber a piece of land. What they actually do is to declare any land transaction invalid against a third party *only in regard to the title to land if it is not recorded.* For example, *A* can agree to sell ten acres of land to *B* and actually deliver a deed for the ten acres to *B*. The contract may be valid and the consideration (payment for the land) accepted, but actual title to the land is not secure until the deed has been recorded. If the seller *A*, in this example, should suffer a heavy casualty loss and be subjected to a court judgment against him before the deed to buyer *B* has been recorded, the ten acres of land would be subject to the claim of *A*'s new creditors since the title would still be in *A*'s name on the public record.

It is important to emphasize that the failure to record an instrument affecting land title does not invalidate the instrument insofar as the parties involved in the transaction are concerned. It places the burden on whichever party is asserting a claim to the land to give notice of his or her claim in the public records, or lose the effectiveness of that claim against any other claimant. The rules apply to all instruments applicable to land titles, conveyances, claims, or debts against the land itself or against the landowner, and, of course, all mortgage instruments. Contracts for deed and leases are instruments affecting land title and can be recorded, but for various reasons of privacy or other interests often are not recorded.

State laws are usually lenient as to what instruments can be recorded, but most require that the signature to the instrument be acknowledged before a duly authorized officer of the state such as a Notary Public, or be properly witnessed. Because any instrument affecting a title to land is a legal matter that can involve many state laws, it is customary, though not always required, that such an instrument be prepared by a licensed attorney. The preparation of any instrument conveying a land title is considered the practice of law in most states and, therefore, is restricted to that state's licensed attorneys. Few, if any, lenders would permit a loan to be made based on a mortgage instrument prepared by anyone other than a qualified attorney regardless of the requirements for recording.

Mortgage Priorities

The expression *first mortgage* or *second mortgage* is so commonly used that it is not unusual for a person to expect to find such an identification spelled out in the mortgage instrument. Such is not the case. The priority by which a mortgage, or any other claim to land, is established is by the time of recording. And this is determined not only by the day of recording, but by the time of that particular day.

In handling a mortgage instrument, the lender is most concerned about the proper priority of his security claim; i.e., what prior claims, if any, could jeopardize the lender's claim to the land. Most lenders do not rely on the record alone, but require an insuring agent to guarantee the priority of the claim backed by an insurance policy, called a *title policy*.

The statutory priorities given workmen and material suppliers in most states may be a source of additional problems for construction loan mortgages. For example, in a mortgage to secure construction money, any work permitted on the land prior to the recording means that a workman may have a claim on the land itself in case of non-payment. Such a claim held by a workman or contractor need not be recorded to establish its priority, but there must be some positive proof that the work was accomplished before the mortgage was recorded. One method of establishing priority for the lender is to photograph the raw land, have the date of the picture certified, and retain the print as proof that the land was untouched prior to recording the mortgage.

Any claim to land that is of lower priority, i.e., recorded or incurred at a later date, is said to be junior to the prior claim. Thus, as noted earlier, second and third mortgages are sometimes referred to as junior mortgages.

Subordination

Another method of establishing priorities for mortgage instruments is by contract. For various reasons it may be beneficial to the parties involved in a land transaction to establish a claim of lower value or lesser importance to another, a procedure called *subordination*.

An example might be a hypothetical case where a piece of land is sold to a developer who plans to erect an office building for lease to one of his customers. The seller of the land, for taxes or other reasons, prefers to take his payment in ten annual installments. But the developer needs to mortgage the land immediately with first priority for payment going to the mortgage lender for construction money to build the office building. In such a case, and assuming credit worthiness of the developer, the land seller would agree specifically to subordinate the land ownership claim to the lender's mortgage, securing the ten annual payments with a second mortgage.

Limitation Statutes

In the codes of law established by the various states, *time limitations* have been established on the validity of most claims or debts. These limitations may vary somewhat, but usually place time limits within which a creditor can file a claim for an open account, such as one to two years, and usually a longer limit within which a written promissory note can be recovered, perhaps five to ten years. Time limits for secured debts may be extended for even longer periods.

There are also limiting statutes imposed for general contractors and subcontractors filing claims for unpaid work and materials on construction projects. Failure to file a claim, usually in the form of a lien recorded in the county records, within the prescribed time limits, would make that claim invalid insofar as the land itself is concerned. It does not void the debt, however.

There are also time limitations in most states affecting title to real property. These have been established in an effort to clarify claims to ownership of land. The time limitations vary with what is called the "color of title" that can be asserted to the land claimed. Two factors are essential to establishing a valid claim to land over a period of time within the statutes of limitation: (1) actual possession and use of the land, and (2) possession and use considered adverse or use without the express consent of the opposing claimant.

An example of a short time limitation might be cited here as, for instance, the purchase of a house from the heirs of a family who previously owned the property. All the known heirs have agreed to the sale of the property and have joined in signing the deed; the purchaser has duly paid the full price agreed to. Then several years later someone claiming to be an heir comes forward to assert his interest in the house that was sold. Because a deed was delivered in good faith and the consideration was paid, the new claimant might be limited to three years within which his claim would be considered by the courts.

The longest time limits are usually granted in any transaction involving minor children or mentally incapacitated persons. Most states draw a line at 25 years and simply rule that possession of land for that period precludes anyone else asserting a claim against it.

The result of these limiting statutes is an effective scrubbing of the records after the prescribed number of years. Title insurance policies lapse after the maximum years within which claims can be filed. Many property owners are careful to establish their own property lines with special markers and to assert their own usage and ownership of land by restricting access to private roadways, etc., for perhaps one day a year, so as to prevent or offset the workings of time limitation statutes.

LAND TITLES

Ownership of land is a right. It is not a deed, it is not a title insurance policy, it is not living on the land. All of these characteristics are important evidences of ownership, but the right itself is broader and covers four definable areas:

1. *Possession*—the right to occupy the land, such as a residence.

2. *Use*—the right to work the land, which covers what may be grown, what minerals may be recovered, and so on.

3. *Enjoyment*—the use and occupancy of the land free of harassment or interference.

4. *Disposition*—the right to sell, lease, or otherwise dispose of the land.

In today's complex living patterns, the free and unfettered ownership of land that once existed in earlier rural areas is difficult to find. Possession is about the only element of ownership that remains clearly distinguishable, and even that has become more difficult to determine.

The usage of land is complicated by leases on mineral rights (oil, gas, coal, and so on) and by restrictions set up by some state governments forbidding the use of water except by separate grants of water rights, as well as by federal restrictions as to what can or cannot be grown on the land. The enjoyment of the land is also subject to many restrictions in urban areas, particularly in the form of zoning laws, health and safety restrictions, and possible conflicts in neighborhood associations.

The rights to dispose of land are complicated by the practice of bequeathing life estates, say, to a widow upon the death of a husband; or by the assignment of property by will to a charitable foundation or educational institution; or by a gift of land to a community for a specific use such as a park, with the land reverting back to the estate of the former owner should his wishes be violated.

With all the complications in land ownership, as outlined above, it becomes necessary to find a way to establish where and in whose hands ownership and control of the land actually lie. In order for a mortgage instrument to be valid and to provide security for a loan, it is necessary that sufficient rights to the land be pledged and that the pledge be made by the person or persons holding the rights to do so. Loans are made against various portions of real property ownership, such as oil production loans on oil leases, development loans on mining claims, and crop loans on surface and water rights. It rarely happens today that much more than a portion of the ownership rights is pledged, but that portion must include the essential rights that would enable a lender to use the property as a last resort in recovering the balance of his loan.

The area under study in this text is land development and the buildings occupying the land, which would mean the ownership rights to at least the surface, the access rights thereto, and protection against infringement by any other user of rights to that land. The researching of these rights of ownership to land is the special province of land title companies, which are basically insurance companies. Title companies sell insurance policies that guarantee to the purchaser a good title to a certain piece of property. The guarantee is in the form of a promise to protect the land title against any adverse claim or to pay the holder of the policy the face amount (purchase price of the property) in cash, should the title fail for any reason. At the time the initial owner's policy is issued, a second policy covering the same property may be purchased that makes a similar pledge of title protection to the lender or mortgagee. The mortgagee's policy runs with the mortgage; i.e., the insurance is in the amount of the balance due on the mortgage note, automatically covers any subsequent holder of the note, and is in effect until the note is paid off. The owner's policy has different terms—it insures the owner for the face amount of the policy for a specified number of years, usually the statutory limit of the owners possible responsibility for the title. The owner's policy continues to protect the owner even after the property has been sold because he or she still carries a responsibility to defend the title that may be passed on under a general warranty deed. The fact that a title policy may exist on a piece of property provides no protection at all for a new purchaser. The new purchaser can only be protected, title insurance-wise, with a new policy issued in his or her name.

A second method of obtaining title information and of determining the validity of a mortgage pledge is to employ an attorney to research the title. In this procedure, the attorney will order an abstract from an abstract or title company. The abstract is a certified collection of all instruments that have been recorded and, therefore, have affected the chain of title since the inception of that title. The inception of the title could be a land grant by a foreign monarch who once claimed the land, or more commonly by a state granting title to a purchaser, or it could be by quit claim deed from the federal government. From its original grant, the land may have been broken into many segments and passed through many hands, and the abstracts can be quite voluminous. The result of the research is an attorney's opinion on the title stating any adverse claims to the land that are exceptions to the title. The opinion will then identify those title problems that must be corrected, or "cured" before a mortgage can be made securely.

In certain areas of the country another method is employed to handle property titles, a method flowing from the Torrens Act procedure. This is a process whereby a state has adopted a program for recording title, mostly for urban property lots, by registering property title in the public record established for that purpose. The procedure is very similar to that used in registering the ownership of a car. Any sale of the property must be registered, and a new certificate of title is then issued by the state. The plan has some inherent advantages in minimizing legal expenses and title costs in the sale of property, but because of the complex nature of land ownership, this plan has not become too widespread in usage.

Accepting the fact that land titles in today's urban society are seldom completely clear, the mortgage lender has learned to live with certain kinds of exceptions. For instance, title insurance companies have standard clauses of exceptions that they customarily make in any insurance policy they issue. One of these exceptions has to do with the rights of anyone then in possession of the property. The title company does not physically inspect the property, leaving that to the buyer. Since the seller is usually in possession of the property when it is sold, his rights are clearly determined when he signs a warranty deed granting title to the buyer. If a tenant is in possession, it is necessary to establish his rights before a sale is consummated.

Another standard exception made by the title company is in the zoning requirements or sometimes in regard to deed restrictions. The title company is not insuring any specific usage of the property; it is only making certain that the ownership rights of possession and disposition are clearly assignable.

The title insuring policy will usually list any easements crossing the property, which are generally utility easements and street rights-of-way. The easements are exceptions to the insurance policy and are simply claims to the land, which are accepted as normal and necessary.

Often the title company will list certain requirements in the initial title opinion that involve a question of encroachments on the property lines, or perhaps a dispute among heirs, or a problem arising from a divorce settlement that is undecided. The requirements must be resolved to the satisfaction of the title company, or the insurance policy can be refused, or it can be issued with the unsatisfied requirement listed as an exception to the coverage.

What these questions involving title problems lead to is not always a completely clear title, but what is called a "merchantable" or "marketable" title. There can be exceptions or unsatisfied requirements, which, at the discretion of the mortgage lender, may be so unimportant or insignificant to the total property value that they can be ignored. The ultimate question is whether or not a knowledgeable buyer would be willing to accept the minor title defects in a subsequent sale should foreclosure become necessary.

In some states, such as Ohio, title companies offer a choice of assurances regarding the land title. A purchaser may require proof of title in the form of a *title guarantee* which is essentially a certification of the information on the subject property as recorded in the county office. The recorded description of the property is accepted and a survey may not be required. If the purchaser requires that the title company also insure the title for a monetary value, an additional charge is made for such coverage.

QUESTIONS FOR DISCUSSION

1. What procedure is used in your state to handle a pledge of security for a mortgage loan?

2. What is the purpose of a promissory note? Of a mortgage instrument?

3. Distinguish between an acceleration clause and an escalation clause in a mortgage.

4. What is the underlying purpose of requiring a borrower to escrow money each month for the annual payment of property taxes?

5. List the costs to a lender that could be involved in a foreclosure action.

6. Describe what is meant by an "open-end" mortgage.

7. What is the principal risk for the buyer-borrower in a contract for deed?

8. Identify the two principal methods by which a lender can be assured that the mortgage pledge is made by the person or persons who have the legal rights to do so.

9. Why is an accurate property description important?

10. Explain a variable rate mortgage, and a graduated payment mortgage.

Chapter 4

Sources of Mortgage Money

The great pools of money that are available in the United States for mortgage loans can be classified into five major sources and a number of lesser sources as follows:

Major Sources

1. Savings and loan associations
2. Mutual savings banks
3. Commercial banks
4. Life insurance companies
5. Government agencies

Lesser Sources

1. Pension and trust funds
2. Individuals
3. Real estate investments trusts
4. Miscellaneous others

Of the principal sources for *all* types of investments, long-term and short-term, business, consumer and mortgage loans, the commercial banks rank as the largest. The second in volume of loans are the thrift institutions or savings banks and associations, followed by industrial corporations. Fourth in size are the investment accounts of the various governments, with the life insurance companies ranking fifth.

What about foreign investments in this country? While it is true that more foreign money is coming in to purchase securities and real estate itself, as a present source of lendable funds, foreign investment has added very little to this country's totals so far. Furthermore, the continuing instability of the world money markets holds poor prospects for any increase of funds from this source for lending purposes.

In examining the major sources of lendable funds, we are limiting our coverage to those making substantial investments in long-term mortgage loans. The industrial corporations, one of the largest sources of investment funds, do not make long-term loans to the general public. Their investments are generally limited to growth within their own organizations and private sphere of business. The need for outside mortgage money by industrial corporations is discussed in Chapter 12, but as a source of funds for the purposes of this text these corporations are not considered.

The sources covered in this chapter are the mortgage lenders—all subject to various regulations that control and direct their loans. But within the rules, each lender is free to exercise individual judgment in the selection of loans that will achieve a maximum yield for the money compatible with the risk exposure. Only a portion of the many government bureaus and agencies making loans have their programs coupled to social and political purposes such as subsidized housing, aid to the victims of a natural disaster, assistance for displaced families, and aid for military personnel. The major thrust of the government programs is to facilitate the flow of money through the private lending institutions and to help protect the savings of the individuals and companies whose cash, in the form of deposits, insurance premiums, and security purchases, is the real underlying source of all our lendable funds.

Institutions making long-term real estate mortgage loans have a variety of reasons for making each loan. They might wish to increase an investment yield, or to satisfy and maintain a business relationship with a particularly good customer; or perhaps they wish to attract some new business from a competitor; or they might want to shift a portion of the investments within their own portfolio of loans; or there could be a need to comply with a statutory requirement or a new regulation. Whatever the specific reason may be for a loan, there are four basic qualifications common to all mortgage lenders, which are as follows:

1. A substantial pool of available cash with a reasonable and predictable inflow.

2. A satisfactory method for controlling the outflow of funds.

3. Adequate personnel knowledgeable in the field of mortgage lending.

4. Legal qualifications permitting long-term loans.

In considering the qualifications listed above, the predictable inflow is excellent with insurance companies and pension funds. Savings associations have grown by being allowed to offer a slightly higher interest rate for savings accounts, but such accounts are subject to withdrawal, legally upon 30-day notice, but in practice, almost on demand. The protection of the outflow for thrift institutions lies in their ability to borrow additional money against their loan portfolio or to sell some of the loans in the secondary market when they are faced with substantial withdrawals. Commercial banks must limit their long-term loans to a percentage of their time deposits rather than their demand deposits. In regard to the outflow of funds, then, the life insurance companies and the pension funds are in almost complete control, whereas the thrift institutions and banks must rely on borrowed funds or the sale of loans to offset any massive withdrawals.

On the succeeding pages, we will analyze those institutions that can be considered sources of mortgage money, relate them to the guidelines indicated above, and discuss the role each one plays in the financing of real estate.

LOAN AMOUNTS BY SOURCE

Table 4-1 illustrates the relative involvement of the various sources of money in the mortgage market. It shows that by 1976 the outstanding real estate mortgage indebtedness in the United States amounted to $755,445 million. The holders of this indebtedness were divided between private financial institutions with $592,398 million or 78 percent, federal and related agencies with $91,975 million or 13 percent, and individuals and others with $71,072 million or 9 percent of the total. Of the total indebtedness, the savings associations hold $286,575 million or 38 percent.

TABLE 4-1.

Mortgage Debt Outstanding by Type of Holder
(In millions of dollars)

Type of holder, and type of property	End of year			End of quarter 1975				1976
	1972	1973	1974	I	II	III	IV	I^r
ALL HOLDERS	564,825	634,954	688,652	695,369	709,153	725,543	741,547	755,445
1- to 4-family	345,372	384,738	412,168	415,607	425,132	436,420	447,350	460,968
Multifamily	76,667	85,296	91,222	91,522	91,733	92,073	92,093	88,887
Commercial	107,349	125,572	140,965	142,701	145,353	149,072	153,119	155,424
Farm	35,437	39,348	44,297	45,539	46,935	47,978	48,985	50,166
PRIVATE FINANCIAL INSTITUTIONS	450,000	505,400	542,552	546,689	558,179	570,049	581,486	592,398
1- to 4-family	288,018	320,420	340,007	342,313	350,198	358,184	365,371	377,038
Multifamily	59,398	64,750	68,161	68,095	68,453	68,688	68,807	65,671
Commercial	92,063	108,735	121,948	123,684	126,634	130,153	134,100	136,305
Farm	10,521	11,495	12,436	12,597	12,894	13,024	13,208	13,384
Commercial banks[1]	*99,314*	*119,068*	*132,105*	*131,903*	*133,012*	*134,514*	*136,186*	*138,304*
1- to 4-family	57,004	67,998	74,758	74,696	75,356	76,149	77,018	78,498
Multifamily	5,778	6,932	7,619	7,176	6,816	6,363	5,915	6,023
Commercial	31,751	38,696	43,679	43,924	44,598	45,694	46,882	47,288
Farm	4,781	5,442	6,049	6,107	6,242	6,308	6,371	6,495
Mutual savings banks	*67,556*	*73,230*	*74,920*	*75,157*	*75,796*	*76,490*	*77,249*	*77,738*
1- to 4-family	41,650	44,246	44,670	44,795	45,175	45,588	46,041	50,344

Multifamily	15,490	16,843	17,234	17,291	17,433	17,593	17,767	13,876
Commercial	10,354	12,084	12,956	12,996	13,112	13,233	13,364	13,456
Farm	62	57	60	75	76	76	77	62
Savings and loan associations	206,182	231,733	249,293	252,442	261,336	270,600	278,693	286,575
1– to 4–family	167,049	187,750	201,553	204,099	211,290	218,483	224,710	230,776
Multifamily	20,783	22,524	23,683	23,831	24,409	24,976	25,417	25,846
Commercial	18,350	21,459	24,057	24,512	25,637	27,141	28,566	29,953
Life insurance companies	76,948	81,369	86,234	87,187	88,035	88,445	89,358	89,781
1– to 4–family	22,315	20,426	19,026	18,723	18,377	17,964	17,602	17,420
Multifamily	17,347	18,451	19,625	19,797	19,795	19,756	19,708	19,926
Commercial	31,608	36,496	41,256	42,252	43,287	44,085	45,288	45,608
Farm	5,678	5,996	6,327	6,415	6,576	6,640	6,760	6,827
FEDERAL AND RELATED AGENCIES	45,790	55,664	72,380	76,010	79,952	84,522	89,039	91,975
1– to 4–family	30,170	35,579	46,322	48,455	51,195	54,697	58,440	60,391
Multifamily	6,063	8,364	11,329	11,995	12,348	12,753	12,954	13,184
Commercial	–	–	–	–	–	–	–	–
Farm	9,557	11,721	14,729	15,560	16,409	17,072	17,645	18,400
Government National Mortgage Association	5,113	4,029	4,846	5,599	5,610	6,534	7,438	7,619
1– to 4–family	2,513	1,455	2,248	2,787	2,787	3,692	4,728	4,886
Multifamily	2,600	2,574	2,598	2,812	2,823	2,842	2,710	2,733
Commercial	–	–	–	–	–	–	–	–
Farmers Home Administration	837	1,200	1,600	1,700	1,800	1,900	2,000	2,100
1– to 4–family	387	550	734	780	826	872	918	964
Farm	450	650	866	920	974	1,028	1,082	1,136
Federal Housing and Veterans Administrations	3,338	3,476	4,015	4,047	4,297	4,681	4,970	5,143
1– to 4–family	2,199	2,013	2,009	1,879	1,915	1,951	1,990	1,922

(continued)

71

TABLE 4-1. (continued)

Multifamily	1,139	1,463	2,006	2,168	2,382	2,730	2,980	3,221
Federal National Mortgage Association	*19,791*	*24,175*	*29,578*	*29,754*	*30,015*	*31,055*	*31,824*	*31,482*
1– to 4–family	17,697	20,370	23,778	23,743	23,988	25,049	25,813	25,562
Multifamily	2,094	3,805	5,800	6,011	6,027	6,006	6,011	5,920
Federal land banks (farm only)	9,107	11,071	13,863	14,640	15,435	16,044	16,563	17,264
Federal Home Loan Mortgage Corporation	*1,789*	*2,604*	*4,586*	*4,608*	*4,944*	*5,033*	*4,987*	*4,602*
1– to 4–family	1,754	2,446	4,217	4,231	4,543	4,632	4,588	4,247
Multifamily	35	158	369	377	401	401	399	355
GNMA Pools	*5,815*	*9,109*	*13,892*	*15,662*	*17,851*	*19,275*	*21,257*	*23,765*
1– to 4–family	5,620	8,745	13,336	15,035	17,136	18,501	20,403	22,810
Multifamily	195	364	556	627	715	774	854	955
INDIVIDUALS AND OTHERS[2]	69,035	73,890	73,720	72,670	71,022	70,972	71,022	71,072
1– to 4–family	27,184	28,739	25,839	24,839	23,739	23,539	23,539	23,539
Multifamily	11,206	12,182	11,732	11,432	10,932	10,632	10,332	10,032
Commercial	15,286	16,837	19,017	19,017	18,719	18,919	19,019	19,119
Farm	15,359	16,132	17,132	17,382	17,632	17,882	18,132	18,382

[1]Includes loans held by nondeposit trust companies but not bank trust departments.

[2]Includes some U.S. agencies for which amounts are small or separate data are not readily available.

Note – Based on data from various institutional and Govt. sources, with some quarters estimated in part by Federal Reserve in conjunction with the Federal Home Loan Bank Board and the Dept. of Commerce. Separation of nonfarm mortgage debt by type of property, where not reported directly, and interpolations and extrapolations where required, estimated mainly by Federal Reserve. Multifamily debt refers to loans on structures of 5 or more units.

Source: Federal Reserve Bulletin, July 1976.

Commercial banks with $138,304 million in mortgage loans outstanding are the second largest source statistically. However, the type of loans held by the commercial bank are mostly short-term types such as construction loans and the holding of mortgage notes as collateral for short-term loans to mortgage companies (called warehouse lines of credit).

SAVINGS AND LOAN ASSOCIATIONS

The number one source of mortgage funds is the savings and loan associations across the country. The origin of this type of institution was the loosely formed associations of people with common interests: farmers, storekeepers, religious groups, fraternal organizations, and others who pooled their capital to provide funds for building houses, improving land, or adding to their farms. The modern counterpart of these groups might be found in company credit unions; although there are differences in the purposes and types of loans of these institutions from those of the earlier associations.

Until the 1930s there was little regulation of these associations, but the Depression showed up many problems. Resources were restricted to local deposits, and the long-term loans allowed little liquidity or flexibility. In 1932 the federal government established the Federal Home Loan Bank system—still in operation today—which provides member associations a continuing source of funds for emergency needs or for financing additional mortgage loans. In 1933 the Federal Home Loan Bank Board was authorized to issue federal charters to newly formed savings associations, charters that required certain standards of compliance and a supervised method of operations. A year later, in 1934, the Federal Savings and Loan Insurance Corporation (FSLIC) was established to provide deposit insurance, and all federally chartered associations were required to belong and to comply with its rules. The insurance coverage now protects any one depositor up to the amount of $40,000.

Along with the efforts of the federal government to improve the savings associations, most states undertook reforms of all kinds to establish regulatory authorities and more stringent lending laws for their own state-chartered institutions. Some states have established their own deposit insurance procedures and have set rules with limits and procedures different from those of the federal patterns. But most states find it a good policy to follow the guidance of the Federal Home Loan Bank Board in order to establish a more uniform set of rules. The growing dependence on the secondary market for the sale of mortgage loans has increased the pressure toward more uniform standards; and unless certain procedures are required by state policies, the lending institution tries to follow the more nationalized procedures.

State-Chartered Savings and Loan Associations

Until 1933 all savings associations were state-chartered and operated under whatever rules and administrative procedures the various state legislatures established. State-chartered associations thus can be found under a variety of rules. They may be either mutually owned by the depositors, or they may be stock corporations owned by stockholders. Further, state charters may be required to carry deposit insurance, or they may not. Some states operate their own insurance funds to protect the depositors; others may require compliance with the Federal Savings and Loan Insurance Corporation. State-chartered associations are permitted to become members of the FSLIC and to be insured by it. To be eligible, the association must also become a member of the Federal Home Loan Bank System and is subject to its supervision. Thus, the state-chartered association would be subject to the rules established by the FSLIC, subject to the supervision of the FHLBB, plus meet the requirements of the state regulatory authorities. In spite of the overlapping of authorities, many state charters elect to join the federal system because of the protection it provides for the depositor.

State regulatory bodies can and do set their own limitations on the types of loans that can be made, the amounts that limit any one type of loan, and the general mix of investments permitted to the associations under their jurisdiction. In practice the upper limits of loans are being set by the federal authorities—the FHLBB and the newer Federal Home Loan Mortgage Corporation, which purchases mortgage loans—in order to maintain a portfolio of loans that can be more easily converted to cash should the need arise.

Federal-Chartered Savings and Loan Associations

The authority granted to the Federal Home Loan Bank Board in 1933 to issue savings and loan association charters created a new pattern that is uniform across the country. All federal-chartered associations until 1975 had to be mutually owned by the depositors. They must be members of the Federal Home Loan Bank system and have their deposits insured by the FSLIC.

The general requirements of the Federal Home Loan Bank Board imposed on its members are (1) an economically sound policy for mortgage loans, and (2) the condition that the interest rates charged be reasonable. The Board also required that a portion of each association's assets be held in liquid form; i.e., cash or demand deposits. Prior to August 1971, this requirement was 7½ percent of savings deposits and short-term borrowed funds. After that date the requirement was lowered to 7 percent in an effort to free more funds to relieve the pressures of the 1969–70 credit crunch. The reserve requirement was later lowered again, this time to 6½ percent, and returned to 7 percent in early 1976.

After many years of review, the Federal Home Loan Bank Board has recently taken some limited steps to permit a few mutually-owned savings associations to switch the form of ownership to that of a stockholder-owned corporation. From the depositors' viewpoint, a change to a stockholder form is important. Over the years these thrift institutions have built up substantial undistributed surpluses, which technically belong to the depositors. Since the individual depositors continue to change through the years, the proper allocation of the accumulated surplus to the current depositors is a major problem to any transition of ownership. From the lending viewpoint, the same rules and regulations would apply to the institution regardless of the form of ownership. A stockholder form of ownership might be considered more aggressive and could tend to channel loans into areas of higher yields.

Investment Policies of Savings Associations

Two important rules guide the thrust of a savings and loan investment policy. One of these is the requirement that 80 percent of a savings association's assets be held in residential mortgage loans, as that is the purpose for which it is chartered. The other is a policy of the Internal Revenue Service that allows a savings association to transfer earnings to a nontaxable surplus account, providing that loans classified as commercial do not exceed 18 percent of the association's assets.

The tax rule was designed to assist the purpose of the savings associations. The pooling of the depositors' funds is intended to provide them with a source of money to purchase or improve their homes. By permitting any earnings to accumulate tax-free, the association's ability to assist its members would be increased, and this would promote the growth of the economy. If any of the earnings are distributed as a dividend to the association's owners, that distribution is taxed at the corporate level and also as income to the member owner. Consequently, many associations prefer to accumulate surpluses.

But surpluses have not always been enough to stabilize the inflow of funds when new deposits slow or reverse themselves into an outflow. From experiences learned in the 1969–70 credit crunch, the Federal Home Loan Bank Board made several changes in the regulations governing member associations to improve their ability to handle fluctuating market conditions. As mentioned earlier, the regular pass book deposits are subject to withdrawal only after 30 days prior notice according to the rules. In practice, no association can really enforce this rule for fear of causing some alarm with a refusal to return a depositor's money upon demand. However, it is this legal limitation on immediate withdrawal that gives an association a technical position to make the long-term loans that cannot be permitted with a commercial bank's demand checking accounts.

To give savings associations greater stability than the 30-day withdrawal notice was supposed to provide, the FHLB in 1971 created a savings certificate to pay 6 percent interest, which was a full 1 percent over the existing pass book rate, provided that the certificate was held for two years. The new savings form was very popular, and some areas of the country reported over half of their deposits were coming from the long-term certificates. Another practice that had a tendency to improve the savings associations' long-term stability of deposits was the increase of branch offices into the smaller communities and rural areas. The effect has been to attract depositors who keep their money in the association and ignore interest-rate cycles.

The FHLBB also relaxed some of the restrictions on the types of loans that savings associations could make, allowing them to finance mobile homes and household appliances and to grant more liberal property-improvement loans. These are short-term loans for the most part, and give the associations a more rapid turnover of their money and greater flexibility in their loan portfolio.

Probably the greatest increase in flexibility for the savings associations has come from the rather sudden opening of the big secondary markets in mortgages. In 1969–70 these thrift institutions had little opportunity to sell the mortgages they held in exchange for cash that they badly needed to take care of new loan commitments. This situation has changed somewhat. In 1971 the Federal Home Loan Mortgage Corporation (nicknamed "Freddie Mac") entered the market for conventional mortgage loans under the direction of the FHLB. Now the savings associations have a new entity which raises capital through the sale of bonds to the general public and can use this capital to buy mortgage loans from the member associations. There has been considerable variation in the individual policies of savings associations utilizing this new market for loans. Some have simply refused to sell any of their loans, while others have arranged to sell off most of their newer loans, holding only the servicing contracts in house.

Another organization that stepped into the market for conventional loans was the Federal National Mortgage Association, which in February 1972, made its first purchase of loans other than FHA- and VA-underwritten loans. Under Chapter 5 of this text, the Federal National Mortgage Association—FNMA, or better known as "Fannie Mae"—is more fully discussed. This organization utilizes an offering procedure that it calls the "Free Market System" by which approved mortgage lenders periodically offer to sell to Fannie Mae blocks of mortgage loans at prices that move competitively with the market for long-term money.

As the rules were being changed to improve the ability of the savings associations to furnish capital for a growing need for mortgage money, the commercial bankers cast a strong competitive eye on the advantages enjoyed by the associations. Principally these have been: (1) government authorization to pay a higher rate of interest on savings deposits than commercial banks were allowed, and (2) the deferment of income tax liability on undistributed profits. In the tight money market of 1973, the banking authorities reduced one of these advantages a bit by allowing commercial banks to increase the rate of interest they could pay on their savings deposits by ½ percent, while permitting savings associations to raise their rates by only ¼ percent. The commercial bankers continue to seek a comparable tax advantage on the income from their own savings deposits.

The results of the changes as sketched above have been to open greater resources for mortgage lending purposes. The effort continues at many levels of our thrift and banking systems. The precise rules and limits will continue to be altered and improved as the need arises and as new ways are found to meet the ever-growing need for mortgage money.

Lending Limits of Savings Associations

The lending powers of both federal- and state-chartered associations are limited by their respective regulatory agencies. Federal charters have dollar limitations on the amount that can be loaned on any one property. The maximum amount permitted on a 90 percent loan is $55,000. The "90 percent" means the amount of the loan in relation to the value of the property, and the value of the property is determined by the appraised value or selling price, whichever is lower. Ninety-five percent loans are restricted to a maximum of $42,000, and any loan over 90 percent must include the addition of mortgage default insurance to protect the lender. It was this requirement that caused the tremendous increase in the sale of private mortgage insurance all over the country, which is discussed in greater detail in the next chapter.

While state regulatory agencies exercise their own authority over lending limits, many choose to follow the guidelines established by the Federal Home Loan Bank Board for its member associations. As pointed out earlier, a large number of state-chartered associations have joined the Federal Home Loan Bank system, since it is much less confusing to follow a sound national policy when possible.

There are fewer dollar limits on the amount of money that may be loaned at ratios of 80 percent or less because the risk exposure of the lending institution is much lower. Some states have simply removed all dollar limits for their own chartered institutions, depending on the prudent judgment of the associations' lending officers to establish their own limitations.

Another limitation on loans is that no one borrower may have more than 10 percent of the association's net worth outstanding. Loans to officers and directors are prohibited by a 1976 FSLIC regulation, except for a personal residence.

A major consideration of most savings associations in establishing their own limits and guidelines is the pattern established for the purchase of loans in the secondary market. Both the Federal Home Loan Mortgage Corporation and the Federal National Mortgage Association have limiting requirements. The ability to sell a block of mortgage loans to either of these organizations at some future date gives an association's portfolio of loans a much greater flexibility. In addition to maximum dollar limitations for various types of loans, the secondary market purchasers are also concerned with the forms used for the note and mortgage instruments. Limitations also apply to the types of loans—the secondary market is not as strong for 95 percent loans as for the lower ratio loans. The market for resort, weekend, or second homes is not as good as for primary houses.

In the matter of geographical limits, some states still confine their thrift institutions to property loans within a maximum of 50 miles from an association's offices. Federal guidelines, which did limit member associations to loans within a radius of 100 miles, were recently expanded to permit loans within 100 miles, were recently expanded to permit loans within 100 miles of the lending institution's agent, which could be an authorized servicing office. Savings associations are restricted in the amount of money they can invest out of state. The long-time limit at 5 percent of their assets that could be invested out of state was raised several years ago to 10 percent and applies only to conventional loans. There is no limit on the amount of money any one institution can invest out of state in FHA- or VA-underwritten loans.

The need for making mortgage loans outside a local geographic area falls primarily on the large savings associations in the big eastern cities, in Chicago, and in some of the cash-heavy midwestern cities, and even in some of the smaller communities with good business activity but not a commensurate residential growth. It is these cash-surplus associations, which provide much of the mortgage money for the growing sections of the country that have generally been short of lendable funds.

Considering the large number of savings associations in this country, it should be noted that the majority are relatively small in assets—under $25 million—and restrict their lending to their local areas. These associations are usually active, enthusiastic participants in local community programs and take considerable pride in using their available funds to promote neighborhood growth.

Investment Table

Table 4-2 shows the distribution of the loan portfolios for savings and loan associations over the past five years. Since they have been required by law to make at least 80 percent of their loans in real estate mortgages, the distribution is mandated. It is more interesting to note the substantial growth in total assets over the period 1971 to May 1976. The increase amounts to $156,997 million, or a growth of 76 percent in the five-year period.

TABLE 4-2.
Savings and Loan Associations
(In millions of dollars)

End of period	Assets					Liabilities					Mortgage loan commitments outstanding at end of period[4]
	Mortgages	Investment securities[1]	Cash	Other	Total assets—Total liabilities	Savings capital	Net worth[2]	Borrowed money[3]	Loans in process	Other	
1971	174,250	18,185	2,857	10,731	206,023	174,197	13,592	8,992	5,029	4,213	7,328
1972	206,182	21,574	2,781	12,590	243,127	206,764	15,240	9,782	6,209	5,132	11,515
1973[5]	231,733	21,055		19,117	271,905	226,968	17,056	17,172	4,667	6,042	9,526
1974	249,293	23,240		22,991	295,524	242,959	18,436	24,780	3,244	6,105	7,454
1975	278,693	30,900		28,802	338,395	286,042	19,776	20,730	5,187	6,659	10,675
1975—May	257,911	30,648		25,520	314,079	262,770	19,128	r19,301	4,105	8,775	12,557
June	261,336	30,880		25,786	318,003	268,978	18,992	r18,863	4,446	6,724	12,363
July	264,458	32,054		26,311	322,823	272,032	19,266	r18,744	4,771	8,010	12,611
Aug.	267,717	31,694		27,127	326,538	273,504	19,495	r19,216	4,995	9,328	12,673
Sept.	270,600	30,786		27,745	329,131	277,201	19,414	r20,031	5,128	7,357	12,585

Oct.	273,596	31,652	28,145	333,393	279,465	19,663	ʳ20,306	5,207	8,752	11,748
Nov.	275,919	32,498	28,610	337,027	281,711	19,919	ʳ20,413	5,164	9,820	11,365
Dec.	278,693	30,900	28,802	338,395	286,042	19,776	ʳ20,709	5,187	6,680	10,675
1976—Jan.	280,071	34,271	29,716	344,058	291,418	19,948	ʳ19,630	5,051	8,011	11,111
Feb.	282,487	36,128	30,251	348,866	295,364	20,162	ʳ18,746	5,134	9,460	12,878
Mar.	286,556	36,722	30,462	353,740	302,436	20,211	18,220	5,379	7,494	14,445
Apr.	290,727	36,437	30,663	357,827	305,234	20,475	17,759	5,787	8,572	15,512
May[p]	294,755	36,998	31,267	363,020	308,276	20,691	17,677	6,151	10,225	16,631

[1] Excludes stock of the Federal Home Loan Bank Board. Compensating changes have been made in "Other" assets.

[2] Includes net undistributed income, which is accrued by most, but not all, associations.

[3] Advances from FHLBB and other borrowing.

[4] Data comparable with those shown for mutual savings banks (on opposite page) except that figures for loans in process are not included above but are included in the figures for mutual savings banks.

[5] Beginning 1973, participation certificates guaranteed by the Federal Home Loan Mortgage Corporation, loans and notes insured by the Farmers Home Administration, and certain other Govt.-insured mortgage-type investments, previously included in mortgage loans, are included in other assets. The effect of this change was to reduce the mortgage total by about $0.6 billion.

Also, GNMA-guaranteed, mortgage-backed securities of the passthrough type, previously included in "Cash" and "Investment securities" are included in "Other" assets. These amounted to about $2.4 billion at the end of 1972.

Note.—FHLBB data; figures are estimates for all savings and loan assns. in the United States. Data are based on monthly reports of insured assns. and annual reports of noninsured assns. Data for current and preceding year are preliminary even when revised.

Source: Federal Reserve Bulletin, July 1976, p. A31.

MUTUAL SAVINGS BANKS

Because the origins of mutual savings banks are so similar to that of savings and loan associations, they are included in the category of thrift institutions: savings and loan associations were organized for the specific purpose of savings intended for home ownership; mutual savings banks were organized simply to encourage saving with no specific usage in mind.

This latter type of bank exists mainly in the northeastern 18 states, plus Oregon, Washington and Alaska, with 75 percent of the total assets located in just two states—New York and Massachusetts. All are state-chartered, and all are mutually owned as the name implies. However, the depositor-owners have almost no voice in management. As presently organized, the mutual savings banks elect their first board of trustees. Subsequent vacancies are filled by the board itself, thus creating a self-perpetuating management.

Mutual savings banks are an outgrowth of a banking method originally popular with new citizens of foreign birth who did not understand or place much confidence in the pieces of paper used as checks. They felt more comfortable dealing in cash. Consequently, the savings banks provided a convenient depository for a savings account and/or cashing pay checks. There was no real need in the beginning for checking account service, and these banks still do not handle this type of demand deposit.

Mutual savings banks, as controlled by the state regulatory bodies, may belong to the Federal Deposit Insurance Corporation (the same as commercial banks) or to one of several state agencies that provide similar account deposit insurance. These insurance agencies exercise authority as to types of investments, limits on amounts for each, and require certain accounting procedures to be followed. They also run periodic examinations of the banks' records to assure that standards are being met.

Investment Policies of Mutual Savings Banks

Mutual savings banks have a wider choice of investments than savings associations. Where the associations are substantially limited to residential mortgages, the savings banks can buy bonds, and make personal, educational, and other consumer-type loans. It is interesting to note that despite the latitude available for investments by this type of institution, the loan portfolios of all savings banks have shown a steady increase in percentage of mortgage loans since World War II. In the period immediately following that war, savings banks held approximately 30 percent of their investments in mortgage loans. An explanation of this relatively low percentage is suggested by the fact that foreclosures accompanying the Depression had left an unfavorable mark on mortgage loans, which was followed by the decreased building volume during the war years of 1941 through 1946, and these factors had correspondingly encouraged heavy investments in government securities. By 1960, however, the investments in mortgages had jumped to a little over 70 percent of the total assets and by 1970 had moved above 75 percent. What accounts for this strong growth of investments in mortgages, which has more than doubled since the 1940s? The following four reasons can be cited, three of which are also keys to the growth of all mortgage lending:

1. The end of World War II brought a selling off of government bonds, depressing the yield from them as compared to mortgages.

2. Changes in the banking laws of the largest states controlling mutual savings banks permitted them to make out-of-state loans.

3. The housing industry expanded following World War II, greatly increasing the demand for mortgage money.

4. Mortgage lenders' attitudes generally changed toward acceptance of FHA and VA commitments, now considering them to be sound and valued procedures.

After 1970, mutual savings banks reduced the rate of increase that they had been making in mortgage loans and turned a bit more to securities, particularly corporate bonds, for the investment of their increasing deposits. As a result, mortgage loans dropped to about 64 percent of their total assets by 1975. Unlike savings associations which have shown a preference for conventional loans, the mutual savings banks invest heavily in FHA–VA underwritten loans. Approximately one-half of their mortgage loans are held in FHA–VA types because these can be made out of state without limits.

The impact of mutual savings banks on our mortgage money market is far greater than the rather regionalized base of their home offices would indicate. With the new authority to make out-of-state investments, the savings banks located in areas of heavy deposits relative to loan demands for housing have been able to profitably channel money to the cash-short growth areas of the south, southwest, and west. The movement of this money to out-of-state investments has been handled through agreements with mortgage bankers and other savings institutions and will be more fully detailed in Chapter 6. The savings banks use both an immediate purchase procedure of buying large blocks of loans on a wholesale basis and a forward commitment method, which is a sales and service type of agreement with an agent, such as a mortgage banker, to accept a block of loans of a specific type at an agreed interest rate over the next four to nine months.

Table of Mutual Savings Bank Investments

Table 4-3 shows the continuing growth of deposits in mutual savings banks and how they are investing their assets. Mortgage loans continue to grow in dollar value but represent a smaller portion of the investment portfolio than in 1970. The reasons for this decline has been as much to diversify their investments as it was a concern over the unsettled conditions in the real estate market in the early 1970s.

COMMERCIAL BANKS

The largest of all lenders with the greatest total cash resources are the commercial banks. But in total investments they seldom carry over 10 to 12 percent of their portfolio in long-term mortgage loans. Before the Depression, commercial banks held a much larger proportion of their deposits in savings accounts, also called *time deposits,* as opposed to the demand deposits or checking accounts. After World War II, the growth of thrift institutions accounted for the greater portion of savings increases. The thrift institutions were permitted to pay a higher interest rate on their deposits, which fostered the movement away from the commercial banks. Being unable to compete for the longer term savings money, the commercial banks concentrated their efforts on the short-term loans they could make with their demand deposits.

In many smaller communities and rural areas, the commercial bank still represents the main source of all money, including mortgage money for farm loans. The banks make the longer term property loans in direct relation to the amount of savings deposits they hold. In the larger urban areas, most commercial banks refuse to make real estate loans for long terms, except, perhaps, as an accommodation to a good commercial customer or for some other appropriate reason such as a civic improvement. Even then, the term of such a loan

TABLE 4-3.

Mutual Savings Banks
(In millions of dollars)

End of period	Loans		Securities			Cash	Other assets	Total assets— Total liabilities and general reserve accts.	Deposits	Other liabilities	General reserve accounts	Mortgage loan commitments[2] classified by maturity (in months)				
	Mortgage	Other	U.S. Govt.	State and local govt.	Corporate and other[1]							3 or less	3-6	6-9	Over 9	Total
1971	62,069	2,808	3,334	385	17,674	1,389	1,711	89,369	81,440	1,810	6,118	1,047	627	463	1,310	3,447
1972[3]	67,563	2,979	3,510	873	21,906	1,644	2,117	100,593	91,613	2,024	6,956	1,593	713	609	1,624	4,539
1973	73,231	3,871	2,957	926	21,383	1,968	2,314	106,651	96,496	2,566	7,589	1,250	598	405	1,008	3,261
1974	74,891	3,812	2,555	930	22,550	2,167	2,645	109,550	98,701	2,888	7,961	664	418	232	726	2,040
1975	77,127	4,028	4,777	1,541	27,964	2,367	3,195	120,999	109,796	2,770	8,433	896	301	203	403	1,803
1975—Apr.	75,259	4,407	3,419	1,121	24,994	1,841	2,780	113,821	102,902	2,849	8,071	913	335	312	538	2,098
May	75,440	4,593	3,616	1,137	25,579	2,077	2,811	115,252	104,056	3,080	8,116	955	383	300	573	2,211
June	75,763	4,492	3,744	1,240	26,470	2,088	2,954	116,751	105,993	2,594	8,164	973	510	195	565	2,243
July	76,097	4,396	3,965	1,436	26,976	1,835	3,004	117,709	106,533	2,970	8,208	957	463	266	526	2,212
Aug.	76,310	4,405	4,187	1,451	27,104	1,730	3,067	118,254	106,745	3,255	8,254	981	431	237	573	2,222
Sept.	76,429	4,487	4,279	1,495	27,033	1,783	3,136	118,643	107,560	2,778	8,304	1,011	372	256	499	2,138
Oct.	76,655	4,481	4,368	1,523	27,106	1,805	3,152	119,089	107,812	2,950	8,328	950	368	275	394	1,987
Nov.	76,855	4,550	4,601	1,551	27,421	1,872	3,223	120,073	108,480	3,215	8,378	972	323	222	379	1,896
Dec.	77,221	4,023	4,740	1,545	27,992	2,330	3,205	121,056	109,873	2,755	8,428	896	301	203	403	1,803
1976—Jan.	77,308	4,839	4,918	1,581	28,473	1,961	3,245	122,325	110,979	2,892	8,455	923	315	195	426	1,859
Feb.	77,413	5,243	5,211	1,765	29,035	1,853	3,301	123,821	112,019	3,275	8,527	930	352	184	401	1,867
Mar.	77,738	5,366	5,452	1,867	30,043	1,740	3,321	125,526	114,090	2,859	8,577	1,092	360	251	427	2,130
Apr.[p]	78,046	5,027	5,533	2,149	30,707	1,647	3,361	126,470	114,752	3,106	8,612	1,175	398	281	436	2,290

[1] Also includes securities of foreign governments and international organizations and nonguaranteed issues of U.S. Govt. agencies.

[2] Commitments outstanding of banks in New York State as reported to the Savings Banks Assn. of the State of New York. Data include building loans.

[3] Balance sheet data beginning 1972 are reported on a gross-of-valuation-reserves basis. The data differ somewhat from balance sheet data previously reported by National Assn. of Mutual Savings Banks, which were net of valuation reserves. For most items, however, the differences are relatively small.

Note—NAMSB estimates for all savings banks in the United States.

Source: Federal Reserve Bulletin, July 1976, p. A30.

would be in the 5-to-15-year bracket rather than 20 to 30 years. During the 1970s, the patterns are changing as banking regulations tend to reduce the former competitive advantages of the thrift institutions and make long-term investments more attractive for the commercial banks.

Regulation of Commercial Banks, State and National

Commercial banks can operate under either state charters or national charters. The distinction to the public lies in the use of the word *national* in the name of the bank.

State-chartered banks operate under the authority of a state banking board or commission, and the rules have considerable variety. State charters in the past have granted greater leeway than national charters in regard to the types of loans, the terms of the loans, the amount of the loan in relation to the collateral offered as security, and the dollar amount of the loan in relation to the bank's assets.

State banks can, and often do, become members of the Federal Reserve System and insure their deposits with the FDIC. If so, they become subject to the regulations and the audits of both the federal and state authorities. Some of the advantages of membership in the Federal Reserve System, such as the right to pass on a fully collateralized loan to the Federal Reserve Bank at the current discount rate of interest, become of less importance when the Federal Reserve Board adopts policies to restrict the ability of their member banks to make loans. At such times, state-chartered banks sometimes find it more profitable for them to simply withdraw from the Federal Reserve System. These withdrawals have the tendency to reduce the effectiveness of policies laid down by the Federal Reserve and may some day bring legislation to place all commercial banks under a single controlling agency.

The authority and responsibility of the state and federal banking agencies over the commercial banks can be listed as follows:

Comptroller of the Currency has authority to grant national charters and to regulate and supervise the 4,700 national banks.

Federal Reserve System is the government bank with authority to examine, supervise, and press corrective action when necessary over the 4,700 national banks and the 1,070 state-chartered banks that are members of the Federal Reserve System.

Federal Deposit Insurance Corporation insures the deposits (up to $40,000 each) in 14,470 banks in the United States. The FDIC does not have examination responsibility over the 5,770 member banks of the Federal Reserve System. It does have examination responsibility over the 8,700 state-chartered banks that are insured by the FDIC and are not members of the Federal Reserve System. Its insurance activities do give the FDIC authority to take actions that will minimize the impact of bank failures on depositors of any insured bank.

State banking agencies have the responsibility of regulating their own state-chartered banks. The degree of regulation and enforcement powers varies among the states, but most try to follow the patterns for investments and accounting procedures as established by federal authorities.

Insofar as real estate loans are concerned, the national banks have always been more restrictive in their regulations than have state-chartered banks. The historical precedent for this difference goes back to 1820. Prior to that time, national banks were not even permitted to make a mortgage loan. The rule has, of course, been changed to allow real estate loans, but generally with lower limits than most state-chartered banks can now permit.

Real Estate Investments of Commercial Banks

In any type of loan, an obvious restriction is the size of the bank and its capitalization. There are about 14,700 commercial banks in the United States with resources averaging $25 million. The range in size is from less than $1 million in deposits to over $10 billion. Regulations limit any single loan of a bank to a percent of its total assets or not to exceed the capitalization (the equity interest) of the bank. In addition, each bank will establish guidelines for its own loans based on its size, which will also include loan minimums. For example, a huge bank such as Chase Manhattan of New York will not consider some categories of loans, such as oil production loans, for less than $1 million, whereas a small local bank could not touch a $1 million loan but can make money on a personal loan for a thousand dollars.

Within their individual limitations, all commercial banks make real estate loans of some form or another. These loans can be generally classified in the following three categories:

1. Direct mortgage loans

2. Construction loans

3. Mortgage warehouse line of credit

Direct Mortgage Loans

While all commercial banks are now legally authorized to make loans using real estate as collateral, the incentives to make such loans vary considerably. Smaller rural banks are still the only source of such loans in many areas. In medium-sized towns and cities, the banks often use their capacity to make long-term loans as an attraction for other business. In large urban areas, the commercial banks find more profitable use for their money in short-term loans that give the portfolio more liquidity. But there are short-term mortgage loans that do attract commercial bank investments.

Some city banks will make short-term loans—3 to 5 years—on raw land for a developer. These are usually limited to 65 percent of the land value and carry higher interest rates than, say, a home loan. Another type of short-term mortgage loan would be on a building fully leased with a fast pay-out assigned to the bank. Service stations can be handled with mortgage loans for up to 15 years, which are secured by a major oil company lease agreement.

Commercial banks often have customers or associated lending firms that are capable of making long-term loans and can lend assistance in accommodating a customer through referrals. A few banks have established real estate investment trusts, discussed later in this chapter, to provide long-term money for their customers outside of the bank's immediate deposits.

Another possible source of mortgage money under the control of most commercial banks is that held by their trust departments. In this field the bank acts as the manager of a trust and would not be investing deposits subject to demand withdrawals, nor would it be subject to the same banking regulations affecting deposits. However, most trusts are guided by the terms under which the money is placed in the bank's care, and the type of investment permitted may be restricted. Trust funds are usually held for specified terms and, as such, make a good source for mortgage money if the trust allows.

Construction Loans

Construction loans are a special form of real estate loan that will be discussed in greater detail in Chapter 12 on loan analysis, but should be noted here as one principal type of mortgage loan offered by some commercial banks. Because of the high risk and specialized construction knowledge required for these loans, not all commercial banks are qualified to handle them. The loans are short-term, generally 6 to 18 months, and return high rates of interest, such as one to five points over the prime rate.

Mortgage Warehouse Line of Credit

With many of the larger commercial banks, the warehousing of mortgage loans for other lenders comprises a major portion of their real estate credit lines. The purpose is to provide immediate cash for a customer such as a mortgage banker, to fund these loans at closing. After establishing a line of credit with the bank, the mortgage banker is able to pledge a note and mortgage obtained from the borrower as security for the cash to fund the loan. Since the mortgage company will be continually adding to the number of loans pledged with the commercial bank, and then periodically shipping groups of these loans on out to permanent investors, the practice has acquired the name of *warehousing*.

The credit lines can run from $1 to $10 million, depending on the strength of the mortgage company. Sale of these loans out of warehouse is usually made in blocks of $250,000 upward to $3 million. A warehouse line of credit will cost the mortgage company for money so borrowed on an interest rate based on the prime rate, or perhaps 1 percent (one point) over prime with a term of 6 to 18 months. Warehousing as a mortgage company procedure is more fully covered in Chapter 6.

Table of Mortgage Loan Activity

Table 4-4 shows the mortgage loans held by commercial banks compared with their total loans and investments:

TABLE 4-4.

Mortgage Loans Held by Banks
(In billions)

Date	Total Loans	Mortgage Loans
1972	558.0	99.3
1973	633.4	119.0
1974	690.4	132.1
1975	721.1	136.1
1976 (1st Qtr)	731.2	138.3

Source: Federal Reserve Bulletin, July 1976.

LIFE INSURANCE COMPANIES

Life insurance companies rank fifth in the nation's total investments by sources, and they have long had a substantial interest in real estate financing—both as an investment in the ownership or equity position and in the making of direct mortgage loans. At one time, life insurance companies equaled the total investments of savings associations in the amounts of their mortgage loans. But life insurance companies were not organized primarily for the purpose of providing mortgage money, as were the savings associations. Their primary interest in using their substantial investment funds has been to provide the highest yield possible commensurate with the safety of their policyholders' money. And this has dictated some flexibility in the movement of their investments from time to time for better returns.

Casualty insurance companies—those that handle fire coverage, automobile insurance, and a host of other types of hazard insurance—have tremendous premium incomes but are not required to maintain the larger permanent reserves demanded for the life insurance companies. Therefore, casualty companies hold their reserves in short-term investments due to the need for liquidity to pay claims. They negotiate practically no mortgage loans and are not a source for our consideration.

Like all sources of mortgage money, the life insurance companies must possess a predictable or controllable cash inflow and outflow with a large pool retained for investment. These companies fully meet this requirement because they have established the need for life insurance protection as a way of life and thus continue to enjoy steady growth of their premium income. The reserves held to assure policyholders that their contracts will be honored upon reaching a specified age, or upon death, provide a multibillion-dollar pool of investment capital that also produces a continuing, and until recently, an untaxed profit for the life insurance company to reinvest.

The outflow of cash is about as predictable as the inflow. What many would consider an uncertain problem is the payment of death benefits; but carefully compiled mortality tables show quite accurately the average rates of death, and on the large number of policyholders that insurance companies deal with, the payment of benefits for any period is readily calculable. Smaller companies usually reinsure their life insurance contracts with the large companies, and even larger companies will spread the risk of a large policy with several other insurance companies.

One of the least predictable outflows of cash for an insurance company comes from the right of policyholders to borrow up to the amount of the cash value of their policy at a low rate of interest. Repayment of such a loan carries a first claim on the insurance proceeds and is a secure investment for the company. But a sudden demand by policyholders for cash can strain a life company's resources and force liquidation of some other portion of its investment portfolio. Demands for loans by policyholders follow money cycles; for example, in periods of tight money, more policyholders seek the relatively lower cost policy loans.

In the United States there are over 1900 life insurance companies and a few from Canada selling policy contracts. They range in size from a very few million in assets to the multibillion-dollar giants that have become household words, such as Prudential, Metropolitan Life, and Equitable.

Regulation of Life Insurance Companies

All insurance companies are under the control of state regulatory bodies. There are no federal charters for insurance. Consequently, the life insurance companies are required to adhere to policies that do vary from state to state, but all the regulations are directed toward protecting the investing public.

The state regulations usually set limits on the types of investment that are permissible, the percent of total portfolio that may be kept in stock, or bonds, or mortgage loans, or the amount of liquidity that must be maintained for each policy dollar outstanding; and most states establish limits on the maximum amount of any one loan or any one property. Some states have limited their own chartered insurance companies to investments within their own states, and others have placed limits on out-of-state companies selling insurance within their state, unless proportional investments are made within the state. Restrictive investment policies based on geography are giving way to regulations designed more for the safeguarding of the policyholder's dollar.

For the most part, state regulations and governing commissions are well conceived and show good intentions to foster sound investment policies. But not all states are able to administer regulations and to police the actual operations as well as a legislature may have intended. Some state insurance boards have been created with substantial investigative capacity but little real authority to correct an abuse if it is discovered. Over the years there have been a few spectacular failures that might have been prevented. Fortunately, the very great majority of life insurance companies are soundly managed and are far more cautious with their policyholders' money than the state might require. Loan applications are carefully scrutinized and objectively judged. A few companies will even refuse to permit their own sales representatives to present a loan application from an individual who also wishes to buy life insurance—the loan underwriters want no pressure exerted on their judgment from the sales personnel.

Investment Policies

The normal pressure on life insurance companies to seek maximum yield from their investments, commensurate with the safety of the money, increased with the introduction of variable annuity policies. This type of life insurance provided for increases in dividends or in the total value of the policy based on the yields from the company's investments. The policy is an effort to compete with the growing interest of mutual funds as a personal investment. Whereas in the past, insurance companies moved their investments from, say, stocks and bonds into mortgage loans or other forms of securities, or vice versa, in order to achieve the highest yields, the pressure increased to do something more.

Many company investment managers had watched the real estate projects that they had made possible with mortgage loans at interest rates of 4 or 5 percent grow in value as land escalated in the 1950s and 1960s, while the insurance company earned only a nominal interest rate in return. Thereafter, the larger companies with greater resources in personnel began to direct their money and their talents into outright ownership and development of real estate as an investment procedure. During periods of scarce money, insurance companies, as well as other lenders, found they could increase yields by demanding a part of the equity interest—the so-called piece-of-the-action stipulation. One way companies have used to protect their investments from inflationary trends is to calculate debt service based on current market rentals for income properties, then take, perhaps, a quarter of any rental income increases that are made.

Another method commonly used by insurance companies expanding their real estate investments is to join with an experienced development company as a partner. Metropolitan Life Insurance Company of New York City joins with such developers as Trammel

Crow of Dallas to acquire land and build multimillion-dollar urban projects, such as the Allen Center in Houston projected at a half-billion dollars. Business Men's Assurance of Kansas City, in addition to making some direct mortgage loans, joins with developers as partners for large commercial ventures, builds housing projects for resale to owners, and builds hotels and motels for the purpose of leasing them to qualified operators such as the Marriott Hotel chain. Prudential uses real estate affiliates to build large urban complexes such as the $150 million residential and commercial complex in the Detroit suburb of Southfield. A few states, fearing the movement of the insurance giants into too much ownership of properties, have enacted restrictive laws to limit the trend; i.e., Texas does not permit an insurance company to own an apartment building except as acquired through foreclosure.

Life insurance companies have in the past maintained their own lending offices in selected locations, and a few still do. Lately, the trend has been more toward working through correspondents or loan representatives. In the handling of direct mortgage loans, the companies can and do make forward commitments to mortgage bankers for specific classes of home loans. Many of the smaller- and medium-sized companies find home loans in their operating territory to be both profitable investments and beneficial to their own company growth.

For the individual borrower, there is little access to an insurance company for a loan such as can be found by walking into a savings and loan office. This is possible with some of the smaller insurance companies, but the larger ones must deal in larger loans or blocks of smaller loans. The volume of money that a company such as Northwestern Mutual Life of Milwaukee must handle with over $2 billion in real estate loans outstanding, makes it impractical to deal directly with, say, a $30,000 house loan.

The investment portfolios of life insurance companies will continue to be influenced by the need for greater yields. Long-term mortgage loans are sound investments for the companies and should always be of interest to them when the yields are competitive with other forms of investment. But yield and security alone are not the only goals; there is also a desire to maintain a particular balance with a company's overall investments. Thus, a higher return from one type of investment would not attract all of a company's money at that time. Looking ahead, it is not likely that states will enact more restrictive legislation to direct an insurance company's investments so as to press more money into the mortgage lending field.

Table of Life Insurance Company Investments

Table 4–5 shows the distribution of life insurance company invest-ments. Roughly one-half are held in business type securities—stocks and bonds. About one-third are held in mortgages of all types. From 1971 to 1975, the percentage of assets held in mortgages slowly de-clined from 34 to 30 percent.

FEDERAL AND STATE GOVERNMENTS

In addition to the private sources of money discussed so far, several federal and state government agencies provide funds for making direct mortgage loans or purchasing them from other lenders.

A few states have established housing agencies with authority to make direct mortgage loans to assist home buyers, and many more are seeking ways to encourage more lendable funds in their states. Money for this purpose is raised by the sale of bonds and with the assistance of various programs developed by the Department of Housing and Urban Development. All states have pension funds and most have specialized trust funds of some kind. These are being utilized increasingly to provide capital for development within the state and to improve housing for its people.

In North Dakota, the state itself owns the Bank of North Dakota. It was established in 1919 by a group of farmers as a service organiza-tion and to avoid using out-of-state bankers who they felt were over-charging for loans. By 1975 the bank held over $390 million in resources and leads the nation in providing financial assistance to college students. It also makes long-term home loans. The bank relies heavily on public deposits with the state government accounting for 75 percent of the deposits. It has been efficiently managed by an Industrial Commission, operates as one of the most profitable banks in the country, and has attracted the attention of several other states.

Another type of mortgage money that is available in some states is that, when authorized, a municipality may issue a tax-exempt type of bond for the purpose of financing industrial growth. One of the more common methods used is for the municipality to establish an industrial park by the purchase of suitable land. Sites for new plants are then sold or leased to acceptable companies, and the municipality will provide the mortgage money for building a new plant.

TABLE 4-5.

Life Insurance Companies (In millions of dollars)

End of period	Total assets	Government securities				Business securities			Mort-gages	Real estate	Policy loans	Other assets
		Total	United States	State and local	For-eign[1]	Total	Bonds	Stocks				
1971	222,102	11,000	4,455	3,363	3,182	99,805	79,198	20,607	75,496	6,904	17,065	11,832
1972	239,730	11,372	4,562	3,367	3,443	112,985	86,140	26,845	76,948	7,295	18,003	13,127
1973	252,436	11,403	4,328	3,412	3,663	117,715	91,796	25,919	81,369	7,693	20,199	14,057
1974^r	263,349	11,965	4,437	3,667	3,861	118,572	96,652	21,920	86,234	8,331	22,862	15,385
1975	289,084	14,582	5,894	4,440	4,248	135,014	106,755	28,259	89,358	9,634	24,389	16,107
1975—Apr.	273,523	12,374	4,608	3,719	4,047	126,256	99,725	26,531	87,638	8,782	23,459	15,014
May	275,816	12,464	4,678	3,739	4,047	127,847	100,478	27,369	87,882	8,843	23,570	15,210
June	278,343	12,560	4,738	3,762	4,060	129,838	101,238	28,600	88,035	8,989	23,675	15,246
July	279,354	12,814	4,843	3,902	4,069	130,298	102,675	27,623	88,162	9,058	23,794	15,228
Aug.	280,482	13,022	4,895	4,039	4,088	130,659	103,496	27,163	88,327	9,112	23,919	15,443
Sept.	281,847	13,150	4,914	4,122	4,114	131,524	104,529	26,995	88,445	9,210	24,048	15,470
Oct.	284,829	13,793	5,505	4,148	4,140	133,237	105,473	27,764	88,655	9,356	24,171	15,617
Nov.	286,975	14,129	5,762	4,210	4,157	134,495	106,385	28,110	88,850	9,464	24,271	15,766
Dec.	289,084	14,582	5,894	4,440	4,248	135,014	106,755	28,259	89,358	9,634	24,389	16,107
1976—Jan.	293,870	15,380	6,446	4,652	4,282	138,965	108,130	30,835	89,395	9,661	24,498	15,971
Feb.	296,479	16,142	6,458	4,790	4,894	140,332	109,321	31,011	89,543	9,726	24,633	16,103
Mar.	299,552	15,723	4,967	5,220	5,536	143,105	111,385	31,720	89,781	9,812	24,755	16,376
Apr.^p	299,983	15,917	5,198	5,100	5,619	143,197	111,757	31,440	89,489	9,852	24,873	16,655

[1] Issues of foreign governments and their subdivisions and bonds of the International Bank for Reconstruction and Development.

Note—Institute of Life Insurance estimates for all life insurance companies in the United States.
Figures are annual statement asset values, with bonds carried on an amortized basis and stocks at year-end market value. Adjustments for interest due and accrued and for differences between market and book values are not made on each item separately but are included, in total in "Other assets."

Source: Federal Reserve Bulletin, July 1976, p. A31.

The federal government has felt a need to assist the people in their living and housing requirements and has long maintained programs of direct loans for such purposes. While a number of agencies provide financing and direct grants of money to assist farmers and ranchers, small businesses, minority businesses, disaster victims, and displaced families, the three most active agencies making direct loans based on real estate mortgages are the Federal Land Bank, the Farmers Home Administration, and the Government National Mortgage Association, discussed below.

Federal Land Bank

Established in 1916 to provide funds to farmers and ranchers—funds that were not always available in the private sector—the Federal Land Bank has provided many billions of dollars for the purchase and improvement of farms and ranches. The system operates through 12 regional offices and smaller district offices somewhat similar to our Federal Reserve organization. At quarterly intervals during the year, the system will sell its own Federal Land Bank bonds, which are secured by the mortgages on properties they finance. These are not government-guaranteed bonds and cannot be classed as *governments.* They are called *agency* bonds because the Federal Land Bank is one of many federal agencies authorized to issue its own bonds and sell them on the open market. The proceeds of each bond sale are allocated to the various regions, as may be required, and are then made available to qualified borrowers.

The Federal Land Bank evaluates a loan application much the same as a private bank and has no real social motivation other than that its money is restricted to loans for farms or ranches. The borrower need not live on the land but must be able to mortgage the property and to show a record of productivity with that land or a previous record of experience. Loans are limited to 85 percent of the Bank's own appraisal and up to a maximum term of 35 years.

The interest rate for these loans is adjusted periodically but is normally held under open market rates. The main reason for the lower rate is that the Federal Land Bank calculates its rates based on an *average* cost of its money as determined from the periodic sale of agency bonds. And the Bank, as an agency of the federal government, is not seeking a profit for an investor with its operations.

Farmers Home Administration

As a part of the efforts of the Roosevelt administration to revitalize the economy from the depths of the Depression, a separate agency was established in 1934 to make direct loans to farmers for land and housing known as the Farmers Home Administration. The loans are limited to rural areas or towns with a population of 20,000 or less, for low and moderate income families who cannot obtain home financing elsewhere. The guidelines established by the Housing and Community Development Act of 1974 permit the FmHA Section 502 single family program to make direct loans up to 100 percent of the appraised value of a house for families with an Adjusted Family Income of not more than $12,900.

The Adjusted Family Income (AFI) is calculated at 95 percent of gross earnings, less $300 for each minor dependent child living at home. For example, a family earning $14,000 per year with three children at home:

Annual earnings	14,000
Less 5%	700
	13,300
Less 3 X 300	900
Adjusted Family Income	12,400

Since the above calculated AFI is less than the maximum 12,900 permitted, the family would qualify for making a loan application. If the AFI is $8,500 or less, the family may receive an interest subsidy or credit, if their housing costs (mortgage payment, insurance, and taxes) exceed 20 percent of their adjusted income.

The FmHA will make loans on new or older homes but the living area cannot exceed 1,300 square feet. The maximum amount of the loan is determined by the applicant's repayment ability.

Evaluation of the loan application is handled in a manner similar to other lending institutions with a complete financial statement required, a history of income, and a credit rating. Each loan is reviewed periodically to determine if the borrower's financial condition has improved to the extent that the loan could be handled by other lending institutions.

Under the Section 515 multifamily program, FmHA will loan money for the construction of new multifamily structures or rehabilitating older ones. A market survey is required to show a need for housing primarily for the elderly and the low-to-moderate income families. This program is restricted to rural communities with a population of less than 20,000.

Government National Mortgage Association

This is a newer agency of the federal government under the Department of Housing and Urban Development (HUD), created in 1968 to carry a portion of the financing chores previously handled by the Federal National Mortgage Association. The Government National Mortgage Association, GNMA or "Ginnie Mae," sells bonds, as do other federal agencies, to raise funds for direct mortgage loans. This agency also has authority to borrow money from the United States Treasury when authorized for specific purposes. And it is the agency that handles direct subsidies for housing programs as appropriated by Congress. GNMA has used its authority to guarantee blocks of mortgages in order to attract more private capital into the mortgage lending field. The impact of this government agency is far broader than the capacity to make some direct loans, and as such, the organization and programs will be discussed in greater detail in Chapter 7.

Federal National Mortgage Association

FNMA (Fannie Mae) should no longer be considered as a source of money under the direction of the federal government as it has been publicly owned and listed on the New York Stock Exchange since 1970. However, as a quasi-public organization it still has strong ties to the federal government and a commitment to various government programs. The bonds it sells to finance purchases of residential mortgage loans are still classed in the financial community as "agency" issues. With its Free Market System of handling mortgage loan offerings from approved lenders throughout the country, FNMA provides an interesting guide to the fluctuations in mortgage interest rates. As a major factor in the secondary markets, buying and selling mortgage loans, the FNMA organization and methods will be more fully covered in Chapter 5.

Federal Housing Administration and Veterans Administration

The FHA and VA are included in this chapter under Sources of Mortgage Money only to dispel the thought that they are. Neither agency makes loans as a continuing practice. The VA does actually make loans in special circumstances. What these two agencies do, in the case of the FHA, is to issue an insurance policy protecting the lender against a default by the borrower; and in the case of the VA, to issue a certificate guaranteeing a specific portion of a loan to enable a veteran to acquire housing without a down payment if desired. Both agencies are of sufficient importance in real estate finance to warrant separate coverage, which will be found in Chapter 7.

To show more specifically where the money comes from to fund FHA–VA type commitments, Table 4-6 gives the distribution among the four major sources of mortgage money plus "others." The amount of loans held by commercial banks would include those secured under a warehouse line of credit and thus of short term.

Pension and Trust Funds

The purpose of a *pension* fund is to accumulate cash and hold it in such a manner that will assure an annual or monthly payment to an individual worker upon retirement or upon reaching a certain age. The purpose of a *trust* fund is to protect an asset over a period of time so as to achieve a specified purpose. While the reasons for creating a trust fund are different from that of a pension fund, the manner in which both funds are held and the need for delivering the assets upon maturity give both a similarity insofar as their possible use as sources of mortgage money.

Both pension and trust fund administrators are guided by the cardinal rule of security for the asset. No pressure exists for them to achieve maximum yields, nor do state or federal laws exercise much control over the type of investments a trust may make. A good administrator is obligated to protect the body of the assets and make sure the funds can be delivered when pledged to do so. Consequently, these assets have tended to be invested in high-grade stocks and bonds, which represent minimum risk and a ready market when they have to be sold for cash. Lately, some of this money is finding its way into the long-term mortgage market as the yields are good and the security is generally acceptable.

As sources of mortgage money, both pension and trust funds represent a near ideal situation in the predictability of inflow and outflow of funds that are needed for any long-term investment. The

TABLE 4-6.

Major Holders of FHA-Insured and VA-Guaranteed Residential Mortgage Debt
(End of period, in billions of dollars)

Holder	June 30, 1974	Sept. 30, 1974	Dec. 31, 1974	Mar. 31, 1975	June 30, 1975	Sept. 30, 1975	Dec. 31, 1975
All holders	137.8	138.6	140.3	142.0	143.0	144.9	147.0
FHA	84.9	84.1	84.1	84.3	85.0	85.1	85.4
VA	52.9	54.5	56.2	57.7	58.0	59.8	61.6
Commercial banks	11.0	10.7	10.4	10.5	9.6	9.7	9.4
FHA	7.6	7.4	7.2	7.2	6.4	6.4	6.3
VA	3.4	3.3	3.2	3.3	3.2	3.3	3.1
Mutual savings banks	27.9	27.8	27.5	27.3	27.2	27.0	27.4
FHA	15.1	15.0	14.8	14.7	14.7	14.5	14.7
VA	12.8	12.8	12.7	12.6	12.5	12.5	12.7
Savings and loan assns.							
FHA	–	–	–	–	–	–	–
VA	} 29.7	} 29.9	} 29.9	} 29.9	} 30.2	} 30.4	} 30.6
Life insurance cos.	13.1	12.9	12.7	12.5	12.2	12.1	11.8
FHA	8.8	8.7	8.6	8.4	8.2	8.1	7.9
VA	4.3	4.2	4.2	4.1	4.0	4.0	3.9
Others	56.1	57.4	59.9	61.6	62.2	65.7	67.8
FHA	–	–	–	–	–	–	–
VA	–	–	–	–	–	–	–

Note—VA-guaranteed residential mortgage debt is for 1- to 4-family properties while FHA-insured includes some debt in multifamily structures. Detail by type of holder partly estimated by Federal Reserve for first and third quarters, and for most recent quarter.

Source: Federal Reserve Bulletin, July 1976, p. A44.

inflow of cash is easily determined by the agreements establishing the fund, and the outflow is an integral part of that agreement.

Pension Funds

Pension funds date back nearly one hundred years, but only recently have they become a factor in real estate financing. The quarter century from 1945 to 1970 showed tremendous growth in corporate pension funds, both insured and noninsured, along with federal, state, and local government pension funds, union funds, and funds of fraternal groups. As recently as 1940, pension funds totaled only $2.4 billion. By 1975 the amount increased to $170 billion with a projection of $215 billion by 1980. The number of employees covered under these plans has increased in the same period from 4.3 million to 30.5 million persons.

Pension funds can be divided into insured or uninsured plans. The insured pension plans are those offered by most large insurance companies. The employer, perhaps with a participating contribution from the employee, pays the premium directly to the insurance company, who is responsible for making future pay-outs to the employee when due. There is usually the added protection of life insurance coverage, and the insurance carrier is obligated to invest the premium payments just as with any other insurance policy.

The majority of pension funds fall into the category of being privately managed and are not underwritten by an insurance company. It is this category of pension plan that brought on some abuses and failures to make the payments to employees when due. Several years of government probing into the question resulted in the enactment of the Employee Retirement Income Security Act in 1974 (also known as the Pension Reform Act). As a part of ERISA, Congress also created the Pension Benefit Guaranty Corporation, chaired by the Secretary of Labor and whose directors also include the Secretary of the Treasury and the Secretary of Commerce. It is the purpose of PBGC to provide mandatory contingent employer liability insurance, at least until such insurance can be provided in the private sector. A small premium is paid by the subscribing pension fund which insures employee benefits at termination.

The Pension Benefit Guaranty Corporation has the right to examine the pension plans insured with them and to take corrective action if proper payments are not being made into the fund, or the investments are causing jeopardy to the future benefits for the employees. The PBGC can create liens on the employers property for collection of the contingent payments.

No requirements have been established for the investment of the pension fund money—only that it be prudent and give proper protection to the employees interest in the fund. The major effort that the government has made to channel pension fund money into real estate mortgages is through the Government National Mortgage Association. GNMA issues a certificate that guarantees a block of mortgage loans called a "mortgage-backed security." Payment of principal and interest is guaranteed by the government on these securities and makes an attractive investment for a pension fund.

Trust Funds

Because trust funds are a practical means of accomplishing a person's objectives in spite of death, and because they hold a means of reducing tax liabilities in estate planning, the usage has grown substantially, and the accumulated assets in the hands of trust administrators have multiplied. Trust funds are usually specific in the purpose to be accomplished and provide guidelines and restrictions as to the ways in which the assets may be invested. Since these funds are essentially a form of private property, there is not much public interest in control or regulation of investments other than for the tax angles involved.

What motivates trust fund administrators is the security of the investment and a fair return. The growing size of the accumulated funds and the near absolute control on withdrawals make long-term mortgage loans practical investments. Mortgage-backed securities, the growing flexibility of the secondary market, the advantages of private mortgage insurance, and the attractive yields over the long term have all added to the appeal of mortgage loans for trust funds. While many funds are administered by competent individuals who may not have expertise in mortgage loans, a growing number of trusts are handled by commercial banks whose trust departments have access to persons of broad experience in this type of loan.

Individuals

The earliest lenders were wealthy individuals. In today's market the terms of mortgage loans are much too lengthy for most individuals to undertake. With a few exceptions, almost all primary mortgage lending by individuals has a motive other than as an investment to earn a return of interest. Some individuals make mortgage loans to assist a member of their family or perhaps a valued employee or associate. By far the largest investment by individuals in mortgage loans stems from a seller accepting a second mortgage as a partial payment for his house or land. The motive is to make a sale rather than an investment. In some areas, such as California, second and even third mortgages are sold to brokers or other individuals at substantial discounts, which increases the yields sufficiently to make an attractive investment.

As investors, individuals come under no specific regulations as to how they must lend money. A mortgage loan must comply with the real estate laws governing such transactions plus the usury laws that limit the amount of interest that can be charged.

Individuals can make mortgage loans on any type of property: residential or commercial, raw land, or development work. Some mortgage companies represent individuals who want to make investments in certain types of property.

With the escalating land values of the late 1960s and early 1970s, urban areas have seen the acreage surrounding them sold on seller-financed deals. In this procedure the raw land is sold by an individual at a fair market price with a small down payment plus interest payments only on the unpaid balance for the next five or ten years. A mortgage is held by the seller until full payment has been made, which makes it in effect a mortgage loan.

Due to the lack of regulation, there is no sound statistical basis for establishing the actual volume of mortgage loans held by individuals.

Real Estate Investment Trusts (REIT)

A relatively new source of mortgage money was encouraged in 1960 when Congress passed the Real Estate Investment Trust Act. The purpose of the Act was to provide more capital to satisfy the growing demand for long-term investment money by opening the field to the individual small investor. In order to encourage a person to buy stock in a corporation that qualified itself as a real estate investment trust, Congress exempted the trust from income taxes, provided that at least 90 percent of the profit is distributed each year as dividends. Also, the income must be derived from real property investments to qualify for the tax exemption. The dividends are taxable to the investor.

The idea was not enthusiastically received at first, but by 1970 many investment trust issues were placed on the market and sold very well. The trusts are formed primarily by leading banks and insurance companies, and many are traded on the nation's stock exchanges. A few of the well-known companies operating in this field are Massachusetts Mutual Mortgage, Northwestern Mutual Life Mortgage, Bank American Realty, Equitable Life Mortgage, MONY Mortgage, Mortgage Trust of America, and many others.

Most of the trusts are controlled by a board of trustees responsible for the integrity of the fund. Actual management of the investment portfolio is contracted to a professional money-management team. The management company is paid a fee for its services, usually about 1 percent of the total assets per year. The managers are all experienced lending officers who have worked with or are well known to the sponsoring bank or insurance company.

Two basic types of REITs have developed—equity and mortgage. The original purpose of Congress was to encourage equity money into the real estate field as owners and operators of income properties. The profit of equity REITs was derived mostly from the operation of income-producing properties they would buy. In the late 1960s, a newer concept developed known as the mortgage type. These newer trusts specialized in the financing of properties and made their profits from the interest income on their mortgages. They operated under the same tax incentives as the equity type.

It was the mortgage type of REIT that created the surge in popularity between 1969 and 1971. Underwriters encouraged banks and insurance companies to establish the trusts because the shares could be easily sold and made good underwriting fees. Loans were easy to make in the real estate boom period of the early 1970s. The REITs borrowed heavily from banks and other lenders to support their demand for more money to lend to construction and development projects. Developers often found a source of mortgage money plus a partner in the REITs to build apartments, office buildings, and shopping centers. Between 1969 and 1973, the relatively new industry increased its assets from about $1 billion to nearly $20 billion.

Serious problems began to surface by 1974 after the bank prime rate had soared past 12 percent and some construction loans on large projects were reaching 18 percent interest rates. The unanticipated high interest costs faced by many of the builders (most construction loans pay interest rates that float from 1 to 6 points over the prime rate) consumed the construction money before the projects could be completed and many failures resulted. By 1975 some of the largest REITs in the country were reporting as much as 25 percent of their loans "not accruing interest"; i.e., a more optimistic way of describing loans in default. The sagging record forced REIT stock prices down to less than book value in some cases and destroyed the market for any new issues. At the same time, major lenders were withdrawing their support for the REITs and many of them faced the same bankruptcy procedures that their builders had faced earlier.

Only a few of the REITs have actually been forced out of business, more have sought mergers with larger REITs, but most of them should survive the shake-out as they become the equity owners of properties forced into foreclosure and those properties recover value in the reviving market. The original purpose is still sound—to provide capital for real estate projects and to enable the small investor to participate in large, well-managed projects. Those REITs that became too heavily involved in mortgage loans are now being forced into an equity position. But it may be a long time before REITs can again sell new stock issues to raise additional capital.

Miscellaneous Other Sources

In different parts of the country various types of companies and institutions have established themselves as a source of mortgage funds, usually limiting the geographic area in which they will loan money. In the following paragraphs the most important of these sources are identified.

Mortgage Bankers. While the great majority of mortgage banking companies operate as a service industry handling funds for other major sources of money, a few of the larger companies have generated their own funds for lending through the sale of mortgage bonds. In the pre-Depression days of the 1920s, the sale of mortgage bonds was quite popular, but the Depression brought many of these issues and their sponsoring companies into collapse.

As the industry has reestablished itself, the sale of mortgage bonds to investors has started to grow again. In the hands of the established mortgage bankers, these funds have provided another source of money for both residential and commercial loans.

Title Companies. Because of the close association and considerable knowledge of the industry carried by the title companies, a few of them have developed direct loan departments or subsidiary companies handling loans. These affiliated companies act both as primary sources in lending their own funds or those raised from the sale of mortgage bonds, and as correspondents or agents for other major lenders.

Endowment Funds, Universities, Colleges, Hospitals. As a group, endowment funds prefer to maintain their assets in high-grade stocks and bonds that have a good record for security, are considered to be more liquid, and, most important, require less administrative attention than a portfolio of mortgage loans. However, many endowments are passed on in the form of land and other real property, and these have required more expertise in the mortgage loan field. The endowment funds can and do assist in the development of their own land by experienced developers, and they are increasing their activities in mortgage lending with such encouragements as the GNMA mortgage-backed security.

Foundations. Foundations have been established primarily by corporations or by wealthy families as a means of continuing charitable or other purposes through the use of income earned from the foundations' investments. The attitude of foundations toward mortgage lending is somewhat similar to that of the endowment funds. They are primarily interested in investing in high-grade stocks and bonds, but are not adverse to mortgage loans, particularly if a purpose of special interest to the foundation can be served.

Foundations have been under substantial legal attack as to their tax obligations and sometimes for the controversial use of their tax-free funds. However, they do represent a limited pool of investment capital that can be used in the mortgage market.

Fraternal, Benevolent, and Religious Associations. Over the years some fraternal, benevolent, and religious organizations have accumulated substantial pools of investment money, which are generally little known and very seldom advertised. The administration of these funds is usually handled on a sound economic basis with security of the loan of more importance than the yield. Some of these organizations limit their lending to their own members and will provide low-cost loans to qualified members in good standing.

Credit Unions. The employees of many companies, labor unions, industry associations, religious organizations, and others have formed credit unions for the benefit of their own members or associates. By the end of 1975 these cooperative associations had piled up $33.2 billion in members' savings and are growing rapidly each year. Most of their loans are to members for the purchase of cars, furniture, or appliances at relatively low interest rates. As the credit unions continue to grow, they have established some expanded goals such as broader trust services, easier withdrawal of funds, and the making of long-term mortgage loans.

QUESTIONS FOR DISCUSSION

1. Discuss the steps that have been taken to improve the liquidity of a savings association loan portfolio.

2. What role does the Federal Home Loan Bank play in the banking system?

3. Why have mutual savings banks increased their investments in real estate loans even though they are not legally required to do so?

4. Discuss the reasons insurance companies are looking more for ownership interests in real estate rather than making direct mortgage loans.

5. Why do insurance companies have such a wide variation in their lending practices?

6. How does the Federal Land Bank raise funds for making loans?

7. Explain the basic lending policies of the Farmers Home Administration.

8. What efforts are being made to attract pension and trust fund money into the real estate mortgage market?

9. Describe the type of loans preferred by commercial banks.

10. Are there any good sources of mortgage money available in your locality outside of the regulated lending institutions?

Chapter 5

Secondary Markets

Prior to the 1940s, mortgage lenders were not able to sell their loans easily and their investment portfolios lacked liquidity; that is, the mortgage loans could not readily be converted to cash. Unlike other forms of capital investment, such as stocks and bonds, there is no national market as yet organized to trade in mortgage loans. Of course, one of the major reasons is the past lack of any common denominator by which mortgage loans could be compared. The evaluation of a mortgage loan has necessarily required some knowledge of the geographic area of the property used as collateral. This has made trading in loans difficult.

ORIGINS OF SECONDARY MARKETS

To make a loan more salable, other means are needed to provide some standardization and a method to protect the secondary lender. The government has succeeded in doing just this with its insured FHA programs and guarantees of VA loans. In this type of loan, the government agencies have established certain standard forms and procedures that are known and accepted by the lenders. And most important, the government agencies provide that necessary common denominator of protection to the lender in the individual insurance commitment.

However, even this was not always the case. When the FHA was initially established, the government effort was not accepted at face value by private investors, and it became necessary to establish a market for government-underwritten loans. Thus the Federal National Mortgage Association was born, and with it the first step toward creating a national market for mortgage loans, or what has become known as the *secondary market.*

The precise delineation between the primary and secondary markets for mortgage loans is difficult to draw as there is an overlap. The clearest line can be made at the origination of the loan, which would be the primary lender. Lenders who buy, or take, a mortgage loan that they did not originate are considered to be the secondary market.

PROCEDURES USED IN SECONDARY MARKETS

Now note the difference in terminology at this point. The originator of a loan speaks to customers, who are the *borrowers,* in terms of *loaning money,* and expresses the cost of the borrowed money as interest plus *points* of discount and fees. Once the originator closes the loan to the borrower, the note and mortgage instrument become marketable paper that can be assigned—and the terminology changes. The mortgage note is now a salable commodity and is negotiated as such. The originator of the loan becomes a *seller,* and the large lending institutions that deal in the secondary market for mortgage loans are called *purchasers.* When a mortgage loan is thus offered for sale, the potential purchaser is interested in only one attribute for loans of similar types, size, and quality, and that is the *net yield.*

Pricing Loans to Adjust Yields

Since the interest and discount on the loan or loans held by the originator have already been established, the only way a seller can change the yield to a purchaser is to adjust the *price* of the loan. For example, if the mortgage note is for $10,000 at 7 percent interest, the yield would be 7 percent. If the seller must offer a higher yield than 7 percent in order to attract a purchaser, he must sell the loan for less than $10,000, that is, discount the face value in order to increase the yield. By selling the $10,000 loan for, say $9500, the purchaser is putting up less cash, but still collects the originally agreed interest and principal reduction applicable to the $10,000 loan at 7 percent, hence, a greater return or yield for the $9500.

The principal balance due on an existing mortgage loan normally changes each month, so therefore the price is quoted as a percentage figure. One hundred is, of course, par. If we were quoting the $10,000 loan mentioned above to sell for $9500, the quotation would simply be "95." This indicates a 5 percent reduction in whatever the principal balance due on the mortgage note may be, or a 5-point discount.

In times of falling interest rates, a loan calling for a higher than current market interest can sell for a premium—at say 102 percent or even 104 percent of its face value. Examples of prices and yields that are used in the secondary market are shown in Table 5-1.

TABLE 5-1.

Price Yield Table Calculated at 7% Interest
for Term of 30 Years

Price	Discount	Yield if prepaid 8 yrs.	Yield if prepaid 10 yrs.	Yield if prepaid 12 yrs.	To maturity
102	+2 (Premium)	6.66	6.71	6.74	6.81
100	0	7.00	7.00	7.00	7.00
96	4	7.70	7.61	7.54	7.41
92	8	8.44	8.24	8.12	7.85

A simple reading of the table shows that the length of time a loan is outstanding has a direct effect on the yield for that loan. Since loans vary considerably in the time for payoff, it is necessary to use some standard. Records of loan payoffs indicate a steadily decreasing length of time due largely to the increased moving that families do. Most mortgage loans are simply refinanced with each sale or after several sales. The average life of a 30-year loan is now under nine years. For simplification, most lenders use a twelve-year term to calculate the actual yield.

Growth Factors of Secondary Markets

The strongest impetus toward establishing a truly national market for mortgage loans must be credited to (1) the Federal National Mortgage Association, (2) the growth of private mortgage insurance fostered by the 1971 change in banking regulations, and (3) establishment of the Federal Home Loan Mortgage Corp. In considering these three major influences in the development of secondary mortgage markets, the largest and most experienced single operator is the Federal National Mortgage Association. In order to examine the background and growth of FNMA, the succeeding portion of this chapter is devoted to the organization and operations of this quasi-private corporation.

FEDERAL NATIONAL MORTGAGE ASSOCIATION

Origin and Purpose of FNMA

By 1938, it had become obvious that private lenders were not looking with much favor on the four-year-old FHA concept of government-insured commitments to assist a credit-worthy but cash-short family in buying a home. Consequently, on February 10, 1938, the National Mortgage Association of Washington was formed as a subsidiary of the Reconstruction Finance Corporation, then changed on April 5, 1938, to the Federal National Mortgage Association, referred to as FNMA, or Fannie Mae. The groundwork had been laid by Congress under Title III of the original FHA Authorization Act.

The basic aims of the Federal National Mortgage Association as determined by the chartering act and subsequent revisions to 1968 included:

1. Establishing a market for the purchase and sale of first mortgages.

2. Providing special assistance on certain residential mortgages and housing programs as designated by the President and by Congress.

3. Managing and liquidating the mortgage portfolio in an orderly manner with minimum adverse effect on the market and minimum loss to the government.

Money needed for the purchase of mortgages was derived from the sale of notes and debentures to private investors. While these FNMA obligations were subject to the approval of the Secretary of the Treasury, they were not guaranteed by the government. Some additional capital was raised by the requirement to purchase FNMA stock in the amount of one-half of 1 percent of every commitment sold. (The present requirement is to purchase stock in the amount of one-fourth of 1 percent of the mortgages delivered.) Operating money was raised through certain fees charged on the purchase of mortgages and through part of the discounts taken.

The initial concept of FNMA embodied the idea that it would serve as a secondary market primarily for buying and selling first mortgages, but over the years the portfolio steadily increased as selling of loans lagged behind. Congress has, from time to time, ordered Fannie Mae to make mortgage purchases to stimulate a lagging economy or to assist in financing new government lending programs as stipulated in the FNMA purposes outlined previously, since these programs were not readily acceptable to private investors as mortgage investments.

Finally, FNMA was charged with the task of management and liquidation, including the handling and disposition of the substantial accumulation of first mortgages in such a manner as not to upset the capital market or cause a loss to the government.

FNMA as Private Corporation

A major change was made in the FNMA establishment when it was transformed into a "private corporation with a public purpose" by Act of Congress in September 1968. Roughly, the FNMA entity was partitioned by this Act in such a way that the first of its three functions—that of maintaining a secondary market—was retained. The other two functions—special assistance programs, and management and liquidation of mortgages—were transferred to a newly formed body corporate without capital stock known as the Government National Mortgage Association (GNMA or Ginnie Mae), designed to operate as a part of the Department of Housing and Urban Development.

The Federal National Mortgage Association began its private corporate life in September 1968, but was not fully transformed until May 21, 1970. At that time the HUD secretary, George Romney, appeared at the annual stockholders meeting, concurred with the finding that at least one-third of the outstanding stock was owned by persons or firms in housing-related industries, and approved the new directors for the corporation.

Relationship with Government

Actually, the "private corporation with a public purpose" is a concept rather than a matter of statute. It is a congressional recognition of the need for continuing a close relationship between FNMA and the government, backing up the latter's efforts to limit the peaks and valleys in the flow of mortgage funds so as to stabilize and increase the supply of housing.

This FNMA–government relationship is unique and has been developed by a number of rules, chartering stipulations, and organization methods, such as:

1. Five of FNMA's 15 directors are appointed by the President of the United States.

2. The HUD Secretary is given regulatory authority to set Fannie Mae's debt limit and its ratio of debt to capital.

3. The HUD Secretary may require that a reasonable portion of the mortgages purchased be related to the national goal to provide adequate housing for low- and moderate-income families.

4. The Secretary of the Treasury has been given authority to buy FNMA debt obligations up to $2.25 billion, which greatly enhances its credit position.

5. While FNMA is a private corporation and its debts are not obligations of the government, by its chartering act, FNMA obligations are lawful investments for fiduciary, trust, and public funds under the control of the federal government.

It might be well to note that this special relationship with the government did much to provide the funds needed for housing in the 1969–1970 financial squeeze when private capital was not readily available. The mortgage portfolio of FNMA, since it was partitioned in 1968, increased from approximately $7 billion to $18 billion by 1972, which vividly underlines the support it gave to our housing programs. By the end of 1975, outstanding mortgage loans had reached $32 billion.

For FNMA, the year 1970 marked not only its conversion to a private corporation and its continuing successful support of the mortgage market but also flagged several milestones with its listing on the nation's major stock exchanges, the first public offering of stock, and the issuing of the first $1 billion in mortgage-backed bonds supported by the credit of the United States. Also, on July 24, 1970, FNMA was given authority to buy conventional home mortgages—in the past it had been restricted to only government-insured or government-guaranteed commitments.

FNMA Standardization of Mortgage Forms

The initial draft of a standard form mortgage instrument was widely circulated within the industry for guidance and comments, including the need to work with the Federal Home Loan Bank System, which provides support to our savings and loan institutions. Considerable protests were raised, and some law suits filed by organized consumer groups against what was termed the "lender-oriented" form, and some revisions were made. The standard forms finally agreed upon modified several provisions, such as allowing interest to be paid on an escrow account if mutually agreed between borrower and lender, dropping the prepayment penalty clause, and allowing the borrower a voice in the settlement of insurance claims. It is important to remember that the primary goal was to attract more private capital into the mortgage market, not to appease consumer groups. Several of these approved forms are reproduced in Chapter 3.

FNMA Purchase of Conventional Loans

On February 14, 1972, the first purchase of conventional loans was made through the free market system. Separate approval of sellers was required for the conventional loan program, and only a very few mortgagees were approved in the beginning. Unlike the FHA/VA type of loans that hold a government commitment as an ultimate recourse, the conventional loans look only to the borrowers and depend heavily on the careful underwriting analysis of the seller to produce sound loans. The purchase of conventional loans by FNMA has been slow in times of plentiful money as the private sources become more competitive. Under such competitive conditions, the rates offered by FNMA, which reflect an average from all sections of the country, are higher than can be found in the competitive big city areas. When money tightens up, the interest rates increase, and many lenders are forced to withdraw from the market for lack of funds. In such times, as in 1969–1970 and in 1973, FNMA's purchases increase sharply. The rates reflected by the national offerings are more stable than those found in most of the high loan-demand growth areas.

Operations

The Federal National Mortgage Association operates from its headquarters in Washington, D.C., with five regional offices in Dallas, Atlanta, Los Angeles, Chicago, and Philadelphia. The regional offices have authority to negotiate loan purchases within their areas and serve as bases for all regional operations.

In order to sell a loan to FNMA, it is first necessary to qualify as an approved seller. Most mortgage companies, some savings and loan associations, and some insurance companies have found it beneficial to be able to do business with FNMA. An approval by the FHA and the VA have been normal prerequisites but do not in themselves qualify a mortgagee for FNMA—a complete file on the capitalization, background, and experience of the qualifying company and its key personnel is required.

All companies doing business with FNMA automatically become stockholders, as one of the requirements is that the seller purchase stock with the one-half of 1 percent commitment fee on each commitment. And the stock must be retained by the mortgagee at one-quarter of 1 percent of its total loans being serviced for FNMA.

FNMA Purchases of Loan Commitments

The Federal National Mortgage Association buys mortgage loans in several ways. The principal vehicle used is the free market system auction (called FMS). With the auction procedures, FNMA issues *commitments* to purchase mortgages on single family homes. It also uses the auction to determine the amount of these mortgages it will purchase and the prices it will pay for them. Formerly, FNMA administratively established mortgage purchase prices by geographic area. However, purchasing at posted prices did not permit a satisfactory method of responding to changes in capital and money markets. The FMS auction stemmed from the recognized need for a freer flow of funds for housing from the capital-surplus areas to the capital-short areas. After careful study, FNMA abandoned the system of spot prices on a regional basis in favor of the issuance of forward commitments through a national, uniform bidding procedure that was more responsive to the mortgage market. The first such auction was held on May 6, 1968, at which time FNMA issued $40.3 million in purchase commitments to 187 successful bidders. Since that date the auction has accounted for well over $25 billion in loan purchase commitments.

The FMS auction is held every other Monday and now accepts bids for forward commitments on both FHA/VA type loans and conventional loans. They are separate auctions but are similar in form and conducted at the same time. Any institution that has met the qualifications to do business with FNMA may submit a bid for their anticipated money requirements over the next four months. The bid that a mortgage company, for example, might submit would be a yield, expressed to three decimals such as 8.875, which is the price the mortgage company would be willing to pay for the money it expects to loan over the next four months. One might call this the "wholesale price" for the money they will loan to home buyers.

The institutions qualified to submit bids to FNMA for loan commitments have a choice of two types of bids; competitive and non-competitive. But only one bid may be made at each auction. The two types are:

1. The *competitive* offering, normally limited to a maximum of $3 million, must specify the yield that the bidder (the *seller* of the loans) will pay to FNMA. An offering fee is required with a competitive bid in the amount of 1/100th of 1 percent of the funds specified in the bid, which is used largely to discourage frivolous bidding. If the offer is accepted, then a commitment fee of ½ of 1 percent must be paid to FNMA immediately upon notice of acceptance. After the auction has closed, the FNMA management reviews the offerings, including the total number of bids, total dollar volume, and the range of the yields offered. In addition, FNMA looks at the mortgage market generally, the range of prices at the time, and FNMA's anticipated financing costs. Management then decides the minimum yield to be accepted and the dollar volume of commitments that will be issued. It is from the range of accepted yields that the weighted average yield is computed.

2. The *noncompetitive* offerings are limited to $200,000 per seller at any one sale and do not specify a yield. These noncompetitive offerings are funded initially from the available funds at that particular sale and are then automatically assigned the weighted average yield as determined by the accepted competitive offers. It is from these noncompetitive offerings that many smaller mortgage companies obtain their assurance of available funds and are able to determine precisely what discount must be charged in order to cover the yield for that commitment of funds.

Both types of offerings are made by telephone to the Washington office using the seller's code number for identification. On the day following each offer date, an announcement is made of the acceptable offers giving the range of yields and the new weighted average yield. Figures 5-1 through 5-4 are copies of actual notices covering several weeks of announcements and results of the free market system. Conditions vary somewhat with each auction as to the length of commitment, eligible mortgages, method of submittal, and money available. Each notice also publishes the results of the previous auction.

FMS AUCTION RESULTS

Table 5-2 shows the fluctuations that occurred in the demand for mortgage money and the yields accepted by FNMA over the first half of 1976. It was a period of relative stability in the movement of long-term interest rates. The peaking in demand for money commitments during May 1976 reflects a seasonal increase in expectations as the next four months are the most favorable for building conditions and completion of houses.

Other Methods Used by FNMA to Purchase Loans

There are other methods besides the free market system auctions used by FNMA to purchase mortgage loans. These are principally project mortgage commitments and convertible stand-by commitments described more fully below:

Project Mortgages. These are the loans for projects such as apartment developments, nursing homes and hospitals and are handled on a project-by-project basis. The project must be insured under one of the specified sections of the National Housing Act. For such a project yet to be constructed, FNMA will issue a commitment to purchase the mortgage loan within the next 24 months. This would be a *stand-by commitment* and would enable a project sponsor to more easily obtain construction financing. The yield requirement for a stand-by commitment is higher than that for a mortgage that can be delivered immediately. If the project is completed and the mortgage loan can be delivered, FNMA uses an *immediate purchase* procedure. The yield requirements for immediate purchase and for stand-by commitments are published periodically with the FMS notices and carefully reflect changes that occur in the national market for mortgages as shown by the auction procedures.

FEDERAL NATIONAL MORTGAGE ASSOCIATION

<u>NOTICE</u>

FNMA No. FMS-FHA/VA 16-76
August 10, 1976

TO: ALL FNMA FHA/VA SELLERS

SUBJECT: FREE MARKET SYSTEM/CONVERTIBLE STANDBY - FHA/VA
           NOTICE OF CURRENT FNMA COMMITMENT INFORMATION
           AND PROJECT REQUIREMENTS

The Federal National Mortgage Association announces that the next Free Market System
(FMS) Auction for commitments to purchase eligible FHA/VA home loans will be as follows:

Date of Auction: August 23, 1976
Hours of Auction: 9 a.m. to 3 p.m., Washington, D.C. time
Telephone Number: (202) 293-7500

The Offer of a Seller for this Auction may not exceed the applicable maximums set forth
below:

Funds Available: NO LIMIT ESTABLISHED
Competitive Seller's Maximum: $3,000,000
Non-competitive Seller's Maximum: $ 200,000

This Auction will be conducted under the general rules which have been established for
FMS Auctions as stated in Section 203 of the FNMA Selling Agreement (Supplement)
and pursuant to the FNMA Selling Agreement and the Supplement thereto.

<u>Results of the FMS-FHA/VA Auction of   August 9, 1976</u>

Type of Contract	Total Offers Eligible *	Total Offers Accepted *	Accepted Yield Range	Weighted Average Yield/ Price of Accepted Offers
4-months	190.1	107.4	8.981-9.261	9.014/96.43

* In Millions

Home Loan <u>Convertible Standby Commitments</u> may be obtained in accordance with Section
204 of the FNMA Selling Agreement (Supplement).

- The current yield required is <u>9.500</u> , effective 12:00 noon, 8/10/76
- The previous yield required was <u>9.550</u> .
- Convertible Standby Commitments issued:
    a) For the two-week period ending 8/9/76: $16,086,000
    b) Year to date volume is: $761,273,000

FIGURE 5-1a.

119

Project Mortgage Requirements

The current Project Mortgage Requirements are as follows for mortgages insured under Sections 220, 221 (d) (3), 221 (d)(4), 223 (e), 233, and 236 of the National Housing Act:

Immediate Purchase Yield required is 9.800 . This yield converts to a price of:

Standby Yield required is 10.600 . This yield converts to a price of:

	Immediate Purchase		Standby
76.67	7 % mortgages	71.54	7% mortgages
82.79	7 3/4% mortgages	77.30	7 3/4% mortgages
84.85	8 % mortgages	79.25	8% mortgages
86.93	8 1/4% mortgages	81.20	8 1/4% mortgages
89.01	8 1/2% mortgages	83.17	8 1/2% mortgages
91.11	8 3/4% mortgages	85.15	8 3/4% mortgages
93.21	9% mortgages	87.13	9% mortgages
97.45	9 1/2% mortgages	91.12	9 1/2% mortgages

With regard to mortgages insured under Sections 207, 213, 213 (j), 223 (f), 231, 232, 232 (i), 234 (d), 241, 242, and Titles X and XI, or insured under any of the foregoing sections or titles pursuant to Section 223 (d), FNMA will deduct 1.50 from both the Immediate Purchase and Standby Commitment prices listed above.

NOTE: SINCE THE ABOVE PRICES ARE BASED ON A 40 YEAR MORTGAGE WITH AN AVERAGE LIFE OF 20 YEARS, ADJUSTMENTS IN PRICE WILL BE MADE FOR MORTGAGES HAVING A DIFFERENT MORTGAGE TERM AND AVERAGE LIFE.

Financing Charge

The required percentage of financing charge in construction loans as referred to in Section 308.05 (b) of the FNMA Selling Agreement Supplement is:

2.35	7 % mortgages	1.09	8 1/2% mortgages
1.93	7 1/2% mortgages	.88	8 3/4% mortgages
1.72	7 3/4% mortgages	.67	9 % mortgages
1.51	8% mortgages	.25	9 1/2% mortgages
1.30	8 1/4% mortgages		

Regional Vice President

FIGURE 5-1b.

Federal National Mortgage Association

RESULTS OF COMPETITIVE OFFERINGS UNDER THE
FREE MARKET SYSTEM - FHA/VA AUCTION

	No.	Amount (000)
OFFERS RECEIVED:	261	$ 192,080
Less (-) Ineligible	(1)	(2,000)
ELIGIBLE OFFERS REC'D ►	260	$ 190,080
% of (Eligible Offers Received / Offers Rec'd)		98.95 %
OFFERS ACCEPTED:		
Competitive	72	$ 85,801
Non-Competitive	122	21,629
TOTAL ►	194	$ 107,430
% of (Total Accepted / Eligible Offers Rec'd)		56.52 %

WEIGHTED AVERAGE YIELD:
PRICE (8.500%): 9.014
96.43
RANGE OF ACCEPTED OFFERS: 8.981 - 9.261

ACCEPTANCE BY REGIONS:	No.	Amount (000)
Southeastern (Atlanta)	33	$ 19,575
Midwestern (Chicago)	42	$ 17,127
Southwestern (Dallas)	42	$ 23,200
Western (Los Angeles)	47	$ 38,751
Northeastern (Phila.)	30	$ 8,777
TOTAL: ►	194	$ 107,430

Date
08-09-76

Home Loan Convertible Standby Yield required is 9.500:
This yield converts to a price of:

83.25	7.00% mortgages	93.20	8.50% mortgages
88.19	7.75% mortgages	94.89	8.75% mortgages
89.85	8.00% mortgages	96.59	9.00% mortgages
91.52	8.25% mortgages	100.00	9.50% mortgages

Project Immediate Purchase Yield required is 9.800:
This yield converts to a price of:

76.67	7.00% mortgages	89.01	8.50% mortgages
82.79	7.75% mortgages	91.11	8.75% mortgages
84.85	8.00% mortgages	93.21	9.00% mortgages
86.93	8.25% mortgages	97.45	9.50% mortgages

Project Standby Yield required is 10.600:
This yield converts to a price of:

71.54	7.00% mortgages	83.17	8.50% mortgages
77.30	7.75% mortgages	85.15	8.75% mortgages
79.25	8.00% mortgages	87.13	9.00% mortgages
81.20	8.25% mortgages	91.12	9.50% mortgages

FNMA Form 889A
Feb. 76

FIGURE 5-2.

121

FEDERAL NATIONAL MORTGAGE ASSOCIATION

NOTICE

FNMA No. FMS-CHM 17-76
August 24, 1976

TO: ALL FNMA CONVENTIONAL SELLERS

SUBJECT: FREE MARKET SYSTEM/CONVERTIBLE STANDBY- CONVENTIONAL
          NOTICE OF CURRENT FNMA COMMITMENT INFORMATION

The Federal National Mortgage Association announces that the next Free Market System
(FMS) Auction for commitments to purchase eligible Conventional home loans will be
as follows:

Date of Auction:	September 7, 1976
Hours of Auction:	9 a.m. to 3 p.m., Washington, D.C. time
Telephone Number:	(202) 293-7500

The Offer of a Seller for this Auction may not exceed the applicable maximums set
forth below:

Funds Available:	NO LIMIT ESTABLISHED
Competitive Seller's Maximum:	$3,000,000
Non-competitive Seller's Maximum:	$ 200,000

This Auction will be conducted under the general rules which have been established for
FMS Auctions as stated in Section 402 of the FNMA Conventional Selling Contract
Supplement and pursuant to the FNMA Conventional Selling Contract and the Supple-
ment thereto.

Results of the FMS-CHM Auction of ___August 23, 1976___

Type of Contract	Total Offers Eligible	Total Offers Accepted *	Accepted Yield Range	Weighted Average Yield of Accepted Offers
4-months	162.1	115.3	9.125-9.200	9.135

* In millions
Home Loan Convertible Standby Commitments may be obtained in accordance with Section
403 of the FNMA Conventional Selling Contract Supplement.

-The current yield required is _9.650_ , effective 12:00 Noon, 8/10/76
-The previous yield required was _9.700_ .
-Convertible Standby Commitments issued:
    a) For the two-week period ending 8/23/76: $1,700,000
    b) Year to date volume is: $166,984,000

Regional Vice President

FIGURE 5-3.

RESULTS OF COMPETITIVE OFFERINGS UNDER THE
FREE MARKET SYSTEM – CONVENTIONAL

AUCTION OF ___08-23-76___

	No.	Amount (000)
OFFERS RECEIVED:	237	$ 163,242
Less (-) Ineligible	(3)	(1,150)
ELIGIBLE OFFERS REC'D ➤	234	$ 162,092
% of (Eligible Offers Received / Offers Rec'd)		99.30 %

	No.	Amount (000)
OFFERS ACCEPTED:		
Competitive	92	$ 102,300
Non-Competitive	76	12,988
TOTAL	168	$ 115,288
% of (Total Accepted / Eligible Offers Rec'd)		71.13 %

WEIGHTED AVERAGE YIELD: 9.135
RANGE OF ACCEPTED OFFERS: 9.125 – 9.200

ACCEPTANCE BY REGIONS:	No.	Amount (000)
Southeastern (Atlanta)	22	$ 7,720
Midwestern (Chicago)	15	$ 5,685
Southwestern (Dallas)	52	$ 35,070
Western (Los Angeles)	61	$ 58,375
Northeastern (Phila.)	18	$ 8,438
TOTAL:	168	$ 115,288

Home Loan Convertible Standby Yield is: 9.650

FIGURE 5-4.

123

TABLE 5-2.

Federal National Mortgage Association Auctions of Commitments to Buy Home Mortgages

Item		Date of auction 1976										
	Jan. 26	Feb. 9	Feb. 23	Mar. 8	Mar. 22	Apr. 5	Apr. 19	May 3	May 17	June 1	June 14	June 28
Amounts (millions of dollars):												
Govt.-underwritten loans												
Offered[1]	103.9	252.2	126.9	299.9	146.3	106.2	132.1	483.3	634.3	349.5	146.6	261.2
Accepted	57.7	179.9	81.2	171.9	121.6	56.2	60.1	222.3	321.4	224.7	98.8	157.5
Conventional loans												
Offered[1]	33.4	57.8	44.0	75.4	46.2	56.4	55.3	110.7	128.8	131.4	77.3	93.6
Accepted	24.7	36.9	23.3	45.0	33.7	31.8	33.4	60.1	68.9	90.5	70.3	59.2
Average yield (per cent) on short-term commitments[2]												
Govt.-underwritten loans	9.07	9.07	9.04	9.06	9.03	8.94	8.83	8.94	9.13	9.20	9.14	9.12
Conventional loans	9.22	9.17	9.14	9.15	9.13	9.05	9.00	9.09	9.24	9.31	9.30	9.31

[1] Mortgage amounts offered by bidders are total bids received.

[2] Average accepted bid yield (before deduction of 38 basis-point fee paid for mortgage servicing) for home mortgages assuming a prepayment period of 12 years for 30-year loans, without special adjustment for FNMA commitment fees and FNMA stock purchase and holding requirements. Commitments mature in 4 months.

Convertible Stand-by Commitments for Home Loans. FNMA will sell commitments to purchase home loans for up to 12 months on both government-backed and conventional home mortgages. The pricing of such commitments is directly related to the auction yields and is published periodically with the bi-weekly notice. Such a stand-by commitment might be used by a builder planning to build a number of houses and in need of some assurance that future buyers will have financing available for them. FNMA may make delivery of the mortgage mandatory with a stand-by commitment or they can permit the owner of the commitment to find a lower cost loan at completion of the project and forfeit the commitment. Forfeiture would mean loss of the commitment fee also.

FNMA Sale of Loans

As a secondary market operation, FNMA must also sell some of its mortgage notes from time to time as conditions permit. Large insurance companies and savings associations are prime customers and deal in multimillion dollar blocks of loans. To improve and broaden its sales, FNMA established the auction technique in 1968 and has found it gives a more accurate indication of the mortgage market. This system proved itself by helping to remove some of the uncertainty about the true state of the mortgage market in periods of fluctuating interest rates.

FEDERAL HOME LOAN MORTGAGE CORPORATION

The credit crunch of 1969–1970 highlighted a problem within the savings associations during periods of tight money. Many depositors simply withdrew their money for investments of higher yields than the fixed rates offered on savings accounts. The outflow of cash could easily exceed the repayments of loans outstanding and make any new loans impossible for an association to make. The Federal Home Loan Bank could not provide sufficient capital to give all the relief that might be needed with loans to members, so an additional agency was created. In the Emergency Home Finance Act of 1970, Congress authorized the Federal Home Loan Mortgage Corporation to *purchase* residential mortgages from members of the Federal Home Loan Bank and other approved financial institutions.

When a member savings association decides to convert some of its existing portfolio of mortgages into cash for any reason, the association can offer the mortgages to FHLMC. The Federal Home Loan Mortgage Corporation, now simplifying its name to "The Mortgage Corporation," will purchase *whole* loans or *participation* loans. A whole loan is 100 percent of the balance due on the mortgage note. A participation loan is the purchase of a part of the loan—FHLMC rules place a minimum of 50 percent and a maximum of 85 percent on the amount of the loan they will purchase under a participation program. FHLMC will purchase home mortgages and multi-family mortgages. Each type of offering requires a slightly different form. Figure 5–5 illustrates the form used to sell a participating interest in conventional home mortgages that are available for immediate delivery. "Immediate" means that all documentation for loans submitted on a purchase contract must be delivered within 60 days. Delivery is mandatory. FHLMC has the right to review each mortgage submitted under a purchase contract and may eliminate from the contract any mortgages that they deem ineligible.

The price of a loan purchased by FHLMC is set by administrative decision based on a careful analysis of the mortgage market. The published figure is a required yield that is announced once a week by FHLMC. Most of the mortgages purchased by FHLMC are serviced by the savings association which sells the loan. So there is a need to allow a *servicing fee* to the association. FHLMC allows a minimum fee of .375 percent (3/8ths of 1 percent) to the association and no longer restricts the fee to that amount should interest rate differentials favor the savings association. To accommodate the servicing fee, FHLMC requires that the minimum gross yield (the rate paid by the home buyer) must be at least .375 percent above the required net yield for the mortgage to qualify for purchase. Using the wholesale-retail comparison, FHLMC is offering money to the savings associations at a wholesale rate amounting to 3/8ths of 1 percent less than the association is charging for loans to its customers.

If the minimum gross yield of the loans held by a savings association is higher than .375 percent more than the published yield required by FHLMC, the loans may be sold at par to FHLMC which would increase the yield to the servicer. But if the loans are held at lower rates, then they would have to be sold at a discount, or at a loss to the savings association. In order to equate the lower interest rates to the required net yield for FHLMC, the discount calculation is made by FHLMC on the presumption of a 30-year loan term with a 12-year repayment period. FHLMC requires that the required net yield and the minimum gross yield specified in a purchase contract

EXHIBIT B

FHLMC Form 57

The Mortgage Corporation

Federal Home Loan Mortgage Corporation

IMMEDIATE PURCHASE CONTRACT
HOME MORTGAGES
CONVENTIONAL PARTICIPATION PROGRAM

Sale: The undersigned Seller hereby offers to sell to the Federal Home Loan Mortgage Corporation ("The Mortgage Corporation" or "FHLMC") undivided interests in Home Mortgages, on the terms stated below and in accordance with the Purchase Documents, as defined in the Sellers' Guide Conventional Mortgages as in effect on the date of this offer, all of which are fully incorporated herein by reference.

Servicing: The undersigned Seller hereby agrees to service all mortgages sold hereunder, in accordance with the Purchase Documents as in effect on the date of this offer, all of which are fully incorporated herein by reference.

Required Yield for Participation in Conventional Home Mortgages as of Date of Offer:_____Percent
(TO 3 DECIMAL PLACES)

Participation % Offered (85% maximum-50% minimum)	Aggregate Principal Amount	FHLMC's Participation Interest (Contract Amount)
_____% (×)	$_____ (=)	$_____

Nonmember Fee: $_____enclosed, if applicable.

Seller's FHLBB Docket No.
or FDIC Certificate No.:_____

SELLER

Date of Offer:_____, 19____

ADDRESS

By_____(Seal)
AUTHORIZED REPRESENTATIVE

This contract is signed pursuant to a telephone offer: Yes_____ No_____

Offer Hereby Accepted by
The Mortgage Corporation

Federal Home Loan Mortgage Corporation

Date of Acceptance:_____

By_____(Seal)
VICE PRESIDENT

Purchase Contract No.:_____

Required Delivery Date:_____

or ☐ Offer Declined by The Mortgage Corporation

Seller's FHLMC Seller/
Servicer No.:_____

Date of Declination:_____

FHLMC-57 4/76

FIGURE 5-5.

must be satisfied by each individual mortgage, not by the delivered package as a whole.

FHLMC is authorized to purchase mortgages from members of the Federal Home Loan Bank and other authorized financial institutions. For a non-member, such as a commercial bank, to sell loans to FHLMC, there is an additional charge of ½ point on the offering.

The possibility of selling a block of mortgages at a loss would be weighed against the advantage of having some additional cash on hand to make new loans at the higher interest rates, earning the origination fees, and adding to the total amount of loans that the seller would be servicing. The seller might also be faced with the need for additional cash to provide funds for commitments made much earlier to a good customer, such as a developer or builder who has continued to send good business to that particular savings association.

FHLMC Sources of Money

While the FHLMC is owned by the Federal Home Loan Bank system and has access to funds raised through the sale of bonds, it also uses two other procedures to raise cash for the purchase of mortgages. These are:

1. *Mortgage Participation Certificates,* also called PC's, are sold every business day through any of the five regional offices of FHLMC in denominations of $100,000, $200,000, $500,000, and $1,000,000. Each PC represents an undivided interest in a large, geographically diversified group of residential mortgages, and is unconditionally guaranteed by FHLMC. PC's pay principal and interest every month and have produced yields in excess of 9 percent.

2. *Guaranteed Mortgage Certificates,* called GMC's, are similar to PC's in quality, denominations, and guarantee, and are aimed for institutions that prefer payment of interest every six months and of principal once a year.

The popular opinion that any agency representing a governmental operation is pumping out money for the benefit of banks or savings associations to use for loans should again be dispelled. There are some subsidy programs, but the beneficiaries are the people, such as those in lower income circumstances with living needs. The Federal Home Loan Mortgage Corporation is not a subsidy operation, and it is expected to raise money in the open market in competition with all other long- and short-term borrowers. Hence, it can only purchase mortgages from the offers presented that will meet the existing market requirements. It does provide an additional outlet for a savings association to achieve some needed liquidity, but always at a price.

TABLE OF SECONDARY MORTGAGE MARKET ACTIVITY

Table 5-3 gives the dollar value of mortgage loans acquired by the Federal National Mortgage Association and the Federal Home Loan Mortgage Corporation. Both organizations *purchase* mortgages from loan originators and operate as a part of the secondary market.

POINTS AND DISCOUNTS

The use of points in discounting loans stems from the need to sell these loans in the secondary market. Hence, a closer examination of the methods and reasons is presented here.

The definition of "points" used in this text refers to the term as a unit of measurement. Thus, the word *point(s)* can be used to identify various fees, such as the origination fee for processing a loan; or it may be used to refer to the costs of private mortgage insurance; or it can be used in reference to the discount. A point is simply 1 percent of the loan amount.

The word point, as used to express a discount, is the percentage that must be added or subtracted from the face value of a loan in order to decrease or increase the yield to a competitive amount. Discounts are increasingly being asked on conventional loans as a method or gimmick to obtain an increase in yield without showing an increase in interest rate. To the borrowing public, the expression is more closely associated with the fixed interest loans underwritten by the FHA and VA. In financial circles, a discount is converted to a "price" for a loan in order to facilitate trading.

Because the FNMA free market system is the most widely publicized arena showing the movements of market yields from mortgage loans, a specific example will be used to illustrate the manner in which points are determined by most mortgage companies.

For this purpose, *yield* can be defined as the return to the investor in percent of the price paid for the note. *Discount* is the difference between the face value of the note and the price the investor paid for the note. Yield includes both the interest earned and the discount taken. So to express the discount as a part of the yield, it must be converted to an annual percentage rate. The discount is a one time

TABLE 5-3.

Federal National Mortgage Association and Federal Home Loan Mortgage Corporation— Secondary Mortgage Market Activity
(In millions of dollars)

	FNMA							FHLMC						
	Mortgage holdings			Mortgage transactions (during period)		Mortgage commitments		Mortgage holdings			Mortgage transactions (during period)		Mortgage commitments	
End of period	Total[1]	FHA-insured	VA-guaranteed	Purchases	Sales	Made during period	Outstanding	Total	FHA-VA	Conventional	Purchases	Sales	Made during period	Outstanding
1971	17,791	12,681	5,110	3,574	336	9,828	6,497	968	821	147	778	64	.....	182
1972	19,791	14,624	5,112	3,699	211	8,797	8,124	1,789	1,503	286	1,297	408	1,606	198
1973	24,175	16,852	6,352	6,127	71	8,914	7,889	2,604	1,743	861	1,334	409	1,629	186
1974	29,578	19,189	8,310	6,953	5	10,765	7,960	4,586	1,904	2,682	2,191	52	4,553	2,390
1975	31,824	19,732	9,573	4,263	2	6,106	4,126	4,987	1,824	3,163	1,716	1,020	982	111

1975—May	29,858	19,251	8,395	247	—	621	6,615	4,773	1,920	2,854	203	38	42	969
June	30,015	19,282	8,498	326	—	557	6,549	4,944	1,936	3,008	210	5	28	700
July	30,351	19,385	8,693	538	—	575	6,119	5,015	1,943	3,072	161	63	139	530
Aug.	30,777	19,507	8,942	594	—	814	5,888	4,942	1,863	3,080	98	145	132	509
Sept.	31,055	19,560	9,122	488	—	575	5,399	5,033	1,852	3,181	148	31	79	403
Oct.	31,373	19,641	9,309	508	—	282	4,685	5,119	1,843	3,276	176	59	45	201
Nov.	31,552	19,648	9,430	372	—	332	4,385	4,971	1,834	3,137	104	225	50	124
Dec.	31,824	19,732	9,573	451	—	517	4,126	4,987	1,824	3,163	69	30	71	111
1976—Jan.	31,772	19,674	9,554	76	55	189	3,170	4,958	1,816	3,142	47	57	42	99
Feb.	31,618	19,541	9,521	56	22	355	3,201	4,686	1,802	2,884	51	296	43	87
Mar.	31,482	19,431	9,473	85	184	405	3,120	4,602	1,787	2,815	95	98	93	128
Apr.	31,389	19,368	9,431	103	—	213	2,788	4,520	1,768	2,752	43	86	209	289
May	32,052	19,296	9,390	877	—	1,305	3,732	......	......	......	......	......	......	......

[1]Includes conventional loans not shown separately.

Note—Data from FNMA and FHLMC, respectively.

For FNMA: Holdings include loans used to back bond issues guaranteed by GNMA. Commitments include some multifamily and nonprofit hospital loan commitments in addition to 1- to 4-family loan commitments accepted in FNMA's free market auction system, and through the FNMA–GNMA Tandem Plans.

For FHLMC: Holdings and transactions cover participations as well as whole loans. Holdings include loans used to back bond issues guaranteed by GNMA. Commitments cover the conventional and Govt.-underwritten loan programs.

Source: Federal Reserve Bulletin, July 1976, p. A43.

charge: a lump sum taken at the time the loan is funded. To determine how much this adds to each year's earnings, or yield, the discount must be spread over the life of the loan. But what is the life of the mortgage loan? While most residential loans, including FHA- and VA-supported loans, are granted for a term of thirty years, the realistic life of the loan is approximately ten years. That is to say, within ten years the average loan is paid off, usually by re-sale and refinancing. So FNMA and FHLMC use a time span of twelve years to determine the yield value of a discount.

The free market system offerings are made in terms of a yield, usually carried to three decimal places. The accepted yield can be converted to a discount mathematically, or more easily, by means of a standard conversion table. Table 5-4 shows several typical yield figures and the sequence of steps showing the fixed interest rate for the note, the price that is used to achieve the yield, and the discount needed to achieve the price.

TABLE 5-4.

For a yield amount	At interest rate	Price must be	Points to achieve
7.862	7%	93.75	6¼
8.044	7%	92.50	7½

The mortgage banking industry is able to use the FNMA free market system yields as solid criteria from which to base its own handling of individual mortgage loans. Based on the above figures and the knowledge that, say, the last yield quoted was 8.04 percent, conservative lenders for a home loan would ask a discount between 7½ to 8 points for a good loan in excess of $25,000. They would ask perhaps another one-half point for a smaller $15,000 to $25,000 loan and a full extra point for any loan under $15,000. Some variation in these points exists due to competitive pressures, but the market for money remains the controlling factor. Loan originators using the FNMA yields as a guide to trends would be watching for an upward or downward movement to further influence their decision as to what discount they might need in order to be making loans at a price, or yield, at which they could be sold.

It should be borne in mind that the normal brokerage fee of 1 to 1½ points is not to be confused with the charge for discount points. Charges for discounts, on the whole, are passed on by the mortgage company to the ultimate lender. The brokerage, or finance fee, is the remuneration earned by the mortgage company for soliciting, processing, and arranging the funding of the loan. Another term for this charge is *origination fee.*

PRIVATE MORTGAGE INSURANCE

One of the essential elements needed to facilitate free trading in mortgage loans is some standard of reliability. The fact that home loans and other property loans are so local in their nature has prevented many investors from moving very far geographically to invest in conventional mortgages. The FHA and VA proved that investors would cross state lines and assist the cash-short growth areas of the country if they had some assurance of protection against the problems incurred in foreclosing a remote property.

The idea of providing insurance against a default in mortgage payments must be credited to the federal programs instigated by the FHA in 1933. It was some years later, during the 1950s, that several entrepreneurs began testing the market for the same type of insurance sold by private insurance companies. Progress was slow at first, and the independents did not really take hold in the mortgage industry until 1971. In that year the regulatory authorities expanded lending limits for conventional residential loans which called for default insurance coverage. Federal-chartered savings and loan associations were permitted to make loans up to 95 percent of appraised value, compared to 90 percent previously, provided that the higher ratio loans were insured. The result was a tremendous growth in private mortgage insurance.

One major insuring company, MGIC, based in Milwaukee, increased its loan coverage volume to $2.8 billion in 1971 and then to $7.5 billion in 1972 with about 40 percent of the coverage in 95 percent loans. The private sector topped the FHA coverage in that year, which in itself amounted to $4.5 billion.

Undoubtedly, adding to the boom in private mortgage insurance, often identified as PMI, was the unfortunate series of abuses revealed in connection with certain FHA home loan transactions occurring in isolated instances in the East and Midwest. In an effort to correct these problems and prevent a recurrence, subsequent new and stringent regulations were imposed and rigidly enforced to a point where it became difficult to sell a house through the FHA programs. Although most of the requirements were later modified, the private mortgage insurance had found its niche and proved its value.

Consider, for example, that under a given set of circumstances, a prospective borrower needing a loan of over $35,000 can actually obtain a smaller down payment through private mortgage insurance procedures than through the FHA. Also it may cost the borrower less overall, with the transaction completed more quickly and involving a minimum of red tape.

What is private mortgage insurance and how does it work? Since it is a fairly new development in general usage, there has been some confusion regarding the facts. Basically, private mortgage insurance covers the top 25 percent of the loan against default. Whereas the FHA insures the total amount of its loan commitment, private mortgage insurance companies limit their exposure to the top portion of the loan, which, of course, is the most risky end.

What they are insuring against is an actual default on the mortgage payments. They are not immediately concerned with the borrower's life, the destruction of the property by fire, or with other hazards. Consequently, the insuring company must make an evaluation of the risk involved with the borrower, the reliability of the borrower's credit record, and the value of the property in question, should foreclosure become necessary.

There are only a few companies capable of selling this type of specialized insurance coverage, and they all work through loan originators: the mortgage companies, savings and loan associations, commercial banks, and other lending institutions. The loan originator must first qualify with the insurance company as an acceptable lender. The insurance carrier normally requires that each mortgage loan undergo evaluation by its own underwriting group before a certificate of coverage is issued. A request for coverage includes submitting (1) a property appraisal made by a professional appraiser approved by the insurance company; (2) a copy of the loan application; (3) a credit report on the borrower; (4) several verifications; and (5) any other data helpful in analyzing the loan. Once the necessary documents and information have been submitted, processing of the application tends to move quickly and is usually completed within 24 hours.

The essence of the insurance certificate is that in case the mortgage loan is defaulted and taken through foreclosure, the insurance company will pay off up to 25 percent of the loan. This means an exposure for the lender of 71.25 percent of the value on a 95 percent loan, and 67.5 percent on a 90 percent loan. The advantage to the lender is obvious in reducing risk to a more practical level wherein full recovery might be made even through an early foreclosure proceeding. The advantage to the borrower lies in being able to borrow a larger percentage of the value than previously obtainable in terms of a conventional loan. Now, for instance, a family might buy a $40,000 house for as little as $2,000 down—a down payment previously available only to a veteran qualifying on a VA guarantee requiring no down payment at all.

In actual operation it has been the practice of at least one insurance carrier, MGIC, to take over the property itself in a foreclosure proceeding and pay off the lender in full, thus relieving him or her of any further management problems. This is the same procedure that is commonly used by the Veterans Administration in similar circumstances and has given much greater acceptance to its guaranty programs. No lender is interested in spending the time and money necessary to take a property through foreclosure, manage and protect it, and make suitable disposition to another user. Mortgage insurance greatly reduces this possibility and has attracted many small investors into conventional mortgage loans.

The cost of private mortgage insurance is paid for by the borrower, the same as under the FHA. While the FHA has only one plan for payment—½ percent annually on the declining balance—private insurors have a variety of methods to offer. This causes some problems in trying to quote loan costs as the insurance rates vary with 80, 90, and 95 percent loan-to-value ratios. The insuring companies also offer single payment plans for different terms of years, such as five, seven, or ten years. Most originators have attempted to reduce this confusion by offering only one or two plans for payment. A common practice is to offer two alternatives—a single payment plan at closing, or a monthly payment plan. On a 95 percent loan the single payment cost is 2½ percent of the loan amount and provides coverage for ten years; for a 90 percent loan this payment drops to 2 percent. On extended payments, the 95 percent loan insurance costs 1 percent at closing plus ¼ percent annually for up to ten years, while on a 90 percent loan the initial cost drops to ½ percent at closing with the same ¼ percent annually for the remainder of the terms. These rates are subject to change.

Conventional loans are usually quoted without discount points, as the full cost is represented in the interest. Using only the interest rate, a current quote might be "8% + 1 + PMI." The one point would be the origination fee or finance fee, as some prefer to call it. To reduce the mortgage insurance cost to a quotation requires knowing which of the payment plans offered will be used by the borrower. Some companies simply add the initial premium cost to the origination fee and then quote the extended payment plan as an increase in the interest cost.

NEW DEVELOPMENTS

In August 1974, the first mortgages were traded through a new nationwide, computerized information net named Automated Mortgage Market Information Network, or AMMINET. The system has over 500 subscribers and is sponsored by the American Bankers Association, the Federal Home Loan Mortgage Corporation, the Mortgage Bankers Association, the National Association of Mutual Savings Banks, the National Savings and Loan League, the U.S. League of Savings Associations and the Department of Housing and Urban Development. The network allows traders to list offers to buy and sell mortgage investments—whole loans, participations, or forward commitment contracts—with a central computer for listings of offers that meet their needs. The subscribers to the system are mortgage companies and savings associations which deal in secondary market offerings.

A second development in secondary market activities is the establishment of futures trading for mortgages by the Chicago Board of Trade in 1975. The trading has been confined to $100,000-unit contracts for GNMA-guaranteed mortgage securities. The pattern of trading is roughly the same as in commodities such as corn, soybeans, gold, and potatoes.

QUESTIONS FOR DISCUSSION

1. Without a national mortgage exchange, how are mortgages traded in the United States?

2. Explain the relationship between the price and the yield on a mortgage loan.

3. Why does the FNMA free market system provide an excellent guide to the cost of mortgage money nationally?

4. Explain the role of the Federal Home Loan Mortgage Corporation and how it operates.

5. What is the purpose of a discount on a loan?

6. Define the meaning of "point."

7. List the different charges that can be required for a mortgage loan which can be quoted in points.

8. How does private mortgage insurance work?

9. Compare the most recent weighted average yields accepted by FNMA with local interest rates and discounts.

Chapter 6

Mortgage Companies

From its origin as a brokerage-type service arranging loans, the mortgage banking industry has grown to a major business, handling well over half the mortgage loans in this country. As early as 1914, the people in this business formed a trade organization, known as the Farm Mortgage Bankers Association, indicating the original emphasis placed on farm loans. The name was changed to its present title of Mortgage Bankers Association of America in 1923, and it now has members from every state and a large permanent staff.

The Association serves as a communications and information center for the industry. Educational programs are sponsored to keep the many persons employed by mortgage bankers up to date on an ever-changing business. And a constant effort is being made to improve the methods and procedures of the industry.

In the early years of this century, mortgage bankers arranged for the sale of their own bonds and used these funds to buy small home and farm mortgages. Because of the thrift-conscious nature of these farmers and homeowners, mortgages were amazingly free of defaults and provided a widely-used medium of investment.

The 1920s brought an increase in mortgage company financing of income properties such as office buildings, apartments, and hotels, perhaps with the firm conviction that a mortgage loan was as secure as gold. And the mortgage companies even referred to the small denomination bonds that they sold to the general public for mortgage financing as "gold bonds."

However, the Depression, triggered by the collapse of prices on the nation's largest stock exchange in October 1929, showed up many basic weaknesses in the mortgage loan system. In the next two to three years most of the mortgage companies that had issued their own bonds, as well as those that had guaranteed bonds for other development companies, were faced with massive foreclosures. Unable to meet their obligations, they were forced into bankruptcy.

From these ruins has arisen a far more enlightened and professionally sound industry—one that today not only arranges for permanent financing of all types of mortgage loans, but also uses its own resources to fund the loans initially, sometimes handling the interim or construction financing, and finally servicing or administering the repayment of the loan for the permanent investor.

MORTGAGE BROKERS

There is a significant difference between the services offered by "loan brokers," and those offered by mortgage bankers working within the mortgage industry. Brokers limit their activity to serving as an intermediary between the client-borrower and the client-lender. While brokers are capable of handling all arrangements for the processing or "packaging" of the loan, they do no funding and have no facilities to service or administer a loan once it has been made. There are some loan-wise individuals who prefer to work on their own as brokers and carry their loan applications to a mortgage banker for verification and funding. They earn a portion of the normal one point finance fee plus an application fee.

Other types of mortgage brokers are companies operating on a national scale who primarily arrange purchases and sales of mortgage loans between originators and investors, or between investor and investor, and in so doing, greatly aid the free flow of mortgages across state lines in the private mortgage market. These brokers seldom originate a loan and do not service them. They are a part of the secondary market in some of their operations.

Occasionally, a mortgage banker, or even a savings association will broker a loan for a customer. Money may not be readily available through regular channels, or the loan request may be for something that the lender cannot handle with its own funds. The lender may then turn to other sources and earn a brokerage fee for handling the loan. This type of extra service is more commonly found in smaller communities.

The lines between a broker, a mortgage banker, and a lender are not always clearly drawn, as brokerage service may be handled by any one of them. Brokerage is essentially the service of processing the loan information for the borrower and arranging for a lender to make the loan. Good brokerage work is done by professionals who respect the confidential nature of the information they must obtain and who earn their fees by knowing which lenders are presently seeking certain types of loans.

MORTGAGE BANKERS

The "full-service" facility offered by the mortgage banker today developed from both the need for a new approach after the Depression collapse and from the desire of the Federal Housing Administration to conduct its programs in conjunction with private industry. The economic pressures of 1930–1931 had dried up lendable funds, construction had been halted, and many banks had closed their doors. The shortage of available funds made the mortgage banker an intermediary for the only remaining sources of cash—cash from insurance companies, from a few large savings banks, and from the Federal National Mortgage Corporation. And the growth of the FHA brought the need for more servicing or loan administration by the mortgage bankers. More than half the mortgage companies operating today were founded after World War II, and in the 1950s four-fifths of all federally underwritten loans held by life insurance companies, savings and loans, and FNMA were serviced by mortgage bankers. The upward trend has continued, and if the government ventures further into the field of real estate financing, it undoubtedly will move through the channels that it helped to create—channels that have helped the government programs to succeed, i.e., the mortgage banking industry.

Qualifications of a Mortgage Banker

At present there are no federal requirements regarding the qualifications or licensing of an individual or a company handling mortgage loans, and few states have established requirements. In most areas any individual meriting the confidence of a lending institution could assist in arranging a loan, thereby earning a fee for his or her services. In practice, however, most mortgage companies and lenders require more concrete proof of ability and integrity.

Some mortgage companies went into business initially to handle only conventional loans for various investor-clients, and not FHA or VA loans. Those companies that specialize in large commercial loans have no real need of approval from FHA, nor do they feel compelled to comply with its regulations. Most mortgage companies, however, feel that a prime requisite for successful loan negotiation is to hold an FHA-approved certificate. The reason for this is that the home loan market, previously dominated by the FHA, is considered to be the most solidly reliable field, the "bread and butter" field, so to speak. In addition, many institutional lenders use the FHA certification of approval as one method of determining the reliability of potential correspondents.

The FHA requires a minimum capitalization of $100,000 (a sum now considered small within the industry), plus relevant details on the background and qualifications of the officers, directors, stockholders, and owners who will control and set policies for the mortgage company. It also requires that offices be made available for serving the general public and that no other business be conducted in those offices. Once the FHA has issued its charter of acceptance, the mortgage company becomes an "approved mortgagee" within the circle of companies qualified to handle federally underwritten commitments. Only approved mortgagees may present loan applications to the FHA for insured commitments. And in turn, the FHA depends heavily on its approved list of mortgage companies to prepare each application properly so as to include the relevant data needed for expeditious processing. Thus the FHA can rely on all information and verifications, the security of any cash required to be escrowed, and the prompt payment of any fees to be collected because it has already carefully examined the company and its official personnel before issuing its approval. A deliberate violation of an FHA requirement could result in the cancellation of the mortgage company's qualifications as an approved mortgagee.

As will become apparent in later chapters, the powerful role of the FHA in real estate finance began diminishing in early 1971, accelerated by a tightening of regulations brought on by abuses caused by a few groups and individuals. At about this same time, private mortgage insurance business was boosted, and its activities became serious competition. Despite the fall from a dominant position, however, the FHA acceptance charter held by a company or institution remains an important credential of a mortgage company's qualifications to transact loans.

Mortgage Company Operations

Although mortgage companies vary widely in their methods, the business organization common to most operates by means of three basic divisions:

1. Administration

2. Loan servicing

3. Loan acquisition

The administrative group supervises and directs all operations and usually seeks out and maintains contacts with its sources of money—the lending institutions. The development of stable, continuing relations with a group of investors is a source of pride with the mortgage companies. And there is always more than one investor, since it is not considered good business for either the mortgage company or the lender to maintain an exclusive arrangement. Lenders are in and out of the market as their particular needs fluctuate, while the mortgage company must maintain a steady supply of funds. The mortgage company officers must know which sources are available for loans and what particular type each lender prefers.

Loan servicing includes the record-keeping section that maintains the customers' or borrowers' accounts. Larger companies have converted much of this accounting to computerized methods for more efficient handling. One part of the records involves the escrow section, which holds the required insurance and tax deposits. Escrow personnel must maintain a continuous analysis of taxes and insurance costs for each property to assure the company that sufficient money will be available when needed to pay the taxes and insurance premiums. Another responsibility of the servicing section is to assure prompt payment of monthly accounts and to send out notifications on delinquencies and in case of a default. All lenders insist on knowing the account status and depend on the mortgage company to use diligence in keeping their accounts current. Laxity in this area could jeopardize a lender's rights in a foreclosure action.

The loan acquisition group, the division best known to outsiders, consists of the loan representatives or supervisors who make the contacts with potential borrowers, real estate agents, banks, accountants, and others in order to seek out the best loans and to handle the actual application for a loan. A loan processor usually works with one of these representatives to maintain the files and to help collect the information required on both the property and the borrower in putting together the complete loan package.

LOAN PACKAGE

Basically, a loan package is all of the data needed to properly evaluate the property and to analyze the borrower as a credit risk. It is the information assembled by the mortgage banker to substantiate a loan. The following is a list of the ordinary requirements that a loan representative would assemble in preparing a house loan package.

Information required on the property

1. Earnest money contract on the sale, which should provide proper legal names of seller and purchaser, legal description of the property, and any special terms.

2. An appraisal by a qualified person.

3. A land survey by a registered surveyor.

4. A title opinion from the title company who will issue the title insurance.

Information required on the borrower (mortgagor)

1. Information questionnaire covering legal names, address, children, employment (for both husband and wife), assets and liabilities, and income and expenses (including fixed payments).

2. Verifications of employment.

3. Verifications of assets and debts.

4. Credit report from accepted agency.

5. Letters of explanation if unusual circumstances are involved.

The mortgage company then adds to this assemblage a covering letter or a report (FHA and VA have a special analysis form). The pertinent details are summarized with an analysis of the borrower's income, subtracting calculable living expenses and installment or monthly payments already committed, to show the cash available for debt retirement. Lenders each have varying requirements as to how this analysis should be presented, and the mortgage company is expected to know precisely what is needed.

For larger loans, the same general information is required but in much greater depth. Usually this borrower is a corporation or partnership, and the loan package would require complete company information, financial statements, and corporate resolutions, if applicable. If the loan involves a project to be constructed, the package must include complete plans and specifications plus an assurance of the contractor's capability. A completion bond is required of the contractor under FHA procedures but is not always used in conventional financing. There is a growing list of certifications needed, such as the status with labor unions, nondiscrimination pledges, impact on the neighborhood statements, and new environmental requirements. Any special participation agreements required by the lender must be worked out in advance of the loan commitment.

A loan package assembled for initial closing under FHA procedure with multifamily projects includes 30 to 40 separate instruments, with all plans and data, and is often assembled under the guidance of an attorney who has specialized in such requirements and can knowledgeably represent the sponsor to the FHA and its attorneys at the closing.

MONEY COMMITMENTS

There are a number of ways for money to be promised or committed to a loan. The nomenclature for basic procedures may differ in some parts of the country, but the intent and purpose are similar and can be classed under the following categories of commitments.

Forward Loan Commitment (Sales and Servicing Contracts)

Since most mortgage bankers represent various institutional investors, some form of understanding or agreement is used to spell out the terms. Such an agreement between a lender and a mortgage company is called a "sales and servicing contract." The agreement recites the type of loan and conditions under which the lender will accept a loan, and also states the services that must be provided by the mortgage company along with the fees charged for these services.

The lender, by terms of the agreement, offers to provide a specified amount of money to the mortgage company for certain classes of loans at a fixed interest rate. The mortgage company is allowed a service charge for handling collections, providing the escrow services, paying taxes and insurance, and for representing the lender if problems occur during the transaction. This service charge, which varies from one-tenth of 1 percent to one-half of 1 percent of the loan depending on the amount of servicing required, is a direct addition (add-on) to the interest rate. For example, presuming that a lender, such as an eastern savings and loan association, agrees to accept a mortgage company's loans for an interest rate of 8½ percent and the mortgage company requires ⅜ percent for servicing the loan, then the quotation submitted by the mortgage company to the borrower would be an interest rate of 8⅞ percent. In the example above, the 8½ percent rate is referred to as *net* to the lender. The lender then sets up a time limit during which the mortgage company may exercise its rights under the commitment, which usually extends from three to six months. This type of commitment can be termed a *forward* commitment, and depending on the relationship between the mortgage company and the lender, it is not unusual for the lender to require a commitment fee.

The commitment fee, when required, is usually 1 percent (or one point) of the total commitment payable upon issuance of the agreement by the lender. Generally this fee is refundable when the commitment is fully used. However, if the mortgage company does not use the full amount of the commitment, it may be required to forfeit a portion of the fee. For example, if a mutual bank makes a $1 million commitment to the M Mortgage Company for four months and the mortgage company deposits $10,000 as a commitment fee, then if at the end of the four-month term, only $750,000 of acceptable loans have been made, the mortgage company may have to forfeit the unfulfilled portion of the fee, or $2500.

Under the forward commitment procedure, a mortgage company may be allowed to submit loans one at a time to the prime lender, but since this is a burdensome procedure, most agreements call for a minimum amount, say $250,000, in a group of loans at any one time. Unless the mortgage company has considerable capital of its own, it will resort to a warehouse line of credit with a local commercial bank to carry the loans until the minimum shipping package has been reached.

Immediate Commitments

Another method employed, and one that accounts for the greatest volume of commitment money, is the immediate or direct purchase of loans from the mortgage company by an institutional lender. Under this procedure the mortgage company funds large volumes of loans with their own capital and credit lines and periodically offers the loans in multimillion dollar blocks to the institutional investor. Immediate delivery usually means within 90 days.

A lender with surplus money to invest will tend to accept a lower net interest rate on a large block of loans where it is possible to make an immediate purchase. In this manner the lender's money is earning interest sooner. Under a forward commitment procedure, the lender may be reluctant to tie up money for future months since interest rates may change.

The large blocks of loans available by means of immediate purchase procedures are of greater interest to the big investors who must move their money in wholesale lots. Most large investors will not undertake a purchase of less than $1 million in loan totals from any single mortgage company.

Mortgage companies are generally able to retain the servicing contracts for residential loans when they are passed on to the institutional lenders regardless of the type of commitment—forward or immediate purchase. The amount of the servicing fee is determined in advance with the forward commitment but can vary somewhat with an immediate purchase commitment. With the latter, the servicing fee to be earned by the mortgage company would amount to whatever the differential is between the interest rate at which the loan was made to the borrower and the net rate acceptable to the secondary lender.

In the large commercial loans, the servicing may be passed on to the secondary lender, or a fee for this service may be negotiated with the mortgage company. Federally chartered thrift institutions and many state regulations require an authorized servicing agent of the lender to be located within 100 miles of the property mortgaged.

Future Commitments

While some of the terms used to describe the various types of money commitments are not always consistent in various parts of the country, probably the most confusing is the difference between a forward commitment and a future commitment. The *forward* commitment as described in the preceding section states a maximum amount for the commitment, then provides for the use, or withdrawal, of that money *during the term* of the commitment. The *future* commitment is a pledge of money, all of which will be made available at a *later specified date*. The future commitment may use terminology such as "on or before July 31, 19--"; or it could provide a time span such as "not before 18 months nor later than 24 months from the date of this commitment agreement." It is the future commitment that is used in making a permanent loan for a building yet to be constructed.

Delivery of the mortgage under a future commitment may, or may not, be mandatory. If delivery of the mortgage is not mandatory, the holder of the commitment may find a lower cost source of money for the permanent loan elsewhere and simply forfeit the commitment fee.

A future commitment almost always costs a nonrefundable commitment fee, which is negotiable. Normally it will be one to two points. The reason for the fee is that the lender is agreeing to have money available for a loan, perhaps one or two years from the date of commitment, and usually at a fixed rate of interest, and the lender feels entitled to a fee for this promise to deliver. As interest rates have become more volatile, future commitments are tending to be tied to a leading indicator of the capital market rather than held to a fixed rate.

It might be well to recall here that the long-term capital market fluctuates far more slowly than the short-term money market. The long-term investor is more interested in the *average* return on the total investments and thus can accept small increases and decreases in periodic new investments. The movement of rates, upward or downward, affects only a small portion of the overall portfolio at any one time. These investments over or under the average return are the *marginal* investments.

Take-out or Stand-by Commitments

A take-out or stand-by commitment is actually a back-up promise to make a loan. It is more popular in periods of tight money and can be applied to any kind of a loan on a projected building, residential property, or income property. It is a commitment that is really not intended to be utilized but is available if needed.

An example of a take-out commitment in operation would be an apartment builder wanting to build in a tight money situation. In this instance a large city may appear to be overbuilt with apartment units and with decreasing occupancy. Let us assume that the major lenders have withdrawn from further apartment loans in the entire city for the time being. However, the builder owns a piece of land in an area of the city that is growing and that shows a real need for more apartment units. In such a case the builder might seek stand-by financing in the form of a take-out commitment from a mortgage company, a real estate investment trust, or another type of lender. A take-out commitment is issued at a higher than market interest rate and lasts for a longer term than the average construction loan commitment. The builder may be allowed three to five years to exercise the rights. To obtain this type of commitment, the builder must pay from two to four points in cash at the time the commitment letter is issued. This assurance of a permanent loan, even though it is at uneconomical rates, is used as a back-up to obtain a construction loan.

The real idea of the take-out commitment is to enable a builder to proceed with the construction of a building, allowing perhaps a year to achieve good occupancy, and with a proven income, then obtain a more reasonable permanent loan and simply drop the higher cost take-out commitment. The builder would, of course, forfeit the initial commitment fee. The idea has worked well when everything clicks and the market analysis has proved accurate. It has also caused some disasters when it hasn't worked.

The idea of take-out commitments has moved into the field of house construction loans as a better protection to the construction lender than a speculative house loan. A commitment for residential house loans would be made at 80 percent of the appraised value of the finished house (usually the same amount as the construction loan itself), to be exercised within one year and at a cost of one point, payable when issued. Sometimes the mortgage company that issues the take-out will allow a portion of the commitment fee to apply on the origination fee if the mortgage company also handles the home buyer's permanent loan. Unlike a take-out commitment for a commercial project, the take-out on a house loan is used by the issuing mortgage company to help secure the *permanent* loan when the house is sold. The borrower then would be the new house buyer.

Permanent Loan

The permanent loan is the final mortgage loan with repayment extended over many years. It can be made from a future commitment or immediate. Conventional loans are made for a period of time extending to 30 years, while some federally underwritten loans extend to terms up to 40 years.

Commercial projects should have a permanent loan assured (or a valid take-out loan commitment as above), before a construction loan will be released. The construction lender wants to know how he or she will be repaid when the building is completed. Only a few builders are financially strong enough to give this assurance without a loan commitment to support them. If a builder is capable of handling the construction costs with personal resources, it is far easier to obtain permanent financing upon completion of the project when the building can be inspected and the income potential more easily ascertained. Such a strong builder would also save paying a commitment fee that would be necessary if the permanent financing is handled as a future commitment rather than immediate.

The permanent loan for a single-family residence is made to the buyer, which may be in the form of a future commitment made prior to actual construction, or more commonly, as an immediate commitment for an existing house.

WAREHOUSING OF MORTGAGE LOANS

In order to accumulate the volume of mortgages needed to satisfy a sales and service contract or to work with immediate sales of blocks of mortgage loans, the mortgagee (mortgage company) must use its own cash to make the initial funding of a loan at closing. Or, as most mortgage companies do, it borrows short-term money at a local commercial bank to provide the cash.

As mentioned in Chapter 4 on commercial banks, warehouse lines are established by mortgage companies on a fully secured basis; that is, each loan advanced by the commercial bank is secured by a note and mortgage assigned to the bank by the mortgage company.

While the credit-worthiness and capabilities of the mortgage banking company will have been fully cleared by the commercial bank before a line of credit is established, there is still a concern as to what will become of the accumulated loans as interest rates fluctuate. If the commercial bank accepts, say $1 million in home loans, which were made at an 8¼ percent interest rate, and the rate then begins to climb upward to 9 percent can the loans be sold without a loss? The answer, of course, is negative unless the loans have previously been committed, or unless the mortgage banker is willing to discount the loans, taking a substantial loss.

Under these conditions, the smaller mortgage companies seek to protect themselves and their warehouse line with a forward commitment; i.e., a sales and service contract with a major lender, or, perhaps, a FNMA commitment. As discussed earlier in this chapter, the commitment by a permanent lending source to accept a fixed amount of certain types of loans over a period of four to six months not only assures the mortgage company of its sale of loans but provides assurance to the commercial bank that the loans in warehouse will be liquidated at an established price.

It is by means of this assurance to the smaller mortgage companies, and to some of the giants, that the Federal National Mortgage Association has played such a dramatic role. If a smaller mortgage company is simply unable to find any lenders willing to furnish a forward commitment because they themselves are short of cash, the mortgage company can then turn to FNMA and acquire, for example, a $200,000 commitment under the free market system procedure by making a noncompetitive offering (see Chapter 5), and accepting the weighted average yield.

The large mortgage companies are capable of playing a different game with their warehouse lines. In the multimillion dollar business of handling large blocks of residential loans and some commercial loans, the commercial banks know that their large mortgage company customers are quite capable of selling big blocks of loans and absorbing substantial losses, if necessary, in an adverse market. Medium to large mortgage companies may have lines of credit at one or more banks totaling from $10 million to $100 million. As the mortgage company makes loans each day and places them in the warehouse line, one or more of the company's officers will be watching the secondary market and discussing possible loan sales with the larger lenders. This procedure is somewhat like a speculation game, for when the market is right the mortgage company may sell off $10 or $20 million in loans at a price that provides a slight additional profit to the mortgage company. In these large volumes, a very slight movement of loan prices has a tremendous effect on the gain (or loss) on the sale.

In view of all this shifting around of the actual note and mortgage, what happens then to the people who borrowed the money to buy a house? They are relatively unaffected and, in most cases, do not know about the movement of the note. This is because the responsibility for the proper servicing of the loan is normally held by the originator of the loan who handles the collections and escrows the necessary tax and insurance money as an agent for the holder of the note. The originator earns a service fee for this work and provides a continuity to the borrower who continues to make monthly payments to the same office.

OTHER SOURCES OF INCOME FOR MORTGAGE COMPANIES

Mortgage companies often furnish other services in addition to their mortgage loan work, and these are usually affiliated with the building industry. The more common of these activities are:

Insurance. The sale of hazard insurance is closely associated with mortgage financing and is often handled by the mortgage company or an affiliated agency.

Appraising. Most mortgage companies have qualified appraisers on their staffs as a service to both their customers and their lenders.

Real Estate Sales. Since many mortgage company loan representatives are also qualified real estate brokers, the sale of real estate is an easy step. However, this represents direct competition to some of the mortgage company's best customers—the other real estate brokers—and is not practical in many cases.

Construction. Some mortgage companies have developed very competent construction divisions and will build both residential housing and commercial buildings for their own use as investments or for sales to others.

Land Development. One of the methods used to move a step ahead of the competition is for a mortgage company to buy land for subdivision development and make the lots available to builders. In this manner the mortgage company can usually retain a first refusal look at all loans and other services that may be required in the new development.

THE FUTURE OF MORTGAGE COMPANIES

Mortgage companies have reached their present high position in the lending field by performing two principal services: (1) a service to borrowers in processing sometimes difficult loan applications and making sure the funds are available to them at closing, and (2) a service to lenders who are too large and remote to undertake processing and servicing of smaller individual loans. The method used by mortgage companies is to actively solicit loan applications through personal contact, through sales and service to the real estate industry, and through the home buyers. But the key to their continuing success lies more in their ability to find lenders willing to work with them and to provide the money for the loans, rather than on their proven sales ability. In periods of tight money, the smaller mortgage company can easily find itself short of funds and dependent on the higher cost sources, which could be mainly the Federal National Mortgage Association. As savings associations continue to grow and spread through their branches into the smaller communities, some have become more aggressive and sales-minded in their approach to lending. The increase in activity of the secondary market and the growing acceptance by savings associations of selling some of their loans have fostered an increase in competition. Mortgage companies without direct affiliation to actual sources of money will find it increasingly hard to compete in a fluctuating market. Many have recognized the trend and are broadening their field of activities into other related businesses, and/or are taking steps to acquire, or be acquired by, a bank, a bank holding corporation, or a savings association.

QUESTIONS FOR DISCUSSION

1. What does the FHA require in the way of qualifications in order for a mortgage lender to receive an approved mortgagee certificate?

2. Name the three basic divisions of operations in a mortgage company and describe what each does.

3. Describe a loan package as assembled by a mortgage company, including what information it must contain.

4. Does your state have any statutes or agencies regulating the mortgage banking industry? If so, how do they function?

5. Describe a forward commitment for money and how it is used by a mortgage company.

6. Define a service fee, and a commitment fee.

7. What are the advantages of an immediate money commitment over a forward commitment for the mortgage company? For the institutional lender?

8. Describe a take-out commitment.

9. For what reasons would a mortgage company borrow money from a commercial bank on a warehouse line of credit?

Chapter 7

Federal Government Programs

FEDERAL HOUSING ADMINISTRATION
(HUD INSURING OFFICE)

The Federal Housing Administration was one of several score agencies spawned during the Depression to help resolve the economic problems that plagued this nation. It is one of the very few that has survived, and it has proved its value over four decades of operation.

The reasons for which the FHA was formed in 1934 are still valid today, although the area of operations has expanded tremendously from the initial assistance program for home buyers. The purposes for the FHA are (1) to encourage wider home ownership; (2) to improve housing standards; and (3) to create a better method of financing mortgage loans. All of these aims have been realized, even beyond original hopes. This was done without making a single loan, simply by sound use of government credit to insure mortgage loans. From its initial widespread rejection by many private lenders, a government-insured commitment now is readily salable to a large number of investors. Even in the tight money market from 1968 to 1970, there was always funding available for a government-insured loan.

When the FHA stepped into the housing picture in 1934, houses had been financed for 50 to 60 percent of their sales price on a first mortgage of three to five years, with a second mortgage and even a third mortgage at increasingly higher interest rates. By offering to insure a single large loan up to 80 percent of value (an extremely high ratio in those days), the FHA was able to insist that the down payment be made in cash, permit no secondary financing, and command a moderate interest rate. The loans were for long terms—up to 20 years at first—and were fully amortized over the life of the loan. Equal monthly payments were charged for principal and interest. Escrow accounts were established for hazard insurance and for taxes, to collect one-twelfth of the yearly cost each month. Each of these monthly payments also included a fee of ½ percent of the unpaid balance annually to cover the cost of mortgage default insurance. Most of these features were later incorporated into the loan guarantee program of the Veterans Administration and have now become normal procedure for conventional loans as well. While none of these ideas actually originated with the FHA, this agency gave them wide usage for the first time and thus brought about a sweeping reform in the field of residential financing.

Over the years, modifications have been made in the mortgage amounts that may be insured, both by the introduction of new programs and by raising the limits on existing programs. Changes in the down payment requirements have the most immediate effect on home buyers in the low- and middle-income brackets with limited cash reserves. On the widely used Section 203 program, the down payment of 3 percent in cash is still adhered to. In 1963 it applied to the first $15,000 of house cost and now applies to the first $25,000. On the next $10,000 of value, the buyer must pay 10 percent down, plus 20 percent of any amount over $35,000 to the maximum permitted. On a single-family residence, the maximum insured commitment that can be issued is $45,000. In calculating the cash requirements, HUD/FHA uses their own appraisal for the value of the property *plus* closing costs (does not include prepaid items) to arrive at the total value for the property.

The following is an example of a down payment calculation for a house with an appraised value of $41,250 plus closing costs of $750 for a total property value of $42,000:

3% of first $25,000	750
10% of next $10,000	1,000
20% of balance ($7,000)	1,400
Total down payment	3,150

Other features have been added to the basic programs. The term of the loan commitment is 75 percent of the remaining useful life of the property to a present maximum of 30 years. In certain instances, a 35-year commitment can be approved if the house was constructed under HUD/FHA inspection procedures. A special program under Section 203 allows an eligible veteran (90 days or more of active duty) to make no down payment on the first $25,000 of property value, pay 10 percent on the next $10,000, and 15 percent on all over that to the maximum permitted commitment of $45,000. However the veteran must pay a minimum of $200 in cash which may apply to closing costs and prepaid items.

The authority to specify maximum permissible interest rates for an insured loan has been granted to the Secretary of Housing and Urban Development. Adjustments are made in the published rate periodically to maintain a reasonable relationship with market interest rates on conventional loans. The workings of the free market further adjust this published rate to a competitive yield through a discount on the loan.

As the FHA gained strength in its housing assistance, more titles and sections were added to its program. While the FHA has over 50 different programs to offer in its portfolio of assistance to home loans, improvement loans, and multi-family project loans, our concern is primarily with loans for single-family residences. Under the assistance programs for home loans, the FHA has special help for servicemen, civilian employees of the armed services, and disaster victims, as well as programs in experimental housing, urban renewal, and condominium housing. Our text will be directed at the most popular of these programs, which are as follows:

1. Title II, Section 203(b)—Home Mortgage Insurance

2. Title II, Section 221(d)(2)—Home Mortgage Insurance for Low and Moderate Income

All programs are implemented by the issuance of a Certificate of Insurance, which protects the lender against default. The differences between the programs are based on the qualifications of the individual who needs the help. There may be lower cash requirements and, in certain programs, an actual subsidy of interest costs. Also, the property must meet certain parameters to qualify for an insured commitment.

Until several years ago, the FHA had been required to analyze each loan on the basis of its economic feasibility and to limit its insured commitments to only those families who presented a reasonable credit risk. The care with which the FHA has exercised its authority over the years is indicated by the fact that it has, in the past, returned over two-thirds of its insurance fees to the Federal Treasury.

In the past few years Congress has seen fit to recognize a growing social need for housing and has introduced a number of new programs through the HUD/FHA which are based not only on economic feasibility but also on a family's need for housing. This country has long supported various types of public housing built by government agencies and rented to lower income families for well-below market rents. Public housing of this sort has not worked out very successfully, and in 1965 Congress altered the direction of the program to place the problem in the hands of private business. Money previously allocated to support public housing was now to be used to subsidize private developers with the expectation that they could do a more effective and efficient job. The programs to activate these social objectives have been channeled through the FHA with the first funding for such a project as far back as 1966.

In January 1973, the Secretary of HUD announced a suspension of all government-subsidized housing programs pending a reevaluation. Abuses and profiteering had been uncovered in some areas, and the Nixon administration felt a better method of giving assistance might be found. Meanwhile, a reduction in spending would be more helpful.

By January 1976, housing shortages and high costs continued to plague the home buyer and President Ford ordered the release of the remaining assistance money that had been impounded three years earlier. The original Section 235 interest subsidy program for home buyers was re-activated, but in a substantially different form. The maximum amount insurable was raised from $21,000 to $29,000 (increased to $33,000 in high-cost areas) but the down payment requirements were raised from a few hundred dollars to 6 percent of the property value. The interest subsidy that did provide government payment of interest costs on the mortgage payment *in excess* of 1 percent has been increased to 5 percent. As in the earlier program requirements, prospective home buyers must qualify for the assistance by showing incomes of roughly 80 percent or less of the median family income for that region of the country. The much higher cash requirement should prevent the high foreclosure rates that marred the earlier program, but it also prevents the program from being of much practical value—few buyers with the lower income needed to qualify will have the cash available to make the down payment.

Program Details

Section 203(b)—Home Mortgage Insurance

Home mortgage insurance under Section 203(b) is the oldest and still the basic program with which HUD/FHA determines qualifications for insured commitments. This insurance can cover one- to four-family residences. The limit on the insurable amount is $45,000 for a one-family unit, $48,750 for two- or three-family units, and $56,000 for a four-family unit. If the buyer does not intend to live in the house, the maximum insurable amount is reduced to 85 percent of that available to an owner-occupant.

The amount of down payment required is 3 percent on the first $25,000 of the HUD/FHA estimate of property value and closing costs, 10 percent on the next $10,000, and 20 percent on any value over $35,000 up to maximum limits. If the buyer is a veteran, and this applies to a single-family unit only, then the down payment is reduced to zero for the first $25,000 of value, 10 percent for the next $10,000, and 15 percent for values over $35,000. The veteran must pay a minimum of $200 in closing costs and prepaid items.

The term of the loan is 30 years or three-quarters of the remaining economic life of the house as determined by the FHA appraiser, whichever is less. The 30-year term can be extended to 35 years if the mortgagor cannot qualify for 30-year term and if the property was constructed subject to FHA or VA inspection. Lesser terms down to 10 years can also be insured.

As an additional help to a buyer 60 years or older, the FHA permits borrowing of the down payment, settlement costs, and prepaid expenses from an approved corporation or individual. Under that age the buyer is expressly forbidden to borrow any of the cash requirements, as this would be considered secondary financing and cause for denial of insurance.

There are additional limitations on mortgage insurance for houses that are not constructed under HUD/FHA inspection procedures. For a house that was started without HUD/FHA inspection and is less than one year old, the mortgage limit is reduced to 90 percent of the first $35,000 of value plus 80 percent (85 percent for veterans) of value above $35,000. If the purchase is an existing house and needs refinancing, the HUD/FHA-insured mortgage can be no more than the greater of the following:

1. Eighty-five percent of the amount that can be insured when the borrower is buying or building a home to live in.

2. The sum of the unpaid balance of the old mortgage and the costs for any repairs or improvements and for obtaining the loan.

In calculating the maximum mortgage amount that HUD/FHA will insure, it is (1) the HUD/FHA appraised value of the property plus closing costs; or (2) acquisition cost; whichever is less. If the purchase price is higher than the HUD/FHA estimate of value plus closing costs, then the home buyer must pay the difference in cash. If the purchase price is lower than this amount, the mortgage limit is based on the acquisition cost rather than on the estimate of value plus closing costs.

Section 221(d)(2)—Home Mortgage Insurance for Low and Moderate Income

This program is a modification of the same basic 203(b) plan with the exception of the cash requirements for closing. It also carries lower maximum loan limits. The requirements are intended as an additional assist in obtaining suitable housing for displaced families and for low- and moderate-income families. The maximum amount insurable is limited to $21,600 on a single-family house, or $25,200 if the house has four bedrooms and the family consists of five or more persons. There are other limits for two-, three-, and four-family units as well as higher limits in areas where cost levels require it.

The insured mortgage can equal 97 percent of the property value. The difference between this program and the 203(b) is that closing costs *and* prepaid items are added to the estimate of value to make the total property value under 221(d)(2). Stated another way, a low- or moderate-income family must make a down payment of at least 3 percent of acquisition cost which amount can be applied to closing costs and prepaid items. If the buyer is a displaced family, the insured mortgage can equal the full value of the property. However, a displaced family must make a down payment of at least $200 in cash, which can be applied to closing costs and prepaid items. (The difference between closing costs and prepaid items is discussed in detail in Chapter 14.)

The net effect of the 221 (d) (2) program would be to reduce the cash requirements for a $25,000 house, for example, as follows:

Where cost of property is:

Estimate of value	24,200
Closing costs	300
Prepaid items	500
	25,000

Item	203(b)	221(d)(2)
Total property value	24,500	25,000 (includes prepays)
Insured commitment 97%	23,765	24,250
Down payment required 3%	735	750
Prepaid items	500	Included
Total cash required to close	1,235	750

In the above example, if the buyer is a displaced family, the insured commitment would be 100 percent, reduced by the mandatory $200 cash requirement, or in the amount of $24,800.

HUD/FHA Loan Analysis

The reasoning used by HUD/FHA in processing a loan is of greater importance to the student of loan analysis than the specifics of various programs. The programs rise and fall, depending about as much on the rules by which the law is implemented, as on the intent of Congress in passing the law. But the processing procedures have remained fairly constant with occasional modifications to stay current with changing conditions and the inflationary economy.

The process starts with the loan application. In this case it is a combination form covering the application for a loan and the application for mortgage insurance. The title is a lengthy one—"Mortgagee's Application for Mortgagor Approval and Commitment for Mortgage Insurance Under the National Housing Act." It immediately indicates several things. The loan applicant does not make the application—it is the lender, the mortgagee, who prepares the application asking HUD/FHA for approval of the borrower and to commit for mortgage insurance on the loan. This is one of the services gladly handled by mortgage companies or any other lender who has qualified with the FHA as a mortgagee. The mortgagee further carries the responsibility of verifying employment and bank deposits of the borrower. The loan application form is designated by No. 2900.

When the home buyer meets with the lender to answer questions necessary for completion of Form 2900, the mortgagee also starts the processing of the Form 2800 which is the "Mortgagee's Application for Property Appraisal." Again the ball is carried by the lender, not HUD/FHA.

The chronological order for an FHA loan commitment would be as follows:

1. Mortgagee prepares Form 2900 from interviews with home buyer-loan applicant. Information submitted by applicant is verified by mortgagee.

Completed form and supporting data are sent to the HUD/FHA mortgage credit examiner. A case number is assigned.

2. Form 2800 is completed by the mortgagee from information submitted by the applicant and sent to the HUD/FHA appraisal section. A staff appraiser is assigned to the case and makes an evaluation of the house to be purchased.

3. When all information has been assembled, the file is examined by an FHA underwriter. If further information is needed, it is normally requested through the mortgagee. If the applicant is approved, a Firm Commitment is issued.

HUD/FHA Form 2900 for Mortgagor Approval

Much can be learned of the detail required for an FHA application by reading the form illustrated in Figure 7-1 which is the first page of the multi-sheet Form 2900. There is a work sheet and instructions on the cover sheet of the form for preliminary work. Page 2900-1 calls for the essential information needed to analyze the borrower—assets, liabilities, employment, and monthly income. On the right-hand side of the form, the mortgagee would list for the borrower the settlement requirements, which is the amount of cash that will be needed to close the loan. Then future monthly payments are recorded to determine how much of the applicant's income will be needed for the housing costs. The blocks for previous monthly housing expense and monthly fixed charges are mostly for comparison purposes. Both mortgagor and mortgagee must sign the certification for each at the bottom of the form. This is the information furnished by the applicant in conjunction with the mortgagee. Now turn to the next form, which is the all important 2900-2, Credit Analysis Page. (Figure 7-2).

It is on the credit analysis page that the FHA processor inserts their figures for comparisons. Note the three extra sets of blanks on 2900-2 under monthly income, settlement requirements, and future monthly payments. The reasoning used by the FHA processor is well established and has been developed from a wealth of underwriting experience. The information submitted by the mortgagee and loan applicant is adjusted by the FHA loan processor to follow their own guidelines. It is the lack of understanding on these changes made by the FHA that causes much of the disagreement when an applicant must be rejected. The recalculation applies to #11 (effective income), #12 (settlement requirements), and #13 (future monthly payments), with the FHA guidelines for each detailed below.

Form Approved
OMB No 63—R1062

U. S. DEPARTMENT OF HOUSING AND URBAN DEVELOPMENT FEDERAL HOUSING ADMINISTRATION	2. FHA Case No.

1.

MORTGAGEE'S APPLICATION FOR MORTGAGOR APPROVAL AND COMMITMENT FOR MORTGAGE INSURANCE UNDER THE NATIONAL HOUSING ACT

☐ SEC. 203(b) ☐ SEC.
(NOTE: See reverse for Privacy Act Statement)

5. MORTGAGEE - Name, Address & Zip Code   *(Please Type)*

(Please locate address within corner marks)

3. PROPERTY ADDRESS

4. MORTGAGORS:

Mtgor. _____ Sex _____ Age _____

Co-Mtgor. _____ Sex _____ Age _____

Address _____

Married	Yrs.	No. of Dependents	Ages

Co-Mortgagor(s)		Sex	Age(s)

(Check One)
☐ White *(Non-Minority)* ☐ American Indian ☐ Spanish American
☐ Negro/Black ☐ Oriental ☐ Other Minority

6. MORTGAGE APPLIED FOR ➔

	Mortgage Amount	*Interest Rate	No. of Months	Monthly Payment Principal & Interest
	$	%		$

7. PURPOSE OF LOAN: ···
MORTGAGOR WILL BE:

☐ Finance Constr. on Own Land ☐ Finance Purchase ☐ Refinance Exist. Loan ☐ Finance Impr. to Exist. Prop. ☐ Other

☐ Occupant ☐ Landlord ☐ Builder ☐ Escrow Commit. Mortgagor

8.   ASSETS

Cash accounts _____ $ _____

Marketable securities _____

Other (explain) _____

OTHER ASSETS   (A) TOTAL $ _____

Cash deposit on purchase .... _____

Other (explain) _____

(B) TOTAL $ _____

9.   LIABILITIES   Monthly Payt.   Unpd. Bal.

Automobile .... $ _____ $ _____

Debts, other Real Estate. .... _____ _____

Life Insurance Loans .... _____ _____

Notes payable .... _____ _____

Credit Union .... _____ _____

Retail accounts .... _____ _____

NAME   ACCOUNT NO. _____ _____

If more space is needed, attach schedule.   **TOTAL** $ _____ $ _____

10.   EMPLOYMENT

Mortgagor's occupation _____

Employer's name & address _____

_____ years employed _____

Co-Mtgor. occupation _____

Employer's name & address _____

_____ years employed _____

11.   MONTHLY INCOME

Mortgagor's base pay .... $ _____

Other Earnings (explain) .... _____

Co-Mtgor. base pay .... _____

Other Earnings (explain) .... _____

Gross Income, Real Estate .... _____

Other (explain) .... _____

TOTAL $ _____

12.   SETTLEMENT REQUIREMENTS

(a) Existing debt (Refinancing only) .... $ _____

(b) Sale price (Realty only) .... _____

(c) Repairs & Improvements .... _____

(d) Closing Costs. .... _____

(e) **TOTAL** (a+b+c+d) Acquisition cost .... _____

(f) Mortgage amount. .... _____

(g) Mortgagor's required investment(e—f) .... _____

(h) Prepayable expenses .... _____

(i) Non-realty & other items .... _____

(j) **TOTAL REQUIREMENTS** (g+h+i) .... _____

(k) Amt.pd. ☐ cash ☐ Other (explain) ········ _____

(l) Amt. to be pd. ☐ cash ☐ Other (explain) ······· _____

(m) Tot. assets available for closing (8) (A) ········ $ _____

13.   FUTURE MONTHLY PAYMENTS

(a) Principal & Interest ·············· $ _____

(b) FHA Mortgage Insurance Premium ············ _____

(c) Ground rent (Leasehold only) ············· _____

(d) **TOTAL DEBT SERVICE** (a+b+c) ············· _____

(e) Hazard Insurance ···················· _____

(f) Taxes, special assessments ················ _____

(g) **TOTAL MTG. PAYT.** (d+e+f) ············· _____

(h) Maintenance & Common Expense ············· _____

(i) Heat & utilities ···················· _____

(j) **TOTAL HSG. EXPENSE** (g+h+i) ············· _____

(k) Other recurring charges (explain) ············ _____

(l) **TOTAL FIXED PAYT.** (j + k) ············· $ _____

14.   PREVIOUS MONTHLY HOUSING EXPENSE

Mortgage payment or rent .... $ _____

Hazard Insurance .... _____

Taxes, special assessments .... _____

Maintenance .... _____

Heat & Utilities .... _____

Other (explain) .... _____

TOTAL $ _____

15.   PREVIOUS MONTHLY FIXED CHARGES

Federal, State & Local income taxes .... $ _____

Prem. for $ _____ Life Insurance. .... _____

Social Security & Retirement Payments .... _____

Installment account payments .... _____

Operating Expenses, other Real Estate .... _____

Other (explain) .... _____

TOTAL $ _____

16. Do you own other Real Estate ☐ Yes ☐ No   Is it to be sold ☐ Yes ☐ No   FHA mortgage ☐ Yes ☐ No   Sales Price $ _____   Orig-Mtg. Amt. $ _____

Unpaid Bal. $ _____   Address _____   Lender _____

17. MORTGAGOR'S CERTIFICATE -- I ☐ have ☐ have not received a copy of the FHA Statement of Value (FHA Form 2800-6) or Veterans Administration Certificate of Reasonable Value (VA Form 26-1843) showing the estimated value of the property described in this application. Have you sold a property within the last year which had an FHA mortgage? ☐ Yes ☐ No. If "Yes" was the mortgage paid in full? ☐ Yes ☐ No. If "No" give FHA Case Number _____, buyer's name _____, property address _____, date of transfer _____, 19 _____, lender's name and address _____ original mortgage amount $ _____ unpaid balance when sold $ _____. Did buyer intend to occupy ? ☐ Yes ☐ No. Have you ever been obligated on a home loan, home improvement loan or a mobile home which resulted in foreclosure, transfer of title in lieu of foreclosure, or judgement? ☐ Yes ☐ No. If "Yes" attach statement giving full details including date, property address, name and address of lender, FHA or VA Case Number, if any, and reasons for the action. If dwelling to be covered by this mortgage is to be rented, is it a part of, adjacent or contiguous to any project, subdivision, or group of rental properties involving eight or more dwelling units in which you have any financial interest? ☐ Yes ☐ No. Not to be rented. If "Yes" give details. Do you own four or more dwelling units with mortgages insured under any title of the National Housing Act? ☐ Yes ☐ No. If "Yes" submit FHA Form 2561. The Mortgagor certifies that all information in this application is given for the purpose of obtaining a loan to be insured under the National Housing Act and is true and complete to the best of his knowledge and belief. Verification may be obtained from any source named herein. *NOTE: The interest rate shown in item 6 is the FHA-VA maximum rate in effect on the date of this commitment and may increase prior to closing unless buyer and lender agree otherwise.

Signature(s) _____ Date _____ 19 _____

18. MORTGAGEE'S CERTIFICATE -The mortgagee certifies that all information in this application is true and complete to the best of its knowledge and belief. Signature _____

Date: _____ 19 _____

FHA FORM NO: 2900-1 Rev. 2/76

FHA COPY — FILE IN CASE BINDER

FIGURE 7-1.

Form Approved
OMB No. 63—R1062

U. S. DEPARTMENT OF HOUSING AND URBAN DEVELOPMENT FEDERAL HOUSING ADMINISTRATION	2. FHA Case No. ▲

1. SPECIAL PROCESSING ▲

1. ☐ Veteran 2. ☐ Assistance Payment 4. ☐ _____

CREDIT ANALYSIS PAGE
MORTGAGE TO BE INSURED UNDER
☐ SEC. 203(b) ☐ SEC.

3

3. PROPERTY ADDRESS

4. MORTGAGORS:

Sex ▲ _____
Mtgor. _____ Age ▲ _____
Co-Mtgor. _____ Sex ▲ _____ Age ▲ _____
Address _____

Married ▲ Yrs.	No. of Dependents ▲	Ages

Co-Mortgagor(s) _____ Sex _____ Age(s) _____

▲ *(Check One)*
1 ☐ White *(Non-Minority)* 3 ☐ American Indian 5 ☐ Spanish American
2 ☐ Negro/Black 4 ☐ Oriental 6 ☐ Other Minority

5.

6. MORTGAGE APPLIED FOR →	Mortgage Amount $	Interest Rate %	No. of Months	Monthly Payment Principal & Interest $

7. PURPOSE OF LOAN: ▲

Finance Constr. ☐ on Own Land	Finance ☐ Purchase	Refinance ☐ Exist. Loan	Finance Impr. ☐ to Exist. Prop.	☐ Other

MORTGAGOR WILL BE: ▲ ☐ Occupant ☐ Landlord ☐ Builder ☐ Escrow Commit. Mortgagor

8. ASSETS

Cash accounts _____ $ _____
_____ _____
Marketable securities _____ _____
Other (explain) _____ _____
OTHER ASSETS (A) TOTAL ▲ $ _____
Cash deposit on purchase . . . . _____
Other (explain) _____ _____
_____ _____
_____ _____
(B) TOTAL $ _____

9. LIABILITIES

	Monthly Payt.	Unpd. Bal.
Automobile	$ _____	$ _____
Debts, other Real Estate	_____	_____
Life Insurance Loans	_____	_____
Notes payable	_____	_____
Credit Union	_____	_____
Retail accounts	_____	_____

NAME _____ ACCOUNT NO _____
_____ _____ _____
_____ _____ _____
(If additional space needed, attach schedule) **TOTAL** $ _____ ▲$ _____

10. EMPLOYMENT

Mortgagor's occupation _____
Employer's name & address _____
_____ years employed _____
Co-Mtgor. occupation _____
Employer's name & address _____
_____ years employed _____

11. MONTHLY INCOME

EFFECTIVE INCOME **MONTHLY INCOME**
▲$ _____ . . . . . . Mortgagor's base pay . . . . ▲$ _____
_____ . . . . Other Earnings . . . _____
▲ _____ . . . . . . Co-Mortgagor's base pay · · · ▲ _____
_____ . . . . . Other Earnings . . . _____
_____ . . . Income, other Real Estate . . . . . _____
_____ . . . . Other . . . _____
▲ _____ . . . . **TOTAL** . . . . ▲$ _____
_____ Less Federal Income Tax . . . . .
▲$ _____ **NET EFFECTIVE INCOME**

12. SETTLEMENT REQUIREMENTS

(a) Existing debt (Refinancing only) . . . $ _____ $ _____
(b) Sale price (Realty only) . . . . _____ ▲ _____
(c) Repairs & Improvements . . . . _____ _____
(d) Closing Costs . . . . _____ ▲ _____
(e) **TOTAL** (a+b+c+d) Acquisition cost _____ ▲ _____
(f) Mortgage amount . . . . _____
(g) Mortgagor's required investment(e—f) . _____
(h) Prepayable expenses . . . . _____
(i) Non-realty & other items · · · · · · · · _____
(j) **TOTAL REQUIREMENTS** (g+h+i) . . . _____ _____
(k) Amt.pd. ☐ cash ☐ Other (explain) . _____ _____
(l) Amt. to be pd. ☐ cash ☐ Other (explain) _____
(m) Tot. assets available for closing (B) (A) . $ _____ $ _____

13. FUTURE MONTHLY PAYMENTS

(a) Principal & Interest . . . . $ _____ $ _____
(b) FHA Mortgage Insurance Premium · · · · _____
(c) Ground rent (Leasehold only) . . . . . . _____
(d) **TOTAL DEBT SERVICE** (a+b+c) . . . . _____ _____
(e) Hazard Insurance . . . . _____
(f) Taxes, special assessments . . . . _____ ▲ _____
(g) **TOTAL MTG. PAYT.** (d+e+f) . . . . . _____ ▲ _____
(h) Maintenance & Common Expense · · · · · _____ ▲ _____
(i) Heat & utilities . . . . _____
(j) **TOTAL HSG. EXPENSE** (g+h+i) . . . . _____ ▲ _____
(k) Other recurring charges (explain) . . . . . _____
(l) **TOTAL FIXED PAYT.** (j + k) . . . . . . $ _____ ▲$ _____

14. PREVIOUS MONTHLY HOUSING EXPENSE

Mortgage payment or rent . . . . $ _____
Hazard Insurance . . . . _____
Taxes, special assessments . . . . _____
Maintenance . . . . _____
Heat & Utilities . . . . _____
Other (explain) . . . . _____
TOTAL ▲$ _____

15. PREVIOUS MONTHLY FIXED CHARGES

Federal, State & Local income taxes . . . . $ _____
Prem. for $ _____ Life Insurance . . . . _____
Social Security & Retirement Payments . . . . _____
Installment account payments . . . . _____
Operating Expenses, other Real Estate . . . . _____
Other (explain) . . . . _____
TOTAL $ _____

16. Do you own other Real Estate ☐ Yes ☐ No Is it to be sold ☐ Yes ☐ No FHA mortgage ☐ Yes ☐ No Sales Price $ _____ Orig-Mtg. Amt $ _____
Unpaid Bal. $ _____ Address _____ Lender _____

17 RATIOS: Loan to Value _____ % Term to Remain. Econ. Life _____ % Total Payt. to Rental Value _____ % Debt. Serv. to Rent Inc _____ %

18. MORTGAGOR RATING

Credit Characteristics _____ Motivating Interest in Ownership _____ Importance of Monetary Interest _____
Adequacy of Available Assets _____ Stability of Effective Income _____ Adequacy of Effective Income _____

Remarks:

☐ Head of Household
Ratio of net effective income to:

Housing Expense _____ %

Total Fixed Payment _____ %

Examiner: _____ Reviewer: _____ Date: _____ 19

FHA FORM NO. 2900-2 Rev. 2/76 FHA COPY - FILE IN CASE BINDER

FIGURE 7-2.

Effective Income (2900-2 #11).   By the FHA rules, the mortgagor's effective income is the estimated amount of the mortgagor's earning capacity that is likely to prevail during the early period of the mortgage risk, that being approximately the first five years of the term of the loan. Although the income reported is confirmed, there may be reasons why the total amount cannot logically be considered a sound basis for future house payments. When the income is temporary in character, or is not of an assured nature, such as child support, the FHA must reduce the stated income in its own analysis. Also, the FHA deducts its estimate of federal income taxes to arrive at its own figure of net effective income.

This estimate of effective income does not attempt to evaluate the possibility of future decrease in income due to weakness of an employer or type of employment—that factor is rated under item #18 (stability of effective income).

More and more wives are taking jobs to help the family improve its standard of living, and in the lower income groups this becomes almost a necessity. A woman's income must now meet the same standards as that of a man and is given identical consideration in the calculation of effective income.

When the co-borrower's income is established by length of employment and/or placement in a particular position for which he or she has had special training, the income is fully allowed. If the continuity of a part of the co-borrower's income appears questionable and cannot be allowed, it is possible in some cases to consider that income as an offset to temporary nonrecurring obligations.

The FHA approaches other than base salary income in about the same way as do conventional lenders; i.e., overtime is not acceptable income unless supported by long experience with a reasonable expectation to continue; and commission or fee types of income are acceptable for an amount that can be stabilized over a longer period of time than would ordinarily be required. An owner of a business would be allowed the amount he or she withdraws as salary, providing this amount does not exceed actual earnings.

Money received for travel expenses cannot be considered as effective income, nor can contributions received, nor the payments received on principal in repayment of a capital investment. And in calculating Federal Income Tax, the FHA bases its estimate on the *effective* income rather than on the current income.

Settlement Requirements (2900-2 #12).   Each application must have an estimate of the net amount of cash needed to close the transaction. Basically, this is the difference between the sales price plus closing costs and the earnest money plus mortgage proceeds. As shown in Form 2900-2, the FHA reserves a separate column for its own calculations.

The sales price would be determined by the sales contract. If the seller agrees to pay any closing costs normally paid by the buyer, and if any nonrealty items such as furniture or a television set are included in the contract sales price, then these would be deducted to determine the actual sales price. The FHA does not insure loans on nonrealty items.

Repairs and improvements, #12(c), include the cost of any repairs or improvements proposed by the mortgagor plus the estimated costs of any additional repairs called for in the appraisal requirements to bring the property up to acceptable standards.

Under closing costs, #12(d), are included the items incidental to the acquisition and financing of the property. These would include the FHA examination fee, the mortgagee's initial service charge, the cost of mortgagee's title policy, charges for preparation of the mortgage documents, recording fees, and similar items. Closing costs do not include the prepaid items, which are the tax and insurance deposits.

The prepayable expenses, #12(h), are the deposits to cover unaccrued taxes, hazard insurance, and mortgage insurance. These are not considered part of the acquisition costs but must be included to determine the adequacy of available assets for settlement. The FHA requires deposits in the amount of two months of the yearly costs incurred. In the case of maintenance fees that are assessed on an annual basis, these too must be included in the prepaid deposits and collected monthly. This practice is becoming more common in the buying of townhouses.

Item #12(i), nonrealty and other items, is where the value of any furniture, appliances, etc., is added back in to show the actual total requirements needed for settlement. The mortgage amount, item #12(f), is calculated on the value of the realty only.

Items #12(k) and #12(l) reflect the amount of money or other value (such as a lot traded) already paid by the mortgagor and the amount to be paid at closing. For item #12(m), the amount shown from item #8(a), other assets, is entered and used to determine adequacy in meeting the cash requirements. The so-called "sweat equity," the cost of actual work done on the property by the mortgagor, is acceptable to apply against closing costs, prepayment, or down payment, if it is reasonably valued.

In reviewing the credit analysis thus far, the settlement requirements must be met in full without resort to any secondary borrowing. If a recent loan appears in the record with the loan proceeds held in a bank account for obvious settlement purposes, the applicant can be rejected.

Future Monthly Payments (2900-2 #13). The monthly payments for debt service, taxes, and insurance are added to reach the total mortgage payment (item #13(g)). To this total is added the anticipated maintenance and the heat and utilities (items #13(h) and (i)). These amounts are estimated by the FHA appraiser and reported in the Form 2800 valuation report returned to the mortgagee. Item #13(k) for other recurring charges includes such items as premiums on life insurance, compulsory contributions to retirement funds, payments on other loans or on real estate (that is, property not to be sold as a part of this transaction), and payments on installment accounts. The last item is not included if the debt is of a nonrecurring nature and will be paid off in less than a year. Car payments for someone who uses the car in his or her work would be considered a recurring payment.

On the income versus monthly payments relationship, the FHA has a general rule that the total fixed obligations, item #13(1), should not exceed 50 percent of the net effective income (that is, FHA's calculated effective income); or the total housing expense, item #13(j), should not exceed 35 percent of the net effective income. As in many of these rules, this too is a guideline. If other factors of credit, such as assets available, manner of living, etc., add strength to the borrower, he or she still could be approved.

Mortgagor Rating (2900-2 #18). The final guide to acceptance or rejection of the applicant is contained in the mortgagor rating. After an extensive review of the many variables involved, the FHA underwriter makes an evaluation of the mortgagor risk. The examination may include questions directed to the mortgagee or to the applicant. The study covers six features;

1. Credit characteristics
2. Motivating interest in ownership
3. Importance of monetary interest
4. Adequacy of available assets
5. Stability of effective income
6. Adequacy of effective income

Formerly, the underwriter made an evaluation of these six features on a five point gradient scale from excellent to reject. Now there are only two grades—acceptable, or rejection. A rejection on any one of the features is cause for denial of the loan commitment.

HUD/FHA Form 2800—For Property Appraisal

At the same time that the application is taken for mortgagor approval (Form 2900), a request is prepared for an appraisal of the property to be purchased. This is another multi-sheet form, No. 2800, which is completed by the HUD/FHA appraiser. The appraiser may be a full-time employee of the FHA as a member of the staff, or may be an independent appraiser employed for the job for a fee. A substantial amount of property information is called for in the form report. The third copy of this report, identified as the FHA Underwriting Report, No. 2800-3, is reproduced in Figure 7-3.

The appraiser's opinion of property value is the key to the amount of the insured loan commitment. However, if the property is sold for less than the appraised value, then the insured commitment is based on the lesser amount. In addition to estimating the property value, the appraiser makes another essential estimate—the monthly expenses that will be incurred in using the house. This report is in Item 7 and includes insurance, taxes, maintenance and repairs, utilities, and any property assessments for condominium-type maintenance. The appraiser's expense estimates are the figures used in calculating the future monthly payments for the mortgagor (Form 2900, item 13).

Another important estimate that is made by the appraiser is that of the condition of the property and the need for repairs. Prior to 1972, the general policy was to report needed repairs as a requirement which must be met for the property to become eligible for mortgage insurance. Some abuses developed in a few areas of the country and in 1972 a system of certifications was introduced into the underwriting procedures. Certain parts of an existing house and its equipment were required to be inspected by licensed specialists and formal certification of their condition became a part of the appraisal procedure. The areas requiring certification are:

1. Plumbing

2. Heating and air conditioning

3. Electrical

4. Roofing

Form Approved
OMB No. 63-R1366

FHA UNDERWRITING REPORT

1. FHA MORTGAGEE NO.

2. FHA CASE ▲ NO.

3. NEIGHBORHOOD CODE
▲1.□ 2.□ 4.□ ▲1.□ 2.□ 4.□ ▲1.□ 2.□ 4.□ ▲1.□ 2.□ 4.□
Core City Other City Sub-urban Model City Peri. of MC Rural URA Code Enf. Blighted

4. ▲ PROPERTY ADDRESS   CENSUS TRACT

MORTGAGE TO BE INSURED UNDER
□ SEC. 203(b) □ SEC. _____

3

LEGAL-LOT ___ BLK. ___ TR./SUBD.

5. MORTGAGEE

6 ESTIMATED VALUE OF PROPERTY .... $_____

8. COMMITTED FOR INSURANCE

COMMITMENT
Issued: _____ 19
Expires: _____ 19

7. MONTHLY EXPENSE ESTIMATE
Fire Ins. ...... $_____
Taxes .... $_____
Condo. Com. Exp $_____
Main & Repairs $_____
Heat & Utilities $_____

9. ESTIMATED CLOSING COST .... $_____

10. COMMITMENT TERMS MAX. MORT. AMT. $_____ NO. MOS _____ MAX. INTEREST _____ %

11. □ EXISTING □ PROPOSED

12. ▲ EXISTING HOUSE 4.□ Name of Occupant (or person to call if unoccupied) Tel. No. Key Encl. □ (If unfurnished)
Mon. & Yr. Completed ▲ _____ □ Never Occup. □ Vacant Occupied by □ Owner □ Tenant at $_____ Per Mo. □ Furn. □ Unfurn.

13. ▲ PROPOSED 1.□ SUBSTAN. REHAB. 2.□ UNDER CONSTR. 3.□
Builder's Name & Address Including ZIP Code Tel. No. Model Identification
Plans: □ First Subm Prob. Repeat Cases □ Yes □ No □ Prev. Proc. as FHA Case No.

14. DESCRIPTION
▲1.□ Wood siding ▲ _____ Stories ▲ _____ Bedrooms □ Store Rm. Mineral Rights Reserved ▲ Type of Heating
1.□ Detached 2.□ Wood shingle 7.□ Split Foyer _____ Liv. Room □ Util. Rm. □ No □ Yes (Explain)
2.□ Semi-det. 3.□ Asb. shingle 8.□ Bi-Level _____ Din. Room ▲1.□ Garage Utilities: Public Comm. Individual ▲1.□ Cent. Air Cond.
3.□ Row 4.□ Fiber board 9.□ Split Level _____ Kitchen 9.□ Carport Water ▲1.□ 2.□ 3.□ 2.□ Wall Air Cond.
1.□ Frame 5.□ Brick or stone ▲1.□ Full Basement _____ No. rms. □ No cars Gas □ □ □ Type of Paving (Str.)
2.□ Masonry 6.□ Stuc. or c. blk. 2.□ _____ % Basement ▲ _____ Baths □ Built-in Elect. □ □ □ □ None
3.□ Concrete 7.□ Aluminum 3.□ Slab on Gr. ▲ _____ ½ Baths ▲2.□ Attached ▲1.□ Underground Wiring □ Curb & Gutter
Factory Fabricated 8.□ Asph. siding 4.□ Crawl Space ▲3.□ Detached Sanitary Sewer ▲1.□ 2.□ 3.□ 4.□ Sept. Cess Tank Pool □ Sidewalk
▲1.□ Yes 2.□ No 9.□ ▲ _____ Living Units _____ % Non-Res □ Storm Sewer

EXTRA FEATURES ▲1.□ Fireplace 2.□ Rec. Room 4.□ Sw. Pool 4.□ Enclosed Porch 2.□ Breezeway 4.□ Fence
▲1.□ Extra Fire Pl. 2.□ Expand Attic 4.□ Fin. Attic ▲1.□ 2.□ 4.□

15. SPEC. ASSESS. Prepayable. $_____ Non-Prepay. $_____ 16. ▲ LOT _____ x _____ 1.□ Irr 2.□ Acres _____ Sq. Ft.
Int _____ % Ann. Pay. $_____ Unpd. Bal. $_____ Rem. Term _____ Yrs 17 GENERAL LOCATION:

18. ANN. R. EST. TAXES $_____ 19. ANN. FIRE INS. $_____ 20. ▲ SALE PRICE $_____ $_____ Mo. _____ Yr.

21. EQUIPMENT IN VALUE: ▲1.□ Range or Counter cook unit & oven 2.□ Refrig. 4.□ Dishwasher
▲1.□ Auto. washer 2.□ Dryer 4.□ ▲1.□ Garb. Disp. 2.□ Vent. Fan 4.□ Carpet

Net variations .... $_____
Basic cost .... $_____
Main Bldg. (Subtotal) .... $_____
Gar./Carport .... $_____
Porches/Terraces. .... $_____
Walks/Drives .... $_____
Ldsp./Pttg./Fin. Gr. ... $_____
Other on-site imp. ..... $_____
2511 Comb. _____ $ x wkmp _____ % = _____ %
On-site imp. adj. ..... $_____
Arch. services .... $_____
Water/sewer tap charges .. $_____
EST. REPL. COST IMP. .. $_____

22. ▲ LOC. CODE
23. BASIC CASE
24. SUB FILE NO
25. REM. LIFE □ ECON. □ PHYS. _____ YRS
26. CONDITION AS APPRAISED
▲1.□ Excellent 2.□ Good 3.□ Fair 4.□ Poor
27. NEIGHBORHOOD DATA
Pres. Land Use _____
Anticip. Land Use _____
Owner Occp. Appeal _____
Demand for Amenity Inc. Prop. _____
_____ % Blt. up _____ % own. _____ % Ten. _____ % Vac.
Age Typ. Bldg _____ to _____
Typ. Mo. Rent $_____ to $_____
▲ Price Range $_____ to $_____
28. ▲ Location □ Acceptable □ Reject □ 223e
Property □ Acceptable □ Reject
29. IMPROVED ▲ LIVING AREA _____ Sq. Ft.

30. COST DATA: 2800-3 for _____ □ Integ. □ 2014
2014-d _____
Cost @ $ _____ Per Sq. Ft. = $_____

31. BLDG. DESC/VARS. — +
Fdns. _____ Frpl. _____
Ext. Wall _____
Shtg _____
Sub. Fl _____ Fin. Fl. _____
Rfg _____ Int. Wall _____
Plg _____
Htg _____ Insul. _____

Equip. _____
Total Variations _____ $_____

32. REPL. COST Review
▲ Repl. cost imp .... $_____
▲ Mkt. Price Eq. site .. $_____
Misc. Allow Costs ... $_____
Mktg. Expense ..... $_____
▲ Repl. Cost ...... $_____

33. COST OF REPAIRS/IMPROVEMENTS
Prop. $_____ Req. $_____

34. COMPARABLE PROPERTIES

	Sq. Ft. Imp. Area	Sto-ries	Rms.	Bed Rms.	Bath	Const.	Gar.	Yr. cond.	Price	Date	S/L	Date Inspec.	+/=	Variations
SUBJECT PROPERTY														
(1)														
(2)														
(3)														

35. CAP. INC. (Mon. Rent $_____ $_____ $_____) — Exc. exp. $_____ = $_____ x Rent mult. of _____ = CAP. INC. $_____

36. APPRAISAL SUMMARY: Capitalized Income $_____ Cost $_____ Market ▲ $_____
VALUE: Val. (Excl. CL Costs) $_____ Closing Costs $_____ Total ▲ $_____

37. LEASE: ANN. GRD. RENT $_____ CAP. AT _____ % = ▲ $_____ Val. of Leased Fee. _____ Val. of Leasehold Est. $_____

38. (1) Remarks (2) Spec. Cond. (3) Rej. Reasons (4) Neigh. Charac. (5) Land excl. From Val. (6) Items Excl. From Repl. Cost

39. INSPECTIONS:
□ Proposed Construction □ Repair
□ Mortgagee's Certificate
□ Appr. Arch. Proc. Date
□ Reject
Review
□ Commit. Staff Val. □ Other
□ Reject
Review Date

WARNING: All persons by signing this report certify that they have no interest present or future, in the property, application or mortgage

FHA FORM NO. 2800-3 Rev. 2/76 NOTE TO PROCESSOR: INSERT CARBON BEFORE COMPLETION OF ITEMS 24 THRU 39 FHA COPY - FILE IN CASE BINDER

FIGURE 7–3.

The purpose of the certification was to prevent a house with serious defects from being sold to an unsuspecting buyer who would then be burdened with overwhelming repair costs. The purpose was unquestionably good, but in operation, the requirement for certification (which originally included warranties of the operating equipment) placed such a heavy expense burden on the seller that many simply refused to sell under an FHA commitment. To help matters, the FHA then offered to pay for the first inspection themselves, providing the appraiser called for such an inspection. However, any repairs that may be needed to meet the FHA requirements would have to be made at the seller's expense.

The rule remains that HUD/FHA will pay for the first inspection that may be called for by an appraiser in the report. But in practice, the appraiser is expected to condition the evaluation on the repair of all deficiencies that are in evidence, rather than call for a separate inspection.

HUD/FHA Reports to the Applicant

Information on the decisions made by FHA personnel regarding an applicant or the subject property has not always been made available to the buyer/applicant. And much of the information has passed through the mortgagee to the real estate broker and then to the buyer. With this procedure the information sometimes becomes distorted and sometimes is misrepresented. To make sure that the buyer receives accurate information, HUD/FHA recently introduced a new procedure that requires an information sheet from Form 2800 to be submitted directly to the home buyer. This is Form 2800-6 (Figure 7-4) which gives the estimated value of the property, a definition of value, and some pertinent advice to home buyers regarding the buyer's obligations and rights. The buyer must certify receipt of Form 2800-6 when he or she signs the initial application form, 2900-1.

Report on Application, Form 2026. This form is used to request additional information on the applicant or the property in order to complete the processing of the application. The same form is also used to report the reasons an application is not eligible for mortgage insurance. Reproduction of this form, Figure 7-5, is made to show the main reasons for rejection of an application.

Firm Commitment, Form 2900-4. When all of the HUD/FHA requirements have been met, a Form Commitment for Mortgage

Form Approved
OMB No. 63-R1 366

FHA MORTGAGEE NO.		FHA CASE NO.

U.S. DEPARTMENT OF HOUSING AND URBAN DEVELOPMENT
FEDERAL HOUSING ADMINISTRATION

**STATEMENT OF APPRAISED VALUE FOR
A MORTGAGE TO BE INSURED UNDER
THE NATIONAL HOUSING ACT**

PROPERTY ADDRESS

☐ SEC. 203(b)   ☐ SEC. _____

MORTGAGEE

**ESTIMATED VALUE
OF PROPERTY .... $ _____**

COMMITTED FOR INSURANCE

Fire Ins .... $ ____	
Taxes .... $ ____	
Condo. Com. Exp.$ ____	
Main & Repairs $ ____	
Heat & Utilities $ ____	

COMMITMENT

Issued _____ 19 ____
Expires _____ 19 ____

**ESTIMATED CLOSING
COST .... $ ____**

DEFINITION OF VALUE

The Federal Housing Commissioner has valued the above identified property for mortgage insurance purposes in the amount equal to the sum of the estimated value of property plus the estimated closing cost.

FHA'S estimate of "Value" ("Replacement Cost" in Section 213 or 220) does not fix a sales price, except when the mortgage is to be insured under section 235(i); does not indicate FHA approval of a purchaser of the property; nor does it indicate the amount of an insured mortgage that would be approved.

"VALUE OF PROPERTY" IS FHA'S ESTIMATE OF THE VALUE OF THE PROPERTY.

"Closing Costs" is the FHA estimate of the cost of closing a mortgage loan on the property. These costs may be paid by either the buyer or the seller.

The maximum mortgage which FHA can insure is based on the sum of the value of the property plus the estimate of closing costs. Under those sections of the National Housing Act (such as 213 or 220) where the maximum mortgage amount must be based on estimated replacement cost, the "Value of Property" shall be deemed to mean replacement cost for mortgage insurance purposes."

"Replacement Cost" is an estimate of the current cost to reproduce the property including land, labor, site survey and marketing expense but excluding payments for prepaid expenses such as taxes and insurance and closing costs.

If the contract price of the property is equal to or less than "Value of Property", and the buyer pays closing costs, a part of the closing costs can be included in the mortgage. IF THE CONTRACT PRICE OF THE PROPERTY IS MORE THAN "VALUE OF PROPERTY" AND THE BUYER PAYS THE CLOSING COSTS, THE BUYER IS PAYING MORE FOR THE PROPERTY THAN FHA'S ESTIMATE OF ITS VALUE.

The law requires that FHA mortgagors receive a statement of "appraised value" prior to the sale of the property. If the sales contract has been signed before the mortgagor receives such a statement, the contract must contain, or must be amended to include the following language;

"It is. . . agreed that,. . . . the purchaser shall not be obligated to complete the purchase...or to incur any penalty...unless the seller has delivered to the purchaser a written statement setting forth...the value of the property (excluding closing costs) not less than $ _____ The purchaser shall have the privilege...of preceeding with...this contract without regard to the amount of the...valuation."

ADVICE TO HOME BUYERS

EXISTING PROPERTIES- WHERE THE APPLICATION INVOLVES AN EXISTING PROPERTY, FHA MAKES AN APPRAISAL ONLY TO DETERMINE THE PROPERTY'S VALUE. AN APPRAISAL DOES NOT IN ANY WAY WARRANT THE CONDITION OF THE PROPERTY. POTENTIAL BUYERS SHOULD EXAMINE THE PROPERTY CAREFULLY AND TAKE ALL NECESSARY PRECAUTIONS BEFORE SIGNING A PURCHASE CONTRACT. THE FHA DOES NOT HAVE AUTHORITY TO PROVIDE FINANCIAL ASSISTANCE IN CONNECTION WITH MAKING NEEDED REPAIRS.

ADVANCE PAYMENTS - Make extra payments when able. You pay less interest and have your home paid for sooner. Notify the lender in writing at least 30 days before the regular payment date on which you intend to make an advance payment.

DELINQUENT PAYMENTS - Monthly payments are due the first day of each month and should be made on or before that date. The lender may make a late charge up to 2 cents for each dollar of any payment more than 15 days late. If you fail for 30 days to make a payment, or to perform any other agreement in the mortgage, your lender may foreclose. You could lose your home, damage your credit, and prevent your obtaining further mortgage loans. If extraordinary circumstances prevent your making payments on time, see your lender at once. If you are temporarily unable to make your payments because of illness, loss of job, etc., your lender may be able to help you. Ask your lender to explain FHA's forbearance policy. **YOUR CREDIT IS AN IMPORTANT ASSET; DON'T LOSE IT THROUGH NEGLECT.**

MORTGAGE INSURANCE PREMIUM - The FHA charges a mortgage insurance premium-in the amount of ½ of 1% a year on the average outstanding principal obligation for the preceding 12 months without taking into account delinquent payments or prepayments. 1/12 of the mortgage insurance premium due each year is collected in the borrower's monthly mortgage payment to allow the lender to accumulate, one month prior to the premium due date, sufficient funds to pay the mortgage insurance premium.

TAXES, ASSESSMENTS, AND INSURANCE-Send your lender bills for taxes, special assessments, or fire insurance that come to you. The fire insurance the lender requires you to carry usually covers only the balance of the loan. Check this with your lender. You may wish to take out additional insurance so that if the house is damaged your loss will be covered as well as the lender's. If your home is damaged by fire, windstorm, or other cause, write your lender at once. Taxes for the coming year can't be known until the bills are received. If they exceed the amount accumulated from your payments, you will be asked to pay the difference. If they are less, the difference will be credited to your account. The same is true of fire insurance. Some States allow homestead or veteran's tax exemptions. Apply for any exemption to which you may be entitled. When it is approved, notify your lender.

CLOSING COSTS - In the heading is FHA's estimate of anticipated closing costs, such as fees for preparation of mortgage instruments, attorney's fees, title insurance, origination fees and documentary stamp taxes. The estimate does not include charges for such prepayable items as taxes, fire insurance.

NEW CONSTRUCTION - When FHA approves plans and specifications before construction, the builder is required to warrant that the house conforms to approved plans. This warranty is for 1 year following the date on which title is conveyed to the original buyer or the date on which the house was first occupied whichever occurs first. If during the warranty period you notice defects for which you believe the builder is responsible, ask him in writing to correct them. If he fails to do so, notify the HUD/FHA Field Office in writing. Mention the FHA case number shown above. If inspection shows the builder to be at fault, the FHA will try to persuade him to make correction. If he does not, you may be able to obtain legal relief under the builder's warranty and where a structual defect is involved the FHA has authority to provide financial assistance in connection with making corrections. Most builders take pride in their work and will make justifiable corrections. They cannot be expected to correct damage caused by ordinary wear and tear or by poor maintenance. Keeping the house in good condition is the owner's responsibility.

IF YOU SELL - If you sell while the mortgage exists, the buyer may finance several ways. Understand how these arrangements may affect you. Consult your lender.

1. You may sell for all cash and pay off your mortgage. This ends your liability
2. The buyer can assume the mortgage and pay the difference between the unpaid balance and the selling price in cash. If the FHA and the lender are willing to accept the buyer as a mortgagor, you can be released from further liability. This requires the specific approval of the lender and the FHA.
3. The buyer can pay the difference in cash and purchase subject to the unpaid mortgage balance. FHA or lender approval is not necessary BUT YOU REMAIN LIABLE FOR THE DEBT. IF THE BUYER DEFAULTS, IT COULD RESULT IN A DEFICIENCY JUDGMENT AND IMPAIR YOUR CREDIT STANDING.

(METHODS 1 AND 2 ARE PREFERABLE TO METHOD NUMBER 3)

OPERATING EXPENSES - In the heading are FHA estimates of monthly costs of taxes, heat and utilities, fire insurance, maintenance and repairs. The estimated figures will probably have to be adjusted when you receive the actual bills. BEAR IN MIND THAT IN MOST COMMUNITIES TAXES AND OTHER OPERATING COSTS ARE INCREASING. The estimates should give some idea of what you can expect the costs to be at the beginning. In some areas FHA's estimate of taxes may also include charges such as sewer charges, garbage collection fee, water rates, etc.

☐ "THIS HOUSING WAS CONSTRUCTED BEFORE 1950. THERE IS A POSSIBILITY THAT IT MAY CONTAIN SOME LEAD PAINT THAT WAS IN USE BEFORE THAT TIME". THE LENDING INSTITUTION IS REQUIRED TO PROVIDE YOU WITH A COPY OF THE BROCHURE ENTITLED "WATCH OUT FOR LEAD PAINT POISONING".

AMOUNT TO BE BORROWED

When you borrow to buy a home, you pay interest and other charges which add to your cost. A larger down-payment will result in a smaller mortgage. Borrow as little as you need and repay in the shortest time.

FHA FORM NO. 2800-6 Rev. 2/76   SEND TO MORTGAGEE FOR DELIVERY TO HOME BUYER

FIGURE 7-4.

U. S. DEPARTMENT OF HOUSING AND URBAN DEVELOPMENT
FEDERAL HOUSING ADMINISTRATION

REPORT ON APPLICATION

MORTGAGOR - *Name, Address and Zip Code*	Date	FHA Case No.

☐ **FEE CREDITED**　　☐ **FEE EARNED**　*(Reconsideration may be requested within 2 months of the last "Fee Credit" rejection or of the initial "Fee Earned" rejection, whichever is later.)*
Fee involved only on initial submissions.

MORTGAGEE - *Name, Address and Zip Code*	Insuring Office (Service Office) Located At:

YOUR APPLICATION CANNOT BE PROCESSED - THE FOLLOWING ITEMS WERE NOT SUBMITTED OR COMPLETED:

R1　☐ Form 2005 - Description of Materials
R2　☐ Plot Plan
R3　☐ Foundation or Basement Plan
R4　☐ Floor Plans (all floors)
R5　☐ Exterior Elevations
R6　☐ Exterior Wall Section
R7　☐ Kitchen Cabinet Details
R8　☐ Stair Section, Fireplace Section and elevation, and Roof Details
R9　☐ Heating Layout and Heat Loss Calculation

R10　☐ Water Supply System Plans and Specs.
R11　☐ Sewage Disposal System Plans & Specs.
R12　☐ Credit report
R13　☐ 2004f - Verification of Deposits
　　　Other –

R14　☐ 2004g - Verification of Employment
R15　☐ Currently dated balance sheet
R16　☐ Copy of sales contract or contract for deed
R17　☐ 2561 - Mortgagor's Contract
R18　☐ 3476 - Certificate of Eligibility (Sec. 221)
R19　☐ DD 802 - Certificate of Eligibility (Sec. 222)
R20　☐ Complete 2800-1:　☐ Mortgage Code No.
　　　☐ Month and year ☐ Never occupied (If applicable) completed
　　　☐ Signature of mortgagee and/or Builder and/or Sponsor
R21　☐ Complete 2900, Item(s)
R22　☐ Complete Amendatory Statement
R23　☐ 2010 - Equal Employment Opportunity Certification
R24　☐ 2011 - Equal Opportunity in Housing Certificate
R25　☐ Mortgagee's Number not shown

YOUR APPLICATION IS NOT ELIGIBLE FOR THE REASONS CHECKED

ARCHITECTURAL

A1　☐ _____ room area does not meet FHA Reqmts.
A2　☐ Does not meet FHA side yard requirements.
A3　☐ Storage space does not meet FHA Requirements.
A4　☐ Stairway head room does not meet FHA Reqmts.
A5　☐ Access to only bathroom does not meet privacy Reqmts.
A6　☐ Extensive inadequacy of framing members.
A7　☐ Dwelling has major deficiencies: visual appeal-livability-natural light & vent.-structural quality-resistance to elements & use-suitability of mech. equipment-conformity with anticipated desires of typical purchasers.
A8　☐ (Proposed) improvements do not meet FHA Reqmts.

MORTGAGE CREDIT

M1　☐ Stability of income not established.
M2　☐ Stable income Mtgr. can reasonably be expected to maintain not in proper relation to total obligations.
M3　☐ Mtgr's. net income not adequate to support prospective housing expense and other fixed obligations.
M4　☐ Income of Co-Mortgagor not considered effective.
M5　☐ Insurable loan limited to $ _____. Mtgr. has insufficient available assets to close.
M6　☐ Exhibits indicate Mtgr. resorting to unacceptable secondary financing; verify source of funds.
M7　☐ Amts. credited to Mtgr. for work or services does not bear proper relation to FHA's est. of val. of work or services.
M8　☐ Work or services unacceptable as "sweat equity."
M9　☐ Proposed withdrawal of funds presently invested in Mortgagor's business could result in financial difficulties which may seriously impair earnings capacity.
M10　☐ Details needed on Notes Payable Outstanding indicating any connection with subject property.
M11　☐ Mortgagor's general credit standing unacceptable.

NOTE: WHEN ITEM "M11" IS CHECKED, A COPY OF THIS REPORT ON APPLICATION MUST BE GIVEN TO THE MORTGAGOR.

☐ In compliance with Public Law 91-508, this is to advise that the above named applicant has been rejected because of an unacceptable credit standing. The determination was made in whole or in part, on the basis of information in a consumer report from: *(Name(s) and address(es))*

VALUATION

V1　☐ Individual water system with insufficient operating experience. Submit: plot plan; signed cert. from builder or subcontractor stating syst. complies with drawings & Specs.; current approval of local Health Authority.
V2　☐ Individual sewage disposal system with insufficient operating experience. Submit: plot plan & as-built drawings & specs.; cert. from builder or subcontractor stating syst. complies with drawings & specs. and sub-surface disposal area is adequate for absorption of all liquids discharged to it.
V3　☐ Unable to gain access to dwelling. Request reopening when arrangements made to complete inspection.
V4　☐ Dwelling not sufficiently complete. May be reopened when construction completed or, submit plans, and Form 2005 covering incomplete items.
V5　☐ Undeveloped location. Subdivision analysis required.
V6　☐ Lot Size: yard area around dwelling inadequate.
V7　☐ Surrounding area too sparsely developed.
V8　☐ Property in area subject to periodic flooding.
V9　☐ Proximity of location to railroad.
V10　☐ Located on heavily traveled arterial street.
V11　☐ Location subject to noxious odors, smoke, noise, etc.
V12　☐ Design is inharmonious with the neighb- 'hood.
V13　☐ Neighborhood transition from single-family residential to rooming house and commercial use.
V14　☐ Inspection reveals location is unacceptable.

GENERAL

G1　☐ Unable to determine acceptability due to contradictory information on _____
G2　☐ A party to the transaction is on a compliance list.
G3　☐ (Application)(committed) under another case number.
G4　☐ Appraisal previously made and case rejected.
G5　☐ Unsatisfactory market condition

☐ OTHER –

FIGURE 7-5.

Insurance is issued on Form 2900-4 as illustrated in Figure 7-6. This commitment must be signed by an agent of the Federal Housing Commissioner, the mortgagor, and the mortgagee. The commitment to insure makes almost certain that a loan can be obtained by the mortgagor from the named mortgagee.

A new provision in the commitment form gives the buyer the right to withdraw from the agreement if the seller has not furnished a copy of the FHA appraised value of the property to the buyer. The buyer has the right to withdraw if the agreed price exceeds the FHA valuation. But the buyer also has the option to consummate the purchase without regard to the appraised value.

VETERANS ADMINISTRATION

The popularly called G.I. Bill of Rights was passed by Congress in 1944. It was designed to give returning World War II veterans a better chance upon resuming civilian life than their fathers had after World War I. While the initial bill, and subsequent additions, provided numerous other benefits such as hospitalization, education, employment training, and unemployment benefits, our interest here will be confined to the home loan section.

Section 501 of the Act provides for a first mortgage real estate loan that is *partially* guaranteed by the Veterans Administration and is subject to the strict rules covering all phases of the loan: the borrower, the lender, the property, the interest, the term and loan amount, plus collections and foreclosures. The primary interest of the VA is to aid the veteran, and to this end the rules are directed.

Unlike the FHA that *insures* up to 97 percent of some loans, the Veterans Administration *guarantees* a portion of the loan, which in effect constitutes a reasonable down payment for the lender. Since the VA does not require a veteran to pay any portion of the closing costs, forbids him to pay any discount, and eliminates the need for a down payment, many veterans can move into their houses with no cash requirements. In the beginning, Congress set the maximum guarantee at $2000, which proved to be much too small. Over the years these limits have been increased periodically to improve the assistance program and to recognize inflationary pressures. In 1975 the present limits were set at 60 percent of the loan or a maximum of $17,500, whichever is least, less any portion of a veteran's entitlement already used.

Form Approved
OMB No 63—R1062

U. S. DEPARTMENT OF HOUSING AND URBAN DEVELOPMENT FEDERAL HOUSING ADMINISTRATION	FHA Case No.

FIRM COMMITMENT FOR

MORTGAGE INSURANCE UNDER THE NATIONAL HOUSING ACT

☐ **SEC. 203(b)** ☐ **SEC.**

PROPERTY ADDRESS

Mtgor._____ Sex____ Age____

Co-Mtgor._____ Sex____ Age____

Address_____

Married	Yrs.	No. of Dependents	Ages

Co-Mortgagor(s)		Sex	Age(s)

(Check One)

1 ☐ White *(Non-Minority)* 3 ☐ American Indian 5 ☐ Spanish American

2 ☐ Negro/Black 4 ☐ Oriental 6 ☐ Other Minority

MORTGAGE APPLIED FOR ➤	Mortgage Amount	*Interest Rate	No. of Months	Monthly Payment Principal & Interest
	$			

☐ **ACCEPTED:** A note and mortgage described above or as modified below will be insured under the National Housing Act provided one of the mortgagors will be an owner-occupant and all conditions appearing in any outstanding commitment issued under the above case number and those set forth below are fulfilled.

☐ MODIFIED AND ACCEPTED AS FOLLOWS:..........	Mortgage Amount	Interest Rate	No. of months	Monthly Payment Principal & Interest
	$	%		$

ESTIMATE OF VALUE AND CLOSING COSTS

VALUE OF PROPERTY $_____

Closing Costs......... $_____

TOTAL *(For Mortgage Insurance Purposes)* .... $_____

ADDITIONAL CONDITIONS

☐ 2544 - Builders warranty required. ☐ Owner-occupancy NOT required. *(Delete (c) - Mortgagor's Certificate)*

(See Item(s)_____ on Addendum to Commitment)

Improved Floor Area	Sq. Ft.

☐ The property is to be insured under Section 221 (d) (2); a code compliance inspection is required.

THIS COMMITMENT EXPIRES: **DATE OF THIS COMMITMENT**

_____,19___   _____,19___

(Expiration Date)   *(Authorized Agent for the Federal Housing Commissioner)*   *(Field Office)*

INSTRUCTIONS TO MORTGAGEE: Forward to the insuring office: (1) this commitment signed by the mortgagee and mortgagor; (2) a copy of the note, bond or other credit instrument; (3) a copy of the mortgage or other security instrument; (4) a copy of the settlement statement, (Form HUD-1) signed by the mortgagee which itemizes all charges and fees collected by the mortgagee from the mortgagor and seller; and (5) FHA Mortgage Insurance Certificate completed with case number, Section of the National Housing Act, mortgage amount, property address, mortgagors' names and mortgagee's name and address.

MORTGAGOR'S CERTIFICATE - The undersigned certifies that:

(a) The mortgaged property, including removable equipment items shown on any outstanding commitment issued under the above case number and those set forth below, will be owned by me free and clear of all liens other than that of such mortgage.

(b) I will not have outstanding any other unpaid obligations contracted in connection with the mortgage transaction or the purchase of the said property except obligations which are secured by property or collateral owned by me independently of the said mortgaged property, or obligations approved by the Commissioner.

(c) One of the undersigned is the occupant of the subject property. (NOTE: Delete item (c) if owner occupancy not required by commitment).

(d) All charges and fees collected from me as shown in the settlement statement have been paid from my own funds, and no other charges have been or will be paid by me in respect to this transaction.

(e) Check Applicable Box:

☐ This was a refinancing transaction; sale of property was not involved.

☐ Purchase of the lot was a separate transaction; dwelling was built for occupancy by me.

☐ The FHA Statement of Appraised Value or VA Certificate of Reasonable Value was given to me prior to my signing the purchase contract for the property.

☐ The FHA Statement of Appraised Value or VA Certificate of Reasonable Value was not received by me prior to my signing the contract to purchase, but the contract to purchase contained the following language: "It is expressly agreed that, notwithstanding any other provisions of this contract, the purchaser shall not be obligated to complete the purchase of the property described herein or to incur any penalty by forfeiture of earnest money deposits or otherwise unless the seller has delivered to the purchaser a written statement issued by the Federal Housing Commissioner setting forth the appraised value of the property (excluding closing costs) of not less than $_____ which statement the seller hereby agrees to deliver to the purchaser promptly after such appraised value statement is made available to the seller. The purchaser shall, however, have the privilege and option of proceeding with the consummation of the contract without regard to the amount of the appraised valuation made by the Federal Housing Commissioner."

(IF THE AMENDMENT PROCEDURE WAS NECESSARY, THE DOLLAR AMOUNT USED IN THE AMENDATORY CLAUSE IS INSERTED IN THE ABOVE BLANK.)

(f) Neither I, nor anyone authorized to act for me, will refuse to sell or rent, after the making of a bona fide offer, or refuse to negotiate for the sale or rental of, or otherwise make unavailable or deny the dwelling or property covered by this loan to any person because of race, color, religion, sex, marital status or national origin. I recognize that any restrictive covenant on this property relating to race, color, religion, sex, marital status or national origin is illegal and void and any such covenant is hereby specifically disclaimed. I understand that civil action for preventative relief may be brought by the Attorney General of the United States in any appropriate U.S. District Court against any person responsible for a violation of this certification. *NOTE: The interest rate shown is the FHA-VA maximum rate in effect on the date of this commitment and may increase prior to closing unless buyer and lender agree otherwise.

Signature(s)_____   Date:_____ 19___

MORTGAGEE'S CERTIFICATE - The undersigned certifies that to the best of its knowledge:

Date _____, 19 ___

(a) None of the statements made in its application for insurance nor in the Mortgagor's Certificate are untrue or incorrect.

(b) The conditions listed above or appearing in any outstanding commitment issued under the above case number have been fulfilled.

(c) Complete disbursement of the loan has been made to the Mortgagor, or to his creditors for his account and with his consent.

(d) The security instrument has been recorded and is a good and valid first lien on the property described.

(e) No charge has been made to or paid by the Mortgagor except as permitted under FHA Regulations.

(f) The copies of the credit and security instruments which are submitted herewith are true and exact copies as executed and filed for record.

(g) It has not paid any kickbacks, fees or consideration of any type, directly or indirectly, on or after May 1, 1972, to any party in connection with this transaction except as permitted under Section 203.7(a)(6) of the FHA Regulations and administrative instructions issued pursuant thereto.

Mortgagee *(Please use FHA imprint stamp, or other approved device.)*

NOTE: If commitment is executed by an agent in name of the mortgagee, the agent must enter the mortgagee's code number and type code number in blocks below.

Code		Type

(Signature and title of officer)

FHA FORM NO. 2900-4 Rev. 2/76   **MORTGAGEE COPY**

FIGURE 7-6.

Eligibility of Veteran

One of the first steps in determining the qualifications of an applicant for a VA guaranty is to check eligibility. The requirements have been changed somewhat over the years and now call for a period of active duty in accordance with the following schedule in order to qualify:

Period of Time	*Days of Active Duty*
September 16, 1940 to July 25, 1947	90
July 26, 1947 to June 26, 1950	181
June 27, 1950 to January 31, 1955	90
February 1, 1955 to present	181

In addition, surviving spouses of persons who died as a result of service are also eligible.

For any veteran considering the purchase of a home, it is a good idea to ask the Veterans Administration to confirm eligibility. This is done by submitting VA Form 26–1880, Request for Determination of Eligibility and Available Loan Guaranty Entitlement.

The Loan Guaranty Entitlement

The amount of money that the VA will guarantee for the veteran is called an *entitlement.* The present limits of the entitlement are 60 percent of the loan amount or $17,500, whichever is the least. If both a husband and wife are eligible veterans, the guarantee may be twice the amount but cannot exceed 60 percent of the loan amount. The entitlement may be only partially used with a balance remaining that may be applied to the purchase of another home. The amount of the entitlement has been increased as follows:

Original act, 1944	2,000
December 28, 1945	4,000
July 12, 1950	7,500
May 7, 1968	12,500
December 31, 1974	17,500

Each increase has added entitlement to all eligible veterans. An example of how this increase might work is a veteran who purchased a home with a $12,500 loan in 1960. The guaranty then would have been $7,500. Because of the increases passed by Congress, the veteran would now have an additional $10,000 in home loan entitlement remaining ($17,500 less $7,500 leaves $10,000).

Restoration of Entitlement

So long as the Veterans Administration remains obligated to the mortgagee, the veteran's entitlement remains pledged and unavailable to the veteran for any further use. If the property is sold and the loan assumed by the new buyer, the VA has no way of obtaining a release from the lender who undertook the loan originally. So the VA continues to hold that portion of the veteran's entitlement that was originally pledged for the loan. There are now two ways that the veteran can regain the use of the guaranty privilege, or to restore the entitlement. These are:

1. Pay off the loan through sale of the property. Restoration of the entitlement cannot be obtained by simply paying off the loan, unless the veteran also moves out. Under a VA guaranty, a veteran can only own one house which must be his or her residence.

2. Under a provision of the Veterans Housing Act of 1974 a new procedure was added which is Substitution of Entitlement. To qualify under this provision, the veteran can sell his or her home on an assumption basis, but only to another qualified veteran. The purchasing veteran must: (a) have the same amount or more of entitlement as the selling veteran; (b) must meet the normal income and credit requirements; and (c) must agree to permit the entitlement to be substituted.

For many years the VA also required that there must be a compelling personal reason for the sale such as a job transfer in order to restore a veteran's entitlement. This is no longer necessary.

Release of Liability

When a veteran sells his or her home and the VA loan is assumed, the veteran remains liable unless he or she asks for a release. The home can be sold to anyone—veteran or non-veteran—and the veteran seller may still be released from the VA obligation.

The release of liability needs a special application, but the law does require the VA to grant the release if the veteran meets the following three requirements: (1) the loan must be current; (2) the purchaser must qualify from the standpoint of income and be an acceptable credit risk; and (3) the purchaser must agree to assume the veteran's obligations on the property. It is good advice for a veteran to make the sale of the house contingent upon the VA acceptance of the purchaser and a release of liability if the sale involves assumption of the GI loan. While the law specifies no time limit for obtaining the release of liability, once a sale is closed the veteran will find little interest from the new purchaser in helping secure the release.

The reason that a release of liability does not automatically restore the veteran's entitlement to a full guarantee again is that the VA remains liable under the original contract of commitment to the mortgagee. Only a payoff of the loan removes this exposure for the VA.

Form 26-1802a—Application for Home Loan Guaranty

Figure 7-7 shows Form 26-1802a, which is prepared by the loan originator for submission to the VA. The form incorporates the essential information on the amount and terms of the loan, the security being offered, the personal and financial status of the veteran, and the certifications by the veteran and the lender to make sure the veteran has been advised of the reasonable value of the property he or she wants to buy.

The application must be accompanied by a number of substantiating documents as follows:

1. A credit report on the veteran from an approved source.

2. Verification of employment as shown in Figure 7-8 which is a standard form used by both FHA and VA. Verifications are needed for both veteran and spouse, if employed, and must show the amount of regular income separately for overtime, commissions, and bonuses. The report should show probability of continued employment.

3. Verification of deposit on the form reproduced as Figure 7-9. This form is used to verify any cash assets claimed by the veteran.

4. A copy of the executed sales or construction contract.

5. The Certificate of Reasonable Value (CRV), Form 26-1813a, which is the appraised value as determined by the VA.

VETERANS ADMINISTRATION
APPLICATION FOR HOME LOAN GUARANTY

1A. VA LOAN NUMBER	1B. LENDER'S LOAN NO.

2A. NAME AND PRESENT ADDRESS OF VETERAN (Include ZIP Code)	2B. RACE OR ETHNIC ORIGIN OF VETERAN	2C. SEX OF VETERAN
	☐ WHITE (Non-minority) ☐ NEGRO/BLACK ☐ SPANISH AMERICAN ☐ AMERICAN INDIAN ☐ ORIENTAL ☐ OTHER	☐ MALE ☐ FEMALE

3. NAME AND ADDRESS OF LENDER (Include No., street or rural route, city, P.O., state and ZIP Code.)	4. PROPERTY ADDRESS INCLUDING NAME OF SUBDIVISION, LOT AND BLOCK NO., AND ZIP CODE

5A. LOAN AMOUNT	5B. INTEREST RATE	5C. PROPOSED MATURITY
$	%	YRS. MOS.

DISCOUNT (Only if veteran to pay under 38, U.S.C. 1803(c) (3) ▶	5D. PERCENT	5E. AMOUNT
	%	$

The undersigned veteran and lender hereby apply to the Administrator of Veterans' Affairs for Guaranty of the loan described herein under Section 1810. Chapter 37, Title 38, United States Code to the full extent permitted by the veteran's available entitlement and severally agree that the Regulations promulgated pursuant to Chapter 37 and in effect on the date of the loan shall govern the rights, duties, and liabilities of the parties.

SECTION I—PURPOSE, AMOUNT, TERMS OF AND SECURITY FOR PROPOSED LOAN

6. PURPOSE OF LOAN- TO:
☐ PURCHASE EXISTING HOME PREVIOUSLY OCCUPIED ☐ CONSTRUCT A HOME - PROCEEDS TO BE PAID OUT DURING CONSTRUCTION ☐ PURCHASE EXISTING HOME NOT PREVIOUSLY OCCUPIED ☐ PURCHASE NEW CONDOMINIUM UNIT ☐ PURCHASE EXISTING CONDOMINIUM UNIT

7. TITLE WILL BE VESTED IN: ☐ VETERN ☐ VETERAN AND SPOUSE ☐ OTHER (Specify)	8. LIEN ☐ 1ST MORTGAGE	9. ESTATE WILL BE: ☐ FEE SIMPLE ☐ LEASEHOLD (Show expiration date)	10. IS THERE A MANDATORY HOMEOWNERS ASSOCIATION? ☐ YES ☐ NO (If "YES", complete Item 11L.)

11. ESTIMATED TAXES, INSURANCE AND ASSESSMENTS		12. ESTIMATED MONTHLY PAYMENT	
A. ANNUAL TAXES	$	A. PRINCIPAL AND INTEREST	$
B. AMOUNT OF HAZARD INSURANCE ON SECURITY		B. TAXES AND INSURANCE DEPOSITS	
C. ANNUAL HAZARD INSURANCE PREMIUMS		C. OTHER	
D. ANNUAL SPECIAL ASSESSMENT PAYMENT			
E. UNPAID SPECIAL ASSESSMENT BALANCE			
F. ANNUAL MAINTENANCE ASSESSMENT		D. TOTAL	$

SECTION II—PERSONAL AND FINANCIAL STATUS OF VETERAN

13A. MARITAL STATUS ☐ MARRIED ☐ UNMARRIED ☐ SEPARATED	13B. CHILD SUPPORT PAID $ PER MONTH	13C. ALIMONY PAID $ PER MONTH	14A. AGE OF SPOUSE	14B. AGE(S) OF DEPENDENT(S)

15. NAME AND ADDRESS OF NEAREST LIVING-RELATIVE (Include telephone number, if available)	16. MONTHLY PAYMENT ON RENTED PREMISES VET. NOW OCCUPIES $	16B. UTILITIES INCLUDED? ☐ YES ☐ NO

17. ASSETS		18. LIABILITIES (Itemize all debts)		
		NAME OF CREDITOR	MO. PAYMENT	BALANCE
A. CASH (Including deposit on purchase)	$		$	$
B. SAVINGS BONDS-OTHER SECURITIES				
C. REAL ESTATE OWNED				
D. AUTO				
E. FURNITURE AND HOUSEHOLD GOODS				
F. OTHER (Use separate sheet, if necessary)		JOB RELATED EXPENSE (Child care, etc. specify)		
G. TOTAL	$	TOTAL	$	$

19. INCOME AND OCCUPATIONAL STATUS			20. ESTIMATED TOTAL COST	
ITEM	VETERAN	SPOUSE	ITEM	AMOUNT
A. OCCUPATION			A. PURCHASE EXISTING HOME	$
			B. ALTERATIONS, IMPRV., REPAIRS	
			C. CONSTRUCTION	
B. NAME OF EMPLOYER			D. LAND (If acquired separately)	
			E. PURCHASE OF CONDOMINIUM UNIT	
			F. PREPAID ITEMS	
C. NUMBER OF YRS. EMPLOYED			G. ESTIMATED CLOSING COST	
			H. DISCOUNT (Only if veteran can pay)	
D. GROSS PAY	MONTHLY $ HOURLY $	MONTHLY $ HOURLY $	I. TOTAL COST (Add items 20A through 20H)	$
			J. LESS CASH FROM VETERAN	
E. OTHER INCOME	$	$	K. LESS OTHER CREDITS	
			L. AMOUNT OF LOAN	$

NOTE—IF LAND ACQUIRED BY SEPARATE TRANSACTION, COMPLETE ITEMS 21A AND 21B.	21A. DATE ACQUIRED	21B. UNPAID BALANCE $

SECTION III—CERTIFICATION (Must be signed by veteran and lender)

THE UNDERSIGNED VETERAN CERTIFIES THAT: (Complete Item 22A and Check Items 22B and 22F in all cases.) (Check Items 22C, 22D and 22E whenever the contract price or cost exceeds the VA reasonable value determination.)

22A. ☐ I have been informed that $ _____ is the reasonable value of the property as determined by the VA.

22B. ☐ I now actually occupy the property identified herein as my home or intend to move into and occupy it as my home within a reasonable period of time after completion of the loan.

22C. ☐ I was ☐ was not ☐ aware of the VA reasonable value determination when I signed my contract.

22D. ☐ Having been informed of the VA reasonable value determination, I do hereby represent that I desire to complete the transaction at the contract price or cost.

22E. ☐ I have paid or will pay in cash from my own resources at or prior to loan closing the difference between the contract price or cost and the VA reasonable value, and I do not now have and will not have outstanding after loan closing any unpaid contractual obligation on account of such cash payment.

22F. ☐ The foregoing information contained in these certifications and in Section II of this application are true and complete to the best of my knowledge and belief.

READ CERTIFICATION CAREFULLY–DO NOT SIGN APPLICATION UNLESS IT IS FULLY COMPLETED

23. DATE	24. SIGNATURE OF VETERAN (Read certification carefully before signing)

THE UNDERSIGNED LENDER CERTIFIES THAT: ALL INFORMATION REFLECTED IN THIS APPLICATION IS TRUE TO THE BEST OF MY KNOWLEDGE AND BELIEF.

25. DATE	26. NAME OF LENDER	27. TELEPHONE NO.	28. SIGNATURE AND TITLE OF OFFICER OR LENDER

FEDERAL STATUTES PROVIDE SEVERE PENALTIES FOR ANY FRAUD, INTENTIONAL MISREPRESENTATION, OR CRIMINAL CONNIVANCE OR CONSPIRACY PURPOSED TO INFLUENCE THE ISSUANCE OF ANY GUARANTY OR INSURANCE BY THE ADMINISTRATOR

VA FORM DEC. 1975 26-1802a   EXISTING STOCKS OF VA FORM 26-1802e. MAR. 1973, WILL BE USED   VA 2

FIGURE 7-7.

FHA FORM NO. 2004-G Rev. 5/75
VA FORM NO. 26-8497 Rev. 5/75

VETERANS ADMINISTRATION
and
U. S. DEPARTMENT OF HOUSING AND URBAN DEVELOPMENT
FEDERAL HOUSING ADMINISTRATION

FORM APPROVED
OMB NO. 63-R1288

REQUEST FOR VERIFICATION OF EMPLOYMENT

*INSTRUCTIONS: Lender – Complete Items 1 through 6. Have applicant complete Items 7 and 8. Forward the completed
form directly to the employer named in Item 1.
Employer – Complete Items 9A through 15 and return form directly to lender named in Item 2.*

PART I REQUEST

1. TO: (Name and Address of Employer):	2. FROM: (Name and Address of Lender):

3. Signature of Lender:	4. Title of Lender:	5. Date:	6. HUD-FHA or VA Number:

I certify that this verification has been sent directly to the employer and has not passed through the hands of the applicant or any other interested party.	I have applied for a mortgage loan and stated that I am employed by you. My signature below authorizes verification of this information.
7. Name and Address of Applicant:	8. Employee's Identification Number: _____
	Signature of applicant

PART II VERIFICATION

9 A . Is applicant now employed by you? ☐Yes ☐No	10A. Position or Job Title:	11. TO BE COMPLETED BY MILITARY PERSONNEL ONLY.	
9B. Present Base Pay is $ _____ This amount is paid: ☐Annually ☐Hourly ☐Monthly ☐Other (Specify) ☐Weekly	10B. Length of Applicant's employment:	Pay Grade:	
		Base Pay	$
		Rations	$
9C. EARNINGS LAST 12 MONTHS Amount $	10C. Probability of continued employment:	Flight or Hazard	$
Basic Earnings $		Clothing	$
Normal Hours worked per Week:	10D. Date Applicant left:		
Overtime Earnings $ _____ ☐Regular ☐Temporary	10E. Reason for leaving:	Quarters	$
		Pro-Pay	$
Other Income $ _____ ☐Regular ☐Temporary		Overseas or Combat	$

12. REMARKS:

13. Signature of Employer:	14. Title of Employer:	15. Date:

RETURN DIRECTLY TO LENDER

FIGURE 7–8.

179

Form Approved
OMB No. 63–R1062

VETERANS ADMINISTRATION
AND
U. S. DEPARTMENT OF HOUSING AND URBAN DEVELOPMENT
FEDERAL HOUSING ADMINISTRATION

REQUEST FOR VERIFICATION OF DEPOSIT

INSTRUCTIONS: LENDER – Complete Items 1 thru 7. Have applicant complete Items 8 and 9. Forward directly to bank or other depository named in Item 1.

ADDRESSEE – Please complete Items 10 thru 13. Return directly to Lender named in Item 2.

PART I – REQUEST

1. TO *(Name and Address of Bank or other Depository)*	2. FROM *(Name and address of lender)*		
3. SIGNATURE OF LENDER	4. TITLE	5. DATE	6. FHA OR VA NUMBER

7. STATEMENT OF APPLICANT

A. NAME AND ADDRESS OF APPLICANT	B. TYPE OF ACCOUNT	BALANCE	ACCOUNT NUMBER
	CHECKING	$	
	SAVINGS	$	

I have applied for a mortgage loan and stated that I maintain account(s) with the bank or depository named in Item 1. My signature below authorizes that bank or other depository to furnish the lender named in Item 2 the information set forth below in Part II. Your response is solely a matter of courtesy for which no responsibility is attached to your institution or any of your officers.

8. SIGNATURE OF APPLICANT	9. DATE

PART II – VERIFICATION

10A. DOES APPLICANT HAVE ANY OUTSTANDING LOANS?	CURRENT STATUS OF ACCOUNTS		

☐ YES ☐ NO *(If "Yes," enter total in Item 10B)*

10B. TYPE OF LOAN	MONTHLY PAYMENT	PRESENT BALANCE	11A. IS ACCOUNT LESS THAN TWO MONTHS OLD? *(If "Yes," give date opened in Item 11B)*	CHECKING	SAVINGS
				☐ YES ☐ NO	☐ YES ☐ NO
SECURED	$	$			
UNSECURED	$	$	11B. DATE ACCOUNT OPENED		
10C. PAYMENT EXPERIENCE			11C. CURRENT BALANCE		
☐ FAVORABLE ☐ UNFAVORABLE *(If unfavorable, explain in Remarks)*			11D. IS ACCOUNT OTHER THAN INDIVIDUAL, E.G., JOINT OR TRUST? *(If "Yes," explain in remarks)*	☐ YES ☐ NO	☐ YES ☐ NO

12. REMARKS

13A. SIGNATURE OF OFFICIAL OF BANK OR OTHER DEPOSITORY	13B. TITLE	13C. DATE

THE INFORMATION ON THIS FORM IS TO BE TRANSMITTED DIRECTLY, WITHOUT PASSING THROUGH THE HANDS OF THE APPLICANT OR ANY OTHER PARTY.

FHA FORM NO. 2004–F (REV. 10/75)
VA FORM 26–8497a, OCT 1975

FIGURE 7–9.

6. The veteran's Certificate of Eligibility, Form 26-1870. This is the statement that shows the veteran's eligibility for assistance and the amount of the entitlement, i.e., the amount of the guaranty available.

7. Any other data or documents as may be required by the VA office. Often clarifications are needed regarding the veteran, and statements giving acceptance of unusual conditions must be submitted.

Other VA Requirements and Procedures

The concern of the Veterans Administration is to make sure that the veteran is assuming an obligation within his or her financial capability, that the property is fairly represented, and that the appraised value (CRV) is fully disclosed. As mentioned earlier, the VA is offering a program of assistance to the veteran as a part of the nation's expression of gratitude for service. It would miss the mark if the veteran were burdened with an impossible debt load or with a grossly misrepresented house. It is with these guidelines in mind that the VA underwriter analyzes the information submitted for approval of a home loan guaranty.

In order to assure the veteran that the home loan will be properly handled and that the government guaranty will not be abused, the VA has a number of specific requirements relating to the loan and how it is handled. Essential areas of VA concern are as follows:

The Lender

To protect against an unscrupulous lender, the VA distinguishes between "supervised" and "nonsupervised" lenders. A supervised lender is one who is subject to periodic examination and regulation by a federal or state agency. Savings and loan associations, commercial banks, and insurance companies would all qualify as supervised lenders. As such, they can process loans on an *automatic* basis. In this procedure, the supervised lender takes all the necessary steps to qualify a borrower, asks for a VA appraisal, and then makes its own underwriting decision. If favorable, the information is submitted to the VA in a Loan Report which the VA is obliged to honor with the issuance of a guaranty certificate.

A nonsupervised lender is anyone who does not qualify as a supervised lender. Mortgage companies, fraternal associations, and individuals would be some examples of nonsupervised lenders. In order to obtain a certificate of guaranty from the VA, the nonsupervised lender would first have to obtain approval from the VA to make a loan to the veteran applicant and would have to submit all required information to the VA office for their underwriting approval.

A third category of lender which was established by the Veterans Housing Act of 1974 is a nonsupervised lender who qualifies for automatic loan processing. Mortgage companies that handle a large number of VA loans would be interested in this category and many have applied for approval. If the VA qualifications are met, the nonsupervised lenders may submit their own approved applications for guaranty in the form of a Loan Report and receive the same automatic issuance of a VA guaranty certificate as a supervised lender.

Interest Rates

In 1975, Congress gave the Administrator of Veterans Affairs the authority to set the maximum rate of interest that would be permitted to a lender under a VA guaranty commitment. The law states that the Administrator should set the rate after consultation with the Secretary of Housing and Urban Development who sets the interest rate for the HUD/FHA programs. In practice, any change in rates is usually announced simultaneously by the Administrator and the Secretary. Adjustment of the interest rate follows the conventional market rather than leads it. There is no fixed rule, but observation indicates that when the spread of interest rates between conventional home loans and the FHA-VA rates exceeds ½ percent (i.e., if the VA rate is 8 percent and conventional loans are exceeding 8½ percent or over 4 points of discount in a rising market), consideration is given to an adjustment. On the down side of rate movements, when conventional rates drop to within ¼ percent of FHA-VA rates (roughly 2 points of discount), there is a tendency to lower the fixed rates allowed on the government-supported programs.

Many other considerations enter into a decision to change the fixed rates besides the general conditions in the conventional market. One of these is the condition of the home building industry, another is the money market in general and its future trends, and not the least of considerations is the current political climate.

Amount of the Loan

The VA sets no limit on the amount of a home loan eligible for guaranty, except that it cannot exceed the reasonable value of the property as determined by the VA appraisal. The veteran may elect to pay more for a house than the reasonable value established by the VA, but this must be done in the form of cash. Regardless of the amount paid for a house, the guaranty on the loan remains limited to $17,500 or 60 percent of the loan amount, whichever is the least.

Term of the Loan

A GI home loan can be obtained for up to 30 years. Shorter terms are approved by the VA if required by the lender and accepted by the veteran. The veteran has the right to repay all or any part of the principal balance due on the loan at any time with no additional interest charges or penalties.

Loan Servicing

The administration of a GI loan is not prescribed by the VA. The approved lenders are expected to follow the normal standards and practices of prudent lenders. The VA expects the veteran-obligor to meet the obligations fully and on time. However, the VA does encourage reasonable forbearance on the part of the lender with the enforcement of its collections. The lender is required to notify the VA of a default within 60 days after nonpayment of an installment. Failure to file the default notice within the prescribed time limits can result in a reduction of the guaranty allowed for the lender.

Once the notification of default has been filed, there is no time limit on when the lender must take action to foreclose on the property. If foreclosure does become necessary, the VA must first appraise the property and set a "specified value." This value becomes the minimum amount for which the property can be sold which serves as a protection for all parties involved. (If a foreclosure does occur and the VA must pay a claim for the veteran as a result, the veteran then becomes indebted to the government for the amount of the claim.)

The Property as Collateral

The VA guaranty applies to the veteran's residence. The residence may be one to four units, but the veteran must live in one of them. The residence may be a farm but it must be personally occupied by the veteran. The VA is normally lenient in accepting a house with some deficiencies so long as the veteran certifies knowledge of any shortcomings and still expresses a desire to buy the property. The basic requirements are that the house be safe, sanitary, and structurally sound.

The VA appraisal of property tends to evaluate the land and building "as is." In an FHA appraisal, the evaluation is made on the basis that certain requirements will be met, or improvements will be made. The VA considers the property value without any improvements being made, but recognizes the need for improvements with a corresponding reduction in the property value.

Sale of Property

Veteran home owners may sell their property to a veteran or non-veteran without VA approval. However, the veteran-seller must obtain VA approval to be released from further liability for the loan, or to obtain a restoration of his entitlement. A GI loan can be assumed by a non-veteran buying the property. There is a substantial difference in the legal consequences of selling a house (or any property) *subject to* an existing mortgage, and in selling with an *assumption of* an existing mortgage. "Subject to" means that the buyer does *not* become personally liable for repayment of the mortgage debt. Assumption of the debt means that the buyer does accept personal responsibility for repayment of the mortgage debt. However, the seller usually remains liable also. The VA is not a party to the sales agreement. Any release of liability for the veteran-seller must follow the rules for that purpose outlined earlier in this section.

Mobile Home Loans

The Veterans Housing Act of 1970 and 1974 authorized the VA to guarantee loans made by private lenders to veterans for the purchase of new and used mobile homes. The same rule applies with the mobile home as with a house—it must be occupied by the veteran as a residence. The unit so acquired may be single-wide or double-wide, and the authorization to guarantee also covers a suitable lot for a mobile home.

Unlike the rules applicable to the guaranty on a house loan, the mobile home loan is restricted by maximum loan amounts. The guaranty *percentage* for a mobile home loan was increased from 30 to 50 percent of the loan amount as of July 1, 1976. The maximum loan amounts effective since 1974 are shown in Table 7-1.

TABLE 7-1.

Maximum Loan Amounts for Mobile Home

Property		Maximum Loan	Maximum Term (years)
Mobile home only	Single-wide	12,500	12
	Double-wide	20,000	20
Mobile home with lot	Single-wide	20,000	15
	Double-wide	27,500	20
Lot only		7,500	12

The interest permitted on a mobile home loan is adjusted periodically as may be needed, but in practice it has remained fairly stable because it follows the higher yields of installment loans. Present rate of interest for the mobile home loan is 12 percent simple interest and 8 percent for the lot. The rate for the lot loan is adjusted the same as for a VA house loan. As in other guaranteed loans, once the interest rate has been established for the loan, it cannot be changed during the life of the loan.

The same rules that apply to regular VA house loans regarding a veteran's entitlement and liability for repayment also apply to the mobile home loan.

VA Policies and Practices

Several of the guiding policies of the Veterans Administration are of interest. One is that, although the guaranty on a home loan is specifically limited and the VA is legally responsible only to that limit, in practice, should foreclosure become necessary, the VA pays off the balance due on the loan and takes title to the property. If the lender elects to re-convey the property on a defaulted loan, the VA is obligated to accept it. It is this assurance to the lender that he or she will not be burdened with the problems of handling property in foreclosure that has encouraged the wide acceptance of the VA programs by private lenders.

Another policy that can be misunderstood is the term of employment required for a veteran to be approved. Since many veterans need housing almost immediately after being discharged from service, it is difficult to show a long employment record with private industry. No rigid requirements for length of time on a job exist. The criterion is more that of underwriters' judgment on the type of work the veteran is doing. If it is a continuation of a general field of expertise that may have been learned in the service, that would satisfy the stability of income guidelines. For example, a control tower operator in the service may continue this type of work as a civilian and have no trouble qualifying for loan approval. But a jet pilot starting out as an insurance sales representative might have a problem convincing the VA underwriter that he or she can make a reasonable living in this new field of endeavor.

The VA performs a very useful service with its assistance program and has helped many veterans find suitable housing. The program is not a gift—the veteran is expected to make full payment of the loan. It is the VA's job to assure themselves that the veteran has a reasonable chance to make the repayment. It is an underwriting philosophy with the VA that in marginal cases, the mortgagee (lender) will be asked to develop more information on the applicant and the property that might permit the resolution of any doubt to be made in the veteran's favor.

GOVERNMENT NATIONAL MORTGAGE ASSOCIATION

In the partitioning of the Federal National Mortgage Association in 1968, the Government National Mortgage Association was established as a part of the Department of Housing and Urban Development. GNMA presently operates from a single office in Washington, D.C. and, under a service agreement, uses all of the FNMA regional offices to handle its field requirements. For these services a fee is paid to FNMA. GNMA is authorized to develop programs as may be directed in the following two areas; (1) special assistance projects, and (2) management and liquidation.

Special Assistance Projects

The broad commission granted by the charter act of the GNMA for special assistance projects gives the president of the United States authority to direct GNMA to make purchase commitments on certain types and categories of home mortgages as he may determine.

GNMA is authorized to buy such mortgages as are insured under other government programs and as may be committed by the Secretary for Housing and Urban Development. Further, GNMA carries special authority to make mortgage purchases in housing programs for the armed services, in emergency areas, for below market interest rate mortgages, for construction advances, and most recently, under the "Tandem Plan," it is empowered to subsidize discounts on government-insured mortgages.

Tandem Plan

One of the important methods that GNMA has used to render special assistance to the housing market in times of tight money and high discounts on federally underwritten fixed-interest loans, is to provide a subsidy for payment of a portion of the discount. This is handled under the "tandem plan," which means that GNMA works in conjunction with the private lenders as a support mechanism rather than as a competitive purchaser of mortgages. Under the tandem plan, early in 1971, GNMA established a purchase price of 97 for all Section 235 mortgages and par (100) for all Section 236 mortgages. As of August 6, 1971, the program was extended to new house loans at 96 and existing house loans at 95, with a limitation of $22,000 on such a loan, or $24,500 if the house is a four-bedroom unit and the family numbers five or more. The program has undergone several revisions.

In its initial concept, the tandem plan was directed at specific programs that the government felt worthy of extra help. With the sharp declines in construction and the real estate market generally in 1973–74, GNMA broadened its programs to provide assistance for all home buyers. A limited amount of subsidy money was provided by Congress to pay the discounts necessary to reduce interest rates for any buyers on a first-come basis. The way this has been handled is for GNMA to offer to buy large blocks of commitments for money which must be loaned at fixed interest rates. For example, GNMA might offer to buy loans totaling $500 million with interest set at 8 percent for a price of 98.5. Since GNMA does not have a large field organization, these offers are handled through FHLMC and FNMA. As soon as such an announcement is made, a local originator such as a savings association, would immediately contact FHLMC requesting an allocation of the special program funds for their own use. (A mortgage company would probably make contact with

FNMA.) The allocations exhaust the funds available for any one program and the originators must then wait for the next special program that may or may not become operational.

To make these subsidized interest rate programs work, the originator is allowed to charge the borrower up to a maximum of 4½ points. The points permitted are 1 point "up front" to pay for the commitment, 1½ points as a marketing fee that goes to GNMA (GNMA buys the loans at 98.5 which provides their fee), and up to 2 points are permitted as an origination fee. In addition to the origination fee, the mortgage company or savings association that originated the loan could retain the servicing of the loans and earn for themselves a 3/8ths of 1 percent servicing fee over the life of the loan.

The tandem plan as presently implemented is a method whereby GNMA makes a commitment to a lender to buy a mortgage at a future date providing the loan is made at a predetermined interest rate which is lower than the prevailing market. GNMA then resells the loan at whatever discount is needed to meet the market rate, absorbing the difference between the purchase and selling prices. In this manner the government pays a portion of the cost of a loan in the amount of discount needed, but does not invest the massive amounts of cash that have been needed for previous plans of outright purchase of low interest rate mortgages. The objectives of the plan are listed as follows:

1. To hold down mortgage interest rates for the home buyer without stifling the flow of private investment funds.

2. To assure the loan originator of a firm price in advance of the loan transaction.

3. To minimize the discount that must be paid by a builder to be assured of loanable funds.

4. To avoid the massive cash expenditures of Treasury funds needed for a direct loan program.

Management and Liquidation of Loan Portfolio

Under the management and liquidating portion of GNMA operations, the Association carries the burden of orderly liquidation of the FNMA portfolio as of October 31, 1954. It is in the interest of the government to transfer these older mortgages into private financing channels as rapidly as possible and return the funds to the Treasury.

Another major function under this section is the authority granted to GNMA to guarantee securities issued itself, or by any other issuer approved for this purpose, in the form of a full government guarantee.

Mortgage-Backed Securities

In an effort to provide greater liquidity to its own pool of mortgages and to tap the growing source of funds in the hands of pension and trust funds, GNMA devised a method to issue a separate certificate of guarantee covering a specific block of FHA, VA, or Farmers Home Administration mortgages, or combinations of these federally underwritten mortgages. The block of mortgages for this purpose can be assembled by a mortgage banker, or a group of them, or by any other approved lending institution in a minimum amount of $2 million. After examination of the block of mortgages by GNMA, if all are found to be in order, a certificate of guarantee is issued for the entire block. For a purchaser of the guarantee certificate, the purpose is to provide a security of a quality similar to a government bond and paying a slightly higher yield for a long term.

After the first four years of operations in this type of certificate, GNMA had guaranteed and sold over $7.5 billion of such securities. In the beginning of the program, most of the purchases had been made by thrift institutions. But, by fiscal year 1974, over 80 percent of these securities were being purchased by pension funds and other nonmortgage-oriented institutions at a rate of over $3 billion per year. The general public also participated in the purchase of certificates which are issued in smaller denominations.

Sources of Money

As a branch of the federal government, GNMA has several methods that it may use to provide money for its purchase of mortgages. These are as follows:

1. *The United States Treasury.* The Chartering Act for GNMA authorizes the Association to issue its obligations and the Secretary of the Treasury to purchase these obligations which are redeemable within five years and at interest rates determined by the Secretary of the Treasury.

2. *Appropriations by Congress.* From time to time, Congress appropriates money to assist home buyers, displaced families, and victims of natural disasters. The housing assistance is in the form of direct subsidies and low interest loans. When GNMA handles such programs, it is under the specific direction of Congress and limited to the amount of money appro-

priated for that purpose. The money used for the purchase of mortgages under the tandem plan is appropriated by Congress. The intention of this plan is to subsidize the discount necessary to provide home buyers with less than market interest rates.

3. *Sale of Securities.* As an agency of the government, GNMA is authorized to issue guarantee certificates and sell securities to investors and the general public.

GNMA is expected to be self-supporting in its operating expenses. The money comes from fees collected on its mortgage transactions, not from the federal treasury.

Continuing Role of GNMA

As an agent of the federal government, GNMA will continue to exercise considerable influence over real estate financing through its various moves in the residential mortgage market. The government effort is in the direction of (1) minimizing the fluctuations in mortgage money that directly affect the ability of the housing industry to operate on a stable basis, and (2) providing the housing the country needs. It can be generally stated that with each successive recession since the depression years of the 1930s, the swings have been a little less violent. While complete stability may neither be obtainable nor desirable, the role of GNMA will continue to be directed toward reducing the cycles and to provide various forms of assistance when money rates climb and the market falls off.

In striving to reduce the extent of housing cycles, GNMA provides the government with one more tool to utilize.

QUESTIONS FOR DISCUSSION

1. How has the FHA achieved the goals for which it was established?

2. What are the present limits on an FHA insured commitment for a single family residence under Section 203(b);

3. How does the FHA handle the present requirements for certification of the plumbing in an existing house?

4. Discuss the guidelines used by the FHA in determining the effective income of a loan applicant.

5. In the FHA settlement requirements, what rules apply to the handling of the down payment? Closing costs? Non realty items?

6. Explain the differences between the loan commitments made by the VA and the FHA.

7. Distinguish between the release of liability for a veteran and the restoration of entitlement.

8. What is a mortgage backed security as conceived by GNMA and how does the program operate?

9. Describe the tandem plan used by GNMA to subsidize discount points so as to reduce interest rates for home buyers.

Chapter 8

Property Appraisal

PROPERTY APPRAISALS

One of the major factors controlling the actual amount of a real estate loan is the appraised value. In the not too distant past a loan officer or other official of a lending institution would determine property value based on personal knowledge and experience in the area. Only in the past few decades has the skill of the professional appraiser been recognized as a valuable addition to the proper analysis of a mortgage loan.

Today, we have two highly professional organizations, both headquartered in Chicago, that qualify members after careful consideration of their educational background, their practical experience in the field, and their passing of extensive tests in this subject. These are:

1. The American Institute of Real Estate Appraisers, which was organized under, and requires an applicant to be a member of, the National Association of Realtors. The Institute issues two basic designations—Residential Member (RM) and Member Appraisal Institute (MAI). The MAI designation is considered by many experts to be tops in the field.

2. The Society of Real Estate Appraisers, developed primarily from the savings and loan group of staff appraisers, now grants three designations—Senior Residential Appraiser (SRA), Senior Real Property Appraiser (SRPA) for commercial properties, and their highest designation, Senior Real Estate Analyst (SREA) qualified to appraise any type of property.

Definition of an Appraisal

An appraisal may be defined as an estimate of the value of an adequately described property as of a specific date, which is supported by an analysis of relevant data. An appraisal is an evaluation of ownership rights. Appraisals can be delivered in three forms: (1) a letter form that describes the main points, (2) a form such as the combined FHMLC–FNMA appraisal report illustrated in Figure 8-1, or (3) a narrative form that goes into considerable analytical detail to substantiate the findings.

Principles of Appraising

How do appraisers approach their problems? What are they looking for in determining values? What analytical details should lenders or borrowers expect to find in written appraisals?

Principles of Appraiser's Analysis. First, let us look at the broad theory behind a professional appraiser's analysis. There are certain principles that guide their thinking in evaluating property. Most important among these are the following:

1. *Supply and demand.* The same theory underlying all economic practice is that scarcity influences supply and that what people want controls the demand.

2. *Substitution.* The value of replaceable property will tend to coincide with the value of an equally desirable substitute property.

3. *Highest and best use.* It is the use of the land at the time of the appraisal that will provide the greatest net return. This requires the proper balance of the four agents of production (labor, coordination, capital, and land) to provide the maximum return for the land used.

4. *Contribution.* This principle applies to the amount of value added by an improvement, such as an elevator in a three-story building, or the value added to a building lot by increasing the depth of that lot.

5. *Conformity.* To achieve maximum value the land use must conform to the surrounding area. An over-improvement, such as a $100,000 house built in a neighborhood of $30,000 homes, will lower the value of the larger house.

6. *Anticipation.* Since value is considered to be the worth of all present and future benefits resulting from property ownership, the anticipation of future benefits has to be evaluated.

RESIDENTIAL APPRAISAL REPORT

File No. _____

To be completed by Lender

Borrower/Client	Census Tract _____ Map Reference _____
Property Address	
City _____ County _____	State _____ Zip Code _____
Legal Description	
Sale Price $ _____ Date of Sale _____ Property Rights Appraised ☐ Fee ☐ Leasehold ☐ DeMinimis PUD(FNMA only) ☐ Condo ☐ PUD)	
Actual Real Estate Taxes $ _____ (yr) Loan charges to be paid by seller $ _____ Other sales concessions	
Lender _____ Lender's Address	
Occupant _____ Appraiser _____ Instructions to Appraiser	

NEIGHBORHOOD

					Good	Avg.	Fair	Poor
Location	☐ Urban	☐ Suburban	☐ Rural					
Built Up	☐ Over 75%	☐ 25% to 75%	☐ Under 25%	Employment Stability	☐	☐	☐	☐
Growth Rate ☐ Fully Dev.	☐ Rapid	☐ Steady	☐ Slow	Convenience to Employment	☐	☐	☐	☐
Property Values	☐ Increasing	☐ Stable	☐ Declining	Convenience to Shopping	☐	☐	☐	☐
Demand/Supply	☐ Shortage	☐ In Balance	☐ Over Supply	Convenience to Schools	☐	☐	☐	☐
Marketing Time	☐ Under 3 Mos.	☐ 4–6 Mos.	☐ Over 6 Mos.	Quality of Schools	☐	☐	☐	☐
Present Land Use ___% 1 Family ___% 2–4 Family ___% Apts. ___% Condo ___% Commercial				Recreational Facilities	☐	☐	☐	☐
___% Industrial ___% Vacant ___% _____				Adequacy of Utilities	☐	☐	☐	☐
Change in Present Land Use ☐ Not Likely	☐ Likely (*)		☐ Taking Place (*)	Property Compatibility	☐	☐	☐	☐
(*) From _____ To _____				Protection from Detrimental Conditions	☐	☐	☐	☐
Predominant Occupancy ☐ Owner	☐ Tenant	_____ % Vacant		Police and Fire Protection	☐	☐	☐	☐
Single Family Price Range $ _____ to $ _____ Predominant Value $ _____				General Appearance of Properties	☐	☐	☐	☐
Single Family Age _____ yrs to _____ yrs Predominant Age _____ yrs				Appeal to Market	☐	☐	☐	☐

Note: FHLMC/FNMA do not consider the racial composition of the neighborhood to be a relevant factor and it must not be considered in the appraisal.

Comments (including those factors adversely affecting marketability) _____

SITE

Dimensions _____ = _____ Sq. Ft. or Acres ☐ Corner Lot

Zoning classification _____ Present improvements ☐ do ☐ do not conform to zoning regulations

Highest and best use: ☐ Present use ☐ Other (specify) _____

	Public	Other (Describe)	OFF SITE IMPROVEMENTS		
				Topo	_____
Elec.	☐	_____	Street Access: ☐ Public ☐ Private	Size	_____
Gas	☐	_____	Surface _____	Shape	_____
Water	☐	_____	Maintenance: ☐ Public ☐ Private	View	_____
San.Sewer	☐	_____	☐ Storm Sewer ☐ Curb/Gutter	Drainage	_____
	☐ Underground Elect. & Tel.	☐ Sidewalk	☐ Street Lights	Is the property located in a HUD identified Flood Hazard Area? ☐ No ☐ Yes	

Comments (favorable or unfavorable including any apparent adverse easements, encroachments or other adverse conditions) _____

IMPROVEMENTS

☐ Existing (approx. yr. blt.) 19___ No. Units _____ Type (det, duplex, semi/det, etc.) _____ Design (rambler, split level, etc.) _____ Exterior Walls _____

☐ Proposed ☐ Under Construction No. Stories _____

Roof Material _____ Gutters & Downspouts ☐ None Window (Type): _____ Insulation ☐ None ☐ Floor

☐ Storm Sash ☐ Screens ☐ Combination ☐ Ceiling ☐ Roof ☐ Walls

Foundation Walls _____ % Basement ☐ Floor Drain Finished Ceiling _____

☐ Outside Entrance ☐ Sump Pump Finished Walls _____

☐ Crawl Space **BSMT.** ☐ Concrete Floor ___% Finished Finished Floor _____

☐ Slab on Grade ☐ Evidence of: ☐ Dampness ☐ Termites ☐ Settlement

Comments _____

ROOM LIST

Room List	Foyer	Living	Dining	Kitchen	Den	Family Rm.	Rec. Rm.	Bedrooms	No. Baths	Laundry	Other
Basement											
1st Level											
2nd Level											

Total _____ Rooms _____ Bedrooms _____ Baths in finished area above grade.

INTERIOR FINISH & EQUIPMENT

Kitchen Equipment: ☐ Refrigerator ☐ Range/Oven ☐ Disposal ☐ Dishwasher ☐ Fan/Hood ☐ Compactor ☐ Washer ☐ Dryer ☐

HEAT: Type _____ Fuel _____ Cond. _____ AIR COND: ☐ Central ☐ Other _____ ☐ Adequate ☐ Inadequate

						Good	Avg.	Fair	Poor
Floors	☐ Hardwood	☐ Carpet Over	☐						
Walls	☐ Drywall	☐ Plaster ☐		Quality of Construction (Materials & Finish)		☐	☐	☐	☐
Trim/Finish	☐ Good	☐ Average ☐ Fair ☐ Poor		Condition of Improvements		☐	☐	☐	☐
Bath Floor	☐ Ceramic	☐		Rooms size and layout		☐	☐	☐	☐
Bath Wainscot	☐ Ceramic	☐		Closets and Storage		☐	☐	☐	☐
Special Features (including fireplaces): _____				Plumbing—adequacy and condition		☐	☐	☐	☐
_____				Electrical—adequacy and condition		☐	☐	☐	☐
				Kitchen Cabinets—adequacy and condition		☐	☐	☐	☐
ATTIC: ☐ Yes ☐ No ☐ Stairway ☐ Drop-stair ☐ Scuttle ☐ Floored				Compatibility to Neighborhood		☐	☐	☐	☐
Finished (Describe) _____ ☐ Heated				Overall Livability		☐	☐	☐	☐
CAR STORAGE: ☐ Garage ☐ Built-in ☐ Attached ☐ Detached ☐ Car Port				Appeal and Marketability		☐	☐	☐	☐
No. Cars _____ ☐ Adequate ☐ Inadequate Condition _____				Effective Age _____ Yrs. Est. Remaining Economic Life _____ Yrs.					

PROPERTY RATING

PORCHES, PATIOS, POOL, FENCES, etc. (describe) _____

COMMENTS (including functional or physical inadequacies, repairs needed, modernization, etc.) _____

FHLMC Form 70 Rev. 9/75   ATTACH DESCRIPTIVE PHOTOGRAPHS OF SUBJECT PROPERTY AND STREET SCENE   FNMA Form 1004 Rev. 9/75

FIGURE 8-1a.

VALUATION SECTION

COST APPROACH

Measurements		No. Stories	Sq. Ft.	ESTIMATED REPRODUCTION COST – NEW – OF IMPROVEMENTS:
x	x	=		Dwelling _____ Sq. Ft. @ $ _____ = $ _____
x	x	=		Sq. Ft. @ $ _____ = _____
x	x	=		Extras _____ = _____
x	x	=		= _____
x	x	=		= _____
x	x	=		Porches, Patios, etc. _____ = _____

Total Gross Living Area (List in Market Data Analysis below) _____
Garage/Car Port _____ Sq. Ft. @ $ _____ = _____

Comment on functional and economic obsolescence: ___•___
Site Improvements (driveway, landscaping, etc.) = _____

Total Estimated Cost New . . . . = $ _____

	Physical	Functional	Economic	
Less Depreciation $		$	$	= $ ( )

Depreciated value of improvements . . . . = $ _____
ESTIMATED LAND VALUE . . . . = $ _____
(If leasehold, show only leasehold value)

INDICATED VALUE BY COST APPROACH . . . $ _____

The undersigned has recited three recent sales of properties most similar and proximate to subject and has considered these in the market analysis. The description includes a dollar adjustment, reflecting market reaction to those items of significant variation between the subject and comparable properties. If a significant item in the comparable property is superior to, or more favorable than, the subject property, a minus (-) adjustment is made, thus reducing the indicated value of subject; if a significant item in the comparable is inferior to, or less favorable than, the subject property, a plus (+) adjustment is made, thus increasing the indicated value of the subject.

MARKET DATA ANALYSIS

ITEM	Subject Property	COMPARABLE NO. 1		COMPARABLE NO. 2		COMPARABLE NO. 3	
Address							
Proximity to Subj.							
Sales Price	$	$		$		$	
Price/Living area	$	$		$		$	
Data Source							
Date of Sale and Time Adjustment	DESCRIPTION	DESCRIPTION	+(–)$ Adjustment	DESCRIPTION	+(–)$ Adjustment	DESCRIPTION	+(–)$ Adjustment
Location							
Site/View							
Design and Appeal							
Quality of Const.							
Age							
Condition							
Living Area Room Count and Total	Total / B-rms / Baths	Total / B-rms / Baths		Total / B-rms / Baths		Total / B-rms / Baths	
Gross Living Area	Sq.Ft.	Sq.Ft.		Sq.Ft.		Sq.Ft.	
Basement & Bsmt. Finished Rooms							
Functional Utility							
Air Conditioning							
Garage/Car Port							
Porches, Patio, Pools, etc.							
Other (e.g. fireplaces, kitchen equip., heating, remodeling)							
Sales or Financing Concessions							
Net Adj. (Total)		☐ Plus; ☐ Minus $		☐ Plus; ☐ Minus $		☐ Plus; ☐ Minus $	
Indicated Value of Subject		$		$		$	

Comments on Market Data _____

INDICATED VALUE BY MARKET DATA APPROACH . . . . $ _____

INDICATED VALUE BY INCOME APPROACH   (If applicable) Economic Market Rent $ _____ /Mo. x Gross Rent Multiplier _____ = $ _____

This appraisal is made ☐ "as is" ☐ subject to the repairs, alterations, or conditions listed below ☐ completion per plans and specifications.

Comments and Conditions of Appraisal: _____

Final Reconciliation: _____

This appraisal is based upon the above requirements, the certification, contingent and limiting conditions, and Market Value definition that are stated in
☐ FHLMC Form 439 (Rev. 9/75)/FNMA Form 1004B filed with client _____ 19 ___ ☐ attached.
If submitted for FNMA, the report has been prepared in compliance with FNMA form instructions.

I ESTIMATE THE MARKET VALUE, AS DEFINED, OF SUBJECT PROPERTY AS OF _____ 19 ___ to be $ _____

Appraiser(s) _____ Review Appraiser (If applicable) _____
☐ Did   ☐ Did Not Physically Inspect Property

FIGURE 8-1b.

The Narrative Type Appraisal

With the theory of the appraisal principles as a background to guide the analysis, the appraiser presents information in a logical sequence. The narrative report, which is the most comprehensive form of appraisal, uses the following pattern and guidelines:

Description of the Property. The property should be defined in accurate legal wording, and the precise rights of ownership must be described. The rights may be a leasehold interest, mineral rights, surface rights, or the full value of all the land and buildings thereon.

The Date and Purpose of the Appraisal. Appraisals can be made for times other than the present, such as when needed to settle an earlier legal dispute. The date of the appraised value must be clearly shown. Also, the purpose of the appraisal should be stated as it will influence the dominant approach to value. In professional appraisals there is no such thing as a buyer's or seller's value—this is not a "purpose" as identified here. An example of purpose would be to estimate value for an insurance settlement, which would involve a cost approach to value as claims are adjusted on the basis of cost. If the purpose is a condemnation action, the most relevant approach would be the market value.

The Background Data. While the standard form and simple letter report will not provide any economic background data, the narrative report discloses the economic information as clues to value. An overall study of the market region, which may be as large as an entire state, is made. The focus is then brought down to the local area—the town or the portion of a city where the property is located. From there the analysis narrows to the specific neighborhood and then to the actual site under appraisal.

The Approaches to Value. Appraisers use three common approaches to determine value: (a) cost, (b) market, and (c) income. All approaches should be used wherever possible, and all should reach approximately similar values, although these values are seldom the same. In certain appraisals, only one approach may be practical, such as valuing a city hall building for insurance purposes. In this analysis only a cost approach would be practical as there is not much buying or selling of city halls to provide market data, nor is there a true income from the building itself to provide figures for an income approach. A single-family residence may appear to lack any income for analysis, but certain neighborhoods have sufficient houses being rented to provide enough data to reach an income approach conclusion. The three approaches to value are discussed in greater detail later in this chapter.

Qualifying Conditions. If in the analysis of the property, the appraiser discovers any material factors that will affect the property's value, these can be reported as further substantiation of the conclusion.

Estimate of Value. This is the real conclusion of the study, the figure most people turn to first when handed a finished appraisal. Each of the approaches to value will result in a firm dollar valuation for that approach. Then, it is the purpose of this estimate to explain why one of the approaches to value is favored over the others. For example, with an income property such as a motel, the value judgment would rest most heavily on the income analysis. The final conclusion is a single value for the property and represents the considered knowledge and experience of the appraiser making the report.

Certification of the Appraiser and His or Her Qualifications. The professional appraiser certifies to his or her opinion by signature, and disclaims any financial interest in the property being appraised that could influence a truly objective conclusion. A recitation of the appraiser's educational background, standing within the profession as indicated by professional ratings, and previous experience such as appraisals previously made and for whom, serves to substantiate the quality of the appraisal for the underwriting officer.

Addendum. Depending on the need for clarification, the appraisal will include maps of the area under consideration with the site pointed out, plus the location of comparable properties referred to in the analysis. Charts may be used to indicate such things as the variables in a market analysis. Photos of the actual property are usually mandatory.

Three Approaches to Property Values

In order to understand more clearly the use of the three approaches to value, which is the essence of an appraisal, each is discussed below.

Property Value as Determined by Cost Approach

The cost approach is developed as the sum of the building reproduction costs, less depreciation, plus land value. The reproduction costs
can be developed the same a builder would prepare a bid proposal
by listing every item of material, labor, field burden, and administrative overhead. Reproduction cost estimates have been simplified in
active urban areas through compilation of many cost experiences
converted to a cost per square foot figure. The offices of active appraisers collect such data in depth for reference.

Depreciation, by definition, detracts from the value and must be
deducted from the reproduction costs. Depreciation consists of three
separate types:

1. *Physical deterioration.* The wear and tear of the actual building—this is
   the type most commonly associated with the word depreciation. Examples would be the need for repainting, a worn-out roof needing new
   shingles, and rotting window casements. These are "curable" items and
   under the breakdown method should be deducted from value as a reha-
   bilitation cost. All other items of physical deterioration are "incurable,"
   that is, not economically feasible to repair. An illustration would be the
   aging of the foundations or of the walls, and this kind of deterioration
   should be charged off as a certain portion of the usable life of the building. Another method of handling physical deterioration, in contrast to
   the breakdown method, is the engineering or observed method wherein
   each major component of the building is listed, and a percent of its full
   life is charged off. This method recognizes that each major component of
   a building may have a different life and the percentage of depreciation
   would vary at any point in time.

2. *Functional obsolescence.* Equally as important as physical deterioration is
   that category of loss in value resulting from poor basic design, inadequate
   facilities, or outdated equipment. These elements, too, can be curable or
   incurable. An example of incurable functional obsolescence would be a
   two-bedroom, one-bath house, which was very popular at the end of
   World War II, but now is a hard item to sell in today's more demanding
   market. There could be an excess of walls or partitions in an office building, which would cost money to remove and modernize, but would be
   curable. Lack of air conditioning in a hotel or office building is another
   example of curable functional obsolescence.

3. *Economic obsolescence.* The third type of depreciation has a more elusive
   quality and really is not in the building at all. Economic obsolescence is
   that set of factors outside and surrounding the property that affect the
   value, requiring the determination of the plus or minus effect of these
   forces. Some are very obvious influences—a new freeway bypassing an

existing service station, the construction of an undesirable industry in an area adjacent to residential property, or the bridging of a stream to open new land for development. The more difficult problem is ascertaining economic impact of the long-term rise or fall of a specific neighborhood. While land owners are able to exercise some voice in protest or encouragement of these outside forces, for the most part what is done with neighboring properties is not controllable and is not curable. And it will always be a force that will affect the value of an individual property.

The other factor to be considered under the cost approach is the value of the land. Lately, almost all land has been marked by a steady appreciation in value. But economic factors can adversely affect land value as well as favorably influence it. Normally, land value can be determined through an examination of recent sales of similarly located properties—the same basic method as used under a market approach to value. However, there are sometimes specific reasons for changes in the appraised value of land. Buildings can and do deteriorate, while the land itself can continue to increase in value due to the same outside factors noted in economic obsolescence above. For example, as urban areas expand, certain intersections become more and more valuable, new throughways and freeways concentrate greater flows of traffic, and huge shopping centers add to the value of all surrounding land. As the suburban sprawl moves outward, former farm land increases in value when it is converted into residential subdivisions; or, as another example, in some older sections of a city the land can become more valuable than the building. The building itself may represent such poor usage of the land that it becomes a liability to the property value, and its removal costs can be deducted from the stated value of the land. It is these fluctuations in land value that bring cost-analysis into step with market evaluation.

Property Value as Determined by Market Approach

Also known as a sales-comparison approach, the value by market approach is determined by prices paid for similar properties. Since no two properties are ever precisely comparable, much of the analysis under this method concerns itself with the detailing of major characteristics and whether these add to or subtract from the value of the property. These details of comparison cover items such as date of sale, location of property, size of lot, type of materials used in construction, and many other factors that the appraiser considers relevant.

The market approach represents one of the most important analyses, as the true worth of any property is the actual amount for which it can be sold. And to this end, accurate information on the present market is essential.

Some confusion does exist in the use of sales prices and asking prices. The appraiser is primarily concerned with completed sales and with sales uncomplicated by extraneous pressures such as forced sales, estate disposals, or transfers within a family. The asking or offering price is considered by most to represent a ceiling or maximum value for the property. Appraisers usually recognize the inherent inaccuracy of an asking price, especially one set by homeowners. This figure is often arrived at by adding the original purchase price, plus the full cost of all improvements that have been made, plus the selling commission, plus the owner's amateur notion of general market appreciation. But every so often an owner actually receives such a sales price from a willing buyer, and this makes the professional feel a bit foolish!

Property Value as Determined by Income Approach

Because the income approach looks at the actual return per dollar invested, it is the most important method for any investment property.

When people buy investment property they normally expect to recover, or "recapture" in appraisal terminology, their money with a profit. They do this from two sources: (1) the annual earnings (excess income over all costs) and (2) the proceeds from a resale at the end of the term of ownership, called *reversion,* or *recapture* of the residual value.

Thus, value of property by the income approach is derived by capitalizing the present worth of an income stream for a certain number of years plus a lump sum reversion at the end of the stream.

Capitalization is achieved by dividing the stabilized income by the rate of return to equal value:

$$\frac{\text{Income}}{\text{Rate of return}} = \text{Value}$$

$$\frac{16,000}{.08} = \$200,000$$

or a reciprocal method,

$$\frac{100}{8} = 12.5 \qquad 12.5 \times 16{,}000 = \$200{,}000$$

Obviously there are many variables to consider in achieving the rather simple illustration above. The income itself is a projection of what the property can reasonably be expected to produce. The rate of return can and should be a composite rate reflecting perhaps one or two mortgage notes to be assumed plus the expected return on the equity investment. One can readily see the importance an appraiser must place in the selection of a rate of return—since a slight variation in this figure produces a wide variation in the calculated value.

The value of the reversion, or recapture of the residual value, is a calculated estimate of the property's value 15, 20, or 30 years from now. It requires knowledge and experience to support a realistic figure of this kind.

SURVEYS

One of the recurring problems in passing land titles and in making sure that a lender is actually receiving a mortgage on the proper land is the identification of that land. Improper identification of the property to be mortgaged, through field error or typographical error, will invalidate the mortgage instrument. It is to physically identify a parcel of land that a survey is made. A survey is an accurate measurement of the property, not a legal description of it.

An example of an error in property description occurred in a motel loan several years ago. In this case, the property described in the mortgage was identified by the perimeter of the building, rather than by the boundaries of the land on which the building stood. The parking areas surrounding the building, which provided the only access to the premises, were not included in the mortgage indenture. When it became necessary to foreclose, the mortgagee learned that he did not have access to the property!

A survey for our purposes is the physical measurement of a specific piece of property certified by a professionally registered surveyor. In processing a mortgage loan, no lender will accept any measurements other than a professional's, as it is a precise business and the loan package requires an accurate description of the land being mortgaged.

When a licensed surveyor defines a piece of property, it is customary to drive stakes or iron rods into the ground at the corners and to "flag" them with colored ribbons. It is not unusual for a lending officer to physically walk the land, checking the corner markers, and thus satisfying himself as to the shape of the parcel, and whether or not there might be any encroachments that would infringe on the mortgage lien. However, the prime responsibility to determine encroachments belongs to the surveyor, which is one of the reasons why a survey is necessary.

LEGAL DESCRIPTIONS

A completed survey is a map showing each boundary line of the property with its precise length and direction. A survey should not be confused with the legal description of a piece of land. A legal description describes property in words, while a survey describes by illustration. Legal descriptions are most commonly found in the following three forms.

Lot and Block

The best known type of legal description is that found in incorporated areas that have established procedures for land development. A subdivider, in obtaining city approval to build streets and connect utilities, submits a master survey of the entire block of land, showing how the subdivision is broken into *lots,* which are then numbered and grouped into *blocks* for easier identification. Once the subdivision plat is accepted, it is recorded in the county offices and becomes a readily available legal reference to any lot in the plan.

For lending purposes, where the need is to identify a specific property over a period of 30 or even 40 years, the recorded subdivision plat is a much better method than a street address. Street names change and numbers can be altered, but the lot and block numbers remain secure because they are recorded. It may be argued that a street address gives a much better picture of where a property lies in discussing various houses or properties, but such identification is not sufficiently accurate to be acceptable to a lender. The common method of clearly identifying property in real estate transactions is, first, to give the legal description, followed by a phrase such as "also known as," and then to provide the street address. To illustrate, a property identification might be spelled out as, "Lot 6, Block 9, Nottingham Addition, Harris County, Texas, also known as 1234 Ashford Lane, Houston, Harris County, Texas."

Metes and Bounds

When recorded plats are not available for identification of land (and sometimes when plats *are* available), it becomes necessary to use an exact survey of the boundary lines for complete identification. This might be true of a recorded lot that has a stream or river as one boundary—the precise boundary being subject to change through erosion or realignment.

The method used is to define a starting corner with proper references to other marking lines, then note the direction in degrees and the distance to the next marking corner, and so on around the perimeter of the property back to the starting point. These descriptions can be quite lengthy and involved. An example of the wording used to describe several boundary lines might be: ". . . and thence along said Smith Street south 61 degrees 32 minutes 18 seconds west 948 and 25/100 feet; thence continuing along said Smith Street south 64 degrees 45 minutes 51 seconds west 162 and 80/100 feet to the point of beginning."

It is obvious that considerable accuracy is required to figure the necessary directions down to a second of a degree and to measure the distances over highly variable and often rough terrain in order to close the boundaries properly. Such a description is acceptable only if certified by a registered surveyor.

In some rural areas, land is identified in the form of metes and bounds by the use of monuments. A "monument" may be something tangible such as a river, a tree, rocks, fences, or streets; or intangible such as a survey line from an adjoining property. Physical monuments such as these are subject to destruction, removal, or shifting, and do not provide lasting identifications for long-term loans.

Geodetic or Government Survey

As long ago as 1785, the federal government adopted a measurement system for land based on survey lines running north and south, called *meridans,* and those running east and west, called *base lines.* The system eventually applied to 30 western states with the exception of Texas. A number of prime meridians and base lines were established. Then the surveyors divided the areas between the intersections into squares, called *checks,* which were 24 miles on each side. These checks were further divided into 16 squares, each measuring 6 miles by 6 miles, called *townships.* The townships were then divided into square mile units (36 to a township), called *sections,* which amounted to 640 acres each. These sections were then divided into halves, quarters, or such portions as were needed to describe individual land holdings. An example is shown in the diagram below.

During the growth years of our country, much of our western land was laid out in this fashion by contract survey crews. Marking stakes were duly placed to identify the corners, and these stakes are frequently used today. The fact that many of the surveys accumulated errors, including the failure to close lines, has created some confusion that concerns principally the oil and mining companies today who are attempting to identify leases, and ranchers claiming property lines against a neighbor.

However, these faulty descriptions have not constituted a serious problem for lending institutions. Land described, for example, as "Section 16, Township 31 north, Range 16 east, New Mexico Prime Meridian," could effectively handle a farm or ranch loan, and a minor inaccuracy in describing such a tract would not undermine the basic security of the collateral.

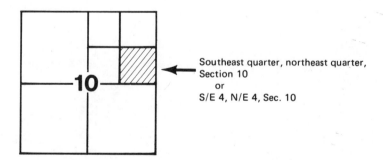

Southeast quarter, northeast quarter, Section 10
or
S/E 4, N/E 4, Sec. 10

In pledging property where there is the possibility or probability that some slight inaccuracy has occurred as to the exact amount of land involved, it is customary to use a qualifying term such as "comprising 640 acres, more or less." Any variation in property size should be considered in the light of what might be termed "reasonable." A few acres out of line among 640 acres would not matter a great deal, but a few feet in a downtown city property could well be of critical importance.

QUESTIONS FOR DISCUSSION

1. Define an appraisal.

2. What qualifications does a mortgage lender require for an appraiser? Identify the leading professional designations for appraisers.

3. What is meant by the "highest and best use" of land?

4. Describe each of the three principal forms in which appraisals can be presented. What are the advantages of each?

5. List the eight steps or sections normally found in a narrative form of appraisal.

6. Describe each of the three approaches to value and given examples of the type property for which each would be most applicable.

7. Name the three categories of depreciation associated with real property. What is the function of each?

8. How would you capitalize an income stream so as to show a property value? What is the reversion value?

9. Distinguish between a survey and a legal description.

10. Give an example of a typical legal description made by lot and block numbers.

Chapter *9*

Analyzing Borrowers

Most mortgage loans are made to individuals or to individual co-borrowers. It is the borrower who is expected to repay the loan, usually from regular income, rather than from the sale of the property. So the lender looks first to the strength of the borrower. The analysis of a borrower is concerned with an individual who has certain rights to privacy under the laws. However, the lender feels an obligation to determine the true credit-worthiness of the borrower to whom he is being asked to lend money—usually money that belongs to other individuals. In the past few years the laws have changed to provide new, and more equitable, guidelines for the granting of credit. Questions that might lead to discriminatory decisions have been eliminated from applications, and the lender is expected to base the analysis on strict financial comparisons. The procedures followed by the FHA and VA in evaluating a borrower have been covered in Chapter 7. This chapter will examine methods used for conventional loans; first, the individual home buyer, then information on credit reports, and finally, some of the problems in analyzing corporate borrowers.

THE LOAN APPLICATION

The basis for an analysis of the borrower starts with the loan application. In 1974, Congress passed the Equal Credit Opportunity Act which prescribes limits on the information that may be asked by a lender in the application for a loan. The act has been implemented under the direction of the Federal Reserve Board and is administered by the Consumer Affairs office of the Federal Reserve. The initial act prohibits discrimination in the granting of credit on the basis of sex and marital status. On March 23, 1976, the ECOA was amended to expand the prohibition against discrimination in credit transactions to include race, color, religion, national origin, sex, marital status, age, receipt of public assistance income, and the exercise of rights under the Consumer Credit Protection Act, of which the ECOA is a part.

Because lenders have always felt a responsibility to obtain full and adequate information about a borrower, the restrictions on what questions may be asked present major problems for an underwriter and have caused extensive revisions in the processing procedures. The areas of greatest concern with the changes are the restrictions on questions regarding marital status, age, and the receipt of public assistance benefits. In the past lenders have undoubtedly given more consideration to a borrower who (1) has a strong motivation to own a home, such as rearing children; (2) who is young enough to have a reasonable expectation of repaying a 30-year loan in his or her lifetime; and (3) who is gainfully employed in a full-time job. The guiding purpose was to make loans with the best expectations of being repaid; not to discriminate. But Congress has now set specific requirements.

The restrictions covering information on sources of an applicant's income do not apply if the applicant expects to use that income as a means of repaying the loan. For example, no questions may be asked regarding alimony, child support, or maintenance payments unless the borrower plans to use this money to make the loan payments. No discounting of income is allowed because of sex, marital status, or because income is derived from part-time employment. In regard to a credit history, an applicant must be permitted to show evidence that facts in a joint report do not accurately reflect his or her individual ability or inclination to repay the loan. If credit is denied, the lender must provide the reasons for denial upon request of the applicant.

The act preempts only those applicable state laws that are inconsistent with the federal requirements. Lenders in states that may impose additional requirements, such as additional prohibitions as to what may be on a loan application, must also comply with the state laws. It should be noted that the requirement of the act for separate liability for separate accounts (married persons can demand that separate credit records be maintained in either a married or a maiden name) cannot be changed by state laws. However, any action taken by a creditor in accordance with *state property laws* directly or indirectly affecting credit-worthiness will not constitute discrimination.

In general, the new laws do not specify how or to whom loans should be made, but do call for lenders to be much more specific with reasons for the rejection of a loan applicant. Generalizations and categories of persons not eligible for credit are no longer permissible. For example, a married person who is separated can no longer be categorized as not acceptable for credit, but must be considered as an individual and judged by the same standards as any other person. There will continue to be a difference in the standards that a lender may use for long-term mortgage credit as opposed to a short-term installment type of credit but the standards must be applied uniformly to all applicants.

Secondary market lenders also have specific requirements for information to meet their own analysis procedures. A standard application form has been sponsored through the cooperative efforts of the Federal National Mortgage Association and the Federal Home Loan Mortgage Corporation. This form is reproduced in Figure 9-1 and should be studied in detail. Its use is mandatory only if the loan is to be sold to either FNMA or FHLMC. However, many loan originators have adopted the same form as it meets all current federal requirements, most other lender requirements, and there is always the possibility that the loan may eventually be sold to one of the sponsoring agencies.

The amended Real Estate Settlement Procedures Act (RESPA) which became effective in June 1976, places two requirements on the lender when a written application for a mortgage loan is received. The first requirement is to give the borrower-applicant a copy of a booklet entitled "Settlement Costs Guide" which has been prepared by the Department of Housing and Urban Development. The guide gives information to the applicant regarding real estate practices and lists the borrower's rights and obligations. The second requirement of the lender is to provide the applicant with a "good faith estimate" of

RESIDENTIAL LOAN APPLICATION

MORTGAGE APPLIED FOR	Type ☐Conv. ☐FHA ☐VA	Amount $	Interest Rate %	No. of Months	Monthly Payment Principal & Interest $	Escrow/Impounds (to be collected monthly) ☐Taxes ☐Hazard Ins. ☐MI ☐

Prepayment Option

SUBJECT PROPERTY

Property Street Address	City	County	State	Zip	No. Units

Legal Description (Attach description if necessary)	Year Built	Property is: ☐Fee ☐Leasehold ☐Condo ☐PUD ☐DeMinimis PUD

Purpose of Loan: ☐Purchase ☐Construction-Perm. ☐Construction ☐Refinance ☐Other (Explain)

Complete this line if Construction-Perm. or Construction Loan ☞	Lot Value Data Year Acquired ____ $	Original Cost $	Present Value (a) $	Cost of Imps. (b) $	Total (a+b) $	ENTER TOTAL AS PURCHASE PRICE IN DETAILS OF ☐ PURCHASE

Complete this line if a Refinance Loan					
Year Acquired	Original Cost $	Amt. Existing Liens $	Purpose of Refinance	Describe Improvement [ ] made [ ] to be made	Cost: $ ____

Title Will Vest in What Names?   How Will Title Be Held? (Tenancy)

Note Will Be Signed By?   Source of Down Payment and Settlement Charges?

BORROWER			**CO-BORROWER***		
Name	Age	Sex**	School Yrs	Name	Age	Sex**	School Yrs

Present Address No. Years ____ ☐Own ☐Rent	Present Address No. Years ____ ☐Own ☐Rent
Street	Street
City/State/Zip	City/State/Zip
Former address if less than 2 years at present address	Former address if less than 2 years at present address
Street	Street
City/State/Zip	City/State/Zip
Years at former address ☐Own ☐Rent	Years at former address ☐Own ☐Rent

Marital Status ☐Married Yrs. ____ ☐Unmarried ☐Separated	(Check One)** ☐American Indian ☐Negro/Black ☐Oriental ☐Spanish American ☐Other Minority ☐White (Non-minority)	Marital Status ☐Married Yrs. ____ ☐Unmarried ☐Separated	(Check One)** ☐American Indian ☐Negro/Black ☐Oriental ☐Spanish American ☐Other Minority ☐White (Non-minority)
Dependents other than Co-Borrower		Dependents other than listed by Borrower	
Number Ages		Number Ages	

Name and Address of Employer	Years employed in this line of work or profession? ____ years Years on this job ____ ☐Self Employed***	Name and Address of Employer	Years employed in this line of work or profession? ____ years Years on this job ____ ☐Self Employed***
Position/Title	Type of Business	Position/Title	Type of Business

GROSS MONTHLY INCOME				**MONTHLY HOUSING EXPENSE**	PREVIOUS	PROPOSED	**DETAILS OF PURCHASE**	
Item	Borrower	Co-Borrower	Total					
Base Income	$	$	$	First Mortgage (P&I)		$	a. Purchase Price	$
Overtime				Other Financing (P&I)			b. Total Closing Costs	
Bonuses				Hazard Insurance			c. Pre Paid Escrows	
Commissions				Taxes (Real Estate)			d. Total (a + b + c)	$
Dividends/Interest				Assessments			e. Amt. This Mortgage	( )
Net Rental Income				Mortgage Insurance			f. Other Financing	( )
Other (SEE SCHEDULE BELOW)				Homeowner Assn. Dues			g. Present Equity in Lot	( )
				Total Monthly Pmt	$	$	h. Amt. of Deposit	( )
				Utilities			i. Closing costs paid by Seller	( )
Total	$	$	$	Total	$	$	j. Cash required for closing	$

DESCRIBE OTHER INCOME

▽ B—Borrower C—Co-Borrower   NOTE: ALIMONY/CHILD SUPPORT PAYMENTS NEED NOT BE LISTED UNLESS THEIR CONSIDERATION IS DESIRED

		Monthly Amt.
		$

IF EMPLOYED IN CURRENT POSITION FOR LESS THAN TWO YEARS COMPLETE THE FOLLOWING

B/C	Previous Employer/School	City/State	Type of Business	Position/Title	Dates From/To	Monthly Salary
						$

QUESTIONS APPLY TO BOTH BORROWERS

If Yes, explain on attached sheet

	Borrower Yes or No	Co-Borrower Yes or No		Borrower Yes or No	Co-Borrower Yes or No
Have you any outstanding judgments, ever taken bankruptcy, had property foreclosed upon, or given deed in lieu thereof?	____	____	Do you have health and accident insurance?	____	____
			Do you have major medical coverage?	____	____
Co-Maker or endorser on any notes?	____	____	Do you intend to occupy property?	____	____
Defendant/Participant in a Law Suit?	____	____	Will this property be your primary residence?	____	____
Obligated for child support/alimony payments?	____	____	Have you previously owned a home?	____	____
Any portion of the down payment borrowed?	____	____	Value of previously owned home	$ ____	$ ____

*Complete this section and all other co-borrower questions about spouse if the spouse will be jointly obligated with the borrower on the loan or if the borrower is relying on the spouse's income or on community property in obtaining the loan.
**This information is requested only for statistical purposes in accordance with the intent of fair housing law. Furnishing this information is voluntary, but borrowers are urged to do so. No lending decision will be made on the basis of this information or on whether or not it is furnished.
***FHLMC requires self employed to furnish signed copies of one or more most recent Federal Tax Returns or audited Profit and Loss Statements. FNMA requires business credit report, signed Federal Income Tax returns for last two years, and, if available, audited P/L plus balance sheet for same period.

FHLMC 65 Rev. 3/76   FNMA 1003 Rev. 3/76

FIGURE 9–1a.

210

This Statement and any applicable supporting schedules may be completed jointly by both married and unmarried co-borrowers if their assets and liabilities are sufficiently joined so that the Statement can be meaningfully and fairly presented on a combined basis; otherwise separate Statements and Schedules are required (FHLMC 65A/FNMA 1003A). If the co-borrower section was completed about spouse, complete this statement and supporting schedules about spouse also.

☐ Completed Jointly ☐ Not Completed Jointly

ASSETS		LIABILITIES AND PLEDGED ASSETS		
Description	Cash or Market Value	Owed To (Name, Address and Account Number)	Mo. Pmt. and Mos. left to pay	Unpaid Balance
Cash Toward Purchase held by		**Indicate by (*) which will be satisfied upon sale or upon refinancing of subject property.**		
		Installment Debt (include "revolving" charge accounts)	$ Pmt./Mos. /	$
Checking and Savings Accounts (Indicate names of Institutions/Acct. Nos.)			/	
			/	
			/	
Stocks and Bonds (No./description)			/	
Life Insurance Net Cash Value *Face Amount ($*			/	
		Automobile Loan		
SUBTOTAL LIQUID ASSETS			/	
Real Estate Owned *(Enter Total Market Value from Real Estate Schedule)*		Real Estate Loans (Itemize and Identify Lender)	╳	
Vested Interest in Retirement Fund			╳	
Net Worth of Business Owned (ATTACH FINANCIAL STATEMENT)			╳	
Auto (Make and Year)		Other Debt Including Stock Pledges (Itemize)	╳	
			/	
Furniture and Personal Property		Alimony and Child Support Payments	╳	
Other Assets (Itemize)			/	
		TOTAL MONTHLY PAYMENTS	$	
TOTAL ASSETS	A. $	NET WORTH (A.−B.) $	TOTAL LIABILITIES $	B. $

SCHEDULE OF REAL ESTATE OWNED (If Additional Properties Owned Attach Separate Schedule)

Address of Property (Indicate S if Sold, PS if Pending Sale or R if Rental being held for income)	Type of Property	Present Market Value	Amount of Mortgages & Liens	Gross Rental Income	Mortgage Payments	Taxes, Ins. Maintenance and Misc.	Net Rental Income
TOTALS →							

LIST PREVIOUS CREDIT REFERENCES

B—Borrower C—Co-Borrower	Owed To (Name and Address)	Account Number	Purpose	Highest Balance	Date Paid
				$	

AGREEMENT: The undersigned hereby applies for the loan described herein to be secured by a first mortgage or trust deed on the property described herein and represents that no part of said premises will be used for any purpose forbidden by law or restriction and that all statements made in this application are true and made for the purpose of obtaining the loan. Verification may be obtained from any source named herein. The original or a copy of this application will be retained by the lender even if the loan is not granted.

I fully understand that it is a federal crime punishable by fine or imprisonment or both to knowingly make any false statements concerning any of the above facts, as applicable under the provisions of Title 18, United States Code, Section 1014.

Signature (Borrower) _____ Date _____ Signature (Co-Borrower) _____ Date _____

Home Phone _____ Business Phone _____ Home Phone _____ Business Phone _____

The Federal Equal Credit Opportunity Act prohibits creditors from discriminating against credit applicants on the basis of sex or marital status. The Federal Agency which administers compliance with this law concerning this _____ is _____
(type of lender)   (regulatory agency and address)
Additionally the Federal Fair Housing Act also prohibits discrimination on the basis of race, color, religion, sex or national origin.

FOR LENDER'S USE ONLY

(FNMA REQUIREMENT ONLY) This application was taken by _____ , a full time employee of
Interviewer

_____ , in a face to face interview with the prospective borrower.
(Name of Lender)

FHLMC 65 Rev. 3/76   REVERSE   FNMA 1003 Rev. 3/76

FIGURE 9–1b.

the settlement service charges the applicant is likely to incur. This estimate must be furnished within three business days of the written application for a loan. The RESPA requirements are covered in greater detail under Chapter 14, "Settlement Procedures."

FINANCIAL EVALUATION OF THE BORROWER

The high loan-to-value ratio (LTVR) of the loan negotiated for house purchases today places a premium on the borrower's repayment ability. The conventional lender, or the private mortgage insurance company selected, cannot expect a recovery of money from the forced sale of collateral in the first few years of the loan. Proper analysis of the borrower to determine total available income, any claims against that income, as well as the credit record, is important for a home loan. A borrower's other assets are helpful as additional security for a loan and can result in a lower rate of interest, but other assets cannot always be counted on for use in repayment. The lender knows that in many cases of actual default in payments the borrower has met with financial problems that were beyond his or her control, such as accidents, job lay-offs, or serious illness in the family; and that such problems can deplete most of the family's financial assets, leaving the lender with few means of recourse beyond the house that has been pledged.

Inevitably then a loan is "good" to the extent that the borrower is good. To initiate the collection of information necessary to analyze a borrower, a loan application is taken. There are some variations of these forms, but the essentials are always there, including (1) identification of the borrower, (2) description of the property, (3) the amount of the loan requested, (4) the borrower's employment and income record, (5) the borrower's assets and liabilities, and (6) the borrower's credit references and certification as to the validity of the information being submitted.

No two borrowers ever present the same credit picture. Analysis of a borrower still defies any attempt to impersonalize the procedure to the point of computerization. But there are some guidelines and general rules, mainly based on common sense, that are helpful in determining whether or not a borrower can make a loan repayment. To make a sound prediction, the underwriter of the loan considers two basic questions: (1) What is the person's ability to pay? (2) What is the person's willingness to pay?

Ability to Pay

More than any other type of loan, the home loan looks to a family's income as the basic resource for repayment. Assets are important but are used in part to determine the spending or saving patterns practiced in the use of that income. Therefore, a careful review of the employment record, present income, and future potential is important. Below are listed some of the income elements considered by a lender, with a commentary on each topic.

Types of Income

In today's multi-job standard that includes more than one jobholder in many families, the actual total income can be difficult to arrive at, as this information suggests:

Salary. The salary is the easiest form of income to determine and generally a more secure type of income.

Bonus. A bonus should not be counted on unless a regular pattern can be established for several successive years.

Commission. A straight commission job can be very lucrative, or it can be a complete bust. Only a past record of income can be accepted as factual, culled from several years of tax returns.

Hourly Wages. The hourly wage is a solid basis for continuing income and one that can usually be confirmed from an employer.

Overtime Wages. This is an uncertain basis for making a larger loan as most employers try to avoid overtime and use it only as an emergency or temporary practice. Again, a consistent pattern of overtime payments for several years would make this an acceptable addition to the gross effective income.

Second Job. Many persons today hold more than one job on a full- or part-time basis. Teachers, policemen, skilled hourly workers, all can have other capabilities and may spend extra hours augmenting their income. If the second job has been held over a period of several years on a regular basis, it provides a substantial lift to the regular income.

Unreported Income. A few people accept extra work, or even become involved full-time, in jobs that pay in cash and on which income is not reported for tax purposes. Such income, if not reported, is illegal and cannot be used under any condition as income to justify a loan. This "borrower" could reach an abrupt end to his free income via the prison route.

Co-Borrower's Income. Prior to the enactment of the Federal Equal Credit Opportunity Act, it was fairly common practice to reduce the effective income that could be accepted from a working wife. The reasoning then was that young married couples who dominate the home buying market were also interested in raising families. And earlier customs generally assigned more of the problems concerned with family emergencies, sickness, pregnancies, and child care to the wife. The new laws recognize changing customs and a lender is now required to apply the same qualification standards to each borrower without questioning marital status or sex.

Income from Children. While many young men and women, living with their parents, earn substantial money at full- or part-time jobs, these earnings are not a recognized addition to the family income for loan purposes. The obligation on the part of the children to contribute to the family finances for support of the home is not a permanent one, since normally they will leave the homestead and set up their own household within a few years. Thus, temporary income supplied by grown children lends no real weight to the loan request.

Pensions and Trusts. Few home buyers in the past have enjoyed pensions, retirement funds, or other work benefits at a sufficiently early age to apply them toward a home purchase. However, the pattern is changing. For instance, many veterans of military and other government services have now completed 20 or 30 years of employment before the age of 50. These benefits are, of course, one of the most reliable forms of income.

Child Support and Alimony. Some states do not permit alimony but provide child support as a matter of court decree. Other states permit both alimony and child support. Such payments can be considered as regular income for a divorcee or remarried person, depending on the court ruling. However, the record of payment must show dependability over a period of time before it would constitute an acceptable addition to total income in full amount. No information need be given on this source if it is not to be counted as income for repayment of the loan.

Self-Employed. Many persons operate their own businesses or work as individuals in professional capacities. Since there is no employer to verify actual income, the only acceptable method of validating this income is by referral to previous income tax reports. Certified copies of these returns can be obtained from the Internal Revenue Service for a small fee upon application by the taxpayer only. Some small businessmen are able to pay certain living expenses from their business (car expenses and depreciation, entertainment, travel, etc.), but weight can only be given to the actual income reported as taxable.

Interest and Dividends. These funds normally represent a stable income but must be considered from the angle of a possible sale of the asset for another purpose. Again, the past record would indicate the probable future pattern in any given case.

Part-Time Employment. Income derived from part-time work has in the past not been accepted at full value towards a person's income applicable to repayment of a mortgage loan. The new ECOA requirements now permit no discounting of this source of income. However, the lender may still require that such income show evidence of stability and reasonable assurance that it will continue.

Welfare Assistance. In the past few years, the concept of welfare as an assist for a disadvantaged person has given way to the idea that this is a right of an individual. Consequently, Congress has determined under the new ECOA requirements that welfare payments must be considered without discount by a lender if the applicant expects to use the welfare assistance as a part of his or her income for repayment of the loan.

Stability of Income

Along with the size of an applicant's income, the assurance that it will be continued must be investigated. Two factors are involved: (1) time on the job, and (2) type of work performed.

Length of Time. Some lenders hold to a policy of rejecting all applicants with less than three years tenure at their present job. There is a basis for this restriction in that any new job may or may not work out, either due to personality factors or to lack of accomplishment. But with the more rapid changes in jobs today, the job tenure can be more fairly judged from the individual's job history. Has the applicant made a record of "job hopping" without noticeable improvement in his income? Is the present job one of greater responsibility and growth potential than the previous job? Has the applicant maintained a record of employment in a chosen field of work and qualifications, or is the present job an entirely new type of work?

The question of job tenure does not lend itself to easily defined limits due to the variables mentioned above. But most lenders hold to some minimum term of employment, generally from one to three years.

Type of Work. While a person with a long record of employment provides the soundest answer to the question of income stability, not everyone seeking loans can provide such a record. The type of work engaged in does give good clues as to future stability.

Persons with salaried jobs with the larger companies and professional people with tenure are considered the most secure. Hourly workers with the protection of union contracts are far more stable (and often higher paid) than lower level management and clerical staff workers. Government employees carry good security as do teachers, policemen, and other service workers. On the lower side of the scale, new sales representatives enticed by stories of high commissions, entertainers, and seasonal workers give poor evidence of continued stable income. To some lenders, socially unacceptable types of work carry unduly low ratings. Self-employed persons should have a record of successful operations to assure stability as more small businesses fail than ever succeed.

For women, only recently has the spectrum of jobs available broadened to include almost every type of work. Rated among the highest for stability are teaching, nursing, and the growing executive group. Secretarial work as a class rates rather poorly, mainly from lack of continued interest; but the top legal, professional and executive secretaries not only command good salaries but are virtually assured of continuous work today. A few of the less stable categories are clerical workers, models, actresses, and waitresses. A growing number of young and older women are going into commission sales work with about the same mixed success as men.

Analyzing Income Factors

Few conventional lenders have established rigid patterns or detailed forms to evaluate an applicant's income. The more common procedure is for the lenders to establish certain basic minimums to guide the loan processor and to base their lending on the record of the agent's results. Every loan underwriter builds a personal record with a lender, and any difficulties or foreclosure may serve to diminish the lender's confidence in the underwriter's analysis and judgment. Broad guidelines for analyzing income stability for loan applications would include such items as:

1. An effective gross income of four or five times the monthly payment.

2. A job tenure of at least eighteen months.

3. Total of all monthly installment obligations, including mortgage payment, less than 40 percent of monthly income.

4. Determination of effective income by including base pay plus all other family income that applicant has stated will be used to repay the loan.

Variations abound in these guidelines, and the only constant is the continued effort of the lender to make sound loans that will be repaid without problems.

Liabilities

All charges or obligations against an applicant's income must be considered in determining the amount available to meet the mortgage obligation. The liability connected with the normal costs of supporting a family and maintaining a house is taken into consideration by limiting the mortgage payment to 20 or 25 percent of the applicant's effective income.

It is the extraordinary charges that must be examined. If other monthly payments exceed one year in pay-off time, they should be deducted against the regular income to arrive at effective income. Such charges as car payments, boat or trailer payments, furniture payments, and loan repayments are all demands upon the monthly income. In conventional lending, these charges can also be weighed against other assets, rather than solely against income.

Assets

Most home buyers are younger couples who have not yet accumulated very many assets. The purchase of a house represents one of the largest investments they will make. But the addition of such values as stocks, bonds, real estate, savings funds, and other assets does indicate an ability to live prudently and conserve a portion of the income. Life insurance is both an asset in its cash value and protection features and a liability in its cost. Cars and boats represent some trade-in value. Furniture and personal property are often overvalued in an applicant's statement of assets because of the owner's personal attachment. Employee trust and pension funds can represent value if the interest is a vested one, i.e., if employees can take the funds with them if they leave the job. An interest in one's own business should be determined by an actual financial statement of that business. Accounts and notes receivable should be detailed for proper valuation.

Willingness to Pay

The element of willingness to pay, sometimes called *credit character*, is the most difficult to analyze and judge. Yet this factor alone can be the cause of a loan rejection. The most tangible information concerning an individual's record of handling obligations comes from the credit bureau report. Information may also be derived from public records regarding litigation, judgments, or criminal actions. Conversations with persons involved in the house sale transaction can sometimes bring to light information on the applicant's manner of living, personal attitudes, and activities that might give cause for a more detailed investigation. The initial loan application often is taken at the lending company's offices, but it can be handled at the residence of the applicant. Some lenders expect a personal call to be made on the applicant by their agents, as a person's manner of living can be most helpful in judging the credit character.

Under the category of "willingness to pay," lenders have always tried to assess an applicant's *motivation* for owning a home. Lenders in the past have felt that the strongest incentive for owning a home came from a family unit committed to the rearing of children. But life styles change and many persons today are not interested in having a family but do want houses. Even prior to the enactment of

the Equal Credit Opportunity Act, lenders were enlarging the qualification standards and making loans to single persons, both men and
women, and non-family units where there was a reasonable assurance
of continuity of interest in owning a house. ECOA has eliminated
sex and marital status as a basis for a loan rejection, but it has not
foreclosed the lender's right to exercise judgment as to the continuing need to repay a mortgage loan. This is an area that does not lend
itself to clear-cut definitions and presents problems for a responsible
loan officer.

Under this category of credit attitude, a formidable barrier must
be surmounted: the problem of invasion of privacy. Attitudes are
changing among lenders but still range over a broad spectrum. The
older, highly personal approach to a loan is still practiced in smaller
communities and by many venerable lending institutions. Some savings and loan associations will not approve a loan without personal
contact with the applicant by at least one, sometimes two, lending
officers.

At the other extreme we find efforts to make the analysis as im-
personal as possible. The thought here is to minimize the effects of
personalities, of likes and dislikes, or of prejudices that have relatively little bearing on the strength of the applicant. These efforts
center around some form of a rating chart with columns such as
"good, fair, and poor" for judging 10 to 20 basic factors on the applicant's credit record. Each factor carries a different value in points
for "good" or "fair," and must total a certain minimum to qualify.
More than one rating in the "poor" column can be an automatic
rejection.

It is in this area of trying to bridge the gap for the remote lender
that the mortgage banker can serve as eyes, ears, and interpreter to
bring all the facts into focus. The true picture can be just as advantageous for the borrower as for the lender and is mandatory in making
proper judgment on any loan. Individuals asking to borrow someone else's money should be willing to provide complete and accurate
information about themselves within the requirements of the Equal
Credit Opportunity Act.

HELPFUL HINTS

Few individuals are experienced in making loan applications. Sometimes raw facts can be misinterpreted, and an explanation is needed
to clarify the situation. Lenders vary considerably in the amount of
cooperation they can or will extend to the borrower in explaining

requirements or correcting omissions. Some of the problem areas and possible answers are discussed below.

Loan Amount versus Income. If the size of the amortization payments is too large for reasonable repayment within the effective income, the lender can suggest a smaller loan. This could well mean a smaller house but still an upgrading in living standards.

Large Monthly Obligations. When a debt load for other purchases, such as a car or furniture, takes too big a bite out of an applicant's income, the lender may suggest a delay in handling the loan for six or eight months to permit the repayment of nonrecurring obligations before undertaking an additional debt.

Failure to Meet All Qualifications. If the applicant fails to qualify under a minimum requirement, such as time on the job, the endorsement of another person may be added to secure the note. In a home loan, it is best that the endorser have a real and sustaining interest in the borrower, such as a parent would have.

CREDIT REPORTS

Individual Credit

In most metropolitan areas there are a number of agencies that furnish credit information on individuals and companies. Credit bureaus, by definition, act as an impartial gathering point of factual information on consumers. Other reporting firms, known as "investigative" reporting companies collect credit information and also data required by insurance companies on the individual. There are also firms which compile records on businesses and these are known as commercial reporting firms.

The mortgage business, for the most part, has followed the lead of the FHA and VA which make contracts with one of the major agencies for each area. The one selected is usually affiliated with Associated Credit Bureaus, Inc. and has ready access to exchange information from other credit bureaus in other areas of the country.

Credit bureaus are heavily dependent on the cooperation of local banks, merchants, and other financial institutions to relay factual data to them. From the information collected, a credit report is assembled and is available to firms which contract for credit reporting service. Each request for a credit report must be for a permissible purpose as outlined in the Fair Credit Reporting Act.

This law, which was passed by the U.S. Congress in 1970, spells out the obligations of the user of the report as well as the credit bureau. Consumers have the right to know the full contents of their file, and may request this information from the credit bureau.

A typical credit report contains four sections. The first two lines contain identifying information. The second section relates to the present employment of the subject of the report. The third section contains data about the individual including former address, former employer, and employment of spouse. The fourth section contains the credit history of the paying habits of the consumer. Each of the 15 columns of the credit history are necessary to provide the reader of the report with a complete picture of the paying habits of the consumer.

Credit reports contain a brief history of past employment, salary or other manner of compensation, and a record of credit experience. In a mortgage credit report it is customary to show a review of the county records for judgments and liens of any kind. Figure 9-2 is a copy of a typical credit report showing how the information is presented by a typical credit bureau. The back of this form explains the abbreviations used in the credit history section.

One of the problems of credit reporting is the possibility of misfiling credit information. The confusion of same names, similar names, changes of married names, and just plain errors can cause an unjustified adverse report, or perhaps fail to give a true picture. Several years ago the use of social security numbers became standard procedure among the credit bureaus, but the new credit laws specifically forbid the lender from requiring disclosure of the applicant's social security number as a condition for making a loan.

Another problem besetting credit reporting is the recent successful legal attacks on credit bureaus when an erroneous report causes damage to a person or company. Information detrimental to a person's credit position can be damaging, and many retail companies follow the easiest route to avoid problems by simply not reporting information. This practice of refusing to furnish any information on credit customers in order to avoid possible damage suits diminishes the value of any cooperative report.

Fair Credit Reporting

The Fair Credit Reporting Act is intended to give an individual the right to examine a summary of the information on file with any credit reporting agency making reports on that individual. The individual may require that erroneous information be corrected. The Act does not give the individual the right to inspect the actual

☐ SINGLE REFERENCE	☐ IN FILE REPORT ☐ TRADE REPORT
☒ FULL REPORT	☐ EMPLOY & TRADE REPORT ☐ PREVIOUS RESIDENCE REPORT
☐ OTHER _____	

Credit Bureau of Anytown
1234 Main Street
Anytown, Anystate   70036

Date Received	**CONFIDENTIAL**
4/1/77	**crediscope® REPORT**
Date Mailed	
4/4/77	
In File Since	
12/68	Member Associated Credit Bureaus, Inc.
Inquired As	

FOR Acme Department Store
Fourth and F Streets
Anytown, Anystate   70034

REPORT ON: LAST NAME	FIRST NAME	INITIAL	SOCIAL SECURITY NUMBER		SPOUSE'S NAME
Doe,	John	G	457-36-5077		Betty

ADDRESS:	CITY	STATE:	ZIP CODE	SINCE:	SPOUSE'S SOCIAL SECURITY NO.
2505 Union	Anytown	Anystate	70030	9/75	436-21-5777

COMPLETE TO HERE FOR TRADE REPORT AND SKIP TO CREDIT HISTORY

PRESENT EMPLOYER:	POSITION HELD:	SINCE:	DATE EMPLOY VERIFIED	EST. MONTHLY INCOME
XYZ Oil Company	Engineer	8/12/72	4/4/76	$ 1200

COMPLETE TO HERE FOR EMPLOYMENT AND TRADE REPORT AND SKIP TO CREDIT HISTORY

DATE OF BIRTH	NUMBER OF DEPENDENTS INCLUDING SELF: 2	☒ OWNS OR BUYING HOME	☐ RENTS HOME	OTHER: (EXPLAIN) ☐
1944				

FORMER ADDRESS:	CITY:	STATE:	FROM:	TO:
1500 Strawberry Rd.	Thattown	Anystate	2/71	9/75

FORMER EMPLOYER:	POSITION HELD:	FROM:	TO:	EST. MONTHLY INCOME
Davel Construction Co.	Engineer	1/71	8/11/72	$ 900

SPOUSE'S EMPLOYER:	POSITION HELD:	SINCE:	DATE EMPLOY VERIFIED	EST. MONTHLY INCOME
First Insurance Company	Clerk	9/75	4/4/76	$ 550

CREDIT HISTORY (Complete this section for all reports)

WHOSE	KIND OF BUSINESS AND ID CODE	DATE REPORTED AND METHOD OF REPORTING	DATE OPENED	DATE OF LAST PAYMENT	HIGHEST CREDIT OR LAST CONTRACT	BALANCE OWING	PAST DUE AMOUNT	NO. OF PAYMENTS	NO. MONTHS HISTORY REVIEWED	30-59 DAYS ONLY	60-89 DAYS ONLY	90 DAYS AND OVER	TYPE & TERMS (MANNER OF PAYMENT)	REMARKS
J	B 142	4/77 A	1971	3/77	5,000	3,550			12				I -$110	
1	C 157	3/77 M	1972	1/77	300	110	$10	1	12				R -$ 10	
J	H 311	3/77 M	1970	1/77	1,250	800			12				I -$ 75	DRP
J	C 85	4/77 A	1969	2/77	180	60	$40	4	12	2		1	R -$ 10	

CIVIL SUIT JUDGMENT
Municipal Court, Docket 296-C
July 8, 1975. Plaintiff - Jackson Auto Repair.
Judgment for $500. Satisfied 12/1/76.

FORM 2000-1/77

FIGURE 9-2.

Copy furnished by courtesy of Associated Credit Bureaus, Inc., John L. Spafford, President.

credit report covering his or her record, but a summary must be shown free of charge if there has been an adverse record filed. The federal agency responsible for administering this act is the Federal Trade Commission headquartered in Washington, D.C. with regional offices in the rest of the country.

CORPORATE CREDIT ANALYSIS

To analyze adequately the credit-worthiness of a company, it is necessary for the underwriter to become acquainted and fully cognizant of every phase of the business under scrutiny: management, sales, production, purchasing, research and planning, personnel policies, and the physical plant and equipment, as well as to make a careful study of the financial statements. There is wide latitude in the quantity and quality of detail needed to answer the fundamental question of whether or not it would be advisable to make a loan to the corporate applicant.

The underwriter expects to have a current, preferably audited, financial statement presented along with the loan application. An *audited* statement is one in which all the pertinent data is verified by the independent accountants preparing the report. The figures are presented in a form and according to rules determined by the accountants, and in which the final conclusions are certified as correct and accurate by the accredited accountants. The principal factors a lender will look for are the record of profitable use of existing assets, the accumulation of cash and property versus outstanding obligations, and the very important working ratio of current assets to current liabilities. The latter indicates both the manner of operation and the immediate cushion of assets available to protect the company against a temporary reversal.

Personal interviews with company officers are utilized to fill in more detail of what the company's plans are and how it intends to carry them out. Where larger loans are involved, it is routine procedure to verify the company's market and its ability to sell its product. Comparative balance sheets and profit and loss statements covering the previous ten years of operations give excellent indications of how the company has handled its business and what the general trend will be. Also, a Dun and Bradstreet report (one of the largest national credit reporting services) can give something of the history on the company, which helps to project future capabilities. It is the long-range ability of the company to operate profitably that is the real key to the trouble-free recovery of a loan.

In order to evaluate the results of the loan on the company's finances, it is customary to prepare a *pro forma* statement—both the balance sheet and the profit and loss statement. These statements are a projection of what the loan will do, such as increase the investment in productivity, add a new product line, provide an additional service, or broaden a market, as well as the expected effects of that loan on the profitability of the company.

To assure the lender that the proceeds of the loan are used as projected, a loan agreement is drawn up that spells out the purpose of the loan and can provide penalties for nonconformance. In addition, certain restrictive covenants are often added to the loan agreement that will place limits on such things as loans or advances to officers or employees until the loan is paid off, control the payment of salaries and dividends, limit any other borrowing, and require approval of the lender before any major assets, patents, or leasehold interests can be sold. All terms of the loan agreement are negotiable and are designed primarily to assure the lender's interest in the company over a period of time during which the ownership and management can change drastically but the loan obligation continues on.

QUESTIONS FOR DISCUSSION

1. List the essential classes of information that a prospective borrower must provide in a loan application.

2. Discuss ability to repay a loan as may be indicated by type of income and stability of income.

3. List four different types of income that a borrower might report on a loan application and discuss the acceptability of each type.

4. What additional information is necessary to verify the income of self-employed persons?

5. How are liabilities against a family income evaluated?

6. What is meant by "willingness to pay" and how can it be evaluated?

7. What information is normally obtained from a credit report on the loan applicant?

8. When a loan application is taken, what two RESPA requirements must be met by the lender?

9. In analyzing corporate credit, what further investigation would an underwriter employer beyond a careful study of the company's financial statements?

Chapter 10

Residential Loan Analysis

GENERAL ANALYSIS OF LOANS

The process of analyzing and approving a loan is called *underwriting.* The individual who assembles and analyzes the necessary data, and usually gives a company's consent to a specific loan, is referred to as the *underwriter.* Properly underwriting any loan requires a complete analysis of all pertinent factors, including: (1) the borrower's ability and willingness to pay; (2) the property, its condition, location, and usage; (3) all relevant economic influences; (4) laws controlling foreclosure procedures and assignments of rent; and (5) any unusual conditions that may exist.

An underwriter must examine the future and estimate the continued stability of the borrower, and must also try to judge the future values in a specific property. The underwriter must look beyond a normal appraisal, which provides an estimate of past or present value, and weigh the forces that affect the future based on the experience of the underwriter in this field.

A loan analysis covers a wide assortment of information; and from these diverse elements, an underwriter must determine the degree of risk involved. There is no such thing as a risk-free mortgage loan. It is the underwriter's prime responsibility to determine the magnitude of the risk, and to compensate for it in the terms and conditions of the loan. The degree of risk determines the ratio of loan to value, the length of time for repayment, and the interest rate required by the lender.

In this and the succeeding chapters, various types of properties will be analyzed to show the economics involved with each type. The conditions an underwriter looks for vary with the properties and the most important one is "where will the money come from to repay this loan and how certain is it that the income will continue?" With a residential loan, repayment can be expected from the borrower's personal income, hence the emphasis on a detailed analysis of the borrower's record of employment and earnings. With income property, the underwriter looks for the capability of the property itself to produce sufficient income to repay the loan. A shopping center has medium- to long-term leases that provide solid information on the stability and continuity of income. An apartment project with few leases and month-to-month tenancy depends on the general occupancy records for the area to provide clues to future income capability. Each of the property types presents its variations. The previous chapter studied the questions involved with borrower analysis with emphasis on his or her income. Now the questions involving the property itself will be discussed, starting with residential loans.

RESIDENTIAL LOAN PRACTICES

Most people borrow money to purchase a home only once or twice in a lifetime, so it is usually a new experience for the average borrower. How should this uninitiated person proceed? What are the normal practices in the field and to whom should the borrower turn for advice? Fortunately, there are many specialists in the business knowledgeable of local practices who can help the home buyer in making decisions.

The Real Estate Broker

Since the house is normally selected before a loan is considered, one of the first knowledgeable experts to look to is the broker handling the house sale. Most states have licensing and bonding statutes to assure the public of the broker's qualifications. The more competent brokers maintain current information on the various local sources of mortgage money, the type of loans each are negotiating, the interest rate, and the current fees charged for service. In the past, some brokers made arrangements with a cooperative lender to send customers to that lender for a split of the fee. The FHA banned this practice as it could be used to the disadvantage of the home buyer. And, in conventional loans, it is not considered to be a good procedure because it limits competition.

In some areas of the country, particularly in the smaller communities, a knowledgeable real estate broker can and does perform a valuable service for the lender by taking a loan application and handling some of the preliminary steps of asking for verifications. For this work the broker earns a portion of the finance fee. When actual work is performed on the loan application by the broker, the FHA permits payment in relation to the services rendered. Payments of this kind are not considered as "fee splitting."

Loan Broker

Independent loan brokers in some areas of the country are very active, maintaining contacts with real estate sales personnel, local savings associations, architects, attorneys, bankers, and any others who would have need for assistance in securing loans for their customers or clients. The independent broker could be called by the real estate broker, for example, at the consummation of a sales contract to assist the buyer in the proper placement of a loan.

The independent broker carries current knowledge of where the best loans can be secured and performs a valuable service for both borrower and lender, earning a brokerage fee, usually ½ to 1 percent of the loan, by taking the loan application from the borrower to make certain it is complete and accurate. The broker assists in the verification of data and assembles the essential information needed in the application package by the lender. The independent broker generally works with small lenders who cannot afford the fixed cost of a salaried representative making calls on potential customers.

Mortgage Companies

Leading the way in the field of merchandizing mortgage loans is the mortgage banking industry. In larger communities, mortgage companies compete heavily with each other through their loan representatives. In periods of easy money, some real estate brokerage firms are besieged with calls from mortgage companies seeking loan business. Those firms that can continue funding loans in periods of tight money gain considerable support from the real estate industry when money becomes more plentiful.

The mortgage company field representative is a trained specialist in the intricacies of loan applications, and sensitive to the points that need clarification or verification for proper underwriting evaluation. The mortgage company representative can take an application at the place and time most convenient to the applicant. It has been this type of assistance to the borrower that has enabled the mortgage companies to handle well over half of all home loans in the country.

Savings Associations

As pointed out in Chapter 4, savings and loan associations—the leading source for mortgage money—handle loans both through intermediaries, such as mortgage companies or brokers, and also directly to their customers. Some of the more aggressive savings associations have followed the mortgage companies' practice of sending loan representatives into the field to call on potential loan applicants. But most savings associations rely on their own depositors and the business contacts made by their officers to attract loan applicants into their own building locations to make applications for loans. Qualified lending officers take the loan applications, obtain the necessary substantiating information, and in most cases, personally present the application to the loan committee for approval. In this manner, the committee can interrogate the lending officer for any details they consider pertinent to their judgment of the loan.

Builders

When a new home is purchased directly from a builder, the builder may already hold a commitment for mortgage money that can be used by the home buyer. Some of the ways these commitments are handled are discussed below.

Competitive Method. The small-to-medium-sized builders may have their construction money secured without any commitment for the permanent loans. For example, a commercial bank carrying the construction financing would have little interest in making a permanent loan. If there is no commitment, the purchaser is free to seek whatever source of mortgage money that may be found.

Commitment Method, Construction. When a builder, and this would cover all sizes of builders, obtains construction money, the lender may request a first refusal right to all permanent loans on the project. The construction lender thus ties up a good source of loans for the future, which is one of the incentives to make the construction loan in the first place. To enforce this right, the lender can add a penalty provision in the construction loan agreement that provides for an extra ½ or 1 percent of the construction loan to be paid for a release of the construction mortgage if the loan is not handled through the same lender. A purchaser cannot be required to borrow money from a particular lender, but it can be a bit more costly to go elsewhere.

Commitment Method, Purchase. Some of the larger builders who can qualify for the lowest rates on their construction money, or use their own funds for this purpose, may purchase a future commitment for money direct from a savings association or other major source to protect future customers needing loans. The builder will pay at least 1 percent of the total commitment amount to hold the money, or may pay additional fees to assure the future home buyers a lower, more competitive interest rate. This expense, which in effect is a prepayment of interest by the builder for the benefit of the buyer, is charged back into the cost of the house. It is in this manner that some builders can advertise lower than market interest rates and obtain a competitive advantage in the housing market.

Associated Companies. A few of the larger builders who are almost national in scope are organized with their own affiliated mortgage companies or money sources to provide permanent loans. The tie-in is generally competitive with the market rates for money and is intended as a convenience for the buyer. These companies seldom press their full range of services upon a customer, but they carry a competitive edge by being available at the proper time.

Other Sources

Every community has a variety of other potential sources that a borrower may find helpful. These would include local loan offices of insurance companies, employee or labor union credit unions, state or city sponsored pension and trust funds that may be utilized for home loans, or perhaps a fraternal or religious organization that the borrower may be affiliated with which has lendable funds available to its members. Most of these lenders do not aggressively solicit home loans. The potential borrower must seek out these sources to obtain a loan as they do not generally provide the helpful assistance that is a hallmark of mortgage companies and savings associations. But the extra effort on the part of the borrower can be rewarded in the form of slightly lower interest rates.

CONVENTIONAL RESIDENTIAL LOANS

In Chapter 7 on government programs, the requirements for and methods used by the FHA and VA in handling residential loans were outlined. In conventional lending, the procedures employed are basically not very different because the goal is the same, namely, to make a sound loan, and this requires adequate information. The variations in conventional lending lie chiefly in the multitude of interpretations and special viewpoints that derive from the vast variety of conventional lenders exercising their individual ideas regarding requirements.

Gradually, however, the individuality associated with conventional loans is giving way to an increasing effort to conform with the outlines for loans prescribed by the secondary market operators. FNMA has its own particular forms, FHLMC requires certain procedures, and the private mortgage insurance companies have their own requirements. All of these agencies have established minimum standards of acceptability and maximum limits, which are subject to change as conditions may require.

In the past few years, the two big government-influenced secondary market operators, FNMA and FHLMC, have worked more closely together and have devised more uniform procedures that are acceptable to both. Two examples of this cooperation are illustrated in this text in the notes and mortgage instruments (Figures 3-1 and 3-2) and in the loan application form (Figures 9-1a and 9-1b). The continuing efforts within the industry to provide more uniform lending standards plus the effects of recent legislation aimed at discriminatory credit practices will tend to reduce the substantial variations in lending procedures.

The expression "conventional loan" is simply a loan that is not government-insured or government-guaranteed. Without such a government commitment, the conventional loan stands more on its own; the credit-worthiness of the borrower and the value of the property held as security become more important to the ultimate lender. Until recently there was nothing else a lender could do in case of default on a conventional loan except turn to the borrower and to foreclose the property. Lenders in distant places were reluctant to accept loans that might require the management and disposal of a repossessed house in a remote place. It is in this area of relieving a lender of the post-foreclosure problems that the FHA and the VA gained strength and acceptability.

Beginning in 1971, during a period in which private mortgage insurance became a requirement for home loans in excess of 90 percent, conventional loans grew more acceptable to the large lending institutions in the secondary market. For the borrower, private mortgage insurance made higher loan-to-value ratios more readily available which permitted lower down payments and broadened the potential market for homes.

Conventional residential loans may be categorized in many ways, including loan-to-value ratio, size of loan, type of property, location of property, and also the present or proposed usage of the property. Following is a discussion of the more important categories and elements affecting residential loans.

Loan-to-Value Ratio (LTVR)

The loan-to-value ratio denotes the amount of the loan as a percentage of the value of the property. The ratio applies to all types of loans. In line with this formula, the value of the property is the single variable. The most common definition of value favored by lenders is the appraised value of the property, or the selling price, whichever is the least. If a loan is being made where a sale is not involved, then the appraised value is the controlling factor.

Banking regulations have long permitted savings associations to make loans up to 90 percent of the property value, but many in the past have used a more conservative 80 percent limit. With the advent of low-cost private mortgage insurance and permission to make 95 percent loans, these ratios are changing and most banks and mortgage companies will negotiate 95 percent loans that are covered by mortgage insurance.

Size of Loan

Federally-chartered savings associations are now permitted to loan up to $42,000 on a 95 percent loan-to-value ratio and up to $55,000 on a 90 percent loan. The Federal Home Loan Mortgage Corporation as well as the Federal National Mortgage Association adhere to the same federally sponsored limits on the size of loans that they will purchase, which sets a firm pattern for the industry.

The separate states set their own limits for state-chartered associations, banks, and insurance companies. Many states elect to follow the pattern set by the national regulatory body, the Federal Home Loan Bank Board. As the controlling authority for member savings associations which are the largest single source of residential mortgage money, the FHLBB holds a dominant position.

There is no real minimum for a loan except pure economics. When a mortgage loan goes under about $10,000, it becomes more expensive to service, and the fee received does not justify the time and expense involved. Of course, the efficiency of organizations varies, and the minimums they can handle fluctuate accordingly. Some mortgage companies consider $20,000 as the minimum conventional loan that can profitably be accepted. To undertake loans of lesser amounts might mean the company would be forced to sell at greater discounts, which would prove unprofitable.

Loans exceeding a lender's limits can be handled by several banks or associations joining together, with one institution responsible for administering the loan. These are called *participation* loans and are more commonly found in the larger commercial loans. But as home loans continue to increase in size, it is not unusual to find several lenders participating in one home loan. For the largest home loans, roughly those reaching to $100,000 and more, the prudent lender would expect a borrower to show a sustaining annual income of about 75 percent of the loan amount, plus some depth in other personal assets.

There are no rules requiring any lender to make loans up to the maximum amounts permitted. Each lender maintains guidelines as to strength of borrower, type of property, neighborhood, etc., that would qualify for a maximum loan. Some states, such as Texas, no longer set maximums on residential loan amounts, and depend upon the lender's good judgment to establish the correct limit for any one loan. However, as interest increases in secondary market sales, lenders are reluctant to negotiate a loan that exceeds the dollar limits established in the secondary market.

Economic Stability

In considering geographic areas for purposes of making residential loans, lenders examine the future growth pattern of the entire region as well as the immediate neighborhood involved. Thus, loans in areas of high unemployment, or where there are mostly seasonal business patterns, or where the population depends heavily on a single industry are considered less desirable by many lenders. Mortgage lenders in such locations cannot expect much lendable funds from the large private institutional lenders. Local banks and savings associations provide some of the needed funds, and mortgage companies may purchase commitments from FNMA for their loans.

In areas of economic strength and sound growth, there are usually many sources of money willing to make loans. Competition for good loans tends to lower the interest rates charged, but the greater demand for money in growth areas keeps the rates in balance and reasonably close to the higher rates charged in areas of lower economic stability.

The Physical Property

Classifications of the physical property cover a multitude of factors. Most conventional residential loans are concerned with single-family units, but also include duplexes, triplexes, and fourplexes. Houses can be identified, too, by the number of bedrooms, or more commonly by the size of the property expressed in square footage of living area.

Townhouses are classified as single-family residences if the land is divided and can be pledged with the building. The use of common walls between the townhouses is acceptable if proper delineation is made in the deed description.

Houses located on unpaved streets are not acceptable to many lenders. One problem that occurs is the decreasing desirability of such a house, in case of a foreclosure sale, due to dust and wet weather inaccessibility. There is also the question of future paving assessments against the land.

For lenders, the classification of materials used in construction is generally confined solely to the exterior or facade of the house. Among the most commonly used materials are aluminum, asbestos, and wood sidings, or brick and stone. Brick and stone are more acceptable to lenders even though some types of wood may have longer lasting qualities.

The utilities available to the house are a consideration. Top preference is shown to an organized, municipally operated water and sewage system. With situations in which a small privately owned water system or private well is the source of water, a lender is concerned about the quality and continuity of the supply. Sewage systems are subject to increasingly rigid requirements as to the quality of effluent that may be released into a river or other waterway. The smaller systems may have difficulty financing an expanded plant. The use of septic tanks does not automatically result in a rejection, though many lenders refuse to make loans on such types of property.

The placement of electrical wires and telephone lines underground serves as an added attraction to the appearance of a neighborhood. However, this feature has little effect on the loan decision. Other niceties (amenities) such as a neighborhood club, swimming pool, or recreation area actually do increase values to some degree and are duly noted in the property appraisals.

Minimum square footage or ground area restrictions are not generally set out as such in a conventional loan. This is in contrast to the FHA, which has a number of such rules detailing minimum room size, number of people per room, maximum amount (one-third) of the lot that may be covered by housing, and other rules, which are not generally disqualifying factors in conventional loans. The overall area of living space is the main concern in conventional loans and many lenders use a thousand square feet as the acceptable minimum. Some lenders may refuse to loan on a single-bedroom detached house. The essential question here is, "Does the property have a sufficiently broad market to facilitate resale if this becomes necessary?"

Location of Property

Lines are drawn by most conventional lenders between urban, suburban, and rural housing. The differences are not always clearly delineated, but they do provide a broad classification that is useful in describing packages of loans.

Due to the sprawl of our great metropolitan areas, the term *suburban* now means almost any location in a recorded subdivision of land in the general area surrounding cities—the region of greatest growth in our country. *Urban* means the downtown and near downtown areas of our cities. *Rural* identifies farm housing and to many lenders, houses existing in the smaller towns. Rural is also occasionally used to identify housing without access to a central water and sewage system.

Neighborhoods. Lenders no longer specify areas or neighborhoods within a city that are acceptable for making loans. It used to be a common practice to delineate acceptable areas from unacceptable areas based primarily on anticipated changes in home values. Obviously, a neighborhood that is allowed to deteriorate does not make an attractive location for a 30-year loan. However, recent federal regulations prohibit lenders from drawing lines on a geographic basis that could constitute discrimination. The practice is known more commonly as "red-lining" from the lines drawn on city maps to guide loan officers. The prohibition is aimed at the elimination of racial discrimination that could result from arbitrary lines drawn around certain neighborhoods. Further, federally regulated lenders are required to disclose the geographic areas in which they have made their loans by census tract or by postal zipcode number.

Flood Prone Areas. The federal government has defined certain areas of the country over the past few years as flood plain zones. These are areas that have been flooded in the past 100 years, or if records do not exist, are calculated to have a one percent chance of being flooded. Any houses built in a designated flood plain may not be financed by any lender subject to any federal regulatory body unless minimum elevation requirements are met. The government will assist a homeowner by providing flood insurance in cooperation with selected private insurance companies in approved areas.

Age of Property

The age of a house is a simple, frequently used criterion for determining acceptable and unacceptable loans. The range varies from an insistence on exclusively new houses, which is very rare, to no fixed limit. Many lenders couple the age of the property with the neighborhood or location of the house. Some neighborhoods maintain their desirability over the years and 30- to 40-year-old houses may qualify for prime loans. However, the big secondary market purchasers of loans usually hold to a maximum age limit of 15 to 25 years to qualify for the best, or prime, rates.

Older houses that are not in the prime neighborhoods may still qualify for mortgage loans but at higher interest rates and for shorter terms. The originator of a loan must always keep in mind what the specific requirements of various sources of money are in regard to age.

Appraisers on conventional loans are expected to specify the actual age of a house in their report. Normally this can be determined from the owner or the builder or from building records. A knowledgeable appraiser can adjust this age to an "apparent age," which could vary in either direction. A neat, well-kept house and yard that has been carefully maintained would have a lower apparent age than a rundown, unkept property.

Another possibility for mortgage loans on the older houses is through the Federal Housing Administration programs. Contrary to the procedure used in conventional loans, the FHA appraiser is asked to give an opinion as to the remaining economic life of the house. The FHA limits its insured commitment to 75 percent of the remaining economic life; i.e., a remaining life of 40 years would permit an insured commitment for 30 years.

Usage of Property

Residential properties can be said to fall into four categories of usage insofar as mortgage loans are concerned. These include:

1. *Owner-occupied.* This property is considered to show prime security usage and accounts for most residential loans. Only owner-occupied units can command the highest ratio loans.

2. *Tenant-occupied.* Such property falls more into the commercial category of loan analysis, though it is still considered a residential loan for savings association tax purposes and so far as banking regulations are concerned. Since a rental house would not command first call on the owner's income, a lender could downgrade the collateral and make a smaller loan of, perhaps, 75 or 80 percent of the value.

3. *Resort Housing.* Until recently, resort houses could be described as cottages, sometimes poorly built of nonpermanent materials, and generally not acceptable as security for loans. The locations often lacked proper fire and police protection, were subject to vandalism and excessive storm damage, and were often not connected to municipal utility systems. In recent years the growth of new, higher class subdivisions in lakefront or mountainous areas has greatly improved the quality and, thus, the acceptability of these homes as collateral. Lenders do, in fact, make many resort home loans, but they adjust the amount downward from, perhaps, 65 to as high as 90 percent loan-to-value ratio.

In resort-type developments, it is not unusual for a developer to buy a loan commitment, paying the discount fee necessary to provide potential customers with a dependable, economical source of mortgage money.

4. *Second Homes.* Second homes are a close corollary to the resort home, though they differ in several ways. The more affluent society of the 1960s and 1970s has produced a growing number of families financially able to live in two different houses. On occasion, the house in the city might be less lived in and less occupied, on the whole, than the so-called second home in the country. With regard to financing, a lender usually makes a careful determination as to which house might be considered the primary housing entitled to preferential treatment, and which one should be downgraded as a second home, receiving an 80 percent or lower loan. A decision such as this would be required where the borrower was interested in making a purchase that is primarily based on a substantial annual income and not enough other assets. The lender must then consider the loan from the viewpoint of a sudden decrease in income due to job loss or working disablement. Which house, then, would most likely have to be forfeited under adverse circumstances?

UNDERWRITING GUIDES

The foregoing classifications of housing help to determine if a particular property will fall within the guidelines acceptable to a particular lender. For example, a lender might advise his correspondent that he is accepting applications for single-family residential loans in certain specified areas, for houses that are not over ten years old, and for loans not less than $20,000. This gives a broad range to work with, but then the evaluation must be focused on the individual property.

The most important piece of information is the appraisal, which provides a professional study of the physical property and the neighborhood. The photographs usually will show one or two views of the house, plus a shot of the street to give some clue to other houses in the neighborhood. The appraised value is compared with the selling price of the property, and a maximum loan limit is determined. The actual amount of the final loan offered is tempered by the borrower's own qualifications. The loan limit, as well as the interest rate and term of the loan, are determined by the amount of risk involved.

An experienced underwriter further checks the property for such factors as:

Location. Assuming the general location has been approved, the actual site within a subdivision can be important. If the property under consideration backs up to an undesirable neighbor, such as an all-night drive-in food store, a lower loan limit might be prudent.

Conformity. A house substantially out of step with others on the block gives cause for refusing or reducing the amount of the loan. The question is one of future resale. A larger, higher-priced house in a neighborhood of smaller homes loses some of its value. A house of an unusual or different design, although very attractive in its proper setting, can present something of a freakish appearance in a conventional neighborhood.

Topography and Soil Conditions. The contours of the land are important as some houses in an otherwise acceptable subdivision might be prone to flooding. As the federal programs for flood insurance grow, this particular problem will become of less importance to the lender. Soil conditions over the country show considerable variation from very solid to highly unstable bases and include geological fault lines. The problems caused by these factors have the same results—the house can become structurally defective and, therefore, unsalable long before the loan is paid off.

Local Regulation. A loan underwriter is always cognizant of the housing codes and should watch for any unusual deed restrictions that can affect future resale. In addition, there are sometimes legal situations that can create problems such as privately owned water districts with their own rules or requirements, flood control districts exercising certain controls, or neighborhood maintenance associations with nearly unlimited authority to raise assessments. As long as the property is occupied and the payments are made, the problems, if any, belong to the homeowner, but the lender must always keep in mind the unfortunate possibility of having to take over the house in a foreclosure.

CONDOMINIUMS

The outright purchase of a vertical or horizontal apartment unit effectively detached from a piece of land has required state-enabling legislation declaring such a unit to be in the category of "real property." By means of these legal provisions, controlled lending institutions are permitted to accept such property as collateral. Legislation allowing condominium sales was initiated in the eastern states and has spread across the country over a period of years. It has only been in the past few years, however, that a nearly explosive growth has overtaken condominium sales, accompanied by the necessary mortgage loan programs. The groups most interested in this type of property purchase are the young marrieds and senior citizens, together comprising over half the adult population.

The increasing popularity of the condominium concept of home purchase stems from the desire for home ownership, with the tax advantages of deducting interest and property taxes against an individual's income. In addition, there is a measure of inflation protection gained in property ownership plus tax deferment (within code limits), or capital gains treatment of a profitable sale. And, finally, the right to rent the unit as a landlord is possible.

The mortgage loan for a condominium is handled similarly to the loan negotiated for a detached single-family residence, using the proper legal description of the condominium, et al. In this case the condominium with no actual physical attachment to a piece of land is pledged as security for the loan.

Since the lender must always foresee the possibility of foreclosure and subsequent resale of the property, it is necessary to examine some additional problem areas peculiar to a condominium. One of the more important items directly involved in condominium-style living that concerns the lender is that of maintenance costs. In order to sell the unit, a developer may be able to hold costs down or may even defer some necessary maintenance in order to show a low monthly charge. Subsequent to the project being sold, however, with the builder no longer responsible for its maintenance, the true problems may show up along with added costs for the unwary purchaser. Therefore the maintenance agreement on the property must be acceptable to the lender.

The voting control of the management board for the project can be held by the developer without a time limitation. It is the general practice for developers to assure proper operation and maintenance during the sell-out period of a project, and provided that the individuals involved have high ethical standards, this is a legitimate selling attraction. The problems of management most often arise under circumstances where not all the units are sold, and the developer must reduce prices, or even rent unsold units, leaving the initial unit owners at a disadvantage. It is good practice to place a time limitation on the developer's absolute voting control; a limitation of perhaps two years would minimize potential problems of this nature.

Utilities should be controlled by the unit owners if at all possible. Unfortunate results may occur when a developer continues to exercise control over all utilities such as gas, electricity, sewer, water, and television channels. Such unwarranted control may expose unit owners to excessive rates and poor performance.

An intention to increase the size of a condominium project should be publicly declared in advance and made known to prospective buyers and lenders. If a developer withholds adjacent land for possible additional units, their later construction might overload existing recreational facilities and reduce the value of all units by the sheer size and numbers of the completed project.

The management contract may affect future values and should be examined by the lender. These contracts are normally written prior to the sale of the units, and it is possible to tie down the rights to sell or lease all units for a lengthy period of time. Any restriction on resale rights would be detrimental to the lender's position.

HOME MORTGAGE DOCUMENTS AS REQUIRED BY FHLMC

As one of the major agencies purchasing home mortgages from savings associations and other approved lenders, the Federal Home Loan Mortgage Corporation (The Mortgage Company) has established a set of requirements for documenting home mortgage loans. Any lender desirous of selling a loan to FHLMC must document that loan in accordance with the rules as listed in the Sellers Guide. The requirements provide a good insight on the kind of information that is needed and the limitations that they have established. The section on mortgages (Part III, Section 5, Delivery of Home Mortgage Documents) is reproduced in Figures 10-1a-10-1d.

PART III—HOME MORTGAGES
Section 5—Delivery of Home Mortgage Documents

As to each conventional Home Mortgage purchased in whole or in part by FHLMC, Seller represents and warrants that the requirements set forth in this Part III, Section 5 have been met.

3.501   Delivery of Mortgage Documentation.

Seller agrees, at its own expense and within the delivery period required under the purchase programs, to deliver to FHLMC or its designee such documents as are required to be delivered under the Purchase Documents, subject to approval of FHLMC as to proper form and execution.

Each group of mortgages delivered shall be accompanied by a Mortgage Schedule (FHLMC Form 12, Part V, Exhibit G) with each mortgage loan submitted listed thereon and by a Contract Delivery Summary (FHLMC Form 381, Part V, Exhibit F) that will list purchase control reconciliation totals. Seller is also requested to give the Applicable FHLMC Regional Office several days informal notice of each delivery.

FHLMC intends to review mortgages submitted to a substantial extent before payment to facilitate an effective transaction. For this reason, Seller should plan for a reasonable review period prior to the FHLMC Funding Date. (Amount of purchase price is adjusted for interest accrued through the day prior to the FHLMC Funding Date.)

Legible photocopies of the following documents (except for mortgages to be purchased in whole by FHLMC, where the mortgage note must be an original) for each mortgage must be adequately stapled at the top of the right side of a legal size manila folder and arranged in the order listed below with the first item on top, and must be forwarded to the Applicable FHLMC Regional Office (all documents must be delivered simultaneously):

a.   Mortgage Submission Voucher (FHLMC Form 13SF, Part V, Exhibit H). This form must be properly completed in detail before a mortgage loan can be processed by the Applicable FHLMC Regional Office.

b.   The Mortgage Note. For mortgages to be purchased in whole by FHLMC, the mortgage note must be the original and must bear an endorsement by Seller: PAY TO THE ORDER OF FEDERAL HOME LOAN MORTGAGE CORPORATION WITHOUT RECOURSE THIS _____ DAY OF _____, 19____.

(month)

_____
(Name of Seller-Endorser)

_____
(Signature of Duly Authorized Officer)

_____
(Typed Name and Title of Signatory)

Such endorsement "Without Recourse" shall, in no way affect Seller's repurchase obligations under the Purchase Documents. The chain of endorsements must be complete from original lender shown on the mortgage note to FHLMC.

For mortgages to be purchased in part by FHLMC, a clearly legible copy of the face of the mortgage note must be delivered and if not closed in Seller's name, a clearly legible copy of the back of the mortgage note as well, in order to show all endorsements from original payee to Seller.

c.   Residential Loan Application (FHLMC Form 65, Part V, Exhibit I). Residential Loan Application (FHLMC Form 65, as revised 3/76), must be used for all mortgage loans closed on or after July 1, 1976. For all mortgage loans closed after April 1, 1974 and before July 1, 1976, Seller must use either this form or FHLMC's Residential Loan Application (FHLMC Form 65, as revised 6/73). For all mortgage loans closed prior to April 1, 1974, Seller may submit loans on his own application form if that form is found acceptable to FHLMC. Regardless of the date the mortgage loan is closed and the application form used, the application must be signed, and dated, by Borrower(s) as shown on the note. If the Mortgaged Premises are currently owned by other than the original Borrower(s), Seller must submit a Residential Loan Application (the date the mortgage loan was assumed determines which application form is required, as detailed above) and a credit report on the current Borrower(s) and a certification of the terms of sale of the Mortgaged Premises.

d.   Credit Report. The credit report must be dated within ninety (90) days of the date of the

FIGURE 10-1a.

note or assumption agreement, if any. Seller must provide copies of written verification of current employment and income whenever the credit reporting agency is unable to verify these items.

÷ **e. Audited Profit and Loss Statements (or Federal Tax Return).** The statements or complete tax return for at least the last year end prior to Borrower's application to Seller for the mortgage loan if Borrower is self-employed. These items must verify income as stated on the Residential Loan Application (FHLMC Form 65) and the Mortgage Submission Voucher (FHLMC Form 13SF).

f. Residential Appraisal Report. (FHLMC Form 70). Seller must use FHLMC Residential Appraisal Report (FHLMC Form 70, as revised 9/75, Part V, Exhibit K) if the mortgage loan is closed after March 1, 1976, and is a Home Mortgage or DeMinimis PUD unit. (See Section 3.501k for mortgage loans on Condominium Units and units in a PUD, other than DeMinimis PUD units.) For all mortgage loans closed after January 1, 1974, and before March 1, 1976, Seller must use either FHLMC Residential Appraisal Report (FHLMC Form 70, as revised 5/73 or 9/75) or FNMA Form 1004.

g. Two Clear Descriptive Photographs. One photograph should be a front view of the Mortgaged Premises, clearly showing the completed improvements, and the second a street scene showing neighboring improvements. (The two photographs must be originals and are to be attached to an 8½ x 11 sheet of plain paper.)

h. Out-of-State Security. In the event the Mortgaged Premises securing the note is outside the state of Seller's principal office, the first such out-of-state mortgage for each state submitted by Seller must be accompanied by an opinion of counsel, addressed to Seller and FHLMC, provided at Seller's expense, stating that:

(1) Counsel is licensed to practice law in the state where the Mortgaged Premises are located;

(2) Counsel has reviewed the procedure of Seller in originating, selling, servicing and enforcing mortgage loans in such state and all laws and documents relevant thereto;

(3) The mortgage is and will remain a valid first lien whether owned by Seller or by a subsequent purchaser, or by Seller in participation with another party;

(4) The mortgage note and mortgage are enforceable by Seller and transfer of the mortgage or any interest therein to any subsequent purchaser will not detract from its enforceability as a result of such transaction;

(5) No licensing or doing business requirements must be met by the Seller or subsequent purchaser as a result of the purchase and ownership of such mortgage note and mortgage by FHLMC, or, if any such requirements exist, such requirements apply only to Seller and have been fully complied with by Seller;

(6) No fees, taxes, or other charges, or any additional requirements of any nature are required to be paid, or met, by Seller or FHLMC.

i. Waiver of Prepayment Fees. For mortgages closed before January 1, 1976, and which Seller desires to sell in part to FHLMC, a copy of any waiver of any prepayment fees, expressed or implied, affecting any mortgage by Seller shall be delivered to FHLMC. Such waiver must be attached to the copy of the mortgage note delivered and Borrower must be notified in writing of such waiver.

j. Flexible Payment Loan. In the event that the Home Mortgage purchased in whole or in part by FHLMC is a Flexible Payment Loan, Seller must:

(1) Indicate on the Mortgage Submission Voucher (FHLMC Form 13SF, Part V, Exhibit H) for that particular mortgage loan, the following information in *Flexible Payment Loan* block of the *Note Data* section—"$_____ Minimum Monthly Pymt. _____ Months" to indicate the amount and term of the reduced installments during the initial term.

The amount entered in the *Monthly Installment Principal and Interest Only* block must reflect the amount due each month after the initial period.

(2) Identify the mortgage loan as a Flexible Payment Loan by placing a "2" after the appropriate Borrower's name on the Mortgage Schedule (FHLMC Form 12, Part V, Exhibit G).

k. Planned Unit Developments and Condominiums. If the mortgage covers a unit in a PUD or condominium:

(1) FHLMC's Appraisal Report—Individual Condominium or PUD Unit (FHLMC Form 465, Part V, Exhibit KK) must be used for all PUD or condominium mortgages closed after November

FIGURE 10-1b.

1, 1974. For PUD or condominium mortgages closed before November 1, 1974, it is recommended that the Seller use FHLMC Form 70 as revised 5/73.

(2) Seller agrees to submit with the delivery of the first mortgage loan in each PUD or condominium project a certification, signed by an authorized officer of Seller, of compliance with the warranties set out in Section 3.207 for Condominium Home Mortgages and Section 3.208 for PUD Home Mortgages. In the event Seller cannot execute such a certification, the Seller shall submit, prior to delivery of the first mortgage, a certification except for those warranties for which Seller specifically requests and recommends a waiver or modification. This certification (and waiver request, if any) must be in the form set out in Part V, Exhibit M and should outline the reasons for recommending either modification or waiver. Seller may also be required to deliver to FHLMC a legal opinion, addressed to Seller and FHLMC, unconditionally confirming the legal conclusions contained in the certification (and waiver request, if any).

(3) If such mortgage is also on a leasehold estate, Seller agrees to submit to FHLMC a Multifamily or Condominium Ground Lease Analysis (FHLMC Form 461, Part V, Exhibit L).

NOTE: In the case of a condominium project on a leasehold (See also Section 3.207m) and a PUD on a leasehold (See also Section 3.208m).

l. Mortgage Loans More Than One Year Old. In the event the mortgage delivered to FHLMC was closed more than one year prior to the Purchase Contract Date of Acceptance, the Seller agrees to submit the following documentation:

(1) Statement of mortgage loan payment record covering the twelve (12) months preceding the Purchase Contract Date of Acceptance;

(2) Seller/Servicer 1-4 Family Property Inspection Report (FHLMC Form 452, Part V, Exhibit P), properly completed in detail, with current photographs of Mortgaged Premises and street scene attached;

(3) A Residential Loan Application (FHLMC Form 65, Part V, Exhibit I), a credit report on Borrower and a certification of the terms of sale of the Mortgaged Premises whenever the Mortgaged Premises are currently owned by other than the original Borrower.

m. Other Documents. Seller agrees to submit such other documents as FHLMC may request.

3.502 Retention of Conventional Home Mortgage Loan File by Seller/Servicer.

The Seller/Servicer agrees to maintain, during the time that FHLMC owns the mortgage loan or a participation interest therein and thereafter for a minimum of three years from the date the mortgage loan is fully paid or, if the mortgage loan is accelerated, six years from the date the mortgage loan is paid, the entire mortgage loan file, which must contain the original of any documentation submitted to FHLMC (except where the original documents are retained by FHLMC) and the additional documents specified below:

÷ **a.** The mortgage instruments.

(1) Original mortgage or deed of trust, complete with recordation notation.

(2) Copy of Note, when original is submitted to FHLMC.

b. For mortgages purchased in whole by FHLMC, assignment of the mortgage to FHLMC in proper form and evidencing recordation, except as provided below:

(1) The assignment of the mortgage is not required to be executed and/or recorded, if such recordation is not necessary under applicable law to perfect FHLMC's first lien interest and is not commonly required by private institutional mortgage investors in the area in which the Mortgaged Premises are located. However, Seller agrees to execute and/or record an assignment of the mortgage at Seller's expense upon request by FHLMC.

(2) Where permitted by applicable law, the assignment instrument may cover more than one mortgage, provided all requirements of the Purchase Documents have been met.

c. Title insurance policy or other evidence of title.

d. Plat of survey meeting the requirements of Section 3.204, unless not commonly required for the type of property by private institutional mortgage investors in the area in which the Mortgage Premises are located.

÷ **e.** Hazard insurance policies properly endorsed and copies of any necessary notices to insurance carriers (as provided in Section 3.203e)

FIGURE 10-1c.

unless Seller carries mortgage impairment insurance instead of maintaining possession of hazard insurance policies. (See Section 2.108 of the Servicers' Guide regarding possession by Servicer of hazard insurance policies.)

f. Stock certificate entitling Borrower to an adequate supply of water, duly endorsed to FHLMC, if the Mortgaged Premises are dependent for assurance of an adequate supply of water upon a water or irrigation company that supplies water only to its shareholders.

g. Closing statement, verification of employment and income, and vertification or acceptable evidence of source and amount of down payment and prepaid items to substantiate such information as shown on the mortgage loan application.

h. Mortgage insurance policy or proof of insurance, if the mortgage is required to be insured.

i. Documents affecting leasehold estate, if any, securing the indebtedness.

j. Legal opinion, addressed to Seller and FHLMC, unconditionally confirming the legal conclusions contained in the certification (and waiver request, if any) of compliance with the warranties regarding a condominium project or PUD.

k. All other documents constituting the mortgage loan file and such other documents as may be requested by FHLMC or as are commonly maintained in mortgage loan files by private institutional mortgage investors or servicers.

For each mortgage covering an individual Condominium or PUD Unit, Seller agrees to possess (but need not maintain in the individual mortgage loan file), such other documentation, in addition to the above, with respect to the condominium or PUD project, as required by FHLMC, e.g., the Declaration of Condominium (or Master Deed or similar instrument) and the bylaws and regulations of the condominium project, and Seller agrees to provide such documentation to FHLMC at any time and at Seller's expense.

FIGURE 10-1d.

QUESTIONS FOR DISCUSSION

1. List the categories of information required for the proper evaluation of any type of real estate loan.

2. Why do the secondary market requirements influence primary market lending?

3. Discuss the various physical aspects of a house that concern the underwriter in determining acceptability of a property as collateral for a loan.

4. What is the economic climate in your community? Does it have a continuing stability that would attract out-of-state mortgage investment money at the lowest market rates?

5. How would you define the term "suburban" as it is used to classify residential loans?

6. Discuss the advantages and disadvantages for the home buyer in using a loan commitment held by the home builder.

7. What is meant by the "apparent age" of a house as it may be determined by an appraiser?

8. How does a lender adjust the amount of a loan and the interest rate when underwriting a resort property or a second home?

9. How does the topography of a neighborhood influence a lender considering a property loan?

10. Discuss the additional problems associated with a condominium loan that would not pertain to a single-family residence.

11. What dollar limits are placed on residential loans and by whom are they placed?

Chapter 11

Loan Analysis of Income Properties

GENERAL INFORMATION

Loans against all types of income properties require the same type of background information as would be needed for analyzing a residential loan. This information package would include a study of the location, the construction and other physical characteristics of the building, the local zoning laws and deed restrictions that may be involved, and the economic potential of the region and local area. In addition, and of greater importance to most investors, is an analysis of the income and expense factors. The lender wants to know how much of the total income is, or will be, available to pay the debt service—those periodic payments of principal and interest on the mortgage loan.

The most accurate method of obtaining the information needed is an *audited statement* by an independent accounting firm showing the actual income and expenses over a period of several years. For new developments such figures, of course, would not be available.

A second method used by many developer-builders is to use actual operating figures but incorporate *adjustments in both income and expenses* to more accurately portray a full year of operation. In this manner expenses might be leveled to show average annual figures. For example, if the exterior of the building was repainted and paid for upon completion, the total expense could be spread over the three-to-five-year life of the paint job to give a more accurate annual expense factor. Annual payments, such as taxes, may have been delayed into the following year and should properly be returned to the current year to give a true picture. Similar adjustments may be made for unusual fluctuations in income. These calculations are often referred to as "stabilized" figures, which are expected to indicate a more accurate operational picture. Stabilized figures should not be confused with adjustments that are intended to mislead the analyst by overstating profit potential.

A third method of preparing an analysis of income property is a *projection of income and expenses*. Obviously, this is the only method that can be used on a new development. It is sometimes called a "pro forma" statement, which is really a knowledgeable estimate of the future cash flow. Since it is a projection, a pro forma statement should be prepared by a professional accountant who is aware of all the facts. It is difficult to accept a property owners's projection as an objective statement.

FEASIBILITY REPORT

The analysis of a new project investment often includes an additional study termed a *feasibility report*. By definition the word feasible means "capable of being used successfully." Therefore, the purpose of such a study is to ascertain the probable success or failure of the project under consideration.

There is a similarity in the background information needed for both a property appraisal and a feasibility report. The difference lies in the focus of conclusions regarding the timing and the usage of the property. A feasibility report seeks conclusions on the profitability of future operations, whereas the appraisal relates future profitability to present property value. A feasibility report is a preliminary study conducted before plans are drawn or financing is obtained. The information is used to guide the builder-developer and also serves as additional material for a potential lender to analyze.

A feasibility study draws certain conclusions concerning cost estimates and then analyzes the market available for the particular project under consideration, such as an apartment building, office building, or other project. The detailed market analysis is the real meat of the study because it attempts to determine the probability of future in-

come. Almost any income property can be projected into an appearance of profitability by using an arbitrarily high figure that may or
may not be substantiated by the actual market available. It is the
purpose of the market study portion of the feasibility report to show
by actual canvass or survey, by charts of population and business
growth, by analysis of present and future traffic and transportation
patterns, and by actual comparisons of occupancy and income of
comparable existing income properties whether or not a need exists
for the proposed project.

Feasibility reports are not guided by any professional group
pressing for accuracy and integrity and are therefore subject to a
wide variety of interpretations. The best reports are prepared by experts in marketing analysis who have no personal interest in the subject property and are therefore able to make objective judgments.
It is not unusual for a report to contain a presentation of information and facts regarding the project and its potential market, leaving
the conclusions to be drawn by the reader.

More in the nature of an illustration, rather than as a standard
pattern that does not really exist, the following outline could represent the material covered in a comprehensive feasibility study:

1. *Conclusions*—Presented first as these are the answers to the practical
   questions that the rest of the study has developed.

2. *Property*—A description of the property, location, type of building or
   buildings, and an estimate of costs showing some detail as to how costs
   are determined.

3. *Market Evaluation*—A study in depth of all factors that affect the marketing of the property, such as traffic patterns, population growth, type of
   income, other services available in the immediate area, direct and indirect
   competition, and any laws, regulations, or other restrictions that will
   affect the project.

4. *Environmental Effect*—As local environmental rules expand, the impact
   of larger projects on the area are becoming the subject of intensive and
   lengthy coverage. The cost of the research and its effect on the cost of
   the project must be considered in the overall investment.

5. *Expense and Income*—An experienced analyst can develop reasonably
   accurate projections of operating costs. These are best approached as
   (1) *fixed*, which covers such items as insurance and taxes that do not vary
   with occupancy, and (2) *operating* expenses such as water, electricity,
   and maintenance that do fluctuate with occupancy. From these figures, a
   breakeven ratio can be determined. The income projection must be based
   on some factual data of comparable rents and occupancy figures, but
   does remain essentially an estimate drawn from knowledge and experience.

A feasibility report does not attempt to recommend financing methods or detail the expenses involved with interest costs. The conclusions stop with an estimate of total cash that would be available for debt service. The timing of the financing, how it is arranged, and under what type of commitments—these are problems for the developer to resolve.

USE OF A LOAN CONSTANT

In discussing a loan, the prospective borrower will find it difficult to mentally convert an interest rate and the term of a loan into a dollar cost for a project. In order to facilitate negotiations, it is customary to use a multiplier, referred to as a *constant,* which means the constant percentage of the original loan that is paid annually for principal and interest. This constant payment is also referred to as *debt service.*

For example, an 8 percent loan with a 25-year term has an annual constant of 9.26 percent. Thus, on a $1 million loan, the debt service amounts to $92,600 annually. Now, if the interest rate is increased to 9 percent, this would change the constant to 10.07 for the same term. If a change occurs in the term from, say 25 years to 15 years, then the original 8 percent rate calculates out at an 11.47 constant.

Tables compiled by statistical experts showing the progression of constants are available at technical bookstores. A variety of other tables are also available for reference on exact mortgage yields, equity build-ups, and amortization statistics.

APARTMENTS

Apartments, or multi-family housing, as the FHA broadly classifies them, can range from a four-family building to upward of 2500 units or more. Since apartments are residential housing, qualifications similar to single-family housing are necessary. This would include location, type and stability of the neighborhood and the region, laws governing foreclosure procedures, and the architectural style of the building itself.

Because an apartment is an investment property as well as a residence, there are many variables involved in determining the risks. Experienced apartment operators judge three factors to be of almost equal importance in a successful operation. These are: (1) location, (2) physical facilities, and (3) management. Obviously, a careful underwriting analysis must consider all three factors in determining the risk involved.

Location is usually the first limiting requirement of an apartment seeker, along with size of the unit and its price. A major consideration of location is easy access to jobs; freeways affect and broaden accessibility. Also important in judging location is proximity to schools and churches. The availability of recreational facilities, such as parks and golf courses, along with restaurants and other entertainment, are all to be considered. Apartment dwellers, as a group, are not as burdened with housework and yard maintenance as a single-family resident would be.

Since location is a major determinant of the available market, it is necessary to evaluate the market in that area. For instance, does the proposed rental structure fit the requirements and will it be competitive? Do the size and type of units meet these demands?

The physical plant must meet the market requirements, not only in size of units, but also in architectural style and amenities available. Amenities would include such factors as playground areas, tennis courts, swimming pool, club room, and entertainment facilities. If the market is primarily a family type, the two- or three-bedroom units would be the most popular choice; if intended for younger singles, the one-bedroom and studio design would be in greatest demand. The elderly, on the other hand, might prefer one or two bedrooms with a minimum of stairs to climb. Sometimes an assortment of units is used with the hope of covering all phases of the market. This "shotgun" approach is a poor substitute for careful analysis of the market as it may result in one type or style of unit easily rented and maintaining good occupancy while others go begging for tenants. Before building begins on an apartment complex, knowledgeable operators (developers) study the market for particular requirements and then use their merchandising power to attract suitable occupants.

Management is a major factor known well to experienced operators and too often underestimated by newcomers to the field. Together with the location and the physical plant, management, too, can be a "make or break" factor. Larger cities throughout the country have companies that specialize in apartment management, offering a complete management service for a fee of 3 to 5 percent of the gross revenues. Maintaining routine cleanliness of the public areas, prompt repairs of equipment or damaged sections of the building, and fair enforcement of tenant rules for the mutual well-being of the tenants are all necessary to achieve and maintain a high occupancy rate. Experienced operators learn how to cope with the special requirements of rental properties such as initial screening of tenants, the most effective methods of collecting rents and keeping them current, the special problems created by domestic pets, the handling of skip-outs and of tenants who create disturbances for other occupants. Consequently, an underwriter will look much more favorably, risk-wise, on a property under the management of competent individuals or companies.

As apartment-style living proliferates in the cities, an underwriter must recognize that the better planned, better maintained facilities are those that will maintain the occupancy in soft or competitive markets. And a continuous high occupancy rate is the key to survival in this business.

Analysis of Income and Expenses

On proposed apartment construction, a projected statement can be prepared to show anticipated gross revenues from each unit and all miscellaneous revenues such as that from laundry rooms, less a vacancy factor and credit losses. This will produce an effective income from which deductions can be made for all expenses. Fixed expenses include such items as taxes and insurance, and operating expenses such as utilities, maintenance, supplies, labor, and management. A special expense that is frequently overlooked or underestimated is the replacement costs—items such as drapes and carpeting, equipment such as stoves or dishwashers, all in continuous use, have a tendency to wear out, and allowances must be set aside for replacements. The cash remaining after these deductions then becomes available for debt service. Any remaining cash, after all expenses and debt service have been covered, serves as a cushion against a loss or a slow period.

It is apparent then that there are many variables among these figures that are subject to interpretation. For example, what occupancy rate may be reliably projected? FHA uses a percentage figure of 93. Conventional lenders generally tend to select an occupancy rate substantiated by actual rates prevailing in a particular area. Most lenders require proof of an occupancy rate near 90 percent before they will entertain a loan application. Rental rates also must be in line with the going market. Expenses can be projected with reasonable accuracy. In general, they range from 36 percent of the gross effective income to 45 percent, depending on the size of the operation and the efficiency of the management.

As previously defined, debt service is the monthly or annual cost of interest and principal payment and should be tailored to insure the timely retirement of the full loan. By careful analysis of the cash available for debt service, the underwriter can determine the most effective loan for the proposed apartment. Adjustable and negotiable factors are the *term,* which under conventional loans ranges from 15 upward to 30 years, and the *loan-to-value* ratio, which determines the equity cash required. The interest rate is generally pegged at current market rates and is less subject to negotiation.

Depreciation as an expense item is expected to be covered under items allocated to maintenance and replacement. However, the principal use of the rules governing depreciation on apartments at the present time is how it can be used as an offset against taxable income. The 1969 Tax Reform Act recognized the need for housing in this country by allowing continuance of accelerated depreciation on residential type property investments, while reducing this type of tax shelter on other investment properties. An investment in a new apartment can qualify for the accelerated double declining balance depreciation. From a loan analysis standpoint, the depreciation allowance against taxes is important in that it reduces the overall tax liabilities but cannot be counted on for the life of the loan. While the amount of depreciation available to apartment investors depends on their income bracket and is complicated by formulas limiting overall tax preference deductions, it is a fair statement that for the first four or five years of a new apartment operation, the interest cost and depreciation deductions will more than offset the available income for tax purposes.

Cooperative Apartments

Cooperative apartments are a variety of apartment in which the ownership of a given unit is vested in the tenant-owner, and the ownership of the land and public facilities is vested jointly with all the other tenant-owners of the complex. The most practical method of operating this type of facility is to set up a corporation with shares of stock representing the jointly-owned interests. Another method would be to place the joint interests in trust with a trust company, which then issues certificates of beneficial interest. Construction of this type of apartment has waxed and waned in the past, primarily stimulated by rising land costs, and the desire for ownership equities. It also is a method of obtaining certain tax advantages, as well as a means of exercising some control in the selection of neighbors and enabling more individually styled apartments. The problem of financing a co-op is finding a means of carrying the costs while the units are in the process of being sold. One reasonable solution to the problem is to require a certain percentage of presold units prior to the release of any loan money.

Rule-of-Thumb Analysis

In order to properly analyze an apartment income property, a detailed study of all information regarding operating costs, fixed expenses, and gross income, with allowances for credit loss and vacancies, must be considered in relation to the total investment required. However, investors have developed certain guidelines that are useful in providing a quick evaluation on an apartment loan application to determine if it is worthy of further analysis. The use of these methods varies among investors and according to practices of the area of the country in which they do business, but some of the more commonly employed ratios and evaluations can be listed as follows:

Mortgage Multiplier. The factor that converts effective gross rent to an estimated mortgage amount ranges from four to six. For example, if a project grosses $2400 per unit annually, it could attract a mortgage loan of $12,000 per unit if a multiplier of five is used.

Loan per Room. The required size of a "room" in an apartment is not standardized. One company might consider a minimum living-room size for a two-bedroom apartment to be 160 square feet with the smallest dimension being 11 feet, or a living-dining alcove combination for a two-bedroom apartment with 200 square feet would be counted as one and one-half rooms. The average loan per room will vary from $2500 to $5500.

Gross Rent Multiplier. This is a rule-of-thumb method for converting gross project rental income into an estimate of value or sales price. The measure varies from 5½ (or 66 months income) to 7 times annual income.

Site Value Ratio. The site value ratio is the ratio of the value of the site to the total value of land and improvements. The percentage varies from 6 to 20 percent.

SHOPPING CENTERS

Shopping in urban areas has relocated substantially from the downtown section to outlying districts and suburbs. The movement dates from approximately World War II and was brought about largely by the automobile which, along with freeway systems, produced a major change in our living patterns and altered our population centers.

Merchants in the downtown areas recognized these changing patterns and, for the most part, were in the vanguard of the development of regional shopping centers. Specialized development companies grew up in this period whose purpose was to organize the merchants, locate proper land sites, arrange for financing, and then handle construction and even management of the completed center.

Size, Services, and Development

The size, shape, and structure of shopping centers, as well as the methods used in their development, show such extreme variation as almost to defy classification. Common observation shows a range from small, localized strips of stores along a frontage road, to a supermarket with perhaps a half-dozen satellite stores served from the same parking lot called "convenience centers," on up to the huge regional complexes.

In terms of financing, the smaller strip-type shopping centers referred to are often built as speculative ventures and remain merely bare-wall shells until suitable tenants are found. Larger centers, however, almost always commence with a major store as a focal point and a traffic generator, and are preleased before construction begins. A developer seldom builds a large facility without leases in hand, for it is the lease that determines the financing. And the type and the amount of the lease supply the key to the money.

Summing up the major varieties of shopping centers from the simplest to the most complex would include: (1) the *neighborhood center,* which provides daily essentials such as food, drugs, hardware, and everyday services; (2) the *community center,* adding to the neighborhood category with apparel, furniture, professional services, and some recreational facilities; and finally (3) the *regional shopping center,* utilizing major stores and scores of lesser shops including a variety of restaurants and substantial recreational facilities, the whole arranged in an attractive manner and esthetically appealing to today's shopper.

Classification for Financing

Shopping center facilities fall into three major categories when considered for financing: (1) owner-occupied, (2) preleased space built by a developer, and (3) space built for speculative leasing. These categories are not always clearly differentiated in that many centers carry a combination of all three types, but they are used here to distinguish differences important to an underwriter's analysis.

Owner-Occupied

While this type of store building is not as common as it once was, there are still many being built. The largest of all retail merchants, Sears, Roebuck and Co., generally leases its smaller stores but buys the land and builds its own facility for the larger centers. A free standing discount store is usually owner-occupied as are many of the newer warehouse-type furniture stores. Some of the largest local merchants undertake development of their own outlying stores. In all cases of owner-occupied facilities, the financial strength and credit record of the owner are the key to good financing. The type of merchandiser capable of building a substantial new facility for sales expansion generally has the experience to know the extent of the market. Regardless of the merchandiser's experience or reputation, however, comprehensive independent market studies are undertaken and made available to the underwriter.

The largest merchants may resort to the sale of bonds for financing expansion rather than a mortgage loan, depending on the cost of the money. In either case, it is the credit reputation of the borrower, rather than the real estate pledged, that determines the interest rate as well as the terms and the amount of the loan.

Preleased

Many merchants prefer to utilize their cash and borrowing capacity for growth in inventory and accounts receivable, rather than for real estate investments. Consequently, they work with investors or builder-developers who are knowledgeable in construction and property management. In order to obtain the physical facility desired, the merchant is often willing to sign a long-term lease ranging from 15 to 25 years, thus assuring the builder-investor of a continuing income. The lease payments must be calculated to cover such maintenance as the owner is held responsible for, plus the debt service. Taxes and insurance increases can be passed on to the tenant with an escalation clause in the lease. The inflationary spiral that began to accelerate in late 1973 has brought about considerable adjustments in the terms contained in all long-term leases. Landlords can no longer give any reasonable assurance that any costs will adhere to a predictable escalation pattern. Consequently, the newer long-term leases contain protective clauses for the landlord which allow any increases in operating costs to be passed on to the tenant in addition to the fixed cost increases which have been normal for taxes and insurance.

The actual lease, the strength of the lessee, and the terms of the lease itself are the keys to financing the building. For a strong lease, a lender will fund a major percentage of the total amount of the lease payments without substantial reference to the building itself. This may run as high as 75 percent of the total amount of the lease payments and can provide for an assignment of the lease payments directly to the lender.

If the lessees are less credit-worthy or of smaller size, the lender will still take an assignment of rentals but also looks more to the strength of the lessor. In this case, too, the size of the loan may be reduced to a percentage, say 70 percent, of the actual investment in land and buildings. The rental from smaller shops such as barber shops, boutiques, and fashion stores, with little established credit would not be considered as a measure for the loan except that such leases in hand would provide an addition to the overall occupancy of a multistore center.

One of the problems that becomes particularly important regarding preleased space is the ability of the developer to complete the building within the projected cost figures. Leases do not provide for rental increases to cover a builder's mistakes. Consequently, the prudent lender must not only determine the accuracy of projected costs of building with the income and expenses that will be generated, but must also be reasonably certain that the builder is sufficiently experienced and capable of completing the project within the specified budget.

Speculative

The substantial growth of all business, and particularly the service-oriented businesses requiring limited store space, has provided a lucrative field for the speculative builder. This is space built in bare-wall form, from the small corner shopping strip to portions of the large regional centers, without a lease or even a prospective tenant. When a tenant is found, the store space is completed to the particular tenant's requirements, either at the tenant's initial expense or added onto lease payments.

From the lender's standpoint, speculative store space rates rather low in desirability and is one of the first types of mortgage loans to dry up in periods of tight money. An empty store, after all, is only an expense. A lender who entertains such a loan must rely on the ability and financial strength of the builder-owner. If the builder is strong, or has an excellent record of finding qualified tenants for previous projects, a lender will look with some favor on the project if money is available.

The building of space for speculative leasing is accepted by lenders when it is a relatively small portion of a large regional center, most of which is already preleased. It has been well proved that major stores generate traffic that benefits and thus attracts many smaller merchants and service-type facilities.

Specific Shopping Center Areas for Underwriting Analysis

There are some problems common to the development and continued successful operation of all types of shopping facilities, from the very largest down to the single-store operation. Problems that must be examined include: (1) location, (2) the physical facilities to be constructed, (3) the management and general plan of operation, (4) tenants and sales volumes, (5) types of leases, and (6) lease terms. Discussion of these problems with possible answers to questions that arise follows.

Location

As in other types of real estate, location of a shopping center dictates the market. The population of the surrounding area should be studied for density, potential growth, family purchasing income, and the number of retail stores per family to determine if there is a real need for the proposed store or shopping center. From this study it should be possible to project the total retail volume in the general area and to reduce this to an estimate of sales per store. With regard to a large-scale center, it would be advisable to employ a market analyst for such a study, as it becomes intricately involved with such facets of the problems as the nature of the center, accessibility, and shopping habits of the prospective customers in or near this location.

The location should also be selected for ease of entry and exit. Long-range plans should also recognize the fact that the flow of traffic at any given center might be substantially altered by future developments.

Physical Plan

There are many ways to build a shopping center, and no single plan insures success. The huge regional centers show great imagination in design, layout, decor, and various attractions offered to the shopper. Many have become recreational centers as well as shopping centers. Entertainment is often provided in the public malls in the form of musicians, demonstrations, art shows, and other types of exhibits. Modern centers exude something of a carnival atmosphere at times in their all-out efforts to attract shoppers and overshadow the competition from smaller centers. Inevitably, middle-level centers are finding it more difficult to compete with the many extra attractions offered by the largest centers. However, the smaller convenience centers in good locations hold onto a local trade and are generally sound investments.

Since parking is one of the big advantages of a shopping center, these facilities should be adequate. As a general rule, three square feet of parking area should be provided for every one square foot of rentable shop space. An alternative rule would be to allow five or six parking spaces for each 1000 square feet of shop. Employee parking is best designated and kept apart from the prime locations. Supermarkets require the most parking space of any type of store.

The physical plan should be carefully examined to make certain that floor plans are of proper size with access readily available, that there is adequate heating and air conditioning, and that sufficient space has been provided for the handling of incoming merchandise and outgoing waste materials. These are mainly architectural and engineering concerns, but if costly mistakes can be prevented, the lender's money will be better secured. Considering the complexities involved, it is always a safer investment to employ experienced builders.

Management and Operations

Management plays a very important role in all types of income properties, and shopping centers are no exception. The larger centers rely heavily on competent management, not only to handle the tenants and maintain the facility, but to provide attractive decorations, timely promotional advertising, control of traffic, policing of crowds, and even some entertainment. The management usually works with an organized merchant's association in providing some of these services. Good promotional organization provides assurance to the lender that there will be a continuity of the entire project as all shopping center store units have a degree of interdependence.

In the area of operations, management can either place much of the responsibility for interior maintenance and daily upkeep on the tenant, or provide the service as a separate charge that can be adjusted as costs change. In the smaller operations and in the single-building facility, the owner usually takes responsibility only for exterior maintenance and the parking areas.

The experience of the operators is very soon evidenced by the manner in which they detail the responsibility for costs: both in how the costs for finishing out a store for a particular lessee are allocated between the owner and the tenant, and in how the operating costs are detailed. Such seemingly minor items as an electric eye-controlled doorway can cause continual maintenance problems. Is this an interior or exterior feature? The knowledgeable operator does not leave such items to later negotiation but spells them out in the written agreement. The lender should have an interest in any potential problem that might be inherited.

In the analysis of a proposed shopping center, the underwriter should definitely determine that adequate allowance has been made for initial planning and start-up costs. The new emphasis on environmental impact adds another cost for the investor who must now prepare studies and submit the necessary reports to authorized officials. Lease-up costs and initial advertising must all be provided for in the financing proposal as well as allowances for probable tax increases on any undeveloped land that is held for future growth.

Tenants

Another area of management responsibility to be examined by the underwriter is the policy used in selecting tenants and locating them within the center. The granting of exclusive franchises is not beneficial to the owner but may be necessary for a large store such as a supermarket. Any franchise granted in broad or general terminology, such as allowing a restaurant an exclusive franchise for "food handling," can be very restrictive to future growth of the center. Tenants should have the financial strength to undertake the lease obligations plus the ability to serve the public in a successful manner. Customer problems involving any single store can cast a poor reflection on the entire shopping center. Also a good diversity of stores is helpful in luring shoppers back again.

As previously indicated in this section, the quality of the tenants in a preleased center is a major factor in securing a mortgage loan. Sometimes there is an overemphasis on the desirability of the national chain-type stores as lucrative tenants. Recent statistical data indicate that localized chains and independent stores are very effective sales producers and that more often than not they turn over a larger volume of sales per square foot of floor space than do national operations. Sales volume is the key to larger rental income on percentage leases. The continued security of the mortgage payments rests to a considerable extent on the ability of the merchants to achieve profitable sales volumes.

Types of Leases

The type of lease used and the detail it contains are vital to the loan analysis. Three main types are: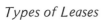

1. *Term Leases*—Term leases are used by most of the smaller shops and by some of the larger stores. This means paying flat monthly rentals figured on a basis of store size or square footage. These leases can allow for automatic increases every year or two and can provide renewal options.

2. *Percentage Lease*—The larger merchants (such as drug stores, supermarkets, and department stores) operate on minimum or base rentals plus a percentage of the gross sales. Percentages can vary from 1 to 6 percent of gross sales depending on type of store and sales volume. A no-minimum lease sets up a risky situation for a lender as the store may be able to operate profitably at a sales volume that does not pay the cost of the space occupied.

3. *Net Leases*—Another form of lease arrangement consists of operating the bare property strictly as an investment for the owner with the tenant paying all maintenance, taxes, and insurance. This type of operation is known as a net lease to the owner, covering only a reasonable return on the property investment. Management and operational problems would all be minimized by passing the entire burden on to the tenant. The net lease procedure is frequently used by individuals or by development com-

panies who have decided to build a facility in a distant location for a major tenant, a supermarket for instance, but simply do not have the personnel available and are not interested in accepting management responsibilities.

Lease Terms

The investment required to furnish a large store requires a long-term lease, which has advantages and disadvantages for the owner. The long term gives the lender good assurance of repayment and makes for better loan terms. The disadvantage lies in the fixed return on an investment over a number of years when costs of all kinds continue to increase over a period of time. Insurance costs also tend to increase and are related to risks that tenants may introduce. Consequently, long-term leases will normally carry escalation clauses that provide for any increase in taxes and insurance to be passed on to the tenant. It is becoming more common to allow increases in maintenance and operating costs to be added to the rental charges.

The smaller stores or shops, such as beauty parlors, florists, and boutiques, generally contract a three-to five-year lease, which is subject to rental increases periodically in anticipation of rising costs. The smaller shops seldom agree to percentage leases as they lack the necessary sales volume and the more complicated bookkeeping procedures required.

There are some lease provisions of special concern to a lender, particularly those that could bring about a premature cancellation of the lease. For example, leases that tie the occupancy of one store to the continued occupancy of another store present an obvious problem. Any type of exclusive clause restricting other shops from carrying competing lines or type of service can be detrimental. Stores can and do change their sales patterns over the years.

Occasionally special leases are permitted a major tenant based on a below-cost figure as a means of capitalizing on the inherent attraction of well-known merchants. The traffic generated by one big store is expected to provide sales for the lesser merchants. From a lender's standpoint, however, this type of subsidized rent structure suggests an undesirable pattern since it places a heavier burden on the remaining tenants to compensate for the loss sustained on the single below-cost lease.

Costs that continually escalate without realistic controls can be set out in a lease agreement as separate expenses, or in clauses allowing an equitable rental adjustment. Such services as heating and air conditioning, participating advertising, waste disposal, janitorial services, and security services may be covered under a separate service contract that can be adjusted for escalation, as may be necessary. Such a contract should contain protective clauses for the tenant to prevent the unscrupulous use of terms as a device for increasing costs unfairly, which might bring about default on the lease itself.

Example of a Shopping Center Lease

An example of a *percentage lease* for a supermarket of 20,000 square feet would be as follows:

> Assume the rental is set at a minimum of $1.50 per square foot, per year, based on a 1½ percent of the gross sales. The $1.50 for 20,000 square feet would amount to a rent of $30,000 per year. So, calculating a gross sales volume of $2,000,000 or less per year, the supermarket would pay the $30,000 per year minimum. If the total volume goes over $2,000,000, the 1½ percent of the gross would apply above that amount.

A typical shopping center deal would vary considerably across the country, depending upon land values and construction costs in a particular area. However, the proportions are similar, and the figures confirm this similarity. Assuming land cost at $1.50 per square foot and using the three-to-one ratio on parking space, the rentable shop space would then cost $6 per foot in land contributed. For a reasonably simple structure, the building costs would come to about $20 per square foot, which includes paving and lighting the parking lot. The total investment, using these figures, would add up to $26 per square foot. At this investment level, base operating costs (those not permitted to escalate) would be limited to $1.15 per square foot per year. Rentals for space such as this would average $4 per square foot per year. Table 11-1 shows how the investment works out using a highly simplified procedure for greater clarity.

Based on the figures in Table 11-1, the investment would show slightly less than 9 percent cash return on the equity investment. However, many unforeseen contingencies could upset this return, such as lower occupancy than expected, failure to collect all rentals due, and run-away operating costs. In the example cited, the cash return cannot be considered as the only profit since the principal payments on the loan are also a part of the profit, and it does not constitute taxable income since the depreciation allowed offers an off-setting deduction. The lender must look to the margin of cash

TABLE 11-1.

Projection for Shopping Center Investment
(Figures are hypothetical using a 50,000 square foot building located on 200,000 square feet of land. Total cost—$1,300,000.)

Capital Investment		
Equity Investment (20%)	260,000	
80% mortgage loan	1,040,000	
Total Investment		1,300,000
Annual Operating Calculations		
Gross Scheduled Income (4.00 per ft.)	200,000	
Less 5% vacancy and credit loss	10,000	
Gross Operating Income		190,000
Less Expenses—		
All operating costs @ 1.15 per ft		57,500
Net Operating Income		132,500
Less Debt Service—		
9-1/2% for 25 year term		
Constant—10.49 X 1,040,000		109,096
Cash flow before taxes		23,404

over-and-above the operating costs and the debt service, in order to estimate the margin of financial safety that can be counted on in any given investment.

OFFICE BUILDINGS

The owners of all types and sizes of office buildings, ranging from the largest to the smallest, acquire or construct them for one of two purposes: (1) their own occupancy, or (2) for lease to others.

Owner-Occupied Buildings

Many owner-occupied office buildings are held by companies or persons with a financial history that makes the decisions on underwriting such a property somewhat easier for the lender. This is due to the fact that the credit reputation of the owner is the major qualifying factor under consideration, whereas the real estate that is to be pledged is of secondary importance. Ultimately, the source of loan repayment is closely tied to the owner-occupant's record of profitability and the manner in which previous financial obligations have been met.

Unlike a shopping center or store, the office building occupied by an owner produces no additional income. But rent and other operating costs can be substantially reduced through more efficient office layouts.

In financing owner-occupied buildings of larger size, an alternative choice to straight mortgage financing would be the sale of first mortgage bonds through an investment banker or a mortgage banker. Acquisition of large office buildings by investing institutions, such as banks or insurance companies, is a common practice. In this way, the owners simply finance large buildings from their own investment funds.

Various local, state, and federal governments and their agencies build office buildings for their own use with legislative appropriations. But some government buildings, such as post offices, are built by private investors under long-term lease contracts and are financed through private sources.

Office Buildings for Lease to Others

The underwriting of buildings intended for lease to others calls for some specialized techniques of real estate mortgage financing and requires extensive analysis of the property involved. In this category there are three main groups: (1) a builder-investor with preleased office space to build, (2) the speculative builder hoping to attract tenants before the building is completed or soon thereafter, and (3) the owner-occupied building with extra space for lease.

Preleased Office Space

The preleased building is the more conservative method and provides the underwriter with a lease to analyze, a tenant to examine for credit-worthiness, and a building and location to study. If the building is specialized to meet a tenant's unusual requirements (such as heavy electrical gear, raised or lowered floors, or special wall patterns), the term of the lease should be sufficient to recover the extra investment. Most underwriters will limit a loan to a percentage of the total lease payments as this is the main source of the loan recovery. Similar to a shopping center, a preleased office building faces an inflexible situation in regard to an overrun on construction costs. The building must be designed and located in such manner that it meets the projected costs, and the contractor must have the ability to complete the project within the contract terms. Bonding of the contractor is a normal requirement. Escalation clauses should be provided in any long-term lease agreement to cover rising taxes, insurance costs, and more recently, maintenance and operating costs. Preleased office buildings for single tenants are usually "bare-wall" leases; i.e., the tenant finishes and furnishes the interior and provides the maintenance.

Speculative Office Buildings

The speculative builder presents a greater risk to an underwriter and only the more experienced and credit-worthy builders can command this type of loan. In addition to the usual analysis of the building and its location, consideration must be given to the market and the regional economic pattern. What are the chances of the speculative building becoming fully leased? The underwriter, however, is not in the business of chance by choice, so a protective restriction can be established that would require the building to have a 75, 80, or perhaps 85 percent occupancy with bona fide tenants before the permanent loan will be released. Of course this throws a real burden on the construction financing and usually means that the builder of a speculative building must have the credit strength or cash reserves to build and lease the building without an assured permanent commitment. It is not unusual for a knowledgeable builder-contractor to build and lease an office building with his own funds, then mortgage-out for more than his costs. In such a case the loan security rests as much on an assignment of the lease income as on the mortgage pledge. With regard to speculative office buildings, lenders often set rental minimums to protect their repayments. Buildings with multi-tenant occupancy usually provide for janitorial service, which can be a separate agreement subject to escalation if costs increase.

Owner-Occupied Building with Space to Lease

The third type of building loan in this office building category is the owner-occupied with space to lease. In this situation there can be a mixture of several types of income including the owner's normal rental payment, plus rent from space for speculative lease, as well as rent from space already preleased. But no one source may provide sufficient revenue to assure recovery of a normal ratio loan. The underwriter must analyze the property as a whole and make certain that the full loan has a reasonable chance of recovery before any portion of that loan is permitted to be released.

General Guidelines

In today's business world, office buildings are under construction in many locations with one major aspect in common—business growth. Even though downtown areas are somewhat congested and offer only limited parking, they are still highly desirable locations for businesses requiring convenient access to banks, accounting firms, attorneys, or other service-oriented facilities, plus easy contact and association with customers, suppliers, other allied businesses, hotel accommodations, and transportation.

As freeway patterns have developed in urban areas, many businesses have opted for outlying locations that provide ease of parking and close proximity to potential office workers. The decline of mass transportation systems, hastened by the increasing use of cars, has made freeway locations in some cases more accessible than downtown. It should be noted in passing, however, that the next generation may very possibly witness a reversal of this trend, especially in view of the energy shortage.

Even though it is a generally accepted idea that the true value of an income property is what it will earn, the physical aspects of the office building should be fully covered in an underwriting analysis. Factors such as the flexibility of interior partitions will affect future ability to rent space. It has been demonstrated that excessive public space may become a heavy burden as the building grows older. Also mechanical equipment can cause problems, and in the case of older buildings may need replacement.

The ability to maintain high occupancy in office buildings is less dependent on economic inducements than on such intangible qualities as prestige and status. For example, ground floor space rented to a dignified, prestigious merchant can enhance the value of upper-floor space. The class of tenants can add to a particular building's value; i.e., a building known for top-rate law firms or a medical office building of high caliber tenancy will attract other professional people. Companies and business concerns seeking a high-class clientele are often willing to pay a few dollars more each month in rentals for the advertising value of a prestige address.

The expenses of operating an office building must be considered in the total loan picture. Unlike other types of real estate properties, office buildings usually furnish a janitorial service for the tenant as well as for the public areas. There are many companies specializing in contract cleaning services and competition will allow some control to be exercised over these costs. If a building is new, projected operating costs must be utilized, but actual operating costs should be available in the records kept on existing buildings. Care must be taken in analyzing any cost figures to minimize distortions that might lead to misleading conclusions. For example, expense items may be omitted, maintenance work can be neglected, incidental repairs may sometimes be capitalized to reduce expense figures, and tenant services can be held to a dangerously low level in order to distort earnings figures in an upward direction. All of these factors should become apparent to the experienced underwriter and properly weighed in the final loan analysis.

Like other properties, the operating management is a key ingredient in continuing success. Poor management can discourage occupancy and drive good tenants away.

Example of an Office Building Loan

Several years ago in a period of tight mortgage money, a mortgage loan was negotiated for a high-rise office building to be built with 150,000 square feet of space. The borrower showed a total investment of $4 million including land and building, and requested a 90 percent loan, or $3.6 million. The financial projections were outlined as shown in Table 11-2.

In this particular example, the lender felt that the high ratio loan request justified a participation of a greater amount than the 9¾ percent interest would yield. The time was a period of very tight money, and lenders were in good position to demand greater yields. Hence, the following features were added to the loan agreement:

1. The land amounting to 100,000 square feet was purchased by the lender for $3 per square foot and then leased back to the owner of the building for a ground rental of $50,000 per year.

2. As additional ground rental, the lender took 3 percent of the gross annual income, which amounted to approximately $21,000 more.

TABLE 11-2.

Projected Statement for Office Building
(Based on 127,500 sq. ft. net rentable space costing $31.50 per ft. Total—$4 million)

Capital Investment		
Equity Investment (10%)	400,000	
90% mortgage loan	3,600,000	
Total Investment		4,000,000

Annual Operating Calculations		
Gross Scheduled Income (6.00 per ft.)	765,000	
Less 5% vacancy and credit loss	38,250	
Gross operating Income		726,750
Less Expenses—		
All operating costs @ 34.5% of gross operating income		250,730
Net Operating Income		476,020
Less Debt Service—		
9.75% interest for 25 year term Constant—10.69 × 3,600,000		384,840
Cash flow before taxes		91,180

3. With the repayment of the loan calculated on a $6 per square foot rental, the lender demanded 15 percent of any rentals earned in excess of $6 per foot as a hedge against inflation.

With the substantial participation protection available to the lender in this loan agreement, there was no requirement for personal endorsement on the part of the borrower.

WAREHOUSE BUILDINGS

Another type of income property that is preferred by many investors because of its relatively low maintenance and management requirements is the warehouse building. The demand for warehouse space has grown substantially in the past decade for several reasons. Many types of companies use general warehouse space to store merchandise in peak seasons or to keep a product closer to its ultimate market, or to house an unusually large stock of a particular raw material.

Somewhat like office buildings, this type of facility can be built for use by an owner, such as a grocery chain operator; or it can be built for use in part by an owner, such as a light manufacturer with portions available for lease to others; or it can be built for speculative leasing as commercial warehouse space. It is the speculative warehouse that requires the most careful loan evaluation of the property. Owner-occupied or partially occupied buildings provide an established business with a source of income to substantiate and undergird the loan analysis. Warehouses are built fully preleased and partially preleased in much the same way as office buildings and shopping centers, so that the analysis of the different types are similar.

There are several basic requirements for effective warehouse space that would make it more easily rentable during the life of a loan. Like all other income properties, location is of paramount importance. The location of a warehouse should include accessibility by roads running in several directions and capable of handling large trucks. The warehouse should also be accessible to rail spurs, if possible. The land need not be in high-density traffic zones as required by shopping centers and some office buildings, but neither should it be locked into small street patterns that limit the size of the truck that can be accommodated. Availability of a rail siding is not essential to every user, but lack of this facility may limit future marketability. Another requirement that must be checked out is the availability of adequate water lines and pressures to support proper fire extinguisher installations. Without adequate fire protection, insurance rates skyrocket and greatly increase storage costs for the prospective tenant.

In the construction design of the building itself, provision should be made for loading docks capable of handling truck and freight-car loadings at the proper heights. The ceilings must be high, generally over 15 feet for more efficient stack storage of merchandise.

The costs of construction of a warehouse building are similar to those for a shopping center building inasmuch as both are fairly high ceiling buildings with little or no interior finishing provided by the builder. Warehouses require heavier floors to support more weight, but use much less parking space than a shopping center building. However, the cost of land suitable for a warehouse is much lower than that required for freeway-accessible shopping sites.

Warehouse leases often provide for a net/net return to the owner, which means the *tenant* pays all maintenance and operating costs, plus all insurance and taxes on the building. In such a lease, management expenses would be held to a bare minimum. The cash available for debt service is thus very easy to calculate. On general warehouses with multi-tenant occupancy, the owner may provide some services and, most likely, will be responsible for taxes and insurance costs.

Miniwarehouses

In recent years a relatively new form of investment has grown up in the building of one story structures partitioned into small rental spaces. The market for such space comes from the more affluent and mobile citizens who accumulate more material goods but, are unable to accommodate them in smaller apartments and houses. The structures usually contain from 100 to 300 rental spaces each ranging in size from 5 × 5 to 20 × 20 feet.

Miniwarehouses can be built for approximately $8.00 per square foot compared with $18.00 or more for apartments. Operating costs are also minimal compared with apartments. The small storage spaces can be rented for 25 cents to 30 cents per month (an 8 × 10 ft. space for $20.00 per month) which compares very favorably with apartment rental rates.

QUESTIONS FOR DISCUSSION

1. What is the purpose of a feasibility report?

2. How is a loan constant used to facilitate a real estate loan transaction?

3. List and explain the importance of the three essential elements for the successful operation of an apartment project.

4. What is meant by the term "debt service"?

5. What is a "mortgage multiplier" as used for a rule-of-thumb guide?

6. Why are the type and quality of leases important to a lender considering a shopping center loan?

7. How does an owner protect himself against construction cost overruns in building a preleased office building? How does the lender protect himself?

8. What procedure is being used to handle the continued increase in both fixed and operating costs when making a long-term lease for building space?

9. Discuss the advantages and disadvantages of owning an office building; a shopping center; a warehouse.

Chapter 12

Loan Analysis of Industrial, Rural, and Development Properties

SPECIAL-PURPOSE BUILDINGS

Buildings erected for specific purposes have more limited marketability or access to income than those categorized in the preceding chapter as income properties. Under this limited usage category falls industrial plants with specially designed floors to support heavy machinery or technical equipment, and/or with overhead structures carrying large cranes and conveyor systems. Also, processing plants such as refineries, and chemical, or mineral handling facilities have singular usage. Other specialized buildings, with a somewhat broader usage because of the large retail markets they serve, are service stations, food franchise outlets, and automobile dealerships.

Large companies, who are the principal builders and owners of specialized properties, have the capability of generating investment money through the sale of bonds or through an increase in their issues/shares of stock. The discussion here focuses only on those circumstances in which an individual or company is seeking a mortgage loan to finance the construction or purchase of a special-purpose plant or building.

In evaluating a building of limited usage for a mortgage loan, the lender will obviously look to something in addition to the real estate value represented in the property itself. There are three methods that can be used to justify such a loan, which are as follows:

Money Good. To establish the amount of a loan that might be made, the "money good" approach would determine at what price the property could be liquidated under a forced sale. This is the amount of money that could be realized through foreclosure.

A loan made for such an amount would be reasonably well secured by the property. But the loan amount would probably be too small, relative to the total investment required, to be of practical value to the borrower. This method is not very common in today's financial markets, but it has been used.

Earnings Record of Borrower. Since the recovery of the loan in an orderly manner depends on the borrower's ability to produce income, the past record of profitable production is of paramount importance in the underwriting of a special-purpose property loan. A large company with established credit presents little problem. A smaller company, seeking to expand with a major investment, would require closer scrutiny. This would not only involve the credit record but also a review of the management personnel with their experience and capabilities.

Any new venture into a specialized area of business or production is generally not suitable for the mortgage lender's portfolio. Such enterprises can find suitable capital in the equity funding provided by the sale of stock. The security required by a mortgage lender limits the loans to reasonably well-proven and experienced people and companies.

Endorsement. The endorsement of a loan either by a customer or by a supplier is a fairly common practice when it proves advantageous to both parties.

An example of a customer giving loan support to a supplier might be a major grocery chain furnishing credit support to a truck gardener or a cattle feeder. Or a large equipment distributor could be giving financial assistance to one of its smaller manufacturing sources. The purpose, of course, is to assure the customer of a continued or enlarged source of product to sell. The method can be in the form of an outright endorsement of the mortgage note for a new facility. Or it can be given in the form of a letter-agreement guaranteeing certain amounts of purchases and providing for an assignment of the payments to a lender if required.

There are many instances in business today of a manufacturer or other supplier of materials assisting its customers by endorsement of their mortgage loans. The reason is to provide the supplier with better marketing facilities through which to sell more products. Examples of this type of assistance abound in the manufacturer-automobile dealer relationship, and also in the pairing of major oil companies and their dealer-owned service stations. Some fast-food franchise operations, motel chains, and equipment rental and distributorships commonly use the endorsement power of the licensing company to facilitate expansion. The endorsement need not be in the full amount of the loan to be helpful, but may entail underwriting a certain portion or specific amount.

By spreading the risk of the mortgage loan over several borrowers or endorsers, the lender may offer a lower interest rate and a longer term for repayment, if that is desirable.

FARM AND RANCH LOANS

At the turn of this century, 90 percent of our country's population lived on farms. Today, farmers make up less than 4 percent of the total population. And the farm loan business has changed, also. Two general categories of farm loans are: (1) the family-resident loan, and (2) the agri-corporate loan.

Family-Resident Farm Loans

The family-resident farm loan has not changed a great deal in the past 30 years. It is still based on the three legs of any good mortgage loan: (1) a credit-worthy borrower, (2) a piece of real estate of sufficient value to provide good collateral, and (3) the ability of the property and the borrower to produce an income assuring repayment of the loan. Judgments on farm land value require good knowledge and experience in a given geographical area. A single-crop farm is the most vulnerable to failure and subsequent loan default. A diversified crop operation, plus some livestock, gives the best security. So the ability of the farm to produce a continued income, regardless of an occasional crop failure or a fluctuating market, is a prime consideration in making a sound farm loan. The land value itself may be distorted by outside pressures such as a city growing nearby, or a large neighboring farm desiring to expand, or possibly a new freeway providing much frontage acreage. But the farm underwriter should confine the analysis to the producing factors: soil conditions, weather, available irrigation, type of crops, nearness to markets, and condition of the markets, for it is these factors that will produce the income from which the loan can be recovered. To give any substantial weight to the rising land values takes the loan into the category of land development.

Agri-Corporate Farm Loans

Our agri-corporate loans show some similarity to special-purpose property loans. Large commercial farm companies control most of the nation's agriculture today and usually provide good business records to assist an underwriter in making an evaluation. Studies of land productivity with various crops and fertilizers, of the most effective methods of breeding and feeding livestock, and of the management techniques of cost control are all helpful in evaluating the operating procedures of commercial farms. These large farms have proved economical in their operations, and they are willing to test new technologies. Equipment can be more fully utilized and better maintained than on smaller holdings. But, along with the advantages, a word of caution: the dependency on hired labor and the management costs of a large commercial farm make them less flexible and more difficult to retrench in periods of lowering prices. The lender should hold the loan-to-value ratio at a conservative level in this type of operation.

The term of a farm loan varies as to need and may run from 10 to 40 years with 33 years a popular term, partly because the Federal Land Bank formerly used 33 years. More leniency is given in the repayment of farm loans than other real estate loans. A farmer's income is subject to greater variation, and a rigid payment schedule can be self-defeating. But any long-term farm loan should have full amortization as a goal.

Ranch Loans

A ranch presents only slight variations to a farm loan in that it produces livestock as the principal source of revenue. Because ranches are predominately in the water-short southwestern regions, an underwriter must take care to analyze the water situation. Often water rights can be of greater value than the land since without water the land may be worthless. A common practice in ranching is to lease public lands for grazing. The acreage so leased becomes of value to the ranch only in the productivity the land can add to the ranch, and this can be limited by the term of the lease. But leased land or grazing rights do add value and should be included in the appraisal for loan purposes. Sometimes ranches produce additional revenues from the sale of timber rights, from mineral leasing, and even from hunting leases and dude ranching. All income has its value but must be considered according to its tenure and stability.

LAND PURCHASE LOANS

With the increasing interest in urban and suburban growth, the purchase of land for the purpose of speculative resale has grown substantially in the past ten years. A limited number of lending institutions do make loans for raw land purchases, notably some commercial banks and a very few savings associations. The loan-to-value limits are generally lower, perhaps 50 to 60 percent of the value, and the term is seldom over three years.

Lenders do not like to look at the actual sale of the collateral as the normal means of recovering on a mortgage loan (exceptions: house construction and land development loans). And lenders are particularly wary of a tract of raw land that may or may not have a market. Hence, such loans are made primarily to persons or companies that represent substantial other assets, and secondarily loans are made where there is a future intended use or sale that can be confirmed.

To expand on the second type of loan mentioned above, the one with a future intended use or sale, the land may be purchased for a housing development, or perhaps a shopping center, and so more time is needed to complete plans and permanent financing. The lender assisting in the immediate purchase of the land is thus in a prime position to make the construction and permanent loans if the conditions meet his requirements.

Sometimes a land broker or a developer will locate a tract of land highly suitable for a particular purchaser. It could be a small tract for a service station, or a larger parcel on which to erect a retail store outlet. But at the time the property becomes available, the ultimate user may not be in a position to consummate the land purchase. In such a circumstance, a binding letter of intent issued to a real estate broker or developer of some substance would greatly facilitate a raw land loan to acquire the chosen site. The land broker would be presenting the lender a reasonably sure sale for the land within a specified time period, with the land itself as collateral.

A loan for the purchase of raw land, regardless of its intended use, classifies as a commercial loan for a savings association and therefore falls into the limited, nonresidential end of the loan portfolio.

LAND DEVELOPMENT

The next step after the purchase of raw land is its development. "Land development" for loan purposes means the building of streets and utilities to prepare lots for resale as home sites. The development work associated with the construction of an apartment or office building project is in the category of "site development" or land preparation and is an integral part of the project construction costs.

Since the work called for in the land development plans can easily identify the project for residential purposes, such a loan is much more acceptable to a savings association than the land purchase itself.

A development loan can be made for as much as 75 or 80 percent of the appraised value of the finished lots, but is seldom permitted to exceed the costs incurred in the land acquisition and construction costs. This is one of several similar types of loans that generate what might be called a certain distortion in values, due to the fact that the very development being financed greatly enhances the value of the raw land. Federal regulations for savings associations permit a loan at 75 percent of the appraised value for residential land development. Conceivably, the appraised value of the completed lots based on an existing market would be substantially greater than the development costs. A 75 percent loan would permit the developer to borrow an amount in excess of the actual investment. In lending terminology, the amount of a loan that exceeds a borrower's actual costs is called "walking money"—money the borrower can walk away with upon completion. The prudent lender is reluctant to permit a borrower to obtain a cash "profit" from a development or construction loan since this has a tendency to lessen the incentive to sell the property as intended.

An integral part of a land development loan agreement is the release mechanism. This is the clause that spells out when, how, and at what price any lot or lots may be released. The release terms may call for an order of priorities by which the land can be developed and will state in what manner the lot will be released, and most important, they will specify the amount of money from each lot sale that must be paid to the lender for the release.

The release itself is a specific release of the mortgage lien on the lot or lots being sold, and is intended to permit the delivery of a clear title to the lot purchaser by the developer. The amount of money required to release a lot may be a percentage of the sales price of the lot, stating a minimum sales price. In this procedure any increase in sales price over the minimum would increase the payment to the lender and amortize the loan more rapidly. Another method is to set a flat sum on each lot for release and let the developer sell at whatever price he or she can. The flat sum per lot is usually calculated so as to repay the development loan with interest in full when somewhere between 50 and 75 percent of the lots have been sold.

Since 1968, the Department of Housing and Urban Development (HUD) has had an Office of Interstate Land Sales charged by Congress with the responsibility of establishing guidelines and procedures for land developers in an effort to minimize deceptive practices and outright frauds. Sale of lots, developed and undeveloped, has grown to $6 billion per year in this country and has brought out some unscrupulous operators. Basically, the rules require nothing more than a full disclosure of the essential facts for the land buyer and can serve as a protection for both buyer and seller. As one explanation goes, a developer can still sell a lot that is completely under water, but he must state in writing that it is under water! The rules apply to any development with over 50 lots for sale, of less than five acres each, and on which no construction is required. Failure to comply with the HUD regulations can involve a fine and imprisonment for the *lender* as well as the developer and his agents.

CONSTRUCTION LOANS

The construction industry employs over 5 million people in this country and depends heavily on the availability of lendable funds. However, several large segments of the construction business are not so dependent on the capital market. These are government projects such as streets, highways, dams, and public buildings, which can be paid for from tax revenues. Various types of bonds, which are usually based on a pledge of tax revenues, might be sold to finance the construction. Another major factor in the construction market is the large corporation which builds industrial plants and utilities. These corporations often finance expansion out of their own revenues or, perhaps, through the sale of bonds.

The type of construction lending discussed in this text concerns a building loan—the money needed to construct a house, an office building, or a shopping center. While these loans vary substantially in size, there is a similarity in the risks involved. All are secured by a first mortgage on the property to be constructed; all are funded only after each stage of construction has been completed; almost all require a permanent loan commitment or take-out of some kind to assure repayment of the construction loan immediately upon completion of the project. So where is the big risk?

The risk to the construction lender is whether or not the building can be completed with the available money and whether it meets all required specifications. Many factors that are difficult to foresee enter into the successful completion of a building. Some are the weather, labor difficulties and strikes, delays in the delivery of materials, changes in the plans or specifications, and the latest requirements, environmental considerations, which have encouraged delaying lawsuits.

Definition

The definition of a construction loan focuses on the special requirements for this type of financing. A construction loan is initially a loan commitment which provides for the money to be disbursed at intervals during construction in a manner that insures payment of all construction costs and finance charges and requires completion of the building in accordance with the plans and specifications so as to deliver a valid first mortgage upon completion.

Further explanation of each part of the definition follows:

Disbursement During Construction.   Unlike other types of loans, a construction loan is not funded when the borrower signs the note. All the borrower has at the beginning is a commitment that funds will be released as construction progresses. There are two basic ways that progress payments are released. One is at regular time intervals, usually monthly. With this method the building progress is inspected each month and the amount of work completed is duly noted. The lender then releases that portion of the loan that has been allocated to the work accomplished. The second method of handling progress payments is by stages of work completed. Under this plan, the lender and borrower agree at the outset on about five stages of progress, which when reached, will release that amount of the loan proceeds. An example of a first stage might be the completion of all underground work and the pouring of the foundation.

Insurance of Payment of Costs.   While it is the borrower's prime responsibility to use the loan proceeds for the payment of charges on the construction, the lender has an important stake in making sure that all labor and materials are paid as the money is released. Every so often, a builder, by design or in error, may mix the records and use the proceeds from one construction loan to pay charges accruing from another project. The result can be labor liens and materialmen's liens filed on the property while still under construction. There are many ways that lenders can use to minimize this risk of improper disbursement. One is for the lender to handle the payments to contractors and subcontractors. Another is to require proof of payment for costs incurred by the borrower before any funds are released from the loan. Another is to require a waiver of lien form signed by each contractor involved with every progress payment. Perhaps the most important protection for the lender on this problem is to know the borrower's reputation for handling building projects. Then make close inspection a standard procedure.

Completion in Accordance with Plans.   Again it is the borrower who is primarily concerned that the building is constructed according to the plans and specifications. But the lender also has a real interest in this question as the failure to meet the plans can be a cause for refusal by the permanent lender to release the loan. The problems are mostly technical ones such as the size of pipes and wiring, the grade and thickness of concrete, the amount of reinforcing used, the compaction of foundation and parking areas, and many others. A construction lender should employ a knowledgeable construction person on its staff who can check the work as it progresses. On smaller projects, the lender may rely on its own staff for inspection approvals. On larger projects it is more common to employ an independent firm or professional to serve as the inspector. Both architects and engineers are used for this purpose and the decision of the professional is usually accepted by both the borrower and the lender as final determination of the acceptability of the project as it is built.

Delivering a Valid First Mortgage. Insofar as the lender is concerned, the goal of the successful construction loan is to complete the project within the money allocated, all bills paid, and no liens filed. The construction loan can then be repaid through funding of a permanent loan, or the sale of the property if it is a house or a condominium.

Additional Comments. It is customary in a construction loan for the lender to withhold 10 percent from each progress payment until final completion. The purpose is to provide a reserve against unexpected liens. Some lenders will hold this reserve until the statutory lien period has expired after completion before releasing it to the borrower. If an unexpected cost is encountered that was not allowed for in the loan committed, the lender will ask, or demand, that the borrower make such payment. The same procedure is used if the borrower decides to make some changes in the plans after the loan has been committed. Such changes must be approved by the lender, and if it should cause an increase in the anticipated cost, the borrower will be expected to use his or her own funds for payment. The lender does not want to have a building only partially completed with all loan funds exhausted.

The personal endorsement of the borrower-owner is almost always required on a construction loan. The same lender may agree to make a long-term permanent loan with no personal endorsement required but will refuse to do so on the construction loan for the same project. The reason is not just the added security given by another endorsement, but in addition, it is the borrower-owner who is in a controlling position during construction to insist on changes in the plans or create costly problems that can upset orderly construction work. The lender just wants to make certain that the borrower-owner carries his full share of responsibility.

The principal sources for construction money are commercial banks with specialized construction loan departments, savings associations, and recently the Real Estate Investment Trusts. The commercial banks' interest is in the higher yields and short terms represented in construction lending; savings associations and the REITs prefer the higher yields, but also are usually in a position to pick up the permanent loans at a minimum of expense to themselves.

There are many variations in the handling of construction loans. Some procedures used in major categories of buildings are outlined below:

Construction Loans for Residential Properties

Single-family detached houses and some townhouse projects are financed by builders on both a contract basis and a speculative basis.

Contract Basis. A house built for an owner under contract represents a reduced risk to the construction lender. The normal sales contract is a firm commitment by the purchaser and includes a permanent loan commitment for closing. Often the permanent commitment is made by the same lender handling the construction financing as a sort of packaged deal, which minimizes paper work. On such a loan the risk to the construction lender is primarily in the builder's ability to complete the house within the contract terms. The builder's record must be known to the lender.

In smaller communities and rural areas, houses are often constructed under contract by a local builder, who also operates a lumber yard, with the builder providing the construction financing from personal resources. A nearby savings association will have already agreed to make the permanent loan when the house is completed.

Speculative Basis. Many builders, mostly in the growing suburban areas, build houses with the expectation of selling them by the time they are completed. To the risk of being able to complete the house within the projected cost figure is added the risk of selling the house at a profitable price upon completion. A lender must look at the strength and capability of a speculative builder before accepting such a loan. As a builder proves himself to the lender, his construction line of credit can be expanded.

When the housing market fluctuates downward, the speculative builder is the first to be hurt. He can be caught with many unsold houses on which the high interest of the construction loan continues to eat at any profits. More and more, construction lenders are seeking to protect themselves against a soft market by demanding a "take-out commitment" before they will agree to the construction loan. As described in Chapter 6, a take-out commitment for a house loan would be an agreement to make the permanent house loan directly to the builder if the house is not sold within one year from the commitment date. The cost of the commitment is usually one point payable at issuance. The loan so committed to the builder would be at the same ratio as the construction loan, usually 80 percent of the sales value of the house, but the rate of interest would be one to three percentage points over the going rate and the term much shorter, probably ten years, than if the loan had been made to the intended occupant-buyer. The builder still has the problem of selling the house, but has a little breather in facing a monthly amortization payment rather than full repayment of the construction loan, while the construction lender is clear with all his money back.

Construction Loans for Income Properties

Apartments, office buildings, shopping centers, and warehouses all use construction financing, sometimes termed *interim financing*, to accomplish the building of the project. As pointed out earlier, only the very strongest builder-developers are capable of commanding construction financing of any income property without a permanent loan commitment to pay off the construction loan at completion. The terms of the permanent loan influence the manner in which the construction money can be handled. Special requirements for funding the permanent loan, such as an 80 percent lease-up before release of the loan proceeds, place the construction lender in a far more risky position. If a permanent lender is currently unavailable, the developer may resort to a standby commitment in the same genre, or identical to, a take-out commitment that calls for much higher payments. The construction lender must have a closing date for the take-out within a reasonable period (one to three years) for proper recovery of the construction loan.

Construction lending calls for highly experienced personnel who can work with builders and who understand construction progress and procedures so as to make timely releases of the loan proceeds. Most lenders will not release a progress draw without physically inspecting the project or having an independent architect inspector submit an estimate of work accomplished. The trick is to be able to complete the project within the money available and still have 10 percent of the loan amount retained at completion to protect the lender against any unforeseen contingencies. When the lender is satisfied that all bills are paid and that no valid liens can be filed, this 10 percent retainage can be released.

MOBILE HOME PARKS

A fairly recent addition to the national scene as a property investment is the mobile home park. This type of project has long been developed in such resort areas as California, Arizona, and Florida, but only since the late sixties has the mobile home park concept spread to most of the country as a way of life.

Mobile home parks considered in this text are those projects that are built for the leasing of land space to the owners of mobile homes. Some mobile home parks are handled much like ordinary subdivisions in that the land is sold to the mobile home owner. As a subdivision development for the sale of lots, the financing would be much the same as discussed earlier in this chapter under the heading of Land Development. The use of the completed park facility for the *rental* of lots presents the problem of permanent financing for the entire development. This can be done either with a conventional loan similar to an apartment loan, or with an FHA-insured commitment.

The original impetus for mobile home parks, outside of resort areas, was to provide a lower cost type of housing. The mobile home, no longer just a trailer that could be pulled behind the family car, became a completely furnished living unit 40 to 60 feet in length. The smaller units can be purchased, including furniture, for $5,000 or $6,000, can be parked in a space that provides little more than a parking lot, and can provide adequate living accommodations at considerably less cost than a normal house. The larger units with "double width" sections can exceed normal housing costs, running $30,000 or $35,000.

So again there is considerable variation in the size of investment involved in a mobile home park. The more spartan projects provide ten or twenty spaces, often built personally by the owner of the land, and can be very lucrative if kept occupied. One of the major attractions to this form of land use is the low maintenance costs.

The middle-size mobile home park has shown the greatest growth and was spurred by a broadening of the Federal Housing Administration insuring requirements in 1969. In an effort to provide more housing for middle and lower income families, the FHA increased their insurable limits to 90 percent of the finished park's value and to terms of 30 years. The insurance provided by the FHA brought in many private investors who would otherwise not have been able to finance such an undertaking. And the FHA set some sound standards of quality for their parks to avoid the "parking lot syndrome." Paved streets were required, minimal landscaping was specified, and some storage space for each housing unit was included. The density of units per acre was limited to a maximum of eight, and recreational facilities such as a clubhouse, swimming pool, or tennis courts were encouraged.

Because the FHA procedures called for a final closing of the permanent loan that would include the entire project, it was necessary to complete all spaces, or pads, in one stage. Lease-up of the large parks thus developed was often slow and caused financial drains to the investors. Foreclosure rates have been unfortunately high.

Conventional lenders for mobile home parks permit the development in stages to allow for lease-up and growth of income before proceeding.

In 1970, the Veterans Administration added a new benefit for veterans to permit a mobile home to be financed and a lot to be purchased under its guarantee programs. The interest rate and term allowed initially were not sufficient to provide much enthusiasm among lenders, but this new development has helped promote some growth in mobile homes as a living accommodation.

Analysis of a Park

Like other forms of income property, a mobile home park must be well located and serve a market demand. The "building" consists of site preparation, underground utilities, connecting streets, and concrete or all-weather pads for placement of the housing units. The only structures involved are usually a clubhouse-office building, a laundry building, and such recreational facilities as the developer elects to provide.

Maintenance requirements are minimal as the tenant is primarily leasing a piece of land. Mobile home parks operate on a cost as low as 20 to 25 percent of their gross rental income.

Mobile home living has been most popular where at least one of the following five situations exists: (1) a military base, (2) a construction project, (3) a college or university, (4) a resort area, or (5) a retirement-oriented community.

One of the problems in the profitable development has been the longer lease-up period. Unlike apartments, which can be leased to good occupancy over fairly short periods in a strong market, the mobile home park tends to lease-up at a slower rate. Sources within the industry have reported an average rate of rent-up at ten to twelve spaces per month for a new park. However, it has also been observed that once a mobile home is moved into location, it seldom moves out of the park. One reason, of course, is that mobile homes are not built for travel, but are actually semipermanent dwellings. Also, where moving is contemplated, the cost of moving at $.75 to $1.50 per mile serves as a deterrent since the moving costs could easily exceed the value of the equity in the mobile home. Hence, it is far more common for an owner who may be transferred to a new location to simply offer the mobile home for sale on its present location and purchase another at the future destination. The result for the owner of a mobile home park is that a more stable income than in an apartment investment can be counted on. Once the pad is leased, there is a security provided by the mobile home itself that provides good assurance of continuous rental payments.

The lending industry does not respond quickly to anything new, preferring instead the comfortable security of a proven good thing. So, in many areas of the country, conventional loans have been slow to surface for the development of mobile home parks. As more experience has demonstrated the values of this type of investment, financing is more easily obtained. A park loan can now be insured against default by private mortgage insurance companies, thus facilitating the trading of these loans in the secondary market.

FINANCING MOBILE HOMES

Mobile homes do not fall in the category of true real estate, but are regarded as personal property in the same way as an automobile. Financing of these homes will be considered briefly here, since they represent some 20 to 25 percent of the housing units built for sale or rental in this country each year.

Partly because they are an outgrowth of the much smaller house trailer, the mobile home is financed in a similar manner to an automobile. Most states will license and tax them as a highway vehicle, causing some dissension and controversy within communities where mobile homes locate and utilize local schools and police and fire protection facilities.

Underwriting programs by both the FHA and VA have provided some impetus to the growth of mobile home sales. And conventional procedures have kept pace. All these loans follow the pattern of a consumer loan, not a mortgage loan, and are secured by an assignment or a lien on the title registered with the state agency for vehicles.

The term for mobile home loans is longer than for a car, generally running for ten to twelve years. But the interest is the same "add-on" type used in car loans. According to this method, for example, a 7.5 percent add-on interest produces a 12.41 percent annual rate for a ten-year loan and a 12.10 percent annual rate for a twelve-year loan.

The majority of conventional lenders handling mobile home loans employ the services of one of several companies specializing in the insuring and processing of vehicle loans. For a small fee, usually a percentage of the monthly payment, the service company sells a default insurance policy similar to that handled by private mortgage insurance for homes. In case of a default on the payments, the service company itself pays off the lender and undertakes the repossession of the mobile home. Some lenders prefer to make their loans through the service company. In this procedure, the service company handles the collections and accounting for the outstanding loans and performs in a similar capacity as that of a mortgage banker for home loans.

QUESTIONS FOR DISCUSSION

1. For loan purposes, what is meant by a special purpose building? Name three types.

2. What is accomplished by the endorsement of a loan by a third party and why is the procedure sometimes used?

3. What do you consider the most important factors for the sound underwriting of a farm loan?

4. Why are raw land loans among the most difficult to obtain? What are the risks involved?

5. In a land development loan, how does a release clause function?

6. What is the importance of the Office of Interstate Land Sales Registration (under HUD) to the lender who is involved with land development projects?

7. Define a construction loan and list the various risks that can be involved.

8. What special problems are associated with a mobile home park development from a lender's viewpoint?

9. What is the best source of funds for use in funding a new business venture?

Chapter 13

Alternative Financing Methods

SALE OF MORTGAGE BONDS

At several points in the text, reference has been made to the sale of bonds as a method of financing a real estate project. In finance, a *bond* is a certificate evidencing indebtedness that is issued by governments and business corporations in return for loans. Money is borrowed by selling the bond certificates. Bonds can be secured, such as mortgage bonds and equipment bonds, or they can be unsecured. Prior to 1929, the sale of mortgage bonds was a principal means of raising real estate investment money. The record of repayment was excellent and the bonds were a popular security for investors. But the collapse of the security markets in 1929, partially due to the unregulated nature of the securities being sold, brought a halt to this source of mortgage money. The rebirth of the mortgage companies after the Great Depression of the 1930s came about through the utilization of existing pools of investment funds such as those held by insurance companies and savings associations, rather than through the sale of bonds to the general public. Gradually the sale of bonds has returned as a method of financing real estate investments.

The creation of the Securities and Exchange Commission (SEC) in 1934 introduced some measure of control to the securities industry, and the enforcement of these regulations was helpful in preventing fraud, deception, and abusive practices in connection with the sale of stocks and bonds. In today's market, only a few of the very largest companies, such as American Telephone, attempt to sell large issues of bonds direct to the general public. The majority of companies work in tandem with investment bankers who are knowledgeable in securities regulations, and whose organizations are staffed with sales personnel capable of handling the distribution.

Because the sale of any kind of security, whether stocks or bonds, requires some established record and credibility, developers taking this step are usually limited to better known companies and individuals of strong financial worth. Considerable initial time and expense are required for the proper registration of a bond issue, involving extensive legal work and accounting data to be submitted to the SEC, which must then approve the issue, clearing it for sale to the public. The cost of registration alone, for instance, can run as high as several hundred thousand dollars.

A bond issue secured by a pledge of real property would be termed a mortgage bond. There are also equipment bonds secured by such things as freight cars or airplanes. A bond that is not secured is called a "debenture" bond and is similar to a promissory note. What the SEC requires is that the issuer fully disclose all information relative to the company and its key personnel, the security behind the bond issue, and how the proceeds of the sale will be used. Failure to comply with SEC requirements is a felony offense, subject to fine and imprisonment.

Once a bond issue has been registered and approved, the investment banker can handle the sale in two different ways. First, an outright purchase of the entire issue can be made at a discount off the full value. The issue is then resold to investor clients at a higher price, usually with the help of a network of associated investment banking firms across the country. With very large issues, several of the major investment houses may join together to underwrite the issue. It takes an intimate knowledge of the market conditions to handle a block purchase with the expectation of making a profit from the mark-up of its discount price.

The second method can be termed the "best efforts" plan. This actually means just what the name implies—the investment banker will sell the issue at whatever the market will bring, retaining a fixed commission.

PRIVATE PLACEMENT OF SECURITIES

The growth of major investors, such as the insurance companies, the mutual funds, and pension funds, has recently dominated the activity on the national security exchanges. However, there is a growing trend to bypass these public markets and place both stock and bond issues directly with an investor. From the point of view of the issuer, the procedure has some advantages, including: (1) no SEC registration required; (2) no publicity—no public pronouncements of proprietary information regarding company products or processes; (3) financial conditions of closely held companies remain confidential information; (4) more flexibility in terms with a negotiated private placement, thereby benefiting both the borrower and the lender; and (5) lower sales costs for the issue.

It is within this field of the private placement of securities that mortgage bankers have become increasingly active and directly competitive with the investment banker. Mortgage companies have good contacts with many sources of money and are familiar with the special needs of each for investments. The sale of a block of securities to their regular investors is a natural expansion of their business relationship.

SEC REGULATIONS FOR REAL ESTATE SALES

The growth in sales of various types of "certificates" to finance real estate developments has brought increased scrutiny by the SEC as to any violations of the securities laws. In general, the SEC considers the sale of any form of a partial interest in land to the general public as a type of security and subject to its regulations. The many forms in which real estate developers present their various "deals" has brought a number of new rulings, all with the purpose to protect the general public against fraud and misrepresentation. In various new rulings, the SEC has considered a predevelopment sale of certificates for lots as a form of securities; the sale of condominium units that may be available for rental purposes has come under registration guidelines; and if the sale of partnership interests is solicited publicly, as opposed to a contact *from* an interested purchaser, then a clearance is needed from the SEC.

In any real estate project involving ownership by a group of persons or companies, the prudent lender will obtain a legal opinion to determine if proper compliance is being made with both federal and state security regulations.

PURCHASE AND LEASE-BACK

One method of financing a real property acquisition is to find a willing investor who will buy or build the property and lease it back to the intended user. Tax laws formerly permitted charitable organizations or tax-exempt institutions to buy land and build for lease without paying property taxes or income taxes. The laws have changed and most states no longer permit such exemptions if a property is clearly intended for commercial purposes, but advantages do remain for both parties to such a transaction. The investor-owner enjoys a secure investment with a sound return. The tenant obtains a building highly suitable for his or her purposes with minimal cash outlay.

The purchase and lease-back procedure is used by major companies, such as oil companies seeking to expand their marketing operations, who will build and lease a property for a particular tenant. Another variation of this procedure is the municipally owned industrial park. A city that wants to increase business and the number of jobs for the community will acquire a suitable tract of land, develop it, and build buildings for lease to acceptable tenants, all for the purpose of attracting more industry. The money for such land purchase and construction is generated by the sale of municipal bonds, not always guaranteed by the issuing community, but always in the tax-exempt municipal category.

LAND LEASES

Businessmen have always felt a strong need for owning something tangible, and with some individuals there has been an almost fanatical pursuit of, and obsessive attraction to, land ownership and the consequent feelings of security such ownership provides. The all-powerful urge to own land simply as land, however, is gradually giving way in this era to a more realistic approach that values land for the uses that can be made of it, instead of just for its ownership alone. Most of the material things we consider essential to sustain and maintain our life style can now be rented, such as houses, cars, appliances, and furniture. Business enterprises have long been accustomed to renting buildings as well as owning them, but they usually insisted on owning their own equipment. Now, through specialized leasing companies, even the most intricate machinery and equipment can be leased. The advantage to the lessee is that his capital is not tied up, the lease payments are all tax-deductible expenses, and the equipment may be more easily exchanged for newer models, thereby reducing the problem of obsolescence.

As land becomes less available there has been a tendency for land owners to lease rather than sell property. Many land areas in Hawaii cannot be purchased at any price, but these areas can be leased for very long terms, thus allowing home building to continue. Some of the more densely populated areas of California, as well as much midtown urban land in all major cities, are subject to acquisition by long-term lease only. Mortgage lenders are able to finance buildings on leased land through agreements that recognize the land lease and provide for certain assignments of rights in case of default. This would not be a first mortgage loan in most states, but is acceptable to some lenders who are permitted to make such a loan. From a practical standpoint, for the lender's protection, the land rental payments can be handled through an escrow account, much the same as property taxes.

USE OF OTHER COLLATERAL

Mortgage loans can be made on the basis of the real property plus some other form of collateral that may be pledged. If the borrower needs more money than the property alone will permit, the lender can ask for more security: additional property, stocks or bonds, an assignment of equipment, or such other assets mutually agreed to by the lender and borrower. With additional collateral, the lender has recourse to other assets for recovery of the loan if it becomes necessary.

Personal Endorsement. The personal endorsement of the borrower for the benefit of a company, relative, or associate is a form of additional collateral to the lender. Large corporate borrowers do not use personal endorsements, but with smaller companies and those under majority control by one stockholder, it is not uncommon to request the personal endorsement of the principals—one or all of them. A personal guarantee on a mortgage loan can be limited. For example, if five men are endorsing a $100,000 loan, each might ask to limit individual liability to $20,000. Approval would be a matter of decision by the lender. Without a specific limitation, each endorser of a note is exposed, or is said to carry a contingent liability, to the full amount of the debt.

Compensating Balances. Cash balances carried in an account with the lending institution, when it is a commercial bank or savings association, can be deemed additional collateral when a minimum balance is required as a condition of the loan agreement. This procedure is also called a *compensating balance.* The requirement to maintain a certain minimum cash balance is not unusual since it gives the lender some assurance that cash is on hand, and this does add some strength to the borrower's financial statement. Many lenders do not acknowledge a compensating balance as any inducement to grant a loan because of the abuses and pressures that can occur. For a one or two point fee, a cash deposit could be transferred to the lender's institution solely to support a loan, but the deposit would not be under the control of the borrower. This does not add strength to the borrower and can encourage lending to an unworthy borrower. But it is hard to deny the importance for a borrower to maintain a sound cash position—and why not on deposit with the lending institution?

Assignment of Life Insurance. Life insurance companies are probably more interested than other lenders in adding the assignment of life insurance policies on the principal borrowers' lives to the list of additional collateral. This practice is a reasonable requirement for any lender when the successful payout of a loan is heavily based on the ability of one or two principals to operate a business. Some home owners also carry mortgage pay out life insurance, a declining balance form that covers the amortized balance due on a loan in case of the premature death of the borrower. However, no lender yet requires this particular type of insurance in conjunction with the granting of a home loan.

SALE OF EQUITY INTERESTS

Two types of equity investment have become popular as methods for financing real estate—syndications and realty funds.

Syndication

In real estate ventures, a syndicate is a form of limited partnership organized to carry out a specific project, and upon completion of that project, is dissolved. Syndicates operate in a number of other businesses, motion pictures for example, and are composed of groups of people or companies formed to carry out a particular enterprise. The purpose is to generate a large amount of capital by increasing the number of investors, or simply to spread the risk of a project and jointly share in the rewards.

The sale of participating interests in the large real estate developments, or in the purchase of a large tract of land to hold for speculative growth in value, has increased substantially over the past decade. Escalating land values have attracted the interest of many smaller investors, and by joining a group the risk is spread and the benefits are a bit more secure.

Most states have set limits on the number of persons that can comprise one syndicate, or in the total amount that can be sold, or in the manner of sale. Any effort to sell a syndicate interest across state lines or through the mails involves the federal rules spelled out by the Securities and Exchange Commission. Competent legal counsel is needed for guidance in any sales effort involving joint ownership interests.

Realty Funds

Whenever a larger group is formed to participate in a real estate venture, and registration with federal and state regulatory agencies is necessary, the participation can be in the form of "units" purchased in a realty fund, formed as a limited partnership.

Realty funds are organized by persons or companies wishing to raise equity money for real estate projects, such as the purchase of raw land, a construction development, or the purchase of existing income properties. The interests are sold in the form of participating certificates at a fixed price per unit. A unit generally costs anywhere from $100 to $5000, depending on the plan of organization, and represents a certain percent of interest in the total fund. Federal and most state laws classify the sale of such participating interests as a sale of securities that must be registered and approved before any sale can be made.

The participant is actually a limited partner and may share in the tax losses and depreciation as well as the profits generated through the fund's investments. The organizer of the fund is usually the general partner, or a company he controls is so designated, and he also serves as the managing agent for the partnership properties.

SPECIAL TYPES OF FINANCING

While most mortgage financing follows a fairly standard pattern of a first mortgage as security based on a reasonable loan-to-value ratio and fully amortized over the term of the loan, there are some interesting variations that can be used in special circumstances. When the situation calls for a more flexible approach to a loan, the following basic methods might be considered, either separately or in combination, as need or imagination may inspire.

Although some proposals become more imaginative than realistic, proper use of specialized financing techniques can rescue a faltering real estate sale or breathe new life into an otherwise stalled project. In the hands of a skilled promoter, some of these procedures reflect the so-called wheeler-dealer concept of development financing. But there is a telling story in an old cartoon depicting a rather seedy looking tramp relaxed on a park bench and picking his teeth with a piece of straw. The caption reads, "I never quite got the hang of it. I was always dealing when I should have been wheeling, and wheeling when I should have been dealing."

Wrap-Around Mortgage

The wrap-around mortgage is a method used to facilitate the sale of a property by encouraging the seller to assist with the financing of the sale. Instead of using a straight second mortgage procedure for a portion of the equity involved in the sale, a special form is used which creates a new note that acknowledges and includes the existing first mortgage in the total. Payment is then made on the new note with a portion of that payment directed towards payment of the first mortgage still existing. The first mortgage holder may be required to approve of the sale and the new note. If such approval calls for substantial escalation of the first mortgage interest rate, the advantages of this procedure are minimized or eliminated. The procedure is most effectively used when the equity has built up substantially over the years and the first mortgage carries an earlier, lower interest rate. The purpose is to hold the advantage of the lower first mortgage interest for the benefit of the seller and, in so doing, to substantially decrease the initial cash requirement for the benefit of the buyer.

To illustrate with a hypothetical example, let us say a building is offered for sale at a price of $100,000, which is acceptable to the buyer. The first mortgage loan, now 10 years old with an interest rate of 6½ percent, is paid down to a balance due of $55,000. On a straight assumption basis, the buyer would need $45,000 cash. Or with a new first mortgage loan on the older building, the maximum loan-to-value ratio being offered would be 75 percent, which would require $25,000 cash. But the buyer does not want to use even that much initial cash in the purchase. Under such conditions a "wrap-around" mortgage might well resolve the problem and make the sale possible. The proposal is for the buyer to pay just $10,000 cash and grant to the seller a wrap-around mortgage on the property for $90,000 at 8½ percent interest, which would acknowledge the exist-ing first mortgage. Under this arrangement the seller is actually undertaking a second mortgage loan in the amount of $35,000, at a fair interest rate, plus earning an additional 2 percent of interest on the first mortgage. Normally, the seller would continue to make the regular payments on the first mortgage obligation, using the proceeds from the "wrap" mortgage payments to do so. The buyer, paying on a $90,000 obligation each month, would of course require some pro-tective clause granting the right to make the first mortgage payments direct to the first mortgagee if a potential default should arise.

Balloon Note

The purpose of a "balloon" payment is to permit smaller monthly installments for the first few years and to retain the loan in a short-term classification for the lending institution. The smaller monthly payments (less than the amount to fully amortize the loan) are made for, say, three years, at which time the full unpaid balance becomes due.

If, for example, the borrower needed $25,000 and offered ade-quate collateral, the lender under this type of loan would accept principal payments of $200 per month, plus accrued interest, for up to three years. At the end of the third year, the final payment due in full would be $18,000, plus interest. (Payments of $200 each for 35 months amount to a principal reduction of $7000.)

It is often assumed that if the payments are promptly made, the lender will renew and extend the final balloon payment for another limited term of small principal payments. But the lender is by no means legally obligated to do so, and circumstances can force the lender to require a full pay off on the note when due.

"Interest Only"

The expression "interest only" covers a variation of the balloon note procedure in that for the first year or so nothing is paid on the principal, and only the interest is due. This method is most commonly used today in the sale of raw land, but is applicable to any kind of loan.

If sellers are commanding a good market price for their land and do not need immediate cash, they have a better chance of selling the property by handling their own financing and making it attractive to the speculative buyer, such as a syndicated group. In such a case, the purchaser, buying the land for resale rather than development, wants as small a cash investment as possible, hoping to resell within several years at a profit.

To use an example: if a person owns 40 acres of land and sells it for $5000 per acre, or $200,000 total, the sales amount may be carried as a loan to the buyer and 8 percent interest collected for the first two years. Thus, the buyer takes title to the property, subject to the seller's mortgage in the amount of $200,000, and each year pays $16,000 to the seller as tax-deductible interest. Before the two years have elapsed, the buyer finds another company who will pay $8000 an acre for the land in cash. Now, the second sale at a later date for $320,000 clears the $200,000 first mortgage and any accrued interest, leaving a substantial profit on a relatively small cash investment. The trick is being able to make that second sale.

Extended Terms

Most companies selling a service or product need their accounts receivable paid promptly and often offer cash discounts for such payments. A few companies utilize credit terms as an incentive to do business with them and, in so doing, provide additional financing for the customer.

In building an apartment, an office building, or even a house, a major supplier such as a lumber dealer, a cement company, or an electrical or plumbing contractor may agree to extend payment terms for 60 or 90 days, or in some cases, until the project is finished and sold. This method does conserve cash for the builder-developer, but usually comes at a higher price—an increase in the product or service price plus interest. And the supplier may be exposed to a payment delay that usually means a forfeiture of lien rights if it exceeds 120 days.

This "extended terms" method of auxiliary finance is not to be confused with slow payment or nonpayment of materialmen's bills; both are very poor procedures. Building supply companies are fully aware of the 90- to 120-day time limits within which to file liens for nonpayment and normally make sure that their interests are protected.

Supplier Loans

In recent years some of the major appliance companies and, in a few cases, utility companies, have given larger builder-developers financial assistance with outright loans secured by second mortgages. The ulterior motive in such cases is always to insure the use of the lender's products. This could be heating and air conditioning equipment, or a full range of kitchen equipment, or it could be a utility company seeking a competitive advantage.

Subordination

Subordination is a procedure used to grant priority to a specific lien so as to permit better financing of a project. In this method, landowners or mortgage holders, for a consideration, might subordinate their position in favor of a specific lending institution in order to meet a loan requirement.

A possible situation wherein this procedure could be used would be a landowner, not wishing to sell the land, but desiring development and income, agrees to a long-term land lease to, say, a motel chain. In order to help finance the construction of the motel building, the landowner would agree to subordinate (to make inferior) his or her ownership rights to the mortgage lien, as arranged by the motel chain. Normally, the motel chain would have to be sufficiently strong financially to give the landowner reasonable assurance of performance under the lease terms. And the landowner would expect to retain the right to step in and assume the mortgage payments, with rights to the motel's income, in case of an act in default by the motel chain.

Leverage

The word *leverage* is defined as the mechanical advantage of a lever. In real estate jargon, the term has several variations, but in essence it means the use of a relatively small amount of cash to induce a large mortgage loan for the purchase of a property. The term belongs more properly in the vocabulary of the promoter-developer who feels the escalation in land value will provide a lucrative return on the equity investment. As long as values inflate, the theory holds up well.

From a lender's viewpoint, the high-ratio loans, i.e., those of low cash equity, are not highly desirable. The rapid rise in land values generally since the mid-sixties has provided a safety margin of its own for existing properties, as the values appreciate instead of depreciate in some areas. But the underwriter cannot always count on a speculative increase in value to prove the soundness of the loan.

QUESTIONS FOR DISCUSSION

1. Describe how the sale of bonds is used to finance a real estate investment.

2. What is meant by the private placement of securities and how does this method compare with public offerings?

3. Discuss the position of the Securities and Exchange Commission in regard to the sale of participating interests in real estate deals.

4. Describe a typical sale lease-back agreement.

5. How can a mortgage loan be made for a property where the land is leased to the loan applicant?

6. What is a syndication and how would it be set up to acquire real property?

7. Describe how a realty fund is organized and operated.

8. What is a "wrap-around mortgage" and how does it work?

9. Describe a "balloon note," and an "interest only" agreement.

10. What is meant by the term "subordination"?

11. Is the use of leverage advantageous for the lender? Why?

Chapter *14*

Settlement Procedures

INTRODUCTION TO RESPA

The closing of a loan is so closely associated with the transfer of title to real property that it is necessary to examine the recent efforts of the federal government to regulate the process. As long ago as 1972, the Secretary of Housing and Urban Development established standards governing the settlement costs allowable in connection with HUD-insured mortgage transactions. The requirements were withdrawn in April 1976. In the meantime, Congress had passed the Real Estate Settlement Procedures Act (RESPA) in 1974, implemented in June 1975, which created such a mass of confusion that its key provisions were suspended within six months. The good intent of the law was lost in the detailed requirements that conflicted with local laws and practices. Unrealistic limits on charges and procedures defeated the purpose of the law, which was to protect the consumer-home buyer. Instead, the intended beneficiary of the law was burdened with inconveniences, delays, and increased costs.

What RESPA is expected to accomplish is to establish national standards for settlement procedures, require full disclosure of all costs involved in the transfer of real property, and to eliminate practices that are deemed detrimental to the buyers' best interests. To

303

resolve some of the chaos created by the original law and the subsequent suspension of key portions, a new amendment was passed taking effect in June 1976. Essentially the new rules do not prescribe dollar limits for any settlement charges but do require the following:

1. Delivery of the HUD-approved information booklet on settlement costs to the loan applicant when application for a loan is made.

2. A good faith estimate of settlement costs to be furnished to loan applicant within three days of the written loan application.

3. A statement of the settlement costs, to the extent known, to be made available to the borrower 24 hours before settlement, if requested by the borrower.

Additional special requirements of RESPA as amended will be detailed in the applicable sections that follow, as they pertain to the mortgage loan.

While RESPA has had a substantial impact on loan closing, it has not changed the requirements for essential information, nor has it altered the basic order of processing. Some additional steps have been inserted along the way.

CLOSING THE LOAN

In the preceding chapters, the text has covered the sources of money and how loan funds move to the borrower, how the lender examines a borrower, and what the lender looks for in the various properties requiring loans. The final step in the process is *closing the loan*—the procedure by which the loan is funded and title to the property is transferred. Real estate loans are made without transfers of title between a seller and a buyer, but the steps are very similar because a mortgage loan always requires a conditional assignment of the title as security for the loan.

The information presented in this chapter is oriented to the closing of a residential loan but the procedures and requirements are essentially the same for a commercial loan. It is the purpose of this chapter to identify the steps necessary for closing and to allocate, insofar as possible, the responsibility for performance and who pays the costs.

PRELIMINARY PROCEDURES

Mortgagor's Information Letter (MIL)

The information contained in the mortgagor's information letter is a part of the closing data needed, but more accurately comes under the listing requirements that a sales agent obtains from the seller when a property is offered for sale. This is the information that is requested from an existing mortgagee, at the time a property is offered for sale, showing the exact amount of loan or loans due on the property, amount of escrow balances, and any premium required for payment of the loan. The letter is normally returned to the real estate broker handling the transaction and becomes a part of the selling proposal. Title companies are normally advised of the existing mortgage lien holders but seek their own information from the county records and directly from the present mortgagee so that a proper pay-off and release of any prior mortgage liens can be handled at the closing.

Preliminary Title Report

When an earnest money contract has been consummated, it is a good idea to "open title" with whatever title insurance company has been selected to handle the closing. Under the new RESPA procedures, the seller may not require that title insurance be purchased from a particular title company as a condition of the sale. But the mortgage lender still has a right to accept or reject a proposed title company. So it is a good suggestion for buyers to make certain that they are selecting an acceptable title company when they decide. Lending institutions are now required to submit a statement to the borrower listing acceptable title companies and attorneys, along with the anticipated charges the borrower might expect. Also, any business relationship between the lender and any settlement service provider must be disclosed. In order to simplify handling, the title company selected is normally one located in the same county as the property being sold.

The preliminary title report is furnished by the title company to both the real estate agent and the mortgage company. The information contained is a confirmation of the correct legal description, and it also includes the names of the owners of the property according to the county records, any restrictions or liens on the property, any judgments against the owners of record, and a listing of any requirements the title company may have to perfect title and issue a title insurance policy. This is an assurance that if the requirements are met, a title policy can be issued. The report is for information only; it is not to be confused with a title "binder," which legally obligates the title company for specific insurance. The title companies normally make no charge for the preliminary report; it is part of their service in anticipation of writing the title insurance policy at closing.

RESPA Disclosure Requirements for the Lender

Information Booklet. Upon submission of a written application for a mortgage loan, the lender is required to give the buyer a copy of the HUD-prepared booklet entitled "Settlement Costs Guide." The booklet contains two parts. Part One is a description of the settlement process, the services that are needed and the nature of the charges for these services. It also gives information on the borrowers rights and the remedies available to him under RESPA. Part Two of the booklet is an item-by-item explanation of settlement services and costs with sample forms that are used.

Good Faith Estimates. When an application is made for a mortgage loan, the lender is required to furnish the buyer a good faith estimate of settlement service charges that the borrower can expect. Three business days are allowed for furnishing this information. A copy of a Good Faith Estimate is reproduced in Figure 14–1.

Truth-in-Lending. While the lender is not required by RESPA to furnish the Truth-in-Lending statement until the loan is consummated, the HUD guide suggests that borrowers ask for the "annual percentage rate" at the time of loan application. The HUD guide gives no clues for the lender on how to calculate this rate accurately before the information needed becomes available. One purpose of the Truth-in-Lending statement is to provide borrowers with an annual percentage rate that they will be paying for their loan which must be calculated to include not only the interest but also the discount points, fees and financing charges, all reduced to an annual percentage.

"GOOD FAITH ESTIMATES"

Name: _____

Re: _____

Property: _____

_____   _____

This list gives an estimate of most of the charges you will have to pay at the settlement of your loan. The figures shown, as <u>estimates</u>, are subject to change. The figures shown are computed based on sales price and proposed mortgage amount as stated on your loan application.

ESTIMATED SETTLEMENT CHARGES

801	Loan Origination Fee	1%	_____
803	Appraisal Fee		_____
804	Credit Report		_____
901*	Interest		_____
902	Mortgage Insurance Premium		_____
1107	Attorney's Fees		_____
1108	Title Insurance		_____
1201	Recording Fees		_____
___	_____		_____
___	_____		_____
1301	Survey		_____

Your contractual agreement with the Seller may limit your payment of the above charges.

*   This interest calculation represents the greatest amount of interest you could be required to pay at settlement. The actual amount will be determined by which day of the month your settlement is conducted. To determine the amount you will have to pay, multiply the number of days remaining in the month in which you settle times _____, which is the daily interest charge for your loan.

THIS FORM DOES NOT COVER ALL ITEMS YOU WILL BE REQUIRED TO PAY IN CASH AT SETTLEMENT. YOU MAY BE REQUIRED TO PAY OTHER ADDITIONAL AMOUNTS AT TIME OF LOAN SETTLEMENT.

FIGURE 14-1.

SETTLEMENT REQUIREMENTS

RESPA sets no requirements on who may close a real estate transaction or handle the "settlement practices." The act acknowledges that procedures vary in different localities and that settlements can be conducted by lending institutions, title insurance companies, escrow companies, real estate brokers, and attorneys for the buyer or seller. Whoever handles the settlement procedures must meet certain requirements of the mortgage lender as to methods used and information required. Following are the major items involved in the settlement procedures with information on the handling of each.

Disclosure of Settlement Costs

Twenty-four hours prior to actual settlement, the borrower has the right to inspect a Uniform Settlement Statement which must itemize the services provided and the fees charged for them. The closing agent who must furnish the statement may not have all the costs available prior to closing but must show what is available. The borrower may waive the right to this advance information but the completed settlement statement must be mailed at the earliest practical date.

Survey

Whenever a loan is involved, a survey may be considered mandatory. It is a good procedure to require an actual survey on any transfer of real property for the buyer's protection. A survey, which must be made by a registered surveyor, will not only show the exact outline and size of the property but will indicate any encroachments that might interfere with full title. An encroachment could be a building on the property erected too close to a property line in violation of a city code requirement, or it could be a fence belonging to a neighbor erroneously placed on the property being purchased. Such usage by a neighbor establishes rights under the statute of limitations through adverse possession and requires sound legal guidance. Because of this possibility, many attorneys require that a survey be available to them before a deed or a mortgage is drawn up.

The close involvement of the survey with the proper title and the legal instruments makes it easier for the title company to order the survey and include the cost in the closing statement of charges. This can be done after the loan has been approved as one of the steps in the settlement process. And this is one of the reasons title companies need a few days to properly prepare for the actual closing.

Insurance

Hazard Insurance. Hazard insurance covers physical damage to the property and is a requirement on mortgage loans. Mortgage lenders must be named as a loss payee on the face of the policy to protect their interest in the property. While the buyer has the right to select the insurance company, the coverage must meet the minimum requirements of the lender. Payment for the policy is a part of the settlement procedures so it is necessary that the mortgage lender be advised who will handle the insurance coverage in advance of closing. The closing agent disburses the buyer's funds for payment of the first full year's insurance coverage. In addition, an escrow fund is established for the borrower's account with the lender which requires two months of insurance premiums as now limited by RESPA regulations.

Mortgage Default Insurance. Mortgage default insurance, when required, is handled entirely by the mortgage company. The method of payment is determined during the loan negotiations, and the premium to be paid at closing is turned over to the mortgage company for remittance to the insurance carrier, be it private mortgage insurance or FHA insurance.

Credit Life Insurance. Mortgage life insurance, sometimes called mortgage cancellation insurance, is a matter between the borrower and personal choice of an insurance carrier. It is not required in residential loans and is not involved in closing procedures. Sometimes such a requirement for life insurance becomes necessary in larger commercial loans where the successful operation and, thus, the loan repayment depend heavily on one or two individuals.

Title Insurance. The title company handling the closing furnishes the title insurance, which is a routine procedure. Rates for such insurance are usually set by a state insurance commission and are well known in advance. The amount of insurance cannot exceed the sales price for the property. It is the seller's responsibility to prove title and pay the insuring costs for the owner's policy. Concurrently, a title insurance policy is issued to the mortgagee and paid for by the borrower (buyer).

Property Taxes

The determination of taxes due at closing always creates some questions. At most closings, this information is obtained by the settlement agent from the court house records. Under the time pressures that most agents work with, the actual figures are not available very much prior to the formal closing or settlement.

As a part of the settlement procedures, the property taxes are pro-rated to date of closing. The buyer pays the taxes as a part of the monthly loan installment—one-twelfth of the annual tax amount with each payment. RESPA rules allow the lender to set up an escrow account for tax payments with an initial deposit of two months of the annual tax amount paid at closing. This provides a cushion for the lender to use in maintaining tax payments on the property.

Since property taxes are payable annually at the end of the tax year, it is the responsibility of the settlement agent to make certain the taxes are paid. Many lenders require that the closing agent guarantee the tax payment.

At the time a property sale is consummated, the real estate broker may be asked for an accounting of closing costs. One of the charges that is difficult to determine is the amount and distribution of the property taxes. How much each party, buyer and seller, are assessed depends on the date of closing the transaction.

Maintenance Assessments

A new form of assessment has developed with the growth of condominiums and neighborhood associations. This is the charge made by an authorized organization, usually established as a part of the home purchase agreement or by a deed restriction to the property, to pay for the maintenance of all common areas. Depending on the restrictions that are placed on the use of money so collected, it may go for landscape maintenance, parking area improvements, trash removal, swimming pool upkeep, exterior building repairs, or any of a number of other needs to maintain a living condition that goes with the purchase of a house or condominium. In most areas, the assessment can be established as a lien on the subject property and, as such, can be made a part of the montly payment the same as property taxes. Two months of the maintenance assessments can be required for escrow purposes.

Prepaid Interest

Another expense at closing that is difficult to determine precisely in advance is the prepaid interest. On mortgage loans interest is normally paid *after* the money has been used; the regular monthly payment on a house loan covers interest for the *preceding* month, plus a reduction in the principal. In order to adjust a payment date to the first of each month (or other agreed monthly date), borrowers are expected to pay the interest on their loan from closing date to the inception date of their normal monthly payment in advance; this means the interest from the closing date to the end of the month in which the closing took place. From the first of the following month the interest would accrue, making the first full monthly payment due on the first of the *second* month following closing. Thus, the actual amount of the prepaid interest due cannot be accurately determined until the closing date.

Since interest might be paid on a loan that may not be funded until several days after closing, an adjustment may be in order. Some mortgage companies, in anticipation of a normal five-day delay in funding, will calculate the interest due, not from the closing date, but from five days after closing until the end of the month when the closing was made. Some companies start the interest at the closing date, even though funds are not released, on the premise that the money has been committed and, therefore, cannot be used for any other purpose during the interim. The FHA and VA, recognizing that abuses in delays can occur and will accrue to the benefit of the mortgage company, have a rule requiring recalculation of the prepaid interest if the loan is not actually funded within five days of closing.

Escrow Accounts or Reserve Accruals

Because the cash to establish certain deposits is required at the time of closing by all mortgage companies, the funds needed have come to be classed as a part of the closing costs. The deposits are to assure the lender that there will be adequate funds on hand to pay *future* taxes and insurance charges. These deposits are also referred to as "pre-pays" or "prepaid items."*

The mortgage company collects one-twelfth of the annual property taxes and insurance costs (both hazard insurance and the FHA or private mortgage insurance premium if involved) as a part of each monthly payment. Therefore, in order to make sure that sufficient money is on hand by the date taxes or insurance payments are due, a cushion is needed. Due dates may not coincide, or there may be a slow payment on the part of the borrower. So the mortgage lender asks for a reserve to be established as a part of the closing or settlement procedures. RESPA regulations now limit the reserve that may be required to an amount that cannot exceed the sum of: (a) an amount equal to the taxes, insurance premiums and other charges that would normally be paid by the buyer up to the due date of the first full monthly mortgage installment; plus, (b) an additional amount not in excess of two months of the estimated annual taxes, insurance premiums and other charges normally paid by the home buyer.

With each monthly payment, the agency servicing the mortgage loan collects one-twelfth of the annual taxes, insurance premiums, and other charges allocated to the reserve account, and credits these collections to the borrower's account. When the annual payments fall due, the servicing agent makes proper payments and charges them to the borrower's account. An accounting of this fund must be made periodically to the borrower, usually once a year, to show what amounts have been paid in and what paid out. If additional funds are needed to pay higher taxes or insurance costs, the servicing agent has the right to increase the amount of the borrower's monthly payments into the reserve account.

The escrow, or reserve account, serves the best interests of both the borrower and the lender. The borrower is assured that taxes and insurance are covered and the lender always has the money available for proper payment when it becomes due. Upon sale of the property and a pay-off of the loan, the reserve account belongs to the seller and is refunded. Sometimes in an assumption sale of a home, the

*The escrow account may be likened to a bank deposit owned by the borrower, but under the complete control of the mortgage lender. It is held for the purpose of paying taxes and insurance owed by the borrower. It should not be confused with the escrow fee which is a small service fee charged by the title company for some of the work performed at closing.

seller overlooks this nest egg and allows it to pass on to the new buyer as a part of the loan assumption. The loan servicing agent does not release the reserve account cash in an assumption because the loan is not paid off. If the seller wants the reserve fund repaid in an assumption sale, the agreement for the buyer to provide reimbursement should be made a part of the sales contract.

Discount

The charge known as the *discount* is one of the least understood costs associated with closing and, as a result, creates more irritations and hard feelings than any other factor. It is simply a charge for the use of money precisely the same as interest would be. For clarification it might be compared to a down payment for the purchase of a car, with the balance paid in monthly installments.

The origin of discounting goes back to the efforts of the government to freeze an interest rate in a fluctuating market. And, since the government does not loan the money itself, the job devolves on private sources of money to fund government underwritten loans. The private sources have to meet the competition of market interest rates and, in order to produce nearly comparable yields to the investor on a fixed interest rate, a system of discounting the loan has been developed. It amounts to a certain percentage reduction of the total loan that is funded; each 1 percent of the loan amount is called *one point.* As the spread between market interest rates and the government specified rate increases, so the points needed to balance are increased.

So far, this procedure would not seem too complicated, but the incongruity becomes apparent in that the government knowingly overlooks the realities of the market. In attempting to protect the purchaser-borrower, the FHA and VA have established the requirement that no discount can be paid by the borrower. From the government's point of view, a discount is regarded as an unnecessary charge for the privilege of using the government insurance or guarantee of payment. From the lender's viewpoint, it is difficult to justify to the association members, trust fund, or stockholders whose money is being loaned, that they should accept a yield substantially under the market rate for comparable conventional loans.

The most obvious answer to resolve the dilemma would be to let the fixed government rates float with the market, a system that has been proposed by many high officials; or to use a direct subsidy of points, a system that has been accomplished through HUD's tandem plan.

But for our purposes, a portion of the loan cost on FHA- and VA-type loans is expected to be paid by the seller as a part of the selling cost. A growing use of discount is coming into conventional lending, but with conventional loans there is no such arbitrary rule placing this cost on the seller.

SETTLEMENT COSTS

The previous section on Settlement Requirements lists the handling and cost allocations for the survey, insurance, property taxes, prepaid insurance, and maintenance charges. In addition to these cost requirements, there are additional charges involved in a settlement which concern the fees charged for the various services that are rendered to both the buyer and the seller. RESPA prohibits anyone from accepting or giving a fee, kickback, or anything of value for a referral agreement or any arrangement to accept a fee or part of a fee where no service has actually been performed. Some or all of the following services will be involved in any loan settlement procedure which in almost all areas of this country have always been handled in a professional manner for a reasonable cost.

Service Fees

In addition to the larger items of cost involved in closing, there are several smaller charges incurred. The *recording fee* is for the purpose of recording with the county the new deed, the new mortgage or deed of trust, and any releases of prior liens that are being paid off at closing. The recording fee, usually charged for by the page, is another item that cannot be determined precisely until the exact number of pages involved is known. The *escrow fee* is another expense consisting of a set charge made by the settlement agent for its services in handling the loan and for providing security for the instruments.

Copies of any property restrictions are normally requested and are furnished by the settlement agent. These are necessary for both the lender and the new owner to know exactly what the subject property might be limited to in its usage. The settlement agent also draws from the county a certificate of the taxes due on the subject property. The costs for reproducing these public records are simply passed on to the buyer or seller, as the case may be, at the time of closing.

Depending on what cost items may have been paid in advance or at time of a loan application, there could be some additional charges remaining to be paid at closing. These would include an appraisal fee, credit report, and photos of the property, all charges associated with securing the mortgage loan and normally paid by the purchaser-borrower.

Attorney's Fees

Each party to the transaction is free to employ an attorney and, in case of any legal questions or disputes, should certainly be encouraged to do so. On most residential property sales, both buyer and seller tend to rely on the selection of attorneys by the title company and/or the mortgage company. The interests of both companies parallel the principal's interest in assuring proper transfer of title and security of the mortgage instruments. It is common practice to rely on the title company to have its own associated law firm prepare all instruments, as it is the title company who actually guarantees that proper title has been passed. The fees involved are divided between the buyer and seller, as they may agree; normally, the seller pays for the warranty deed and any title clearing instruments (releases, etc.), and the buyer pays for the note and mortgage instruments needed to secure the loan.

Finance Fees

The charge by the mortgage company for handling the loan processing and funding is called a finance fee, an origination fee, or occasionally, loan brokerage. The charge is 1 to 1½ percent of the loan amount and is normally paid by the buyer.

Sales Commission

The charge by the real estate agent for selling the property is usually listed as the *commission* and is whatever fee the seller has agreed to, ranging from 5 to 8 percent of the sale price.

Inspection Fees

The sales contract may call for certain inspections to be made on the subject property with the costs paid by either the buyer or the seller. A termite or pest inspection is a fairly common requirement, particularly in southern climates. An inspection for structural soundness may be called for, or for any of the mechanical equipment being sold with the house. If the lender introduces any inspection requirements as a part of the loan commitment, such charges could be paid by either the buyer or the seller but would normally be considered a buyer's cost as a part of obtaining the loan.

SETTLEMENT STATEMENT

As a part of the new Real Estate Settlement Procedures Act, the federal government has established a new standard form to be used in all real estate settlements. The Department of Housing and Urban Development has developed the new Uniform Settlement Statement which is reproduced in Figure 14-2, revision dated May 1976. The first portion of this statement calls for information concerning the loan, the property, and the parties to the transaction. Section J of the form pertains to the buyer-borrower's side of the transaction and details all costs payable by him or her, concluding with the net cash to be paid by the borrower. The right-hand side of the form, Section K, pertains to the seller. All costs attributable to the seller are deducted from the sale price due to him or her with the bottom line showing the cash due to the seller. The second sheet of the form is Section L which lists all the settlement services that will be required and provides columns to allocate these charges to either the buyer's or seller's column. The totals from Section L are transferred back and become a part of Sections J and K on the first page.

In addition to the Settlement Statement, the form provides for a settlement costs worksheet for the buyer to use in comparing costs that may be charged by various service providers. The worksheet is essentially a reprint of Section L of the settlement statement listing all services that may be needed.

The Uniform Settlement Statement is the same form that is used to meet the RESPA requirements for disclosure of settlement costs to the buyer 24 hours prior to closing. If all costs are not known 24 hours prior to closing by the settlement agent, and they seldom are, then the requirement calls for all *available* costs to be dis-

A. U.S. DEPARTMENT OF HOUSING AND URBAN DEVELOPMENT	B. TYPE OF LOAN:

B. TYPE OF LOAN:

1. ☐ FHA   2. ☐ FMHA   3. ☐ CONV. UNINS.
4. ☐ VA   5. ☐ CONV. INS.

6. FILE NUMBER	7. LOAN NUMBER

8. MORTG. INS. CASE NO.

U·LIFE TITLE COMPANY of Houston

SETTLEMENT STATEMENT

C. **NOTE:** This form is furnished to give you a statement of actual settlement costs. Amounts paid to and by the settlement agent are shown. Items marked "(p.o.c.)" were paid outside the closing; they are shown here for informational purposes and are not included in the totals.

D. NAME OF BORROWER	E. NAME OF SELLER	F. NAME OF LENDER

G. PROPERTY LOCATION	H. SETTLEMENT AGENT	I. SETTLEMENT DATE:
	PLACE OF SETTLEMENT	

J. SUMMARY OF BORROWER'S TRANSACTION		K. SUMMARY OF SELLER'S TRANSACTION	
100. GROSS AMOUNT DUE FROM BORROWER:		**400. GROSS AMOUNT DUE TO SELLER:**	
101. Contract sales price		401. Contract sales price	
102. Personal property		402. Personal property	
103. Settlement charges to borrower *(line 1400)*		403.	
104.		404.	
105.		405.	
Adjustments for items paid by seller in advance:		Adjustments for items paid by seller in advance:	
106. City/town taxes to		406. City/town taxes to	
107. County taxes to		407. County taxes to	
108. Assessments to		408. Assessments to	
109. Maintenance to		409. Maintenance to	
110. School/Taxes to		410. Commitment Fee to	
111. to		411. to	
112. to		412. to	
120. GROSS AMOUNT DUE FROM BORROWER:		**420. GROSS AMOUNT DUE TO SELLER:**	
200. AMOUNTS PAID BY OR IN BEHALF OF BORROWER:		**500. REDUCTIONS IN AMOUNT DUE TO SELLER:**	
201. Deposit or earnest money		501. Excess deposit (see instructions)	
202. Principal amount of new loan(s)		502. Settlement charges to seller *(line 1400)*	
203. Existing loan(s) taken subject to		503. Existing loan(s) taken subject to	
204. Commitment Fee		504. Payoff of first mortgage loan	
205.		505. Payoff of second mortgage loan	
206.		506.	
207.		507.	
208.		508.	
209.		509.	
Adjustments for items unpaid by seller:		Adjustments for items unpaid by seller:	
210. City/town taxes to		510. City/town taxes to	
211. County taxes to		511. County Taxes to	
212. Assessments to		512. Assessments to	
213. School/Taxes to		513. Maintenance to	
214. to		514. School/Taxes to	
215. to		515. to	
216. to		516. to	
217. to		517. to	
218. to		518. to	
219. to		519. to	
220. TOTAL PAID BY/FOR BORROWER:		**520. TOTAL REDUCTION AMOUNT DUE SELLER:**	
300. CASH AT SETTLEMENT FROM/TO BORROWER:		**600. CASH AT SETTLEMENT TO/FROM SELLER:**	
301. Gross amount due from borrower *(line 120)*		601. Gross amount due to seller *(line 420)*	
302. Less amounts paid by/for borrower *(line 220)*	( )	602. Less total reductions in amount due seller *(line 520)*	( )
303. CASH (☐ FROM) (☐ TO) BORROWER:		603. CASH (☐ TO) (☐ FROM) SELLER	

HUD-1 (Rev. 5-76)

FIGURE 14-2a.

L. SETTLEMENT CHARGES	PAID FROM BORROWER'S FUNDS AT SETTLEMENT	PAID FROM SELLER'S FUNDS AT SETTLEMENT
700. TOTAL SALES/BROKER'S COMMISSION Based on price $ @ % =		
Division of commission (line 700) as follows:		
701. $ to		
702. $ to		
703. Commission paid at settlement		
704.		
800. ITEMS PAYABLE IN CONNECTION WITH LOAN.		
801. Loan Origination fee %		
802. Loan Discount %		
803. Appraisal Fee to		
804. Credit Report to		
805. Lender's inspection fee		
806. Mortgage Insurance application fee to		
807. Assumption Fee		
808. Commitment Fee		
809. FNMA Processing Fee		
810. Pictures		
811.		
900. ITEMS REQUIRED BY LENDER TO BE PAID IN ADVANCE.		
901. Interest from to @ $ /day		
902. Mortgage insurance premium for mo. to		
903. Hazard insurance premium for yrs. to		
904. Flood Insurance yrs. to		
905.		
1000. RESERVES DEPOSITED WITH LENDER		
1001. Hazard insurance mo. @ $ per mo.		
1002. Mortgage insurance mo. @ $ per mo.		
1003. City property taxes mo. @ $ per mo.		
1004. County property taxes mo. @ $ per mo.		
1005. Annual assessments (Maint.) mo. @ $ per mo.		
1006. School Property Taxes mo. @ $ per mo.		
1007. Water Dist. Prop. Tax mo. @ $ per mo.		
1008. Flood Insurance mo. @ $ per mo.		
1100. TITLE CHARGES:		
1101. Settlement or closing fee to		
1102. Abstract or title search to		
1103. Title examination to		
1104. Title insurance binder to		
1105. Document preparation to		
1106. Notary fees to		
1107. Attorney's fees to to		
(includes above items No.:		
1108. Title insurance to		
(includes above items No.:		
1109. Lender's coverage $		
1110. Owner's coverage $		
1111. Escrow Fee		
1112. Restrictions		
1113. Messenger Service		
1200. GOVERNMENT RECORDING AND TRANSFER CHARGES		
1201. Recording fees: Deed $ Mortgage $ Releases $		
1202. City/county tax/stamps: Deed $ Mortgage $		
1203. State tax/stamps: Deed $ Mortgage $		
1204. Tax Certificates		
1205.		
1300. ADDITIONAL SETTLEMENT CHARGES		
1301. Survey to		
1302. Pest inspection to		
1303.		
1304.		
1305.		
1400. TOTAL SETTLEMENT CHARGES (entered on lines 103, Section J and 502, Section K)		

SELLER'S AND/OR PURCHASER'S STATEMENT

Seller's and Purchaser's signature hereon acknowledges his/their approval of tax prorations, and signifies their understanding that prorations were based on figures for preceding year, or estimates for current year, and in event of any change for current year, all necessary adjustments must be made between Seller and Purchaser direct; likewise any DEFICIT in delinquent taxes will be reimbursed to Title Company by the Seller.

We approve the foregoing settlement statement, in its entirety, authorize payments in accordance therewith and acknowledge receipt of a copy thereof.

Signature _____   _____

           Seller

Address _____   _____

                Purchaser

_____

          Escrow Officer   HUD-1 (Rev. 5-76)

FIGURE 14-2b.

closed. The fully completed statement must be available at closing and a copy given to the buyer and seller.

Distribution of Costs

In regard to how the various costs are allocated between the buyer and seller, RESPA has no requirements. It is still a matter of negotiating between the parties involved. Some builders in an effort to sell their houses will undertake to pay all closing costs as a part of their sales promotion. But in most transactions, the following generalization would apply:

Seller pays:

1. For any title requirements to perfect good title.
2. Costs of preparing the warranty deed.
3. Owner's title policy and any fees required.
4. Any discount points required on FHA/VA loans.
5. Sales commission.

Buyer pays:

1. Loan brokerage fees and costs to secure loan.
2. Mortgagee's title policy.
3. Costs of preparing mortgage instruments and filing fees for same.

Negotiable charges:

1. Cost of survey.
2. Cost of appraisal.
3. Inspection fees.

FINAL CLOSING INSTRUCTIONS

Mortgagee's Closing Instructions

Once a loan has been approved, the mortgage company prepares a sheet of instructions for delivery to the settlement agent handling closing procedures. The instructions detail such items as the correct legal name of the mortgagee, the name of the trustee for the deed of trust, the terms of the mortgage note, and special requirements to be included in the mortgage or deed of trust (that is, if the mortgage company is not submitting its own forms for a note and mortgage), specific instructions on monthly payments to be given to the borrowers, details of the escrow requirements, and details of disbursement procedures. Along with the instructions, the mortgage company will send the buyer-seller affidavits as may be required, which certify to the actual down payment (cash and/or property exchanged) and to the use of the loan proceeds, which must be acknowledged by the notarized signatures of all buyers and sellers. Also, a truth-in-lending statement is prepared for the purchaser-borrower signature at closing. Some mortgage companies require certifications of occupancy (for homestead information). The forms vary between companies according to how their legal counselors interpret the state laws.

The instructions of the mortgage company invariably call for a certain amount of work on the part of the settlement agent closing the loan, if only as a means of clarifying the loan requirements. This is in addition to the other details of closing that a settlement agent must handle, such as assembling the title information, preparing or reviewing the note and deed of trust, verifying tax requirements, and determining the insurance payments needed.

It is advisable to allow the settlement agent a reasonable time for its work in preparing for a closing. A forced deadline can induce errors and omissions.

Setting the Closing

When the mortgage company has approved the loan and prepared its closing instructions, it is the responsibility of the real estate agent, or agents, involved to arrange a mutually agreeable closing time. Practices vary in different parts of the country—in some areas all parties meet around a table for the settlement procedures; in other parts, no actual meeting is required and escrow agents are authorized to request that the necessary instruments be delivered to them. The agents then take the steps required to pay off existing loans, adjust taxes, buy insurance, all as called for in the escrow agreement. If all parties make timely delivery of the instruments and monies that have been agreed upon, the escrow is considered "closed."

Whenever the local practices require a meeting of the parties involved, it is usually held in the offices of the company or person designated to handle the settlement procedures. This may be a title company, an attorney, a real estate agent, an escrow agent, or the lender itself. Whoever handles the loan closing must have the approval of the lender as it is its money that is generally most involved. Closings can be accomplished with separate meetings, the buyer at one time and the seller at another, leaving the settlement agent to escrow the instruments and consideration until the procedure is completed and distribution can be made.

It is easier for the agents involved, as well as providing greater clarity for both buyer and seller, to arrange for a single meeting. Although a closing is no place for negotiations, if any misunderstanding should crop up, it can be more readily resolved if all parties are immediately available for decisions.

DISBURSEMENT OF FUNDS

In many parts of the country, a closing is just that; instruments are signed and funds are disbursed before anyone leaves the closing table. In some areas, it is more common to execute and acknowledge the instruments at the closing but delay the disbursement of funds until later.

The purpose for any delay in releasing funds is twofold: first, to give the lender an opportunity to make a second review of all instruments and to verify proper signatures and acknowledgements, and second, to allow the settlement agent time to clear any checks that may have been submitted by the parties involved before releasing its own disbursement checks. One interpretation of state regulations governing title insurance companies calls *any* check paid to a title company an "escrow receivable," rather than a cash item, until the check has actually cleared the bank. However, there is growing pressure to handle a closing in its proper sequence and not call for the parties to meet until all the loose ends have been accomplished and the money is available for distribution.

The actual disbursement of funds at or following the settlement procedures is usually made to several different individuals and companies as well as the cash due to the seller. One of the reasons an escrow agent is employed in the settlement is to make sure that all parties with claims in the settlement are paid. The mortgage lender wants to be certain that taxes are paid, that the insurance coverage has been paid for, and that no subsequent claims can be filed that might cloud their right to a first mortgage lien securing their loan.

Sales agents, inspectors, attorneys, and the service agents all expect to receive their fees from the closing agent. After all required payments have been made, the balance due the seller is then disbursed, the required instruments are filed of record, and the transaction is considered closed.

QUESTIONS FOR DISCUSSION

1. Discuss the purpose of the Real Estate Settlement Procedures Act and how it attempts to accomplish it.

2. Does RESPA prescribe any limitations on fees that may be charged in closing a loan?

3. Discuss the importance of a survey in the settlement procedure.

4. Distinguish between the four types of insurance that may be involved in a loan closing.

5. What is the reason for a prepayment of interest at the time of settlement procedures?

6. Where are loan closings normally held in your community? Who is the agent usually selected to represent the mortgage company at the closing procedure?

7. What information is furnished to the settlement agent (closer) by the mortgage lender just prior to closing?

8. Discuss the use of the disclosure statement and the settlement statement as now required by RESPA.

9. Give a general rule on allocation of settlement charges between the purchaser-borrower and the seller.

Glossary

The following terms are those most frequently used in real estate financing, which are considered essential in understanding the material presented in this text.

Acceleration. A clause in a mortgage instrument permitting demand for full payment of principal upon default of the obligations.

Acknowledgment. For real estate purposes, a signature witnessed or notarized in a manner that can be recorded.

Amortization. The systematic and continuous payment of an obligation through installments until such time as that debt has been paid off in full.

Appraisal. An estimate of property value by a qualified person.

Assessment. A charge against a property owner for purposes of taxation; i.e., the property owner pays his share of community improvements and maintenance according to the valuation of his property.

Assessed Value. Property value as determined by a taxing authority.

Assets. Real and personal property that may be chargeable with the debts of the owner.

Assignment of Mortgage. Transfer by the lender (mortgagee) of the mortgage obligation.

Assumption Agreement. A contract, by deed or other form, through which a buyer undertakes the obligations of an existing mortgage.

Balloon Payment. A debt repayment plan wherein the installments are less than required for a full amortization, with the balance due in a lump sum at maturity.

Basis Points. The movement of interest rates or yields expressed in hundredths of a percent; i.e., a change in yield from 7.45% to 7.55% would be termed an increase of 10 basis points.

Basket Provision. Regulations applicable to financial institutions that permit a small percentage of total assets to be held in otherwise unauthorized investments.

Blanket Mortgage. A type of mortgage that pledges more than one parcel of real estate.

Bond. A form of security that guarantees payment of the face value with interest to the purchaser (lender), and usually secured with a pledge of property or a commitment of income such as a tax revenue bond.

Borrower. A person or company using another's money or property, who has both a legal and moral obligation to repay the loan.

Broker. An intermediary between buyer and seller, or between lender and borrower, usually acting as agent for one or more parties, who arranges loans or sells property in return for a fee or commission.

Capitalization. The conversion of an income stream into a property valuation for purposes of appraisal.

Cash Flow. The amount of cash received over a period of time from an income property.

Chattel. An article of property that can be moved; personal property.

Chattel Mortgage. A type of lien (legal claim) that applies to personal property as distinguished from real property.

Closer. The individual responsible for making final settlement of the property transaction and disbursement of the loan proceeds.

Closing. The consummation of a real estate transaction wherein certain rights of ownership are transferred in exchange for the monetary and other considerations agreed upon. Also called *loan closing*.

Collateral. Property acceptable as security for a loan.

Compensating Balance. A minimum balance held on deposit in accordance with a loan agreement.

Commitment. A pledge to grant a loan based on an acceptable application.

Commitment Fee. Money paid in return for the pledge of a future loan.

Conditional Sale. An agreement granting title to property after all payments have been made.

Condominium. A unit in a multifamily structure or office building wherein the owner holds a fee simple title to the unit he or she occupies and a tenancy in common with the other owners of the common elements.

Consideration. The cash, services, or token given in exchange for property or services.

Constant Payment. The payment of a fixed sum periodically, which money is applied to interest, and second to principal reduction, in a manner calculated to amortize a debt.

Constant Rate. Also called *constant*, which is the factor or multiplier used for easy computation of the equal monthly or annual payments to amortize a loan.

Construction Loan. A type of mortgage loan to finance construction, which is funded by the lender to the builder at periodic intervals as the work progresses.

Contingent Liability. The responsibility assumed by a third party who accepts liability for an obligation upon the failure of an initial obligor to perform as agreed.

Contract for Deed. An agreement to sell property wherein title to the property is delivered to the buyer only after all installment payments have been made.

Contract for Sale. An agreement between a buyer and a seller of real property to deliver good title in return for a consideration.

Conventional Loan. A loan that is not underwritten by a federal agency.

Conveyance. The written instrument by which title to real property is transferred from one party to another.

Debenture Bond. An unsecured pledge to repay.

Debt. An obligation to be repaid by a borrower to a lender.

Debt Service. The periodic payment due on a loan, which includes principal, interest, mortgage insurance, and any other fees required by the loan agreement.

Deed. A written instrument by which real estate is transferred to another owner. The deed is signed, sealed, and delivered by the seller.

Deed of Trust. A type of mortgage that conveys real property to a third party for holding in trust as security for payment of a loan.

Deed Restriction. A clause in a deed that restricts the use of the land being conveyed.

Default. The failure to perform on an obligation as agreed in a contract.

Delinquency. A loan payment that is overdue but within the grace period allowed before actual default is declared.

Development Loan. Money loaned for the purpose of improving land by the building of streets and utilities so as to make lots suitable for sale or use in construction.

Discount. The amount expressed in points that is subtracted from the face value of a loan in order to increase the effective yield.

Earnest Money. A portion of the down payment delivered to the seller or an escrow agent by the purchaser of real estate with his offer as evidence of good faith.

Encroachment. Any physical intrusion upon the property rights of another.

Equity. The ownership interest—that portion of a property's value beyond any liability therein.

Escalation. The right of a lender to increase the rate of interest in a loan agreement.

Escrow. Property, money, or something of value held in custody by a third party in accordance with an agreement.

Execution. The act of signing by the involved parties of an instrument, usually witnessed or notarized for recording purposes.

Fee Simple. A legal term indicating title to property without encumbrances.

FHA Loan. A loan insured by the Insuring Office of the Department of Housing and Urban Development; formerly known as the Federal Housing Administration.

Fixture. Personal property so affixed to the land as to become a part of the realty.

Foreclosure. Legal action to bar a mortgagor's claims to property after default has occurred.

Graduated Payment Mortgage. A type of mortgage agreement that provides for lower payments than a constant amortization rate in the early years and higher payments in the later years.

Gross Income. The total money received from an operating property over a given period of time.

Guarantee (verb). The act of pledging by a third party to assure payment.

Guaranty (noun). A pledge by a third party to assume the obligation of another.

Hazard Insurance. The insurance covering physical damage to property.

HUD. The Department of Housing and Urban Development.

Income Property. Real estate capable of producing net revenue.

Instrument. A legal document in writing.

Interest. The payment for the use of money.

Interim Financing. An in-between (intermediate) loan—the money loaned for construction in anticipation of the permanent loan.

Land Loan. Money loaned for the purchase of raw land.

Late Charge. A fee added to an installment as a penalty for failure to make a timely payment.

Leverage. The capacity to borrow an amount greater than the equity in property. The larger the loan in relation to the equity, the greater the leverage.

Lien. A legal claim or attachment, filed on record, against property as security for payment of an obligation.

Limitations. A period of time as fixed by state statutes within which certain acts are to be performed to render them valid.

Liquidity. The extent to which assets held in other forms can be easily and quickly converted into cash.

Loan. A granting of the use of money in return for the payment of interest.

Loan-to-Value-Ratio (LTVR). The relationship between the amount of a loan and the value of the property pledged.

Marginal Property. Capable of making only a very low economic return.

Maturity. The date that payment on a loan is due.

Mechanic's Lien. Also known as Mechanic's and Materialmen's Lien, or M & M Lien; a claim for payment of labor and/or materials filed on record in the County.

Mortgage. A conditional conveyance of property as security for a debt.

Mortgaging Out. Securing of a loan upon completion of a project sufficient to cover all costs: a 100% loan.

Mortgagee. The lender of money and the receiver of the security in the form of a mortgage.

Mortgagor. The borrower of money and the giver of a mortgage as security.

Mortgage Note. A description of the debt and a promise to pay—the instrument that is secured by the mortgage indenture.

Mortgage Release. A disclaimer of further liability on the mortgage note issued by the lender.

Multifamily Mortgage. An FHA term designating an apartment or any housing with more than four family units.

Net Income. That portion of gross income remaining after payment of all expenses.

Option. The right to purchase or lease a piece of property at a certain price for a designated period.

Origination Fee. The amount charged for services performed by the company handling the initial application and processing of a loan.

Participation Loan. A loan funded by more than one lender and serviced by one of them.

Permanent Loan. A mortgage loan granted for a long term based on the economic life of a property.

Partial Release. The removal of a general mortgage lien from a specific portion of the land that has been pledged.

Personal Property. A possession: any item of value that is not real estate.

Points. A unit of measure for charges that amounts to one percent of a loan. One point is one percent of the subject loan.

Possession. Occupancy: the highest form of "notice."

Principal. The amount of the mortgage debt.

Real Estate. Land and that attached thereto, including minerals and resources inherent to the land, and any man-made improvements so affixed as to become a part of the land. Also known as *realty* or *real property*.

Realtor. A registered word designating a member in good standing of the National Association of Real Estate Boards.

Recording. To file a legal instrument in the public records of a county.

Reversionary Clause. A restrictive provision in a deed to land that causes title to return to the grantor if violated.

Secondary Market. Large investors who buy and sell mortgage loans that they do not originate.

Servicing (Loan Servicing). The work of an agent, usually a mortgage company, comprising the collection of mortgage payments, securing of escrow funds, payment of property taxes and insurance from the escrowed funds, follow-up on delinquencies, accounting for and remitting principal, and interest payments to the lender.

Settlement Procedure. The steps taken to finalize the funding of a loan agreement and a property transfer. Also called a loan closing.

Single-Family Mortgage. A mortgage loan on property occupied by one family; and for classification purposes, can include up to four family units.

Spot Loan. Money loaned on individual houses in various neighborhoods, as contrasted to new houses in a single development.

Statutory Redemption. A state law that permits a mortgagor a limited time after foreclosure to pay off the debt and reclaim the property.

Subordination. To make a claim to real property inferior to that of another by specific agreement.

Survey. The measurement and description of land by a registered surveyor.

Sweat Equity. An ownership interest in property earned by the performance of manual labor on that property.

Syndication. The organization of a group of investors for the purpose of acquiring a specific property.

Take-out. A type of loan commitment—a promise to make a loan at a future specified time. It is most commonly used to designate a higher cost, shorter term, back-up commitment as a support for construction financing until a suitable permanent loan can be secured.

Term. The time limit within which a loan must be repaid.

Time Deposits. Money held in savings accounts not subject to demand withdrawal.

Title. The legal evidence of ownership rights to real property.

Tract Loan. Individual mortgage loan negotiated for houses of similar character located in a new development.

Trade Fixture. Personal property, peculiar to a trade, which remains personal even though affixed to real property.

Underwriter. The person or company taking responsibility for approving a mortgage loan.

Usury. Excessive interest as determined by state law.

Variable Rate Mortgage. A type of mortgage agreement that allows for periodic adjustment of the interest rate in keeping with a fluctuating market.

VA Loan. A loan made by private lenders that is partially guaranteed by the Veterans Administration.

Vendor's Lien. A lien securing the loan of money used to purchase property.

Warehousing. The practice, mostly by mortgage bankers, of pledging mortgage notes to a commercial bank for cash used to fund the mortgage loans.

Whole Loan. A term used in the secondary market to indicate the full amount of a loan is available for sale with no portion, or participation, retained by the seller.

Yield. The total money earned on a loan for the term of the loan computed on an annual percentage basis.

Index